# The Writing of Weddings in Middle-Period China

SUNY series in Chinese Philosophy and Culture
Roger T. Ames, editor

# The Writing of Weddings in Middle-Period China

## Text and Ritual Practice in the Eighth through Fourteenth Centuries

Christian de Pee

State University of New York Press

Published by
State University of New York Press, Albany



Printed in the United States of America



For information, address State University of New York Press, 194 Washington Avenue, Suite 305, Albany, NY 12210-2384

Production by Judith Block
Marketing by Fran Keneston

**Library of Congress Cataloging-in-Publication Data**

De Pee, Christian.
The writing of weddings in middle-period China : text and ritual practice in the eighth through fourteenth centuries / Christian de Pee.
p. cm.—(SUNY series in Chinese philosophy and culture)
Includes bibliographical references and index.
ISBN-13: 978-0-7914-7073-2 (hardcover : alk. paper)
ISBN-13: 978-0-7914-7074-9 (pbk. : alk. paper)
1. Marriage customs and rites—China. 2. Weddings in literature.
3. China—History—Tang dynasty, 618-907.
4. China—History—Song dynasty, 960-1279. I. Title.

GT2783.A2D42 2007
392.50951—dc22

2006025531

10 9 8 7 6 5 4 3 2 1

To Lara

# Contents

# Illustrations

## Figures



## Tables

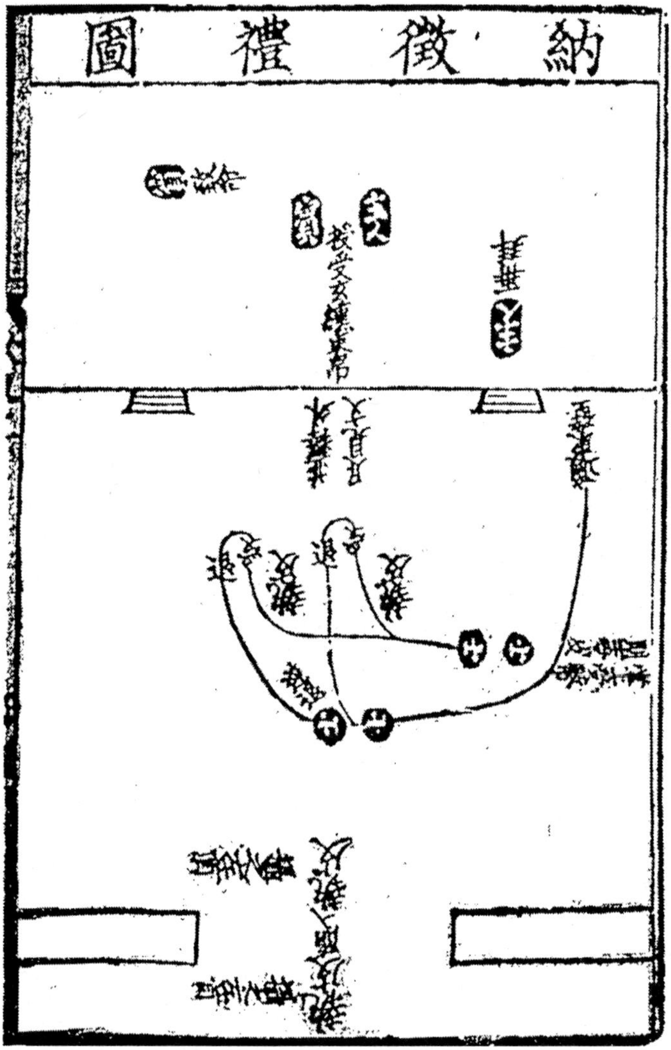


"Ritual choreography of Submission of the Betrothal Gifts," from Yang Fu's *Ceremonies and Rites Illustrated* (*Yili tu*, 1228). Yuan-dynasty edition. Courtesy of the National Central Library, Taipei.

# Preface

This book attempts to preserve the fragile traces of the practice of weddings during the Middle Period, from the late Tang (618–907) through the Yuan dynasty (1272–1368). The ephemeral configurations of grooms and brides and wedding guests, the unique sounds and sights and fragrances of Middle-Period weddings, have by nature ever defied the limitations of the written page. But where writing was a ritual practice, and where the text was a ritual object, texts do yet preserve, amid their configurations of written signs, traces of the practice of Middle-Period weddings. The detailed choreographies of ritual manuals allow the reader, now as then, to merge through symmetrical, centered time and space with the perfect ceremonies of legendary antiquity. The lavish display of wit and erudition in engagement letters creates linear hierarchies of literary production and linear successions of literary fashions that are replicated in the linear time and space of their ritual narratives. The recondite cosmological calculations of calendars and almanacs assume a cyclical time and space in which the revolutions of noxious dangers and bright opportunities determine auspicious and inauspicious dates, hours, and locations for weddings. Legal verdicts reconfigure local wedding ceremonies according to the universal categories of imperial law, in the ritual time and space of imperial government, yet in the process of that translation, in the margins of those judgments, become dimly, briefly visible unwritten cultures of colloquial practice. These incompatible notions of time, space, and bodies, configured in incommensurable wedding ceremonies, converge in tombs in which deceased spouses have been buried together. The material ambiguity of the tomb allows a juxtaposition of discourses that the determinate conventions of the Middle-Period text prohibit. The Middle-Period text, in other words, has preserved configurations of time, space, bodies, and writing, without indicating how these might be refigured in the ritual practice of weddings.

This is a book about the practice of the text. It examines the intersections between the practice of writing and the practice of weddings during the Middle Period, and in the process reassesses the relationship between the Middle-Period text and the practice of the historian. The particularities of writing as a cultural practice during the Middle Period, and the particularities of the transmission of texts during late imperial times, have created a textual legacy that differs markedly from the textual legacies of the European and the American past. It stands to reason, therefore, that the received narratives and idioms of European and American historiography are not always suitable to render the history of the Middle Period, and that the historian should consider metaphors and modes of emplotment that accommodate the particularities of Middle-Period texts. This book attempts a description of fragmented discourses, in a style that allows an active, dialectical engagement with the extant texts. With every chapter, each shorter than the previous, the distance between the practice of the text and the practice of ritual widens, as also the transmitted texts become fewer and more fragmentary. Each chapter, moreover, spans a different stretch of time, from the origins of a genre to its demise, or from one founding text to another. The designation "Middle Period" is broad enough to encompass these different spans of time, while being specific enough to suggest the era of a growing market economy, an increasing population, the spread of printing, the new prominence of the imperial examinations, the changing nature of the elite, and the re-evaluation of the classical tradition—all factors that shaped the narratives of the discourses that are the subject of the chapters of this book.

The research and the composition of this book, begun as a dissertation, have in the course of time been subvened by the Center for Chinese Studies in Taipei; the American Council for Learned Societies/Chiang Ching-kuo Foundation Fellowship Selection Committee, with funds provided by the Chiang Ching-kuo Foundation; the Mrs. Giles Whiting Foundation; the Fang-Tu Teaching Fellowship in East Asian Studies, Heyman Center, Columbia University; and a postdoctoral fellowship at the Center for Chinese Studies, University of California at Berkeley. The research for this book has also benefited much from a yearlong affiliation granted by the Institute of History and Philology at Academia Sinica, in Taiwan. I am grateful to all these institutions for their support.

I am also pleased to acknowledge the help I have received over the years from librarians in Taiwan, Mainland China, and the United

States, specifically the staff of the Rare Books Collection of the National Central Library and the National Palace Museum Library Rare Book Room in Taipei, the Fu Ssu-nien Library of the Institute of History and Philology at Academia Sinica, the C. V. Starr East Asian Library at Columbia University, the East Asian Library at the University of California at Berkeley, the East Asian Library at Princeton University, the Kroch Asia Library at Cornell University, the library of Yunnan University, and the Gejiu Municipal Library.

A number of passages in this book have previously been published in "The Ritual and Sexual Bodies of the Groom and the Bride in Ritual Manuals of the Sung Dynasty (11th through 13th Centuries)," in *Chinese Women in the Imperial Past: New Perspectives*, ed. Harriet T. Zurndorfer (Leiden: E. J. Brill, 1999); "Premodern Chinese Weddings and the Divorce of Past and Present," *positions: east asia cultures critique* 9 : 3 (winter 2001); "Material Ambiguity and the Hermetic Text: Cities, Tombs, and Middle-Period History," *Journal of Song-Yuan Studies* 34 (2004); and "Till Death Do Us Unite: Texts, Tombs, and the Cultural History of Weddings in Middle-Period China (Eighth through Fourteenth Centuries)," *The Journal of Asian Studies* 65 : 4 (November 2006). Those passages are reprinted here with the kind permission of Koninklijke Brill, *positions: east asia cultures critique*, the *Journal of Song-Yuan Studies*, and the Association for Asian Studies.

Robert Hymes offered incisive criticism during the important early stages of my dissertation. In later years, my work on the book was helped by the comments and encouragements of many, among them Alain Arrault, Robert Ashmore, Bettine Birge, Peter Bol, Miranda Brown, Lucille Chia, Astrid de Pee, Hilde de Weerdt, William Hanks, Ton Hengeveld, Lionel Jensen, David Lurie, Jennifer Purtle, Sarah Schneewind, Anna Shields, Patricia Thornton, Walter van de Leur, Lothar von Falkenhausen, Stephen West, and the two anonymous readers for the State University of New York Press. I am grateful also for the suggestions and criticisms offered by audiences at the workshop on the History of Chinese Women at Leiden University; the 1998 and 2000 annual meetings of the Association for Asian Studies; the Traditional China Seminar and the Society of Fellows in the Humanities at Columbia University; the Department of East Asian Languages and Civilizations at the University of Chicago; the Center for Chinese Studies at the University of California at Berkeley; and the seminar on New Approaches to Chinese Studies at the University of California at Los Angeles. Nancy Ellegate and Judith Block of the State University of New York Press have been encouraging, helpful, and accommodating in the preparation of this book for print.

To Angela Zito and to Michael Nylan I owe special debts of gratitude. Angela Zito helped me understand the substance and argument of my book, and it is doubtful that without her friendship I should have attained many of the book's crucial insights. Without the persistent, and insistent, kindness of Michael Nylan, this book might never have been published.

The greater part of this book was written, eventually, on a remote mountain plateau in southern Yunnan, at a pleasant yellow table with a view of a steep cliff and a prefectural hotel. In the memory of that happy time, I dedicate this book to Lara Kusnetzky, for reasons both obvious and ineffable.

# Introduction

## The Practice of the Text

He who does not understand words cannot understand others.

—*The Analects* XX.3[1]

To understand oneself is to understand oneself in front of the text.

—Paul Ricoeur (1975)[2]

The practice of wedding ritual is irretrievably lost; the practice of wedding ritual survives to the present hour. The classical written language and the well-defined genres of the eighth through fourteenth centuries could not accommodate the individual, colloquial practice of contemporary wedding ceremonies. Yet where writing was itself a ritual act and where the text was itself a ritual object, the written page has preserved into the present a living trace of Middle-Period weddings, as vigorous as when the author put his brush to paper, as distinct as when the printer carved his blocks. On the solemn pages of ritual manuals, in the impeccable meter of engagement letters and wedding poems, in the esoteric calculations of calendars and almanacs, and in the stately diction of legal codes and verdicts stand immutably inscribed the time and space into which authors placed their scripted grooms and brides and wedding gifts. If in these fragments the practice of the text coincides with the practice of ritual, however, the practice of ritual extended across and beyond the determinate limits of the classical text. The material remains of joint burial—the unification of the ritualized bodies of deceased spouses in the ritualized time and space of a tomb—suggest how the ambiguous simultaneity of mute objects and ritual choreography allowed a juxtaposition of incommensurable notions of time, space, bodies, and text that remain strictly segregated in writing. A reflexive, dialectical hermeneutics reveals the temporal and spatial multiplicity that informs the wedding narratives in Middle-Period texts, and exposes the violent imposition of a universalist, linear temporality and spatiality on these texts by modern historians. But the embodied "sense of ritual" that coordinated this multiplicity of time, space, bodies, and text in individual wedding ceremonies is irretrievably lost.[3]

## The Practice of the Classical Text: The Writing of Weddings in the Middle Period

Authors of ritual manuals (chapter 1) reinscribed the wedding rites of remote, sacred antiquity to enable the reincorporation of these rites in the present. The compilers of imperial protocol and manuals of letters and ceremonies (*shuyi*) during the Tang (618–907), Five Dynasties (907–960), and early Song (960–1279) deemed that ritual changed with the times, and attempted to rewrite the untried precedents and novel practices of their day in accordance with the ritual scriptures of antiquity, thus contributing to the long series of careful adjustments that connected living practice to the distant past. In the eleventh century, the study of ancient bronze vessels and stone inscriptions convinced canonical scholars that it was possible to "bow, yield, and turn among the ancients" and that true, immutable ritual established, not an extended organic connection, but an immediate identity between the present and antiquity. Sima Guang (1019–1086), Zhang Zai (1020–1077), Lü Dajun (1031–1082), Cheng Yi (1033–1107), and others therefore rewrote the fragmented wedding ceremonies of the ritual scriptures into complete, seamless ritual narratives that appeared alien and dangerous to their bewildered contemporaries. Although the compilers of ritual manuals, both in the Tang and in the Song, reinscribed the scriptures of antiquity in hopes of restoring its incorporated practice to living ritual, theirs was an eminently textual discourse. Their detailed choreographies script an embodied exegesis that merges text and performance, the reading eye and the performing body, past and present. In this text/performance of ritual manuals, the groom and the bride move through interlocking systems of symmetrical ceremonies and through a ritual grammar of walls, thresholds, and stairs to become husband and wife at the spatial and temporal center of the narrative.[4] The time of the ritual, both symmetrical and porous, is the time of the text, and ancient ritual definitively merges with Middle-Period text when Zhu Xi's (1130–1200) *Family Rituals* gains recognition as a new scripture by a contemporary sage, first among his disciples, then at the imperial courts of the Yuan (1272–1368) and Ming (1368–1644) dynasties.

In wedding correspondence (chapter 2), the family of the groom and the family of the bride exchanged ceremonial letters whose erudition and elegance confirmed the education of the sender and, therewith, the prestige of the match. Sometime in the eleventh century, letters in exuberant parallel prose composed in the public formats of official communications began to replace the staid, private engagement letters of earlier ages. This compulsory display of cultural capital made writing a ritual act, producing the ritual object that was the calligraphed letter in its elaborate box or tube. In these letters, and in the wedding poems contributed by friends and relatives, the written bodies of grooms and brides (mere traces of the author's educated hand) move through written time and space toward a metaphoric rite of public consummation. The linearity of this parallel, anterior, written time and space is the linearity of literary fashions, whose passing tastes abandoned the practice of social correspondence in parallel prose during the fourteenth century.

Calendars and almanacs (chapter 3) chart safe paths through liminal space and time for the vulnerable and dangerous bodies of the groom and the bride. Their calculations transcribe the cyclical movements of baleful stars and deities that loom above wells and thresholds, inflicting illness and death on careless revelers and on the virgin bride. Extant almanacs and calendars (and medical texts and miracle tales) preserve a mere fraction of an expansive culture of practice in which writing served but as an aid in calculation and in which the printed page provided only one site of competition between astrologers and geomancers, doctors and diviners. Transmission has favored the most academic of cosmological systems, recorded in lasting tomes by imperial bureaus and literati dilettantes. The chance survival of illicit calendars and cheap pamphlets in the caves of Dunhuang and the sands of Turfan, however, supplements those scholarly works to suggest the myriad calculatory systems generated by a limited number of cosmological principles, shared by vying experts from the lofty halls of the imperial court to the market stall by the village well. The dark, grinding cycles that in their timeless revolution determined the blessings and dangers of weddings also determined the fate of the texts that transcribed them, obliterating thousands of almanacs with the birth of new stars and deities, and tens of thousands of calendars with each passing year.

The laws and legal codes promulgated under the Tang, Song, and Yuan dynasties (chapter 4) formulated a hierarchical structure in which official rank, degree of kinship, age, and (under the Yuan) ethnicity determined the rights and obligations of each imperial subject. Marriage laws served to contain the complications wrought in this transparent structure by the transfer of persons and property during betrothals and weddings. Marriage introduced the bride and, to a lesser extent, the groom into new mourning circles, and this change of ritual status bore with it new rights and obligations: rights to property, to the use of violence, to mourning, burial, and sacrifice, and obligations to the continuity of the ancestral line. In verdicts, this universalist imperial order confronts the local practice of weddings and marriage. Within the safe confines of the written page, the local official translates colloquial language and vernacular practice into the written discourse of imperial law, and redistributes persons and property according to legal stipulations often unknown to plaintiffs and defendants. In the margins of verdicts become briefly, dimly visible unwritten ceremonies, at the blurred distance that always already separates the universalist practice of the legal text from the local practice of wedding ceremonies. In legal discourse, writing is a ritual act in the ritual performance of imperial government, and the verdict is a ritual object, posted for public instruction or offered to superiors with all due formulas and stamps. Its space is the imperial space of county courts and prefectural capitals, its bodies are the imperial bodies of circumscribed subjects, and its time is the imperial time of mourning obligations, assizes, amnesties, and dynastic change. Each new dynasty destroyed the legal archives of its predecessor, preserving for the present an incomplete, incommensurable miscellany of edicts, codes, verdicts of literary merit, and precedents that impedes an understanding of the local practice of imperial law—let alone the local practice of weddings.

With every chapter of this book (each shorter than the previous) the surviving texts become less representative of the culture of writing and printing that produced them, while at the same time an increasing remove separates the practice of the text from the practice of ritual. The tightly scripted time, space, and bodies of ritual manuals and imperial protocol have been carefully, respectfully transmitted across the centuries. Literary merit and lasting reputations have saved from oblivion the anthologies and collected works that contain wedding letters and nuptial poems—their calligraphy and ceremonial trappings erased from the uniform printed text, but the cultural capital of their wit and allusions intact. The limited, instrumental function of text and writing in mantic practice left its cosmology imperfectly inscribed and barred its thousands of short, fleeting pamphlets from inclusion in enduring collections. The few scattered formulas and diagrams for the calculation of auspicious matches, propitious hours, and unthreatened spaces assume nuptial practices that are now forgotten. The sparse verdicts and precedents to survive from the Song and Yuan uphold the universalist order of imperial law against the perverse intrusion of local customs, and reduce disorderly vernacular practice to the transparent categories of written law. Where writing is a ritual act and where the text is a ritual object—in the meticulous choreographies of ritual manuals, in the elegant erudition of wedding correspondence, in the divinatory diagrams of cosmological calculation—the time, space, and bodies of the text are the time, space, and bodies of wedding ritual. In legal codes and verdicts, text and writing are ritual technologies of imperial rule whose hierarchies of time, space, and bodies bear no necessary relationship to the local practice of weddings. When the distance between the practice of the text and the practice of ritual increases further, in the writing of "local customs" (and in fiction), weddings become a mere function of the text.[5]

Because this book is concerned with inscribed traces of ritual practice, its chapters exclude the writing of local customs (*fengsu*). A brief exposition on this discourse, however, may provide the reader with an illustration of the relationship between the practice of the text and the practice of ritual, alleviating the summary abstraction of the above paragraphs with a measure of concrete detail.

Local gazetteers, travel diaries, and notebooks (*biji*) constitute the imperial center through a negative discourse on regional difference.[6] Each of these genres places the imperial capital at the center of the world, on the level ground of the present. The traveler who leaves the civilized Central Plain ascends into time, from the imperial present of the capital through the simple, recent past of the undulating countryside to the prehistory of steep borderlands. The towering cliffs, torrential rivers, and intemperate climes through which the traveler passes have detracted their hoary inhabitants from the civilizing transformation of the imperial court. Wedding practices, in this cultural geography, serve as one index of local character and relative civilization. The practice of the text, in other words, reduces unfamiliar wedding ceremonies to negative signs of difference, performed in alien time and space by crude, foreign bodies.[7]

Notebooks collect everything that lacks a place in other genres and thereby become an instantiation of this landscape: a marginal genre that writes the uncentered, whether geographic, political, literary, moral, or metaphorical—forgotten poems, oral traditions, humor, violence, miracle tales, strange foods, lost texts, scabrous anecdotes, exotic products, puns, writing on walls, gossip, local customs. As Zhuang Chuo (fl. 1090–1150) writes in the preface to his notebook *Collected Chicken Ribs* (*Jilei bian*, 1133):

> After Cao Mengde [i.e., Cao Cao, 155–220 CE] had pacified Hanzhong [in the Northwest] he wanted to conquer Shu [in the Southwest], but was unable to advance, while at the same time he realized that the region, if conquered, would be difficult to defend. When he stepped out to instruct his officers, he merely said, "Chicken ribs!" Nobody understood what he meant, except Yang Xiu who explained, "One does not derive any satisfaction from eating chicken ribs, yet throwing them out is a regrettable waste. Our lord has retreated for further deliberation." One will search the records in vain for Aman's [i.e., Cao Cao's] achievements, but this idle phrase of his was belatedly written down, much like some dry bit of chicken ribs. If one chances upon it, sitting hungry at home after gathering turnips and water chestnuts, it may not be quite as good as a rabbit shoulder, but it is better than a stark ox bone. Since this book of mine rather resembles this state of affairs, I have entitled it *Chicken Ribs*.[8]

Among the riddles and palindromes, monks and diviners, unknown plants and local technologies, and other odds and ends saved from the crevices of classical writing, Zhuang Chuo also includes local customs and regional character:

> Generally speaking, human nature takes after the surrounding landscape. The Northwest is mountainous, and its people are therefore dignified, sincere, and simple. The Jing and Yang regions [present Jiangsu, Anhui, Hubei, and Hunan] are rich in water, and its people are likewise bright, scintillating, and versatile, with an unfortunate tendency toward superficiality and shallowness. A man's character can be read from his face. Only the sagely and wise are able to resist the destabilizing force of local customs.[9]

Into this written geographical space (where the plain northern landscape with its slow rivers merges with the smooth surface of the page), Zhuang Chuo places certain dislodged wedding practices of his day:

> Never before have rites and ceremonies been as deficient as they have been in recent times. The unevenness of wedding and mourning practices is especially pronounced. Even imperial princes who take a wife follow customary rites such as Bowing to the Spirits of the Ancestors and Joining the Topknot. When [the *History of the Han* writes that] Li Guang "waged war on the Xiongnu after tying up his hair," it means to convey that he was still young, having barely reached the age of the capping ceremony.[10] Therefore Du Fu's [712–770] "Departure of a Young Bride" says, "After I tied up my hair I became your wife."[11] Later generations, however, have at weddings combed the hair of the groom and the bride together into one topknot and have called this "Tying up the Hair." This is ridiculous. One cannot begin to explain how uncanonical it is.[12]
>
> The customs of the South are even more bizarre than the old practices of the Central Plain. After the Emperor moved the capital to Yue a few years ago [to present Hangzhou, in 1127], for example, there was at some point a wedding in the family of an official from Wu [present Jiangsu province], conducted according to the manner of this official's hometown. He had several hundred envelopes of red paper filled with a mixture of lime and crushed clam shells, and instructed the bride to begin tossing these into the roadway as soon as she ascended the carriage. This was called "Powder to Protect the Mother-in-law." When the bride reached the gate of the groom's house, the official began summoning spirits, then sacrificed wine and food, and ordered a shaman to burn paper money and to recite exorcist spells, in order to drive away the bride's ancestors. As the bride descended from her carriage, her male and female relatives were told to carry her to the bedstead. After the parents of the groom had drunk three cups with the assembled guests, their son left the banquet to pay his respects at the bridal seat. Someone spread a mat for him next to the bride.[13] They drank three cups, and then proceeded to conduct Joining the Topknot and all other such ceremonies, with numerous outrageous elements.

> Commoner brides are not elaborately covered, and all kinds of strangers will stare at them. A virgin will sit on the dais; a bride who has been married before will sit in front of it. If onlookers praise her, and even if men fondle her, she will be pleased and not deem it improper.[14]

In this passage, contemporary wedding practices afford Zhuang Chuo an occasion for political criticism. The unified, timeless ritual of the ancient sages, preserved in canonical texts and at the imperial court, is threatened by the meaningless diversity of vulgar, changeable customs that have begun to affect the nuptial rites of metropolitan officials and imperial princes. The practice of the text excludes the practice of ritual: its deviation from the canon invalidates unwritten vernacular custom (the false etymology of Tying up the Hair only adds to its absurdity), and the cultural geography of the text reduces the inscribed practices to a disjointed series of incomprehensible ceremonies. Just as the absence of the author from these passages makes it impossible to locate him in the ritual narratives (Was he present at the wedding in Hangzhou? Did he witness the ceremonies in the bedroom?), so the distance between the practice of the text and the practice of ritual prohibits any knowledge or understanding of the adumbrated ceremonies.[15]

The strange, exciting detail of travel diaries is conceived in similar contrast with a civilized center. In the preface to his *Xuanhe Embassy's Illustrated Gazetteer of Koryo* (*Xuanhe fengshi Gaoli tujing*, 1124), for example, Xu Jing (1091–1153) explains that in writing his account of the 1122 mission to the kingdom of Koryo (in present Korea) he has "made broad selections from the many stories, based on what I have perceived with my own eyes and ears, abridging or omitting all that is similar to our Middle Kingdom and choosing instead what is different. . . . In this illustrated gazetteer my hand has laid out what my eyes have seen, beginning with the most remote corners and the strangest regions."[16] Xu Jing's rudimentary observations about weddings in Koryo hold its betrothal gifts and marital practices against the universalist standard of ancient ritual and Song civilization: "Cappings, weddings, mourning, and sacrifice are seldom restrained by ritual. . . . When aristocrats and officials marry, they use betrothal gifts of a sort, but commoners exchange only wine and rice. Wealthy men, moreover, take up to three or four wives and divorce them at the slightest disagreement."[17]

Particularly lewd, violent, or otherwise beguiling practices receive lengthier treatment, such as the wedding ceremonies of the Liao in *By*

*Way of Answer to Queries about the Land beyond the Mountains* (*Lingwai daida*, 1178), by Zhou Qufei (1163 *jinshi*):

Entering the Cabin

> The inhabitants of the creeks and caves of Yongzhou [present Guilin, Guangxi province] all intermarry. Since many of the indigenous officials are surnamed Huang, their intermarriage unites families of the same surname. In their wedding ceremonies they place the highest value on crude ostentation and physical violence. The rites and ceremonies that attend the bestowal of betrothal gifts often involve as many as a thousand people. Although the gifts never include gold, silver, or money, they comprise prodigious amounts of wine and dried fish, so that the expense may rightly be called extravagant. When the groom comes to fetch the bride, the bride's family builds more than a hundred straw huts some two miles from their home, where the groom and the bride may live. This is called "Entering the Cabin." The groom's family accompanies the groom to the cabin with drums and music, and the bride's family likewise conveys the bride to the cabin with musicians. The bride's maids and concubines number over a hundred, and the groom brings several hundred servants. On the wedding night, the families of the groom and the bride cover themselves with weapons, and at the slightest disagreement they cross blades. After the wedding, the groom always carries a dagger in his sleeve. If one of his wife's maids displeases him in any way, he kills her on the spot. This is called "Manifestation of the Brave." Only half a year after entering the cabin is the bride taken to the groom's house. The bride's party will fear the groom only if he kills several dozen maids upon entering the cabin. If he fails to do so, he will be considered a weakling.[18]

This passage forces Liao wedding practices into a narrative that reduces them to perversions of universalist, civilized ritual. The Liao do not observe the law that prohibits marriage between people of the same surname, they disregard elegance and moderation, they do not use money or precious metals, they play music at weddings, and the bride does not enter the groom's family until half a year after the nuptials. The straw huts and the incomprehensible violence function as ultimate signs of difference, epitomized in the unfamiliar, exotic phrases Entering the Cabin and Manifestation of the Brave. The author stands at the same remove from the ceremonies as does the reader, and imparts to him a pleasurable combination of amusement and horror that confirms a shared confidence in their superior civilization.

But even when authors write about their hometown, the emphasis on unique local character and peculiar, colorful customs forestalls, by its implication of deviance from a grounding center, the independent creation of meaning in local practice. Fan Chengda (1126–1193), for example, compiled his *Gazetteer of Wu Prefecture* (*Wujun zhi*, 1192) in a deliberate effort to record the particularities of his native region, during a formative period in the history of the local gazetteer when compilers negotiated this very relationship between center and periphery.[19] In the section on local customs, he embeds a mention of marital practices in the cultural geography familiar from notebooks and travel diaries:

> Wuzhong [present Wu county, Jiangsu province] has long been famous for its abundance. Cultivated fields line valley and hillside, and there is not a plot of barren soil anywhere in the outskirts of the town. Since all have their own property, there are no great discrepancies in wealth. The region's customs are therefore extravagant rather than frugal. The locals vie for seasonal products, and they like to go on outings and to entertain. At the beginning of the year, they gather at the Buddhist temple. This is called "the Yearly Confession." The temple grounds throng with men and women, leaving barely space to walk. Friends and relatives who have not seen one another all year often meet on this occasion, some with congratulations, some with condolences. There is also much fevered negotiation of marriage and scrutiny of prospective grooms and brides, and often final arrangements are made on this occasion.[20]

And even in the *Record of Dreaming of Hua in the Eastern Capital* (*Dongjing meng Hua lu*, 1147), a nostalgic memoir of life in Kaifeng "that, for an instant, breaks the traditional grasp that hierarchical ordering holds on textual representations of space," wedding practices function as a sign of difference.[21] In his preface, the pseudonymous Meng Yuanlao explains that he has attempted to preserve in writing the sights and sounds and smells of his Arcadian youth before his fading memories dissolve into the false recollections of his wistful relatives:

> I have arranged my adumbrated notes into this volume in hopes that the reader who opens its pages may see the splendor of that time. The ancients sometimes dreamt that they roamed in the land of Hua Xu, where joy was boundless. Whenever I think back to those days, I return to the present in sorrow, as though awakening from a dream of Hua Xu. Therefore I have named this book *A Dream of Hua*.[22]

On the pages of *A Dream of Hua* unfolds, indeed, a dreamscape of detached bliss, devoid of poverty and crime, in which people work only to sustain the pleasures of others. A bright haze of prosperity and peace envelops the bustling streets and the crowded shops, creating a space that strongly resembles the transcendental Kaifeng of the famous scroll painting "Upstream during the Third Moon" (*Qingming shang he tu*).[23] Through these ephemeral alleys winds a generic wedding sequence of prodigious gifts, decorated carriages, and colorful ceremonies:

> When the bride descended from the carriage, there would be a yinyang expert with a basket full of grains, beans, coins, fruits, herbs, and shoots, which he would toss toward the gate while reciting spells, and small children would scramble for them. This was called "Scattering Grains and Beans." It was commonly said to exorcise the Black Goat and other such baleful deities. When the bride alighted from her carriage or sedan chair, she had to step onto a strip of cloth or a mat. She could not tread the ground. Someone would walk backward holding up a mirror, leading the bride to the place where she had to step over a saddle, across herbs, and over a balance. Then she would enter a room in whose center a curtain was suspended. This was called "Sitting under the Empty Curtain." Or she would immediately be led into the bedroom and be seated on the bed. This was also known as "Sitting on Wealth and Nobility." The women and girls who had accompanied her would retire after three quick cups of wine. This was called "the Running Send-off."[24]

As innocent bits of folklore, evil deities are powerless to affect the oblivious, brilliant ceremonies of enchanted memory. The picturesque series of named acts illuminate briefly the streets and buildings of a lost city, as do the names of gates, avenues, shops, dishes, and entertainers in other sections of *A Dream of Hua*.[25] Like those other sections, the wedding sequence is "stunning for its extremely specific detail and for its lack of comprehensiveness."[26] Although it accommodates small variations (differences in expenditure, a carriage or a sedan chair, a strip of cotton or a mat), it makes no mention of the pertinence of social distinctions or the tremendous regional variety of the transient official population. The time, space, and bodies of these generic ceremonies are the carefree youth, the prosperous capital, and the nameless grooms and brides of the author's blurred, nostalgic memory.

The cultural geography of generic convention allows regional difference to be written only as a negative sign.[27] The learned brush and the lettered page place author and reader at the center of imperial civilization whence local customs must always appear marginal and incomprehensible. Even *A Dream of Hua*, an unconventional text by an unskilled author, does not attempt a comprehensive description of the practical space and time of Kaifeng. Instead, it recollects unique and irreplaceable aspects of a remote city, in implied contrast with the present of the new capital at Hangzhou. The scholarly, cumulative nature of the writing of local customs, moreover, further increases the distance between the written center and the vernacular margins. Notebooks, local gazetteers, and even travel diaries often comprise unidentified layers of older texts on whose authority the writer silently relies. In his entry on Liao wedding practices, for example, Zhou Qufei merely inserts a few phrases into a passage copied from Fan Chengda's *Records of a Forester at Guihai* (*Guihai yuheng zhi*, 1175), a work that was itself largely the product of "Schreibtischarbeit."[28] The writing of local customs, in other words, reduces wedding ritual to a function of the universalist practice of the text. The historian must stand with the author in the ordered landscape of classical prose. The passages translated above outline the dim, receding contours of the limits of historical knowledge, beyond which stretch unknown, unknowable cultures of local practice.

Local practice cannot be written, since the standardized genres and universalist discourses that inform classical writing can accommodate neither its locality nor its practicality.[29] Only when a written narrative accords with the universalist notions of time, space, bodies, and text of the genre and the discourse in which it is inscribed, does it point toward an historical performance, namely the refiguring performance in reading or in ritual of those prefigured universalist notions, mediated by the inscribed configuration of the ritual narrative.[30] Ritual manuals, engagement letters and wedding poems, calendars and almanacs, and legal codes and verdicts all place their grooms and brides within the time, space, and text of encompassing discursive formations: the symmetrical, centered, porous time and space of exegetical discourse, where the groom and the bride merge with sacred antiquity; the linear time and space of literary discourse, where the written bodies of the groom and the bride proceed through an anterior, metaphorical time and space; the cyclical time and space of cosmological discourse, in which calculations and diagrams chart a safe path for the liminal groom and bride through liminal time and space; and the imperial time and space of legal discourse, in which codes and verdicts carefully inscribe the groom and the bride into a transparent hierarchy of imperial subjects.[31] Only when writing is a ritual act or when the text is a ritual object—in ritual manuals, in wedding correspondence, and in cosmological calculation—is the text part of the refiguration of time, space, and bodies through the performance (in body or in mind) of wedding ritual, and is the text therefore an historical trace of the ritual practice of weddings. Legal codes and verdicts are traces of the ritual practice of imperial government, whose order the inscription of weddings aims to perpetuate. In the geographical discourse of local customs, writing disperses ritual practice into a series of meaningless, incomprehensible vignettes.

The text, however, cannot determine the refiguration of time, space, bodies, and writing in the reading or performance of inscribed ritual narratives. The simultaneity and material polysemy of ritual practice, moreover, allows a convergence of discursive formations in ritual time and space that remain strictly segregated in the time and space of classical writing.[32] In the material remains of joint burial (conclusion), sometimes traces of archaic ritual, literary display, and cosmological calculation converge under the shared motifs of filial devotion, reproduction, and immortality. The reunification of the gendered, ritualized bodies of deceased spouses in the ritualized time and space of the tomb bears explicit parallels to wedding ritual. It is therefore possible that archaic ceremonies, literary display, and cosmological calculation converged in the ritual practice of weddings as they do in the material remains of joint burial. But the sense of ritual that coordinated these incommensurable notions of time, space, bodies, and writing in satisfactory, individual wedding rites has been irretrievably lost.

## The Practice of the Academic Text: The Writing of Weddings in Modern and Postmodern History

Historical studies published in Mainland China, Taiwan, and the United States disregard the multiplicity of time, space, bodies, and writing in ritual narratives of the Middle Period, and instead inscribe Middle-Period weddings and marriage in the linear time and space of modernity. As heirs to eighteenth-century Enlightenment rationalism and nineteenth-century historicism, these studies assume a discontinuity between the modern present and the unenlightened past, between the discerning eye of the knowing scholar and the performing body of the unconscious native. Since only the modern scholar is cognizant of the universal truths that underlay the events of the past (whether it be the truth of historical materialism, of psychoanalysis, of medical science, or of structuralist anthropology), Middle-Period texts dissolve into a mass of lifeless, unresisting data, to be gathered by the thick-soled historian across the craggy generic boundaries and rough discursive formations of expansive centuries, then to be labeled at the learned desk according to their true, enduring scientific categories.[33] The untenable assumptions about text and ritual that inform the resulting studies of Middle-Period weddings and marriage have passed unnoticed only because their historical and ritual narratives conform to widely shared modern notions of time, space, bodies, and text. The common sense of the historian produces a history that the reader recognizes as lively and real. In fact, the native's unconscious is the historian's own, and the obliviousness to the practice of the historical text rehearses the historian's obliviousness to the practice of academic writing.[34] The severance of the present from the past forecloses the unrealized "potentialities of the present" opened up by the historical text, and condemns the historian to solipsist homologies that are both invalid and uninteresting.[35]

Few books and articles published in Mainland China and Taiwan are dedicated in their entirety to Middle-Period wedding ritual.[36] Most discussions of Middle-Period weddings are embedded in more encompassing studies of the history of *hunyin*, a binome whose meaning scholars in the early twentieth century expanded from its classical denotation of wedding ritual to marriage in the broadest sense: marriage patterns, wedding practices, and marital relations, with connotations of family organization, concubinage, chastity, and divorce.

Historical monographs published during the 1920s and 1930s provided the Republic of China, the young nation-state, with a past that befit its modern present, inscribed in newly acquired subject positions such as women, family, nation, and China, and in an unfamiliar academic discourse of shifting neologisms.[37] Lewis Henry Morgan's (1818–1881) *Ancient Society* (1877) afforded Republican historians a universal, scientific narrative of the linear development of marital practices by which they could measure the historical progress of China toward its recent enlightenment—from the promiscuous matriliny during the stage of savagery, through the patrilineal monogamy that defines the stage of civilization, to the hygienic, scientific practices of romantic love in the blissful present.[38] After this first configuration of the Chinese past and its sources according to Morgan's insights, his narrative (and its summary rewrite by Friedrich Engels in *The Origin of the Family, Private Property and the State*, 1884) has continued to shape studies of *hunyin* in the People's Republic of China and in Taiwan.[39]

The universal, linear narrative of *hunyin* creates a predetermined history that can be read through the transparent sources:

> When we uncoil the long scroll that depicts Chinese marriage customs through history, all kinds of marriage patterns appear in their manifold curious and wondrous shapes. Different concepts of marriage assert themselves in their multifariousness, and all manner of wedding customs display their radiant splendor and endless variations. If we direct our penetrating gaze to see through the historical ideas behind marriage customs and to reveal their deepest layers of meaning and their profound mysteries, then we may realize that traditional Chinese marriage customs are like a prism, refracting the motley rainbow of traditional Chinese culture and providing us with a profound historical enlightenment.[40]

The historical text has no real existence. Under the historian's gaze it disintegrates into a collection of data (*cailiao*, *ziliao*) that are held together only by the historian's preconceived framework, which also gives them meaning. The historian recognizes neither wedding rites nor the sources nor his own writing as works of discourse. Texts preserve data of wedding ceremonies that reflect (*fanying*) objective, universal developments, and these the historian dutifully transcribes in objective, universal categories.

Just as objectivist linear history collapses writing and ritual performance with the society they refract, it collapses historical time and geographic space. Within the discrete periods defined by universal, objective transitions (social, political, technological), only insignificant regional variations can exist in marital practices.[41] Histories of *hunyin* published in Mainland China and Taiwan therefore either uphold one or two privileged texts as representative of the wedding ceremonies of a particular period, or they invent a generic, composite sequence that merges a number of disparate sources. The privileged texts for the Middle Period are usually Zhu Xi's *Family Rituals* and Meng Yuanlao's *Dream of Hua*. To those historians who hold *Family Rituals* to be representative of the age, the adoption of this text by the Yuan and Ming imperial courts does not mark the acceptance of Zhu Xi's exegetical authority and his claims to sagehood, but the acknowledgment of his abridgment of canonical ritual as a timely means for the perpetuation of feudal oppression.[42] *A Dream of Hua* appears to derive its historical authority from the rare detail and the illusory realism of its wedding sequence.[43] Some historians, misrecognizing discursive difference as social difference, identify, the wedding ceremonies in *Family Rituals* as the ritual practices of the elite, and the wedding ceremonies in *A Dream of Hua* as popular practice.[44]

Where the selection of a privileged text reduces the ritual practice of several centuries to the misconstrued ritual time and space of one or two texts, composite narratives devise sequences of ceremonies entirely divorced from historical time and space, as well as from inscribed ritual time and space. In such sequences, faceless grooms and anonymous brides float through a nondescript landscape of selfsame centuries, performing disjointed, incomplete, repetitive ceremonies (painted with bright, false colors). The generic, composite bride may thus be submitted to Scattering the Curtain in the bedroom before having entered the groom's compound (due to the careless historian's equation of Scattering the Curtain [*sa zhang*] with Scattering Grains and Beans [*sa gudou*]) or pay her first visit to the groom's ancestral temple both during and after the wedding (maintaining the incompatible ceremonies of Bowing to the Spirits of the Ancestors [*bai xianling*, or *bai tang*] and Visit to the Temple [*miao jian*]). The sole meaning of such composite sequences lies in their instantiation of certain social or political conditions that the historian has designated as defining of the age.[45]

American historians of the Middle Period have been critical of the shortcomings of Chinese scholarship on their subject, but they have often failed to notice that these shortcomings derive from structuralist assumptions not very different from their own. Although social history generally lacks the overt teleology of historical materialism, its notion of the social is conceived in similarly objectivist terms. In the early pages of their articles and monographs, social historians of the Middle Period consistently introduce universalist concepts (women, education, social mobility, bureaucracy, and so forth) to create a three-dimensional past that operates according to contemporary notions of psychology and social behavior, and that precedes the sources. Middle-Period texts are reduced to a reflection of this preconceived past. Between the modern present and its universalist past, the texts are prevented from creating meanings and histories of their own.

In one important American monograph on Song-dynasty marriage, for example, it is not the universal progress of technological development that abolishes historical discourse, but certain timeless patterns of structuralist anthropology. Its aggregate wedding ceremony, staged as a rite of passage, combines fragments from eleventh- and twelfth-century ritual manuals, the twelfth-century *Dream of Hua*, fourteenth-century writing manuals, and a Ming-dynasty short story set in Song times, and other texts, in a sequence that disregards the ritual narrative of each of its sources.[46] The silent, solemn bride of *Family Rituals* transforms into the fiery, fictional heroine of a fifteenth-century tale, who then finds herself carried in a sedan chair through nameless streets in Northern Song Kaifeng, to change at the groom's gate into a nervous young woman who finds "opportunities to express reluctance and resistance" in a fourteenth-century song cycle of which she is in fact a lifeless, two-dimensional creation.[47] Although the monograph is partial to the linear time and space of literary discourse, it eliminates the compelling sexual drive of the narrative of public consummation by sending the groom to fetch the bride at her house (in the manner of *Family Rituals*) and by placing him next to the bride at the family altar upon her arrival at his house (combining Sima Guang's *Letters and Ceremonies* with *A Dream of Hua* and a Yuan-dynasty writing manual), instead of allowing them to meet for the first time in the bedroom. The removal of the ceremonies from the ritual time and space of the text severs them from historical time and space, and yields an exercise in timeless structuralism, masked by the beguiling realism of colorful data.[48]

The prefigured linearity of modernity, whether of the historical materialism of Chinese scholars or the structuralist social history of

American historians, precludes the multiplicity of time, space, bodies, and text configured in Middle-Period ritual narratives. The presumption of universalist, objectivist truth renders both text and ritual transparent, and places the modern scholar's own writing outside history. This denial of discourse in both the past and the present deceives modern scholars into accepting any text that appears to converge with their preconceptions as literal truth, and to dismiss any unfitting text as corrupt, contrived, or irrelevant. They misrecognize the polemic distinction between ritual (*li*) and custom (*su*) as a real, social difference between elite and popular practice; inflate with ghoulish life the surface narratives of nuptial songs and *A Dream of Hua*; and in general neglect real traces of ritual practice, such as wedding correspondence and cosmological calculations, for the benefit of those texts in which the writer stands (or, rather, is believed to stand) at a descriptive remove from ritual practice. Because the cultural geography of local customs coincides perfectly with nineteenth-century notions of time, space, bodies, and writing, the historical materialist and the social historian accept its uneven, polemic observations as fact. Much like the writer of local customs, the modern scholar assumes that the advanced present and the modern world are separated from backward regions and periods in both space and time, and that this remove affords the modern the right to inscribe the inferior bodies that populate those remote spaces and times into their linear narratives of progress.[49] Like the writer of local customs, the modern scholar presses foreign ceremonies into an ill-fitting, preconceived ritual narrative that reduces them to exotic, amusing, meaningless signs of difference.

The recognition of writing as a ritual practice and of text as a ritual object re-establishes the organic connection between ritual and history, and between the past and the present. The configuration of prefigured time, space, bodies, and text in ritual narratives has created an enduring trace of discursive practice that ever allows the reader to refigure its living contents in the present. It is as such a living trace of historical practice that the text discloses the past. The historian may follow this trace, from a modern typeset edition or a facsimile reprint or a manuscript, through the shifting corpora created by transmission, to the brush and the hand that wrote the text, in a distinct historical time and space, in a determinate genre and discourse.[50] The refiguration of the "world of the text" requires a critical, dialectical, reflexive hermeneutics in which the coherence of the trace, not the presumption of the reader, guides explanation and interpretation. Only thus does the reader allow the unfolding of the "worlds in front of the text" and the unrealized "potentialities of the present."[51] This results, not in a more truthful rendition of Middle-Period wedding ceremonies, but in a narrative description of fragmented discourses, in which authors and texts (not grooms and brides) create ritual time, space, and bodies that have been preserved, misread, edited, and obliterated by later generations.[52] The preservation of this multiplicity of narratives and discourses in a historical monograph of course befits the postmodern mood, with its rejection of the modern confidence in linear progress and singular truth. But this postmodern reading is founded on a solid hermeneutics and validated by an effective heuristics, as historical materialism and social history are not.[53]

The material remains of joint burial are merely a different kind of trace of historical practice.[54] The incomplete evidence of burial practices, the fragmented context of the landscape, and the selective destruction of tombs by natural decay, grave robbers, and archaeologists require a critical, reflexive, dialectical hermeneutics not essentially different from that of the historian, who places incomplete texts in fragmented discursive formations that have been diminished by selective transmission.[55] Yet the "simpler but more ambiguous language" of material culture distinguishes artifacts from documents.[56] The mute simultaneity and the silent ambiguity of architecture, stone carvings, murals, grave goods, and human remains allow a juxtaposition of incompatible notions of time, space, bodies, and writing that the determinate text precludes. This convergence of incommensurable discourses in the ritual time and space of the tomb opens up the conceptual possibility of a similar convergence of discourses in the ritual time and space of weddings—but only as prefigured discourses, not as configured texts. The convergence of discourses in the tomb marks the practical limitations of the classical text; it does not legitimate the conjecture of composite ritual narratives.[57] The material remains of joint burial and the inscribed narratives of transmitted texts represent different kinds of historical fragments of ritual practice: the configuration of time, space, bodies, and writing in tombs is individual and ambiguous but incomplete, and in the end only similar, not identical, to wedding ritual; the configuration of time, space, bodies, and writing in texts is fuller and more explicit, but also determinate and generic. Together, these material and written traces, fragmented and incomplete, allude to individual configurations of prefigured time, space, bodies, and text in the ritual practice of Middle-Period weddings, informed by a sense of ritual that was embodied, unwritten, unwritable, and irretrievably lost.[58]

This book presents an attempt to write Middle-Period weddings in American academic prose without rupturing the organic connection between the present and the past. Each chapter places wedding ritual within a distinct discursive formation and describes the writing of weddings within that discursive formation as it developed across the centuries, from its origins through its disintegration, or from one founding text to another. The narrative, the ritual theory, the language, and even the metaphors of each chapter accord as much as possible with the sources as written, printed, and transmitted. This is a history of the writing of weddings: a history of writing as cultural practice, of conventional genres and encompassing discourses, of the obliteration of manuscripts by generic printed texts, of the transforming corpora created by the process of transmission, and of the joyful retrieval of living traces of the past in the present. Perhaps more elegant literary forms exist that could preserve the discourses of the past, but the disjoined chapters of this book, with their disjointed times and spaces, in a pleasing way point to another disjunction, namely the remove between Middle-Period texts and the Western historiographical tradition. The organic connection that exists between Western historiography and its sources—the cumulative canon of Herodotus and Livy, Gregory of Tours and Bede, Voltaire and Gibbon, Tocqueville and Carlyle, extending across the spatial and temporal, religious and philosophical rifts between kingdoms and calendars—does not exist between Western historiography and Middle-Period texts.[59] This divide between the received narratives of Western history and literature and the uncompliant discourses of Middle-Period texts requires a reconsideration of modes of emplotment, and that is what this book attempts.[60]

Texts connect the present to the past, their words enduring traces of historical practice. He who "understands words" may hope to understand the "others" who wrote those words—"as though meeting face to face" across the centuries, as Li Jike (fl. 1158) imagines in his reading of that final phrase of *The Analects* (*Lunyu*).[61] Yet in the end it is not the reader who explains the text, but the text that illumines the reader, as it unfolds in front of the page the proposed worlds of the text and the unrealized potentialities of the present.

# Chapter One

## Ritual Manuals

### Exegetical Hermeneutics and the Re-Embodiment of Antiquity

> Often I bewail the difficulty of *Ceremonies and Rites* [*Yili*]. And but few are those who practice its injunctions today. Transmissions of ancient practice have grown apart, so that one cannot investigate how the rituals of antiquity might be restored. Today, truly, we lack all means to put *Ceremonies and Rites* to use. Yet it contains in crude form the structures laid down by King Wen and the Duke of Zhou. . . . How regrettable! that I did not live to see those times, advancing and retreating, bowing and yielding in their midst. Alas! Such boundless sorrow!
>
> —Han Yu (768–824 CE)[1]

> For half my life, I studied in different places, reading *Ceremonies and Rites* till late at night. After so many years of immersion, I suddenly experienced a feeling of discovery. Now, every time I open a section, it is as if in my heart-mind, inside my eyes, I can actually see the ancients, across more than a thousand years, and it is as if I bow, yield, and turn in their midst. Many a time I must have waved my arms and stamped my feet in joy without knowing it.
>
> —Ao Jigong (1301)[2]

In 726, four years after Emperor Xuanzong (r. 712–756) of the Tang dynasty had ordered the compilation of a new ritual code, Secretarial Receptionist Wang Yan proposed to edit the *Record of Ritual* (*Liji*) into a contemporary protocol in which current precedent would replace arcane passages. Zhang Yue (667–730), Right Aide at the Academy of Scholarly Worthies, protested this proposal: "The *Record of Ritual* was compiled during the Han dynasty and has been transmitted across the centuries as an unassailable scripture. Today we stand far removed from the sages of antiquity, and I am afraid that it will be impossible to inflict such alterations." Instead, Zhang Yue proposed to return to *Rites of the Zhenguan Period* (*Zhenguan li* or *Da Tang yili*, 637) and *Rites of the Xianqing Period* (*Xianqing li*, 658), and to reopen based on those protocols the debate about the relationship between current precedent and ancient ritual. The emperor endorsed Zhang Yue's proposal.[3]

*Rites of the Kaiyuan Period of the Great Tang* (*Da Tang Kaiyuan li*), completed in 732, merged imperial precedent with canonical ritual in seamless ritual narratives. The new ceremonies designed by the Academy of Scholarly Worthies overlay the palace grounds and imperial bodies with the spaces and choreographies of ancient ritual scripture, thus combining the authority of the canon with the detailed protocol of the imperial court. Although subsequent generations of ritual specialists emended parts of *Rites of the Kaiyuan Period*, they honored its hermeneutical principles. The ritual codes compiled in the tenth and eleventh centuries at the Song imperial court still bore a significant resemblance to the Kaiyuan code.[4]

But in 1078, Chen Xiang (1017–1080) completed a revision of imperial sacrificial rites in which he denounced his predecessors' attempts at merging canon and precedent:

> Your humble servant Chen and his fellow compilers of *Detailed Investigations into the Rites and Texts of the Imperial Altars and Temples* [*Xiangding jiaomiao liwen*] observe: The ceremonies of the seasonal offerings to the illustrious spirits at the Altar of Heaven and the sacrifices to the imperial ancestors at court in outline all follow Tang ritual. Even the placement of spirit tablets on the altar, the imperial conveyances, and the trappings of the ceremonial guard are devised according to a combination of precedents from different eras. When one compares these ceremonies to the rituals of the ancient kings, the differences are immediately apparent. Moreover, the insistence on the combination of precedents from different eras has resulted in countless conflicts, both in the words used and in the emotions conveyed. For a long time, ritual specialists have transmitted protocol with only minor, insubstantial changes, and those who insisted on reform relied entirely on the practices of their own day.[5]

Chen Xiang wrote his denunciation of ritual precedent in a time when scholars were gaining confidence in their ability to recover ancient ritual. The ancients who had seemed forbiddingly remote to Zhang Yue and Han Yu in the eighth century, to eleventh-century scholars had become a visible, tangible presence. Since the canon had been first committed to print in 953, its texts had become available to a growing community of scholars.[6] This community gathered not only in bookshops, libraries, and academies, but it existed in the written and printed space of letters and books. Into this printed space Ouyang Xiu (1007–1072) introduced in 1063 his *Record of Collecting Antiquities* (*Jigu lu*), an annotated collection of stone inscriptions he had gathered over several decades. A few years later, Ouyang Xiu's friend Liu Chang (1019–1068) ordered the contours of eleven ancient bronze vessels engraved in stone and circulated rubbings from these engravings under the title *Record of Pre-Qin Vessels* (*Xian-Qin guqi ji*).[7]

The works of Ouyang Xiu and Liu Chang inspired an enthusiastic following among their contemporaries, who began collecting and reproducing inscriptions and vessels with abandon. The reproductions made private collections accessible to remote scholars. In this space of paper and ink, a community of epigraphists and archaeologists assisted one another in deciphering inscriptions and classifying vessels, comparing items from different collections, and corroborating their surmises with canonical citations. Within a few decades, Song scholars identified the names and ritual functions of all types of ancient bronze vessels and acquired a proficiency in reading and writing ancient script forms.

The cauldrons and beakers created a connection between Song literati and the ancients that was both historical and timeless. The patinated vessels found on riverbanks and in ancient burial grounds had stood in distant times on royal altars and in noble temples. But the vessels also held a universal truth, an understanding of cosmic patterns that had informed the ritual, music, institutions, and social structure of antiquity and that could not be expressed in words. As Fan Zhen (1008–1088) memorialized in 1037, in a debate about musical reform, "Music is harmonic *qi*. Harmonic *qi* is conveyed by sound, and sound originates in formlessness. Therefore the ancients transmitted the system of sound by means of concrete objects, that men in later times might study them."[8]

Ancient bronze vessels and musical instruments instantiated a cosmic order that the ancients embodied in ritual performance. Ritual allowed man to conform to the natural order and to attain his proper place in society and the cosmos. Culture had thus merged with nature in ancient civilization, in a perfect, lasting order. But whereas vessels had survived intact across the millennia to convey timeless truths through their enduring proportions, ritual had been imperfectly inscribed, in texts that subsequently had suffered fragmentation, neglect, and corruption at the hands of careless scholars. In his preface to the monograph on ritual and music in the *New History of the Tang*, published around the same time as his *Record of Collecting Antiquities*, Ouyang Xiu sets forth this degeneration of ritual from a pervasive, inherent order to a bounded, meaningless practice:

> Until the Three Dynasties, order issued from one source, and ritual and music pervaded the realm. But since the Three Dynasties, order has derived from two sources, and ritual and music have become mere words.
>
> In antiquity, halls and carriages served as dwellings, robes and caps as clothes, ewers and beakers as vessels, and metal bells, stone drums, silk strings, and bamboo flutes as musical instruments. With these, the ancients approached their altars and temples, surveyed the court, and served the spirits, and thus instilled order among the people. . . . Every single act of the common people issued from ritual. The instillment in the people of filiality and compassion, friendship and brotherliness, loyalty and trust, and humaneness and duty could therefore simply proceed through their dwellings, actions, clothing, and food. Ritual inhered in their every action, morning and night. This is what I mean when I write "order issued from one source, and ritual and music pervaded the realm." . . .
>
> After the Three Dynasties had come to naught, the Qin dynasty perverted the legacy of antiquity, and all those who possessed the realm since referred to the Qin, whether in the matter of emperor and officials, nomenclature and rank, imperial institutions, or the structure of palaces, carriages, clothing, and vessels. . . . The ritual and music of the Three Dynasties, their names and implements, were carefully stored away by officials, to be produced periodically for use at the altars and temples and at court, and one would say, "This is ritual. Herewith we instruct the people." This is what I mean by "order derives from two sources, and ritual and music are mere words."[9]

In order to retrieve the incorporated knowledge of the ancients, to recreate the permanently ritualized bodies of antiquity, to realign human civilization with the cosmic order in an enduring empire, scholars in the eleventh century engaged in a dialectical investigation of the historical remains of the Three Dynasties and the timeless truths revealed in nature and the cosmos. Combining archaeology, epigraphy, philology, and exegetical hermeneutics, literati of the late Northern Song attempted to reconstruct ancient texts, understand their meaning and context, and embody their injunctions in the present. They re-inscribed canonical texts in order to be able to reincorporate their cosmic truth in the present. Like the ancient vessels, ritual created a direct, physical connection with the ancients that collapsed a distance of millennia into a shared, timeless, embodied truth. Thus, Zhai Qinian (fl. 1142) wrote in his *History of Seal Script* (*Zhoushi*) of the archaic rites performed under Emperor Huizong (r. 1100–1125):

> With one stroke he wiped away the vulgar speculations of the scholars of the Han and the Tang. After a myriad generations, the classification of the vessels of the Three Dynasties was finally restored, so that the matters recorded in the canon were no longer mere words.[10]

Yet the archaic rites of Huizong failed to establish a lasting peace. In 1114, Huizong performed the summer solstice sacrifice at the Altar of the Earth with twenty-eight reproductions of ancient bronze vessels, inscribed with archaic texts honoring deities and ancestors.[11] Twelve years later, Jurchen armies besieged Kaifeng and conquered the northern half of the Song empire. In the caravans of imperial kinsmen, conducted by Jurchen soldiers to the northern steppes, traveled Emperor Huizong and hundreds of ancient bronzes looted from his palace. Private collectors abandoned their antiquities on their flight to the south. Although southern scholars occasionally obtained ancient bronzes through trade with northern merchants, the study of antiquities did not regain the fervor of the Northern Song. To some, the lost collections symbolized a decadent culture of material excess, epitomized by an extravagant emperor who in the pursuit of his oblivious obsessions lost his empire and his life.[12]

Paper and ink proved more durable than bronze and stone. The reproduction of steles and vessels ensured the preservation of many important collections for scholars of the Southern Song. Antiquity was once more reduced to text. Epigraphy, archaeology, philology, and canonical exegesis operated on the level surface of the written page, where scholars of the Southern Song could bow and yield among the ancients through commentaries, illustrations of ancient vessels and dress, plans of classical courtyards, and reconstructions of ritual choreography. By the thirteenth century, *Family Rituals*, compiled by Zhu Xi and emended by his disciples, gained acceptance as a new scripture, a ritual text that transposed the cosmic patterns inscribed in the ancient canon onto contemporary spaces and contemporary bodies.

The ritual manuals of the Tang and Song dynasties reinscribe canonical texts to allow reincorporation of the timeless knowledge of the ancients. As an interface between performing bodies of the past and the present, the ritual manual is a provisional text that dissolves when its written bodies and spaces assume concrete shape. But despite the ambition of the authors to make their texts disappear, the ritual manual remains a text—the historical product of exegetical convictions and hermeneutical techniques. Like the ancient bronzes scrutinized by Song literati, ritual manuals are both historical and timeless. As products of exegetical scholarship, they betray the scholarly fashions and political ambitions of their time. Yet, as scripts for performance, they merge past and present, text and body, reader and performer, in a space where the literatus may bow and yield among the ancients and into which the present reader, too, may enter.

Weddings in ritual manuals belong to a ritual cycle that repeats endlessly through the generations to produce and reproduce the ritual bodies of family and society. But unlike cappings and pinnings (ceremonies marking the adulthood of boys and girls), funerals, and sacrifice, weddings also produce biological bodies. Although the permanently ritualized bodies envisioned by some Tang and Song exegetes merge biological sex and ritual subject position (just as nature and culture merge in the permanently ritualized civilization of antiquity), sexual bodies and ritual bodies remain logically distinct as male and female (*nannü*), and husband and wife (*fufu*). While capping and pinning create ritual bodies by initiating boys and girls into the ritual cycle, weddings create the legitimate sexual bodies necessary to sustain the ritual cycle itself. In the words of the chapter "The Meaning of Weddings" in the *Record of Ritual*:

> Only after establishing respect and gravity does wedding ritual allow the groom and the bride to become intimate. Such is the general purport of the rite: it is thereby that the distinction between male and female is completed, and it is thus that

> proper relations between husband and wife are established. Only after male and female have been differentiated can husband and wife have proper relations; and only after husband and wife have established proper relations can father and son achieve intimacy; and only after father and son have achieved intimacy can ruler and minister attain their proper stations. Therefore it is said, "Weddings are the root of ritual." Truly, ritual begins with capping; has its root in weddings; achieves its utmost gravity at mourning and sacrifice; confers the greatest honor at court audiences and official missions; and establishes harmony at archery and community wine drinking ceremonies. This is the general purport of ritual.[13]

The sexual bodies of male and female set the ritual cycle in motion, yet these sexual bodies themselves remain outside the cycle. The proper placement of sexual bodies in the ritual time and space of weddings therefore posed difficulties to authors of ritual manuals in the Tang and Song dynasties. An understanding of their ruminations and solutions in this matter yields insights into the important hermeneutical changes that informed the ritual manuals of the eighth through thirteenth centuries. But an understanding of these solutions requires an acquaintance with the raw materials and basic techniques of exegetical hermeneutics.

## Canonical Weddings: Fragments and Hermeneutics

Of all canonical texts, the second chapter of *Ceremonies and Rites*, "Wedding Rites of an Ordinary Officer" (*Shi hunli*), contains the most comprehensive wedding sequence. From this chapter, authors of ritual manuals in the Tang and Song dynasties derived the basic ritual narrative for wedding ceremonies.

The sequence (see fig. 1.1) opens with a series of rituals commonly designated the Six Rites (*liu li*): Submission of the Choice (*na cai*), Asking the Name (*wen ming*), Submission of the Auspicious Result (*na ji*), Submission of the Betrothal Gifts (*na zheng*), Requesting the Date (*qing qi*), and Fetching the Bride (*qin ying*). In the first five ceremonies of this series, a representative of the groom's family (the guest) communicates his family's intentions to a representative of the bride's family

**FIGURE 1.1. Schema of Wedding Ritual according to *Ceremonies and Rites.***

Submission of the Choice (*na cai*)

- Host arranges the messenger's seat outside the gate
  - Guest arrives, communicates through host's assistant
    - Host meets guest at the gate; they enter and ascend
      - Guest conveys message and goose; host bows
    - Guest descends and exits; host descends
  - [Guest communicates through host's assistant]

Asking the Name (*wen ming*)

  - Guest communicates through host's assistant
    - Host meets guest at the gate; they enter and ascend
      - Guest conveys request and goose; host bows
    - Guest descends and exits; host descends
  - Guest announces the end of the rite through assistant
- Host rewards the messenger with a meal

Submission of the Auspicious Result (*na ji*): same as Submission of the Choice.

Submission of the Betrothal Gifts (*na zheng*): same as previous, but with gifts of cloth and deerskins instead of a goose.

Requesting the Date (*qing qi*): same as Submission of the Choice.

Fetching the Bride (*qin ying*)

- Arrangements at the groom's chamber
  - Departure of groom and followers
    - Groom arrives at the bride's gate
      - Bride, duenna, and followers assume their places
        - Host meets groom at the gate; they bow, enter, ascend
          - Groom presents goose and bows
        - Groom descends and exits
      - Bride descends
    - Groom, bride, duenna, and followers depart
  - Groom, bride, duenna, and followers arrive at groom's gate
  - Groom and bride enter the groom's chamber
    - Groom and bride wash, sacrifice, eat, drink, bow
  - Groom leaves the chamber; bride remains
  - Groom and bride disrobe, followers spread mats, pillows
    - Groom re-enters, loosens bride's tassel
  - Followers leave the chamber with the candles
- Followers consume the leftovers of the nuptial meal

Bride Meets Her Parents-in-Law (*fu jian jiugu*)

Parents-in-Law Receive the Bride (*jiugu xiang fu*)

Bride Visits the Ancestral Temple (*miao jian*)

(the host) and conveys their gifts. This ritualized dialogue and exchange of objects take place at the center of symmetrical space (the center of the platform of the host's family temple) and symmetrical time. The choreography of bodies through ritual space and time in fact creates this center: the guest enters and exits, announces the beginning and the end of the ritual, ascends and descends. Even the acts that prepare and dismantle the ritual site (and that therefore, strictly speaking, lie outside ritual time and space), become implicated in this symmetrical structure: the host arranges a seat for the guest outside the gate prior to the guest's arrival, and after the guest has announced the end of the ceremony, the host invites the guest for a meal. (During this meal, the guest no longer represents the groom's family but only the messenger in the capacity of messenger; thus, in this separate ceremony the guest replicates the host's bows as he does not in the central ceremony.)

Fetching the Bride employs the same ritual grammar of spatial and temporal symmetry in a longer, more complex choreography of bodies and clothing, vessels and foods. On the evening of the wedding, the groom's family prepares for the arrival of the bride, arranging foods, vessels, and other objects inside and outside the groom's chamber. The host of the groom's family sends off the groom, who subsequently assumes the role of host, setting out at dusk with carriages and followers to fetch the bride. When the groom arrives at the bride's gate, the ritual role of host passes to the bride's father, who instructs the bride before welcoming the groom. The groom presents a goose at the temple and bows toward the north. When he descends the steps, the bride follows him, accompanied by her duenna and followers, to be led to her carriage. At his compound, the groom (at certain points helped by ritual assistants) leads the bride through the gate, into his chamber, and through a ritual washing, and then through sacrifices, libations, and a ritualized meal (Sharing the Meal [*tong lao*] and Sharing the Nuptial Cup [*he jin*]). After the meal, the groom leaves the chamber. The bride's followers receive the groom's clothes and spread his mat while the groom's followers do the same for the bride. After the groom has re-entered the chamber and loosened the bride's tassel, the followers leave the chamber to finish the leftovers of the nuptial meal, taking the candles with them.

The next day, the bride engages in a series of ritual exchanges of food and drink with the groom's parents (The Bride Meets the Parents-in-Law [*fu jian jiugu*], The Bride Feeds Her Parents-in-Law [*fu jun jiugu*], and The Parents-in-Law Treat the Bride [*jiugu xiang fu*]). The groom's parents then reward the followers with a meal and gifts. In the third month after the wedding, the bride visits the groom's ancestral temple for the first time (*miao jian*).

The wedding sequence as a whole consists of a series of interlocking symmetries rather than one overarching symmetrical structure. The separation of the bride from her natal family (begun three months before the wedding with her instruction in the family temple) and her integration into the groom's family (starting with the groom and the groom's parents, and completed with her visit to the groom's ancestral temple) suggest an overarching, symmetrical structure that places the night of the nuptial meal at the exact temporal center. Yet within that structure exist symmetrical entities that do not center on the wedding night but rather on acts that are peripheral to other symmetrical structures. Every preparatory act finds its completion, and every core is embedded in peripheral acts, both in complete ceremonies and in ritual details. The wedding sequence as a whole, however, combines circular and linear time in a complex texture that defies simple analysis and univocal interpretation (see, for example, Fetching the Bride in fig. 1.1).

The exposition of the basic ritual choreography in "Wedding Rites of an Ordinary Officer" is followed by a section of notes (*ji*). Some of these notes supply ritual details for the wedding sequence, including the precise words of all formalized dialogues. But the notes also provide general injunctions about timing (all ceremonies should take place at dawn or dusk), space (all ceremonies should take place in the temple), words (all words should be beautiful, not offensive), and food (all foods should be fresh and whole).

The exegetical hermeneutics of Tang and Song scholars assumed not only that the notes to "Wedding Rites of an Ordinary Officer" should be integrated into the basic sequence, but that injunctions and details from other scriptures supplemented the wedding sequence of *Ceremonies and Rites*. Tang and Song exegetes held that all canonical texts preserved traces of antiquity, and the cosmic unity of that legendary time implicated its textual traces which, even when corrupted and incomplete, partook of a similar coherence.

This hermeneutics provided Tang and Song scholars with a miscellaneous array of ritual details and interpretative statements concerning ancient wedding ritual. *Rites of Zhou* (*Zhouli*) lists the office of matchmaker and explains that the matchmaker collected the birth records of all boys and girls in the realm so that they might be timely and properly married—men at the age of thirty and women at the age of twenty.[14] The *Guliang Commentary* (*Guliang zhuan*) and the *Record of Ritual* mention the same ages for male and female marriage, and "Cutting an Axe-Handle," in the *Book of Songs* (*Shijing*), emphasizes the indispensability of a matchmaker in the conclusion of a marriage:[15]

> How does one cut an axe-handle?
> Without an axe it is impossible.
> How does one take a wife?
> Without a matchmaker she cannot be got.[16]

References to matches and wedding ceremonies during the late Zhou occur throughout the historical records of the *Spring and Autumn Annals* (*Chunqiu*), with opinions by the early commentators about the appropriateness of these various undertakings.[17]

Longer passages on wedding ritual appear in several chapters of the *Record of Ritual*. "Summary of Ritual Details" (*Quli*) explains that wedding ritual establishes proper differentiation between male and female through the matchmaker and betrothal gifts, through announcements to authorities, spirits, and the local community, and through exogamy.[18] In "Master Zeng Asked" (*Zengzi wen*), Kongzi ("Confucius") and Zengzi discuss several aspects of weddings: a three-day candlelight vigil at the groom's house and a three-day prohibition of music at the bride's house; the first sacrifice by the bride in the third month of marriage; and the contingencies caused by deaths in the families of the groom or the bride, or by the death of the groom or the bride themselves between Submission of the Choice and the bride's first visit to the groom's ancestral temple.[19] A long passage on cappings and weddings in the chapter "Sacrificing a Single Beast at the Ramparts" (*Jiao tesheng*) places weddings in a context of cosmic reproduction and proceeds to discuss the meaning of different stages in the wedding sequence: the betrothal gift as an expression of trust and fidelity, the precedence of male over female, and the cultural and cosmic significance of a balance between intimacy (of the groom and the bride) and differentiation (of male and female), and between equality and inequality. It also decrees that there be no music or congratulations at weddings.[20] The chapter "Miscellaneous Records" (*Zaji*) includes notes on the combination of cappings and weddings with various stages of mourning,[21] on the bundle of cloth presented as a betrothal gift, on the introduction of the bride to the groom's relatives after meeting the parents-in-law, and on the incomplete pinning that marks the adulthood of unmarried daughters at the age of twenty.[22] "Fundamentals of Sacrifice" (*Jitong*) argues that through wedding ritual one recruits outside assistance for one's sacrifices,[23] and according to "Explanation of the Canon" (*Jingjie*) weddings prevent debauchery by enforcing differentiation between males and females.[24] In "Duke Ai Asked" (*Ai gong wen*), Duke Ai and Kongzi debate the appropriateness of the sacrificial garb donned by the king at Fetching the Bride. Kongzi argues that the solemnity of the occasion, the ensurance of continuity in royal sacrifice, justifies the sacrificial robes.[25] In "Notes on Barriers" (*Fangji*), Kongzi voices his despair over the occurrence of elopements in times when proper wedding ritual still enforced differentiation, over transgressions of the clear prohibitions against same-surname marriage during the Zhou dynasty, and over the occasional disappearances of brides despite the practice of Fetching the Bride.[26]

Song scholars read "The Meaning of Weddings" (*Hunyi*), a systematic exposition that constitutes one of the last chapters of the *Record of Ritual*, as an early Han commentary on "Wedding Rites of an Ordinary Officer" in *Ceremonies and Rites*. The chapter explains that wedding ritual forges a bond between two families and ensures patrilineal continuity in ancestral sacrifice. The simultaneous production of the legitimate sexual bodies of male and female (through differentiation) and of the ritual bodies of husband and wife (through intimacy) makes weddings the root of all ritual. "The Meaning of Weddings" also explains the symbolism of individual acts and ceremonies, with especial emphasis on obedience (*shun*) as the principal virtue of the bride. The chapter ends with a discussion of the segregated living space and cosmic duties of the queen and the various levels of imperial consorts on one hand, and the king and his palace officials on the other hand.

Although scholars in the Tang and the Song shared important hermeneutical assumptions, their interpretations of individual passages could differ significantly. According to some, the goose presented in ancient wedding ceremonies symbolized the bride who followed the groom as the goose follows the sun (the groom and the sun both being yang), while according to others the goose symbolized marital fidelity (since geese mate for life). Yet others argued that the goose corresponded to the rank of Ordinary Officer and that other ranks offered different kinds of fowl. Some held that in antiquity males and females had married at the exact ages of thirty and twenty (and opinions differed further about the specific cosmological and biological reasons for this practice), while others deemed that the ages of thirty and twenty had been the upper limits of timely marriage.

Inconsistencies in the diverse canon further complicated these debates. The matchmaker mentioned in *Rites of Zhou* and the *Book of Songs*, for example, does not appear in the detailed wedding sequence of *Ceremonies and Rites*. And according to the *Record of Ritual*, The Bride Feeds Her Parents-in-Law should be held on the day after The Bride Meets the Parents-in-Law, but *Ceremonies and Rites* does not specify this. Scholars also disagreed about the place of weddings in larger ritual structures. Some took pinning to be the female, inner equivalent of public male capping, while others argued that capping and pinning were asymmetrical because girls did not achieve full adulthood until marriage. And some proposed that weddings should precede cappings in the ritual cycle, as some canonical passages indicate.

The hermeneutical assumptions of Middle-Period scholars not only suggested particular approaches to the concrete detail of the transmitted texts, but construed particular silences and lacunae, a particular incompleteness. The hermeneutical assumptions about the texts that had survived suggested what had been lost, creating complementary text as real and as legitimate to the exegete as the extant corpus. The legitimacy of the canon (the very notion of a canon, in fact) depended on the assumption of its historical coherence: its compilation in the latter days of the Zhou as an effort to preserve the embodied knowledge of the ancients, and its final redaction by Kongzi, the last sage. Under this assumption of completeness, silence could acquire the status of text, as in Lu Dian's (1070 *jinshi*) hermeneutical argument, "The reason that the text does not say that one can take a wife before the end of the third-degree mourning period [i.e., nine months], is that one cannot take a wife before the end of the third-degree mourning period."[27]

Drawing on this exegetical hermeneutics, Tang and Song authors of ritual manuals construed comprehensive wedding ceremonies. The wedding rituals in these manuals combine concrete detail from canonical texts with exegetical inferences. The supplementation of the wedding sequence in *Ceremonies and Rites* with passages from other canonical texts, hermeneutical extrapolations, and interpretative contemporary substitutions of arcane details, allowed the reinscription of ancient ritual for reincorporation in the present. Realized in ritual performance, the exegetical text dissolves as time and space, past and present, vessels and bodies merge in a timeless cosmic pattern.

## *Rites of the Kaiyuan Period*: The Merging of Canon and Precedent

Although the demise of earlier ritual codes prohibits verification of later assertions about their contents, Tang and Song scholars alleged that *Rites of the Kaiyuan Period* inaugurated a new approach to ritual protocol. More than four centuries after the promulgation of *Rites of the Kaiyuan Period*, the Southern Song statesman Zhou Bida (1126–1204) wrote:

> No period since the Three Dynasties had debated order as abundantly as did the Tang. Many of its views on ritual therefore deserve attention. . . . When the Kaiyuan Emperor [Xuanzong] reigned the land and guarded the well-being of his subjects, Academician Zhang Yue memorialized that the ritual codes were marred by contradictions. It would appear that he had devised ways of resolving this matter. The emperor then ordered Xu Jian, Li Rui, and Shi Jingben to make emendations. They were succeeded by Xiao Song, Wang Zhongqiu, and others, and only after several years was the code finished. It received the title *Rites of the Kaiyuan Period of the Great Tang*. The auspicious rites, inauspicious rites, military rites, guest rites, and joyful rites were then complete. . . . Only the Kaiyuan Emperor, reigning with an order both powerful and subtle, possessed a will to expansive peace that enabled him to select the scholars and ministers for the correction of ponderous codes. And only because Xu Jian and his peers in their erudite debates and in their pursuit of a unifying thread embodied the intentions of the emperor were they able to complete the work without petty disagreements. Whenever thereafter doubts arose at court, the matter could be settled by reference to this work, without assembling scholars for a debate. . . . The reader feels as though provided with a map that suddenly enables him to establish the compass points.[28]

When completed in 732, *Rites of the Kaiyuan Period* comprised 152 ceremonies, in 150 fascicles, divided into six sections of unequal length: a section of general ritual precedent (*xuli*, fascicles 1–3, treating general matters of divination, arrangement of ancestral tablets, vessels, carriages, clothing, and prayer); auspicious rites (*jili*, fascicles 4–78, treating sacrifices and prayers); guest rites (*binli*, fascicles 79–80, treating the reception of foreign embassies); military rites (*junli*, fascicles 81–90, treating rites of war, hunting, and archery); joyful rites (*jiali*, fascicles 91–130, treating cappings, weddings, New Year's ceremonies, ceremonies at the Luminous Hall, and investitures); and inauspicious rites (*xiongli*, fascicles 131–150, treating rites for bad harvests and mourning).[29]

The permutation of the order of the Five Rituals points to the tension between canon and precedent in *Rites of the Kaiyuan Period.* In placing the inauspicious rites last, the compilers followed the precedent of the Zhenguan and Xianqing codes rather than *Rites of Zhou* or the *Book of Documents* (*Shangshu*), where the inauspicious rites follow immediately upon the auspicious rites.[30] In relegating the rites of death to the final fascicles of the code, the compilers not only exercised exegetical prerogative, but they placed the auspicious symbolism of the imperial court above canonical integrity. Although the text does not explain the motivations for the rearrangement of the Five Rituals, the omission of ceremonies for the mourning and burial of the emperor suggests that the decision was informed by a reluctance to write of imperial death.[31] *Rites of the Kaiyuan Period* restored ancient ritual to the present, but the code also represented in writing the established hierarchies of bodies and space of the Tang empire. The omission of imperial burial (and of the rites of accession to the throne) excluded suggestions of discontinuity and death from this written representation of the empire.

In the structure of the individual sections and in the choreography of the individual ceremonies, the tension between canon and precedent is negotiated through the relationship between imperial rank and canonical detail. Rank supersedes the canonical sequence of ceremonies as an organizing principle in the arrangement of the individual sections. The section of joyful rites, for example, treats the emperor's capping, wedding, New Year's rites, rites at the Luminous Hall, and investment ceremonies before proceeding to the joyful rites of the heir apparent, princes, princesses, and ranked officials.

In individual ceremonies, canon and precedent often merge in hermeneutical extrapolation. Through the fragmented canon, Tang scholars discerned a ritualized society intricately divided by rank, but the obliteration of ancient protocol precluded full knowledge of the ritual enactment of this hierarchy. In their construction of individual ceremonies, the compilers of *Rites of the Kaiyuan Period* therefore extrapolated ranked difference from indications within the canon, but they also relied on the expressions of rank that obtained in their own time. Through this hermeneutics of canon and precedent, *Rites of the Kaiyuan Period* merges written bodies and spaces of antiquity with the living present.

In their reconstruction of ancient imperial and royal wedding ritual, the compilers of *Rites of the Kaiyuan Period* extrapolated in the main from "Wedding Rites of an Ordinary Officer." They identified the ordinary officer of antiquity with contemporary officials of ranks six through nine, so that the wedding ritual for this group bears the closest resemblance to the wedding sequence in *Ceremonies and Rites*. The wedding rituals for officials of different ranks (1–3, 4–5, 6–9) are distinguished by clothing, by the make of mats and carriages, by the amount and type of gifts exchanged, by the number of vessels used, and by the kinds of food served. With the increase of rank—from officials to princesses and princes, the heir apparent, and the emperor—increase the number of ceremonies and ritual actors, the refinement of clothes and ritual implements, and the costliness of gifts. The increase in rank also involves a growing divide between the family of the groom and the family of the bride. Adjustments in the ritual choreographies of the host and the guest, and the groom and the bride, lend form to that disparity.

The ritual schema of the emperor's wedding (fig. 1.2) reveals the extent of hermeneutical extrapolation in the wedding ceremonies of *Rites of the Kaiyuan Period*. Exegetical hermeneutics combines with imperial precedent to expand the canonical sequence with additional ceremonies and to adjust its choreography, fitting it to the ritualized and gendered spaces of the Tang imperial palace. The hierarchical arrangement of imperial insignia, ranked officials, and foreign embassies in the ceremony for the Imperial Appointment of Messengers represents the empire and creates an empty center in time and space that only the emperor can fill. In Submission of the Choice and subsequent ceremonies, the main messenger faces south at the center of the host's temple and reads aloud an imperial edict, rather than engaging with the host in a ritual dialogue. The edict, written in the imperial hand, represents the overflowing presence of the emperor that cannot be contained even by the ritual bodies of his sundry messengers. In Fetching the Bride, too, an edict represents the emperor, because the emperor will not venture from the palace to assume the role of a guest.[32]

When compared with imperial wedding ceremonies, the wedding rituals for ranked officials reveal a similar conjunction of exegesis and

## FIGURE 1.2. Schema of Imperial Weddings according to *Rites of the Kaiyuan Period.*

Divination of the date: accords with regular protocol.

Announcement at the Altar of Heaven: same as imperial capping.

Announcement at the Altar of the Earth: same as previous.

Imperial Appointment of Messengers:

- Arrangement of the throne, seats, music, ranked sections
  - Dancers, musicians, and ritual assistants enter
    - Imperial insignia and officials enter
      - Preparation of the central ritual site
        - Emperor enters (from the west)
          - Announcement of thc messengers by edict
        - Emperor exits (to the east)
      - Messengers exit by carriage, with edict, etc.
    - Officials and imperial insignia exit by rank
  - [Dancers, musicians, and ritual assistants exit]
- [Removal of seats, music, ranked sections, throne]

Submission of the Choice

Asking the Name

Submission of the Auspicious Result

Submission of the Betrothal Gift

Announcement of the Date

Announcement at the Temple

Investment of the Empress

Ordering the Messenger to Fetch the Bride

Sharing the Meal

Empress's Memorial of Gratitude

Empress's Audience at the Empress Dowager

Empress Receives Congratulations from the Ministers

Empress Receives the Ministers

Empress Receives Outer Noblewomen

Final Ritual for the Ministers

Empress Visits the Temple

precedent. The matchmaker of *Rites of Zhou* and the *Book of Songs* becomes a go-between, conveying the documents one finds in Tang manuals of letters and ceremonies: "In wedding ritual, first send a matchmaker and wedding letters. Initiate Submission of the Choice only after the family of the bride has given consent."[33] The extrapolation of the gifts and other forms of material display in the weddings of ranked officials coincides with concerns expressed in the sumptuary laws of the Tang empire.[34] Between the bride's first meeting with her parents-in-law and the departure of the followers, *Rites of the Kaiyuan Period* inserts a reception of the family of the bride by the family of the groom that lacks a basis in the canon but that mimics the language and choreography of canonical ritual.

The wedding ceremonies in *Rites of the Kaiyuan Period* are thus in the first place a matter of textual practice: an exercise in exegesis, a careful fusion of canon and precedent, that produces hermetic choreographies of written spaces and written bodies. In the detailed ritual scripts, text and performance coincide and become interchangeable: the text becomes the performance, the reader becomes the performer, and the written spaces and bodies acquire a ritual efficacy of their own. The fascicles dedicated to the weddings of ranked officials, for example, confine their differences entirely to the small print of double-column notes, leaving the main text of these three fascicles identical. Later redactions of *Rites of the Kaiyuan Period*, such as the thirty-five-fascicle condensation in *Comprehensive Records* (*Tongdian*) by Du You (735–812), excise all such repetition by means of fused commentaries and cross-references.[35] But in *Rites of the Kaiyuan Period*, the coincidence of text and performance, of reader and performer, of the written page and ritual space, forbids such abridgments, as they would create lacunae in the continuous choreography of the text.[36]

Tang and Song scholars praised *Rites of the Kaiyuan Period*, not as a return to the ritualized society of antiquity, but as an endeavor of exegesis. Zhou Bida commends it as a work of reference and compares it to a map that orients its reader in three-dimensional space.[37] According to David McMullen, *Rites of the Kaiyuan Period* as a text possessed a prestige that extended beyond its ceremonies and scholarship to encompass the virtue of its times:

> The continued high standing of the code, however, did not mean that the full range of its directives was in any sense mandatory in the imperial ritual programme. . . . The public

deference of scholars towards the Kaiyuan code in the post-rebellion period [i.e., after 755] is thus to be understood largely as a public expression of reverence and nostalgia for the politically prosperous, stable and expansionist era in which it had been produced.[38]

## Manuals of Letters and Ceremonies: The Hermeneutics of Practice and the Preservation of Ritual

Ritual manuals produced outside the Tang imperial court propose a merging of canon and precedent similar to that of *Rites of the Kaiyuan Period.* These manuals of letters and ceremonies, dating from the seventh through the tenth century, rewrite contemporary practice to configure it with canonical ritual.[39] Published under an array of similar titles and ascribed to a small number of prestigious authors, these manuals vie to establish claims to authoritative reworkings of contemporary practice. Titles and prefaces emphasize comprehensiveness, currency, and scholarly pedigree. The preface to *Newly Established Letters and Ceremonies of the Great Tang for Auspicious and Inauspicious Occasions* (*Da Tang xinding jixiong shuyi*), ascribed to Zheng Yuqing (746–820), sets forth the discursive context of manuals of letters and ceremonies, while according a privileged place to itself:

> "When ritual obtains among men, peace reigns. But when ritual is wanting, danger looms."[40] Such is the understanding of ceremonies and ritual among those of discriminating intelligence. Therefore great families accord grave respect to ritual at auspicious and inauspicious occasions.[41] Yet the expansive, detailed complexity of canonical ritual encumbers convenient reference. The worthy men who compiled and extracted letter formats and ceremonies for auspicious and inauspicious occasions, in order to preserve ritual still in use, certainly rendered an obliging service. Yet although some dozen authors wrote such manuals, only Metropolitan Governor Mr. Du [Youjin] compared the ceremonies and rites compiled by all various authors, and it has now been in use for seventy-six years.[42] . . . Therefore I have made selections from the array of ceremonies and compared them with the scriptures. From the wealth of

> writing samples I first selected those that represent the essence of our time, and then I chose the most admirable among them.
>
> With Li Cao, Aide to the Court of the Imperial Stud; Pei Chai, Director of the Bureau of Merit Titles; Li Ying, former Commandant of Quyao; Lu Zhi [754–805], Vice Director of the Secretariat and Jointly Manager of Affairs with the Secretariat-Chancellery; Yang Huan, Attendant Censor; Han Yu, Vice Director of the Transit Authorization Bureau; and others, I discussed the practices of our time and the redaction of ceremonies and rites for auspicious and inauspicious occasions. Then, with anguish, I attacked those ignorant customs from close range, since that is the heart of the matter. . . .[43]

This preface claims to supersede earlier manuals of letters and ceremonies not because it applies new or superior standards, but because it is recent and comprehensive. It explicitly shares with earlier manuals a concern with preserving ritual from the encroachment of "ignorant customs." The continuous change in practice, however, necessitates periodic measuring of current ceremonies against the ritual scriptures and the compilation of new manuals that aid the great families in their discrimination between canonical practice and vulgar custom. The exegetical hermeneutics of *Newly Established Letters and Ceremonies* assumes that ritual inheres in changing practice. A dialectical investigation of living practice and scripture allows the perspicacious scholar to discern ritual from custom, and to rewrite current practice to conform to the enduring standard of canonical ritual. Contemporary practice thus becomes a text, isolated from its practical associations, to be disassembled and rearranged in a textual environment.[44]

The treatment of weddings in the manuals of letters and ceremonies merges canonical exegesis with contemporary practice. The untitled Dunhuang fragment S1725, for example, addresses well-established exegetical matters such as the meaning of the goose, the timing of the various wedding ceremonies, and the proper sequence for Fetching the Bride, but it also discusses, in the same section and in the same language, practices not found in canonical texts, such as the distinction between a "wife's letter" and a "wife's provisory note," the proper presentation of a goat or rice, and posthumous marriage:[45]

> Question: What is a "wife's provisory note"? Answer: If the wife has met her husband's party, it is called a "letter," but if

> she has not met her husband's party, it is called a "provisory note." Question: What is meant by "has met"? Answer: When a son who lives on his own takes a wife, propriety requires that he Fetch the Bride and induce her into his house according to ritual. For three months she does not leave to pay a visit, but each morning she sends word to her parents-in-law. . . . Only after the third month does she leave to visit her husband's ancestral temple. . . . If the wife has submitted to Fetching the Bride and the induction into her husband's house, she has "met her husband's party." Should she need to inquire about an auspicious or inauspicious matter, she should send a "letter" immediately. But in recent times many do not perform Fetching the Bride or the induction into the house. Instead, they conduct all ritual at the bride's house and sometimes do not return to the groom's house for several years. . . . When an auspicious or inauspicious event occurs, a wife ought to send a letter or note, and although the wife has completed the ritual at this point, she has not met any of the husband's party. In such cases one speaks of a "provisory note."[46]

Although the author of this passage takes exception to certain practices of his day ("more often than one cares to admit," he writes about couples who fail to return to the husband's ancestral house, "they even have children"), he endeavors to fit such undesirable practices into proper terminology and into a larger framework of proper family relations. The ritual structure of the family endures even if its constituent ceremonies change.

The use of written exchanges occupies a prominent place among such contemporary ceremonial practices. In the above passage, the bride sends letters or notes to her parents-in-law to substitute for her physical presence in their household. Other passages in this untitled fragment provide detailed descriptions of the labels attached to gifts and of beribboned boards with ceremonial texts. Other manuals of letters and ceremonies preserved at Dunhuang contain model letters exchanged between the family of the groom and the family of the bride, with elaborate instructions about proper formats and stationery.[47] Writing here becomes a ritual act that parallels or replaces choreographies of bodies through ritual time and space, and thereby becomes subject to the same hermeneutics of canon and precedent.

In *Newly Compiled Letters and Ceremonies for Auspicious and Inauspicious Occasions* (P2646), attributed to Zhang Ao, the exchange of letters and the hermeneutics of canon and current practice converge in a full ritual sequence (see fig. 1.3).[48] The rich gifts that accompany the proposal composed by the groom's family (horses, cloth, cash, livestock, foods) suggest that the two families have already agreed to the marriage and that the proposal is primarily a ritual object. Indeed, the opening of the wooden casing that encloses the letter (and whose measurements possess cosmological significance) and the reading of the proposal occupy the temporal and spatial center of the engagement ceremony.[49] The creation of this center through choreography and ritual space bears a strong resemblance to canonical ceremonies such as Submission of the Betrothal Gifts, even if the gifts and other ritual objects differ markedly from their canonical counterparts.

The ceremonies of the wedding night also construe a ritual core through a combination of canonical and contemporary elements. The canonical grammar of symmetrical time and space enfolds the groom's presentation of the goose in the bride's hall within fertility rites and other symbolic and metaphoric acts. The boys who toss fruit and coins at the empty canopy while intoning blessings, return to witness the draining of the nuptial cups. And the groom's men who sing taunting songs and dance outside the bride's house, reappear at the canopy to chant suggestive poems:

> After the nuptial cups have been emptied, the groom rises and undresses in the next room. He lays off his ritual dress and cap, his ornamental sword, his footwear, and so forth, and re-enters in his underwear, with his official tablet. The groom sits down on the eastern part of the canopy, the bride on the western side. The bride hides her face behind flowers and a fan. In front of the canopy, the groom's men chant three or five poems enjoining the groom to remove the bride's fan and to pluck her flowers. After removing the fan, the groom pushes away the flowers in the bride's hair with his [phallic] official tablet.[50]

Modern scholars such as Patricia Ebrey, Zhao Heping, and Zhou Yiliang have ignored the exegetical hermeneutics of Tang manuals of letters and ceremonies, and have instead claimed them as repositories of historical practice or as the last, desperate defenses of an embattled aristocracy.[51] Yet the ritual sequence in *Newly Compiled Letters and Ceremonies* not only maintains canonical elements (such as the goose, the parental injunctions, the shared meal and the nuptial cups, the

**FIGURE 1.3. Schema of Wedding Ritual according to *Newly Compiled Letters and Ceremonies for Auspicious and Inauspicious Occasions.***

Ceremonial Reception of the Proposal by the Bride's Family:

- Groom's family composes a marriage proposal (*tonghun shu*) and dispatches messengers with proposal and gifts
  - Arrangements at the bride's house, guests arrive
    - Guests enter, display the gifts, and take their place
      - Guest bows and conveys the proposal
        - Host ascends the hall and reads the proposal
      - Guests exit
    - Host's assistants remove the gifts
  - Host exits and rewards the guests with meal and gifts
- [Messengers return]

Bride's family composes a reply (no ceremony specified)

Wedding Night:

- Groom's host and bride's host announce the wedding at their ancestral temple

- Groom's men taunt and dance at the bride's house
  - Young boys toss fruit and coins at a canopy and chant
    - Bride enters the hall, behind fan and screen
      - Groom and assistants enter
        - Bride takes place on a saddle, behind a low screen
          - Groom throws goose across screen into the hall
        - Groom's assistants give money to release the goose
      - Bride receives parents' instructions
    - Bride exits the hall
  - Groom and bride eat and drink at canopy, boys chant
- Groom undresses, groom's men chant, groom removes bride's fan and flowers

- All assistants exit with candles; end of the ritual

Congratulatory notes of commiseration

ritual undressing, the final removal of the candles, the avoidance of congratulations) within an overall canonical ritual grammar, but it concludes with an explication of its exegetical ambitions:

> The kings of yore established ritual, and later generations practiced it. Therefore, males and females perform wedding ritual to complete the Way of husband and wife, lest human relations be reduced to chaos. Here, the wedding rites are presented in outline, not in full detail, but the true gentleman [*junzi*] who performs them with care will not go astray.[52]

Such assertions would be meaningless unless supported by contemporary hermeneutics: canonical scholars would recognize the claim as spurious, while those ignorant of the canon would be unlikely to take much interest in following its injunctions in the first place.

Rather, modern scholars seem to have applied to the Tang manuals an anachronistic standard, derived from an exegetical hermeneutics developed during the Northern Song. This later hermeneutics assumes that ritual inheres in the detail of ancient choreographies and objects, and cannot be transposed indiscriminately to contemporary implements and practices. It also places the male-female binary outside ritual and removes the sexual bodies of the groom and the bride from ritualized time and space. This strict hermeneutics of text informs Ouyang Xiu's condemnation of the manuals of letters and ceremonies as the products of a degenerate age:

> The wedding rites in Liu Yue's *Letters and Ceremonies* include a ritual in which "the bride sits on the groom's saddle and her parents braid her hair." First I wondered on what kind of interpretation of the canon this was based. But when I read in the preface that Yue has "supplemented [canonical ritual] with practices currently esteemed," I realized that this must simply be a custom of his day. Yue, however, lived in the violent times of the Five Dynasties, times that abandoned and perverted the rites and music. He should not have dabbled in discussions of the structures laid down by the Three Kings and he should not have integrated into those structures an arbitrary selection of the auspicious and inauspicious ceremonies practiced in the custom of his day. Certainly this manual cannot serve as a model for later generations.[53]

The compilers of manuals of letters and ceremonies in the seventh through tenth centuries believed that the importance of canonical ritual lay in its general structure and intention and that this structure and intention could be transposed onto contemporary practices. A continuous dialectical investigation of contemporary practice and canonical texts resulted in a series of manuals that rewrote current customs into canonical structures. Wedding letters, copious gifts, fertility ceremonies, symbolic defloration, and other contemporary practices found a place in the wedding sequence. But by the end of the eleventh century, changes in exegetical hermeneutics resulted in ritual manuals that dismissed almost all contemporary practices and constructed archaic ceremonies far removed from the ken of their day. While the Tang hermeneutics of practice assumed an historical, organic connection between ancient ritual and current practice, the Song hermeneutics of text posited an immediate identity of the present and the past.

## The Hermeneutical Shift in the Northern Song: Epigraphy, Archaeology, and the Identity of Past and Present

In their brief genealogies of Northern Song epigraphy, philology, and archaeology, Zhai Qinian, Feng Zizhen (b. 1257–d. after 1314), and Xiong Penglai (1246–1323) identify Tang scholars as the earliest known ancestors. But Shi Xinwen's epigraphic studies during the Kaiyuan period, resulting in his *Explanation of the Ancient-Text Book of Documents* (*Guwen Shangshu shiwen*, eighth century), had been either ridiculed or neglected, and subsequent epigraphic studies in the Tang remained restricted to scattered finds and the occasional colophon to a cherished rubbing. The philological dictionaries compiled in early Northern Song by the brothers Xu Xuan (916–991) and Xu Kai (920–974), and by Xia Song (985–1051), could therefore hardly have been expected to be accurate or comprehensive.[54]

In the latter half of the Northern Song, however, a scholarly community grew that in a few decades deciphered ancient scripts, classified ancient ritual vessels, and compiled extensive dictionaries and glossaries on ancient inscriptions. All members of this community acknowledged their debt to the pioneering efforts of Ouyang Xiu and Liu Chang.[55] Ouyang Xiu's preface to his *Record of Collecting Antiquities* conjures the image of a solitary figure indiscriminately gathering eroded inscriptions and hoary objects in remote woods and desolate marshes.[56] But the publication of Ouyang Xiu's collection created a community of scholars who ventured into the countryside to collect their own rubbings, which in turn they exchanged, examined, and published.[57]

While Ouyang Xiu had confined himself to stone inscriptions from the imperial period, epigraphic studies soon expanded to include inscriptions on ancient bronzes. Liu Chang's *Record of Pre-Qin Vessels* was the first publication to combine bronze inscriptions with illustrations of the vessels from which they were taken. Yet, his preface already posits the existence of a textual community, extending through space and time, in which knowledge circulates and grows—and in which antiquity seems to draw nearer:

> The eleven objects in this *Record of Pre-Qin Vessels* are subtle and intricate in structure, and their inscriptions in tadpole script bear evidence to their ancient origins. No scholar today is able to understand them entirely. With the help of other works, I have managed to decipher fifty to sixty percent of the inscriptions. These deciphered passages, combined with current genealogical reconstructions, suggest that these vessels may date from the time of King Wen and King Wu of the Zhou, more than two thousand years ago. Alas! Hardly a thing survives from the times of the Three Kings. Thinking of what the sage kings founded and of what the *Book of Songs* and the *Book of Documents* describe, one can only sit and sigh. How can one say that these are mere vessels! . . . Kongzi said, "I observe much, and remember it. This is a lower level of wisdom."[58] Most cannot aspire to this standard, but there may well be one in this realm who is able to decipher these inscriptions. Therefore I ordered them copied and inscribed in stone, with illustrations of the vessels, to await erudite gentlemen who cherish antiquity. Eventually, a ritualist may understand the structure of the vessels, a philologist may identify the characters, and a genealogist may place the names and generations in proper order. Only then will our understanding be complete.[59]

The works that followed upon the *Record of Collecting Antiquities* and the *Record of Pre-Qin Vessels* grew in size and in sophistication. Collections multiplied and expanded, and their vessels and inscriptions were published, deciphered, supplemented, recompiled, and republished. Around 1090, Li Gonglin (1049–1106) set a new standard in this field of endeavor with the publication of his *Investigations of Antiquity Illustrated* (*Kaogu tu*). This work contained an immaculate illustration of each vessel and provided a transcription, glosses, and an explanation of each inscription, as well as notes on the ritual use of the vessels. "Literati knew that the interest in the study of vessels from the Three Dynasties really began with Boshi [i.e., Li Gonglin]."[60] Li Gonglin, moreover, proposed a new way of reading vessels:

> According to Boshi, the sages devised their vessels as images [*xiang*]. In writing the Way and handing down their injunctions, they implied untransmittable subtleties in the shape and use of these vessels so as to leave a record for later generations. Men of expansive knowledge thus might through the vessel retrieve the image, and through the image retrieve the meaning. By applying mind and eye to the intent of these sacred objects, such men would understand the unspoken secrets of ritual, music, and law.[61]

Only a few years later, in 1092, Lü Dalin (1044–1093) elaborated the implications of this theory in the preface to his monograph (in ten fascicles), likewise entitled *Investigations of Antiquity Illustrated* (*Kaogu tu*):

> According to Zhuang Zhou [trad. 369–286 BCE], classicists [*ru*] lose the real in their obsessive pursuit of traces, and in their studies they cannot cope with change. Therefore he wrote the story of Wheelwright Pian and the parable of the straw dogs.[62] . . . [Yet] Yao, Shun, Yu, and Gaotao all spoke of a "search for antiquity," and Kongzi himself said, "I cherish the past and seek it with diligence."[63] Although what is called "antiquity" may be the visible traces of the kings of yore, those who seek them and cherish them always seek that which made the traces. Structures and images are metaphors for the subtle intentions of the sages. These, antiquity and the present share in common. A hundred intervening generations have not been able to change them. One cannot dismiss them with tales of straw dogs or Wheelwright Pian.
>
> When the Han became heir to the charred remains of the Qin, they looked upon the Three Dynasties as on a new morn one looks upon last night's dream. The editing of scattered fragments yielded only a few texts. And as customs changed with the generations, as people died and books vanished, hopes of finding remains of the kings of yore became remote, even absurd. Yet unexpectedly, after centuries had passed, vases and vessels, cauldrons and cups emerged from mountains and walls, from ditches and graves. . . . Alas! If Heaven had indeed destroyed this culture of ours, why would these vessels

> emerge? . . . When one contemplates these vessels and recites their words, it is as though their countenance conveys an echo from the Three Dynasties—as though one can see its people.[64]

Within a few decades, the ancients had become a physical presence in Song society. Their vessels lent substance to the scriptures and elucidated obscure ritual passages. Their inscriptions corroborated, supplemented, and corrected corrupt transmissions. Most important, the vessels created a direct, bodily connection between Song literati and the ancients, a connection that had never before existed in imperial times. The Song was the true heir to antiquity.

In the final decades of the Northern Song, illustrated catalogues of antiquities continued to appear. The publication of philological dictionaries facilitated the study of inscriptions and yielded new insights into canonical texts. The collection of ancient vessels and inscriptions gained such popularity under Emperor Huizong that they became precious goods in a commodified antique market, leading to widespread grave robbery and to forgery. These related trends of scholarly inquiry and sumptuous excess combined in *Broad Researches of Antiquity Illustrated* (*Bo gu tu*, 1107, 1123), a work compiled under the auspices of Emperor Huizong, with plates and descriptions of more than five hundred vessels.[65]

By the time the private collections of Northern Song literati were scattered and "the numinous ox cauldrons and elephant vases, the elegant dragon pots and goose lamps [from the imperial collection] had all been reduced to troughs for barbarian horses," the ancient vessels had been translated into text.[66] Not only did collections survive in the rubbings, illustrations, and descriptions of published catalogues and private libraries, but the vessels themselves had become readable as text. The conviction, among Northern Song scholars, that the ancients had devised their vessels as images and metaphors (*yu*) placed the vessels on the same plane as the written word. The readability of vessels in turn lent a materiality to text. This dialectic between text and vessels allowed an engagement with the ancients through text that had never before been envisioned.

Generations of imperial literati acknowledged Liu Chang not only as the first scholar to have published a collection of ancient vessels and inscriptions, but also as the first to have subjected the integrity of the canon to rigorous inquiry and to have suggested changes in its composition and wording.[67] The philological insights gained through epigraphic studies gave rise to further suspicions about the transmitted texts of the canon. The destructive policies of the Qin had not only decimated the received texts of antiquity, but its reform of the script had resulted in the loss of the inherent truth of the ancient language and ancient writing. Song philologists set out to recover these real characters which they believed to have been drawn directly from nature. A knowledge of the shape and meaning of the ancient script would yield insights into the wisdom of the ancients in much the same way as the bronze vessels:

> Writing, I have been told, was invented to replace knotted cords. Many centuries passed from Cang Jie's first imposition of structure and order on the ten thousand things, through the manifold increase [of his script] under Yao, Shun, and the Three Dynasties, yet the system was respectfully transmitted and the meanings carefully handed down: brilliant and numinous, naturally resplendent. The rites and music, and the codes and ordinances were kept complete through continuous revision; words and things, and volume and measurements were held aloft with unremitting constancy. But as antiquity receded into the past, the origins were lost in the flow of time, and scholars and noblemen tended toward the vernacular in their pursuit of convenience. . . . The writing of Cang Jie was lost.[68]

The ritual of the ancients was just such a language. Like the vessels, like the script, like the trigrams of the *Book of Changes*, the choreography of ancient ritual gave shape to inherent cosmic patterns. Ritual, too, was designed as an image. As Zhou Xu (1073 *jinshi*) writes in the introduction to his *Explanation of the Record of Ritual* (*Liji shuo*):

> Verily, ritual is the perfect embodiment of man's natural endowment: the Way, virtue, humaneness, and propriety issue from man's natural endowment; and ritual in turn issues from the Way, virtue, humaneness, and propriety to become their patterned expression. . . . Therefore it is said, "Only through ritual can the Way, virtue, humaneness, and propriety be perfected." Such indeed is the nature of ritual. Words cannot fully express the difference between auspicious rites and

> inauspicious rites, or the distinction between military ritual and guest ritual. Their meaning must needs find expression in images. What one garment or one vessel conveys in its volume and measurements we call "image," and image is none other than pattern [*wen*]. Reasoning from the specific to the general, one may say that volume and measurements are the outward, visible expressions of meaning, and this meaning is none other than human emotion.[69]

Ritual, in other words, is both natural and historical. Although ritual gives natural expression to timeless, inherent, moral structures, only the ancients had possessed such insight into these cosmic patterns as to enable them to devise their proper embodiment by man. Song literati attempted to recover this inherent ritual through a dialectical inquiry into the fragmented remains of antiquity and into timeless cosmic truths. Ancient texts and artifacts aided them in penetrating universal truths, while insights into universal truths enabled them to understand and reconstruct the traces of ancient wisdom. Thus, on one hand, Song scholars wrote copious commentaries on the ritual scriptures and published illustrated compendia of topical passages from these scriptures, such as *The Images of Ritual* (*Li xiang*) by Lu Dian and the *Book of Ritual* (*Li shu*) by Chen Xiangdao (1053–1093).[70] On the other hand, they attempted to restore the practice of ancient ritual, in which the embodiment of ancient ritual was both an end in itself and a hermeneutical tool. This hermeneutics of text, with its dialectic between canonical exegesis and the embodiment of cosmic patterns, marked a fundamental departure from the earlier hermeneutics of practice.

## Ritual Manuals of the Northern Song: The Hermeneutics of Text and the Embodiment of Antiquity

The ritual codes compiled at the Song imperial court during the first century of its reign were based on *Rites of the Kaiyuan Period*. The compilers of the *Comprehensive Rites of the Kaibao Period* (*Kaibao tongli*, 973) removed passages from the Tang ritual code and added new materials. During the ensuing decades, continued emendation resulted in the *New Compilation by the Hall of Rites* (*Lige xinbian*, 1020s), *New Rites of the Court of Imperial Sacrifices* (*Taichang xinli*, 1040s), and in a bewildering, disorderly array of unedited supplementary edicts and loose-leafed additions that discolored, tore, and vanished. This state of affairs moved Ouyang Xiu to compile a new comprehensive code, *Cumulative Rites of the Court of Imperial Sacrifices* (*Taichang yin'ge li*, 1065). Using the *Comprehensive Rites of the Kaibao Period* as their basic text, he and his fellow editors combined old and new rites to create a full, coherent, and accurate code.[71]

Despite his commitment to antiquity and his explicit condemnation of the historical perversion of ancient ritual, Ouyang Xiu proved unable to implement his views at court. When the Princess of Yan married in 1056, Ouyang Xiu, as the head of the Rites Agency, gathered ritual scholars to discuss reform of the received wedding ceremonies. It was agreed that a bride's family, even if it were the imperial family, ought not announce the match, submit betrothal gifts, or divine the wedding date, and that a reintroduction of the Five Rites (i.e., the Six Rites minus Fetching the Bride) into imperial weddings could supply at least a reference to proper ritual relations. The reintroduction of the Five Rites remained a token addition, however, compressed into the day prior to the wedding and further reduced by the imposing uxorilocal context of the imperial palace and imperial ritual.[72] Emperor Renzong (r. 1022–1063), meanwhile, worried about finding proper historical precedent for the wedding of unprecedented lavishness that he intended to give his daughter.[73]

As the early interest in the material remains of antiquity created a sense of physical proximity to that brilliant period, fervent debates raged at the court of Emperor Shenzong (r. 1068–1086) about the possibilities of implementing policies that would fashion the Song empire in the image of the Three Dynasties. In formulating his controversial New Policies, Wang Anshi (1021–1086) envisioned a society ordered according to *Rites of Zhou*. His opponents disagreed, not with his grand vision of a return to antiquity, but with his particular selection and interpretation of legitimizing scriptures. The failure of many of Wang's reforms strengthened his opponents' critique of his exegetical hermeneutics, by the dialectical logic of the time: the poor harvests, the starvation, and the resistance to Wang Anshi's reforms indicated that his efforts did not accord with the timeless truth of the ancients.[74]

The debates extended to ritual reform.[75] Emperor Shenzong appointed Lu Dian, a protégé of Wang Anshi and author of *The Images of Ritual*, to advise on the design of new imperial robes and caps.[76] But in 1078 the Emperor appointed Chen Xiang (1017–1080), an outspoken opponent of Wang Anshi's New Policies, as Editor of a special bureau within the Court of Imperial Sacrifice, responsible for aligning imperial sacrifice with ancient practice. In his insistence on scripture as a guide to ritual practice (and, indeed, to everyday life), Chen Xiang dismissed the languorous adherence to historical precedent that had rendered all earlier ritual codes mere documents of their own times, not repositories of timeless truth.[77]

Changes in the wedding ritual of imperial princesses under Shenzong accorded with this movement from precedent to canon. Rejecting the established priority of imperial rank over proper ritual relations, Shenzong decreed that imperial princesses should perform the full canonical ceremonies of the daughter-in-law:

> During the reign of Emperor Yingzong [r. 1064–1068], Huihe, Princess of Yan [d. 1085], was wedded to Wang Shiyue [1044–1102]. In former times it had been the custom that families who married an imperial princess lowered themselves by one generation to convey their respect. Emperor Yingzong disapproved of this practice: "This ordinance disregards the proper order of human relations and ought not be maintained." Concerned with the improvement of customs, he ordered the matter corrected forthwith, but he was unable to draw up the edict [prior to his death]. Only after Shenzong ascended the throne was an edict handed down stipulating that all imperial princesses at their wedding were held to perform the rites of Meeting the Parents-in-Law. At this time Wang Shiyue's father, Wang Kechen [1014–1089], served as Administrative Assistant in Kaifeng prefecture [and thus resided near the palace]. On the day prior to the ritual, Imperial Commissioners prepared Wang's residence for the arrival of the princess. After the princess had performed the rites of serving her parents-in-law, a full orchestra of court musicians rang out, and the realm rejoiced. All sighed when the carriages of the palace women returned through the streets of Kaifeng.
>
> This event has exerted a profound influence upon recent marriages among the elite: until Huihe no person as exalted as an imperial princess had ever practiced the Way of the wife. . . . Only the ancestors of the present imperial house have accorded such importance to the regal force of transformation, and with majestic splendor they have perfected custom.[78]

A new era had dawned in the late-eleventh century. Even if scholars engaged in fierce debates about policies and hermeneutics, they agreed that their age stood closer to antiquity than any previous period. In the words of Cheng Yi:

> Our dynasty is the first since the Three Dynasties to be able to leap from the present to antiquity, and it is the cultivation of the five practices [i.e., bearing, speech, sight, hearing, and thought] that has made this possible. . . . After perspicacity [of thought] had been established as a basis, the spirit of the age distinguished itself of its own accord.[79]

The concern with the embodiment of antiquity was not confined to the ritual codes of the imperial court. In fact, the compilation of these ritual codes owed much to the initiatives of committed scholars such as Ouyang Xiu and Chen Xiang, who vied with the court for moral and exegetical authority. The practice of ancient ritual and the cultivation of ancient virtues outside the palace walls, however, posed challenges not encountered at court. The imperial palace was a permanently ritualized space, inhabited by permanently ritualized bodies, which did not admit of a distinction between ritual and the mundane. Moreover, the court had at its disposal sufficient material resources and skilled craftsmen to create and alter space, clothing, and ritual objects in any manner deemed necessary. The lack of such resources and the difficulty of ritualizing everyday existence encumbered efforts at the embodiment of antiquity outside the palace.

The life and writings of Chen Xiang illustrate how the timeless practices of the ancients in the eleventh century could inspire alienation, fear, and aggression. When, in his youthful days, Chen Xiang traveled with three friends to proclaim the Way of the ancients in their native region in Fujian, "the people were at first afraid, and ridiculed them."[80] One of these three friends, Chen Lie (fl. 1060–1086), went to extremes that shocked his contemporaries: "When the mother of Cai Junmo [Cai Xiang, 1012–1067] passed away, Chen Lie crawled all the way from his house to attend the mourning ceremonies. When asked about this, he explained, 'This is what the *Book of Songs* means by "Whenever others were in mourning, I went on my knees to help them."' This is the sort of thing he used to do."[81] Explaining in a letter to Xu Hong (1026–1057) the difficulties entailed by his commitment to learning and ritual, Chen Xiang himself offers the following arresting images:

> The sage [i.e., Kongzi] was never deterred by difficulties. Among his disciples, however, only Yan Yuan was fond of learning. Therefore Kongzi told him, "Look at nothing in defiance of ritual, listen to nothing in defiance of ritual, speak of nothing in defiance of ritual, never stir hand or foot in defiance of ritual." Only thus may the realm return to humaneness.[82] Therefore I say that one may not attain it except with the gravest difficulty. Heaven has not endowed me with riches or with longevity, but it has given me this: I cannot turn away from learning.
>
> Of late a man dwells in these parts who is naked and walks backwards. Those who see him point at him and say that he is delusional and has lost his mind. But if someone who is committed to learning loses his mind, not only will he be unable to correct it, but there will be nobody to see him and point at him. This ought to be cause for the gravest concern, a guiding thought in self-examination.
>
> One ought really find a place where a few people could subsist, living on a wooded mountain, chanting and singing the remaining songs and writings of the ancients, so that one might gain a better understanding of their intentions. And once the community grows to some forty or fifty, it will become clear how the ancients sustained themselves. But no outsiders should ever see it, and I do not know whether such utter seclusion would be possible.[83]

Although Chen Xiang compares the deluded naked man in his neighborhood to the wayward scholar, he is fully aware that wayward scholars constitute the majority, and that his contemporaries would regard his archaic mountain community as deluded and threatening.

The literati of the Northern Song who wished to restore ancient ritual to the present thus faced two daunting obstacles. First, the ancient, fragmented, and corrupted texts of the canon left many uncertainties about the precise form and meaning of ancient ritual. Its reconstruction through exegetical hermeneutics required an authoritative confidence that most literati lacked. Second, the limited material resources and the social confines of contemporary society restrained and circumscribed the performance of archaic rites. The necessary adjustments to financial means and contemporary material conditions, moreover, added to the demands on exegetical authority, because only scholars with an extraordinary understanding of ancient ritual could hope to map its structures and meanings onto contemporary spaces, bodies, and objects. Yet, men such as Sima Guang, Zhang Zai, Cheng Yi, Lü Dafang (1027–1097), and Lü Dalin possessed such confidence in their grasp of the canon that they took it upon themselves to compile ritual manuals that offered solutions to these predicaments.

Sima Guang completed his *Letters and Ceremonies* (*Shuyi*) around 1081, only a few years after Chen Xiang submitted his *Detailed Investigations into the Rites and Texts of the Imperial Altars and Temples* to the throne.[84] Where Chen Xiang dismissed the attempted fusion of canon and precedent in imperial ritual codes since the compilation of *Rites of the Kaiyuan Period*, Sima Guang attacks the hermeneutics of the manuals of letters and ceremonies of the Tang and the Five Dynasties. Sima Guang's manual does not rewrite contemporary practice according to canonical structures; it rewrites ritual scripture according to an exegetical hermeneutics that allows the re-embodiment of ancient ritual in the present. For Sima Guang, as for Chen Xiang, ritual does not change with time. Rather, it inheres in particular physical and temporal structures, in objects and attire, in volume and measurements, in the detail of the ritual scriptures.[85] Through his reinscription of canonical texts he intended to reinscribe contemporary space, time, and bodies—a project diametrically opposed to that of earlier manuals of letters and ceremonies.[86]

In his reconstruction of ancient wedding ritual, Sima Guang relies on a distinct set of hermeneutical techniques. In order to create a continuous ritual narrative, he supplements "Wedding Rites of an Ordinary Officer" with passages from other scriptures, as well as with contemporary practices that he holds to retain the essence of ancient ritual. His exegetical choices supply concrete ceremonial detail where fragmentation and ambiguity leave lacunae in the wedding sequence of *Ceremonies and Rites*. Sima Guang also relies on exegetical hermeneutics to reduce the duration, complexity, and cost of the canonical sequence by condensing the narrative and by substituting arcane or costly ritual objects with affordable contemporary equivalents. In supplementing his canonical sequence with contemporary practices, Sima Guang creates a strict distinction between ritual (*li*) and custom (*su*). The few contemporary practices he recognizes as textual, respectable, ancient, unified, and indigenous he designates as ritual, and these he inscribes in his ritual narrative. Contemporary practices he deems to

## FIGURE 1.4. Schema of Wedding Ritual according to Sima Guang's *Letters and Ceremonies.*

Submission of the Choice, Asking the Name, Submission of the Auspicious Result, Submission of the Betrothal Gifts, Requesting the Date: all according to canonical choreography

Fetching the Bride:

- Bride's family decorates the groom's chamber
  - Arrangement of vessels in the groom's chamber
    - Host and groom ascend the hall
    - | Groom sacrifices, bows, receives host's command
    - Groom descends and departs

    - Groom arrives; bride and others assume their places
      - | Bride sacrifices, bows, receives instructions
      - Bride, duenna, and followers retreat
        - Host receives groom; they enter and ascend
        - | Groom presents a goose and bows
        - Bride appears and descends with groom and followers
      - Groom leads bride and duenna to the carriage
      - | Bride ascends the carriage
    - Groom, bride, and followers depart for the groom's house

    - Groom leads bride into the temple, before parents
    - | Sacrifice and announcement to ancestors
    - Groom and bride leave the temple

    - Groom and bride enter the groom's chamber and wash
    - | Groom and bride sacrifice, eat, drink
    - Groom leaves the chamber, bride stays
  - Followers remove the vessels and consume the leftovers

  - Groom re-enters
  - | Groom and bride disrobe
  - Followers exit with candles
- Groom's parents reward the followers with a meal

The Bride Meets Her Parents-in-Law

The Bride Feeds Her Parents-in-Law

Parents-in-Law Feed the Bride

The Groom Meets His Wife's Parents

be illiterate, illicit, regional, foreign, and vulgar he condemns as custom or, more commonly, ignores.

The wedding sequence in Sima Guang's *Letters and Ceremonies* opens with a specification of the proper ages of grooms and brides, an exposition on the consequences of mourning obligations for the timing of weddings, and an explanation of the imperative use of a matchmaker, all of which are based on scriptures other than *Ceremonies and Rites*. Elsewhere, Sima Guang provides a description of the layout of the temple, stipulates that the host of the groom's family should report to the ancestors prior to Submission of the Choice, and reads a measure of ritual primogeniture into the ceremonies that relate to the future succession of the groom's parents by the groom and the bride. Sima's comment on the announcement to the ancestors during Submission of the Choice states the hermeneutical principles applied:

> Although "Wedding Rites of an Ordinary Officer" makes no mention of such an announcement, all of the Six Rites are conducted at the temple. According to *Mr. Zuo's Commentary on the Spring and Autumn Annals* [*Zuo zhuan*], Hu, son of the Duke of Zheng "was first mated and then announced the thing in the ancestral temple. The officer Chen said, 'These are not husband and wife; he is imposing on his fathers.'"[87] But when Wei, son of the Duke of Chu, married in Zheng, the text says, "Wei then set forth his offerings on the stands in the temples of [his fathers, the kings] Zhuang and Gong."[88] Thus we know that in antiquity an announcement to the ancestors always preceded the wedding. Indeed, a wedding is a matter of great importance in a family, and propriety requires that it be announced.[89]

This inference, from two brief passages in *Mr. Zuo's Commentary on the Spring and Autumn Annals*, of the universality in ancient weddings of the announcement to the ancestors illustrates two important hermeneutical assumptions: first, the assumption of the historical unity of ancient practice and the resulting consistency of canonical fragments; second, the assumption of certain general principles that may be deduced from canonical fragments, subsequently to be applied to other fragments as a heuristic device.

Sima Guang further elaborates the wedding sequence with interpretative decisions. He determines that the ages of thirty and twenty are the upper limits, not absolute numbers, for the marriage of males and females, and that the pinning ceremony for girls is equivalent, rather than asymmetrical, to the capping ritual for boys. Interpreting the goose as an animal whose trek follows yang, Sima Guang stipulates that it may be replaced with a wooden substitute, but not with other types of living fowl.

This alternative presentment of a wooden goose also serves as an example of the substitutions and condensations at which Sima Guang arrives, again through his exegetical hermeneutics. He reduces the number of steps in certain ceremonies, substitutes words in the dialogues, and replaces certain types of food and wine with cheaper equivalents. He also uses substitutes to adjust for perceived anachronisms. While he insists on maintaining the use of a wheeled carriage in Fetching the Bride (rather than indulging the contemporary preference for the sedan chair), he finds detailed substitutes for the changes in the make of such carriages. In the canon, the groom proffers a rope to help the bride climb into the vehicle, and the duenna presents the bride with a piece of cloth to protect her from the dust of travel; in *Letters and Ceremonies* the groom holds open the curtain of the carriage for the bride, and the duenna closes it for her. Other substitutions pertain to architectural space (front substituted for south, left for east, etc., in spaces not built along a south-north axis), divination techniques (modern techniques may replace archaic ones), and the design of the box offered by the bride to her parents-in-law on the morning after the wedding night. Sima Guang also silently introduces chairs, tables, and incense into his archaic ritual.

Sima Guang's most significant alterations of "Wedding Rites of an Ordinary Officer," however, derive not from his exegetical hermeneutics, but from his introduction of elements from contemporary ritual practice. Elsewhere, in a long memorial to the throne, Sima Guang argues that acquired practices (*xi*) through habit naturalize all practices of the age and thereby obscure the essential difference between custom and ritual. Ritual is inherent and timeless, and therefore exists beyond practice and knowledge, while custom exists only in practice.[90] His *Letters and Ceremonies* includes certain practices from his day that Sima Guang has identified as ritual, isolated from their practical context, and inscribed into his ritual sequences. Thus he writes in the section on cappings,

> The capping ceremony has long been abandoned. During my childhood I heard that among the people of the villages and the

> fields there were still those who practiced it under the name of Unto the Head [*shang tou*]. But in the cities it is extinct. This is what is meant by "If a ritual is lost, seek it in the fields."[91]

Such dispersed remains of ancient ritual, preserved among the corrupt practices of the day, instantiate the same timeless truths as the incomplete rites of the fragmented canon, and exist on the same plane. Sima Guang therefore reinscribes such practices in the same manner as he reinscribes canonical ritual, combining contemporary ritual and canonical ritual in a written narrative that enables the reader and performer to embody patterns ancient and timeless.

Sima Guang inscribes three contemporary ceremonies into his wedding ritual: the arrangement of furnishings in the groom's chamber by the bride's family on the day prior to Fetching the Bride (Decking the Room, *pu fang*); the bride's visit to the ancestral shrine immediately upon entering the groom's house (Bowing to the Spirits of the Ancestors, *bai xian ling*); and alternate bows exchanged by the groom and the bride upon entering the groom's chamber. He also alters the canonical sequence in two places to accord with contemporary practice: he insists that the bride sit to the west during Sharing the Meal (rather than to the east), and he advances the banquet for the followers of the groom and the bride to the wedding night (from the day after Fetching the Bride). In his explanation of Decking the Room, Sima Guang suggests the extent of his reinscription of contemporary practice:

> One day prior to Fetching the Bride, the bride's family sends people to hang the curtains and display the furnishings in the groom's bedroom. [Comment:] In common usage this is called "Decking the Room." Although this did not exist in antiquity, it is practiced in current custom, and it should not be abandoned. The groom's family should provide beds, mats, tables, chairs, and the like, while the bride's family is responsible for bedding, curtains, coverlets, and so forth. Lay out only those items needed [on the day of Fetching the Bride], such as the bedding, curtains, and screens, but keep things that are not needed, such as clothes, socks, and shoes, locked in the trunks. In current custom these are all displayed to boast extravagant wealth, but that is the habit of maidservants and the common man, not worthy of imitation.[92]

Although Sima Guang introduces Decking the Room as a contemporary practice that "should not be abandoned," he empties it of what he perceives to be its conventional ceremonial function, namely the display of wealth. Through Sima Guang's reinscription, the ceremony becomes a solemn occasion, a counterpart to the elaborate arrangement of vessels and foods by the groom's family in the same room the following day, and is thereby inscribed into the interlocking symmetries of canonical wedding ritual.

The comments on Bowing to the Spirits of the Ancestors and alternate bows emphasize their resonance with ancient ritual:

> In antiquity this ritual did not exist. Presently it is called "Bowing to the Spirits of the Ancestors." This, too, should be preserved.[93]
>
> In antiquity the ceremony of alternate bows between the groom and the bride did not exist. In present custom, they bow alternately when they see each other for the first time. Bowing communicates respect, which is the appropriate principle of the occasion, and it should not be abandoned.[94]

To Sima Guang, Bowing to the Spirits of the Ancestors is a ritual, entirely without the taint of custom, and he inscribes it, in canonical language, as the core of his wedding sequence. The comment on alternate bows bears a trace of a more forcible reinscription: the groom and the bride in current custom "bow alternately when they see each other for the first time," says the text, indicating that Sima Guang has removed the alternate bows from a wedding sequence in which the groom does not fetch the bride but instead encounters her first in his own bedroom.[95]

A proper understanding of the consequences of Sima Guang's introduction of reinscribed contemporary practices into his exegetical hermeneutics requires an analysis of the wedding sequence as a whole, with its symmetries and asymmetries (see fig. 1.4). In *Ceremonies and Rites*, Fetching the Bride consists of two symmetrical parts: the departure of the bride from her natal home, and her induction into the home of the groom (see fig. 1.1). Fetching the Bride itself in turn fits into a larger symmetrical structure in which the bride's first visit to the groom's ancestral temple mirrors the bride's initial instruction at the temple of her natal home. Within this second, larger symmetrical structure, Fetching the Bride becomes linear, with the consummation of the marriage as the ritual core, equidistant between the bride's parting from her parents and her meeting with her parents-in-law, and so forth. In Sima Guang's sequence, Bowing to the Spirits of the Ancestors becomes the ritual center, enfolded within the bride's meeting with the groom (first at the carriage, then in his chamber), the decoration of the groom's chamber and the feasting of the bride's followers, the bride's parting from her parents and her ceremonial encounter with her parents-in-law. Rather than being both symmetrical and linear, Fetching the Bride in Sima Guang's wedding ritual is only symmetrical because its center coincides with that of the wedding sequence as a whole. The consummation of the marriage thereby becomes a marginal affair, removed from ritual time and space.

This marginalization of the consummation, however, this exclusion of the creation of the legitimate sexual bodies of male and female from ritual space and time, shows that Sima Guang's hermeneutics of text does not allow him to escape from the hermeneutical circle in which earlier (and later) authors of ritual manuals were caught.[96] In reinscribing the timeless ritual of antiquity, whether by the Tang hermeneutics of practice or the Song hermeneutics of text, the authors of ritual manuals rely on the historical hermeneutics of their day: time necessarily mediates timelessness and predisposes exegetes to particular interpretations of canonical texts. Sima Guang's distinction between ritual and custom, which relies entirely on internalized exegetical principles, is a good example of the inevitable hermeneutical tautology. His segregation of ritual bodies from sexual bodies allows a more extensive comparison of historical hermeneutics.

The ritual narrative of Fetching the Bride in the canonical *Ceremonies and Rites* combines the production of ritual and sexual bodies. After the groom and the bride have entered the groom's chamber, they are washed by each other's followers. The groom and the bride then share food and drink, the last serving of wine being drunk from cups made from a gourd split in half. The groom enters the adjoining room where the bride's followers assist him in undressing, while the groom's followers assist in the undressing of the bride. The duenna hands the bride a towel. The followers spread out the sleeping mats, the groom's followers again arranging the bride's side and vice versa. The groom re-enters the chamber and loosens the bride's tassel before all assistants leave the room, bearing the candles. While the groom and the bride are left together in the dark, the followers, again crosswise, consume the food and wine left over by the groom and the bride.[97] "The Meaning of Weddings" in the *Record of Ritual* explains that the shared food and the nuptial cups "join the bodies" (*he ti*) of the groom and the bride and eliminate status distinctions in order to make them intimate (*qin*). But the text also stresses that the ritual instills propriety, establishing differentiation between male and female, and proper relations between husband and wife.[98]

According to the Tang subcommentary by Jia Gongyan (fl. 650), the crossovers between the followers of the groom and the bride coincide with a reversal in the regular gendered seating arrangement. Associating the east with yang (male) and the west with yin (female), Jia Gongyan concludes that the repeated choreographic reversals, from the assisted washing to the consumption of the leftovers, symbolize "the gradual process of copulation" (*jiaojie you jian*). As the assistants spread the bed mats side by side, Jia observes:

> When the assistants arranged the seats for Sharing the Meal, the husband was seated in the west and the wife in the east. Only here does the husband take the east and the wife the west. The initial reversal of positions showed the gradual merging of yin and yang. Therefore the male was in the west and the female in the east. Here [the text] takes yang and moves it toward yin. Therefore male and female each take their proper station.[99]

In Jia Gongyan's reading, the production of sexual bodies (male and female) intertwines with the production of ritual bodies (husband and wife). The symmetrical structure of Sharing the Meal, from its preparation to the consumption of the leftovers, produces the ritual bodies of husband and wife, while the linear "process of copulation" creates the sexual bodies of male and female within shared ritual time and space.[100]

Similar assumptions inform the hermeneutics of Tang manuals of letters and ceremonies found at Dunhuang. The untitled fragment S1725, for example, presents the following explanations for the presentation of three rolls of dark cloth, three rolls of red cloth, and five rolls of silk as betrothal gifts:

> The dark cloth mimics heaven and symbolizes the male, while the red cloth mimics the earth and symbolizes the female. The rites of yin and yang conjoin, and thus male and female

> copulate [*jiaotong*]. . . . The bundle of silk consists of five rolls of gauze, each forty feet long and rolled up from both sides into two halves of twenty feet each. . . . This is called the "bundle of silk," and it mimics the union of husband and wife: unrolled, they separate, but rolled up, they are united.[101]

The ritual narrative of the Wedding Night in *Newly Compiled Letters and Ceremonies for Auspicious and Inauspicious Occasions* combines the symmetrical rites of husband and wife with a linear, and explicit, narrative that creates the sexual bodies of male and female (see fig. 1.3).

Sima Guang, however, excludes the sexual bodies of the groom and the bride from ritual time and space through a judicious reordering of ritual symmetry and choreography. Although he maintains the crossovers between the followers during the meal (to overcome shyness, says Sima Guang, proposing a nonsymbolic reading that circumvents the male-female binary), the ceremony as a whole produces only the ritual bodies of husband and wife.[102] The exchange of bows between the groom and the bride, appropriated from contemporary practice, sets the tone of distanced respect. Then, reading east and west as left and right (rather than as yang and yin), Sima Guang restores the groom and the bride to the orientations proper to husband and wife. The advancement of the consumption of leftovers to precede the ritual undressing, finally, renders Sharing the Meal a symmetrical structure onto itself, producing only the ritual bodies of husband and wife. The ritual undressing, as the sole remains of the production of sexual bodies, is thus separated from Sharing the Meal. Sima Guang's alterations in the consumption of food and wine reinforce this desexualization of the ritual sequence. The followers eat and drink the leftovers as part of the cycle that produces husband and wife, while the segregated consumption of untouched foods at the remunerative banquets hosted by the groom's parents are dissociated from the sexual union of the groom and the bride.[103]

Sima Guang regards weddings as joyous occasions of a solemn kind. Although the function of weddings lies both in the production of ritual bodies and in the legitimation of sexual bodies, the latter do not belong within the ritual cycle, and should be excluded from ritual time and space. The ritual bodies of husband and wife perform outside the conjugal circle in the public space of ritualized relations, but their sexual bodies hide in darkness to produce new moral, ritual bodies for the continuity of positioned ritual subjects.[104] This view of a ritualized society, instantiated in antiquity and existing beyond time, Sima Guang inscribes into his wedding sequence by means of his hermeneutics of text. Through his reinscription of contemporary practices, he imparts to his canonical wedding sequence certain universal principles absent from "Wedding Rites of an Ordinary Officer." Thus revolves the hermeneutical circle: general principles gained from the canon are subsequently reinscribed in ritual. The immutable, timeless truths of the ancients are accessible only through changeable, historical hermeneutics; no objective standard exists by which the validity of these hermeneutics may be assessed.[105]

Sima Guang applies his hermeneutics of text to both scripture and contemporary practice in order to reinscribe ancient ritual in such a way that its timeless cosmic patterns may be reincorporated in the present. Whereas ritual experts in the Tang and early Northern Song deemed that ritual evolved with time and that its connection with antiquity was historical, to Sima Guang ritual was immutable and inherent. This immanent truth of ritual inhered not only in general ideas and overarching structures, but in subtle detail, and the wedding sequence Sima Guang devised to maintain those material and choreographic details impressed his contemporaries as archaic. If even his adaptations of contemporary ceremonies transformed living practice into arcane text, his retention of ancient dialogue (written on cue cards), the display of deerskins during Submission of the Betrothal Gifts, and the use of a wheeled carriage stood far removed from the practice of his day:

> Fortunately, women today can ride in a felt carriage. Yet current custom attaches importance to the use of a sedan chair and spurns this carriage. Would it hurt to sit in a felt carriage for a little while during Fetching the Bride? The disposition of some people will not allow them to ride in a carriage since it causes them to vomit, and such people of course should travel by sedan chair. But with a sedan chair one cannot perform the ceremony in which the groom replaces the driver for the first three revolutions of the wheels, nor is there any use for the duenna.[106]

Zhang Zai, the brothers Cheng Hao (1032–1085) and Cheng Yi, and the brothers Lü Dafang, Lü Dajun, and Lü Dalin studied with one another and shared a commitment to a return to antiquity. Although in this respect they resembled contemporaries such as Chen Xiang, Sima Guang, and Wang Anshi, they grew disillusioned with the grand imperial projects of reform with which the latter involved themselves. Instead, they envisioned a process of reform that began with the individual, the family, and the local community, as outlined in the chapter "The Great Learning" (*Daxue*) in the *Record of Ritual*:

> In antiquity, those who wished to manifest their manifest virtue in the realm first brought order to their state. Those who wished to bring order to their state first regulated their family. Those who wished to regulate their family first trained their bodies. Those who wished to train their bodies first rectified their heart-mind. Those who wished to rectify their heart-mind first made their intentions sincere. Those who wished to make their intentions sincere would first extend their knowledge. The extension of knowledge lies in realizing the nature of things.[107]

Peter Bol explains that Cheng Yi understands this extension of knowledge as a dialectical process which "combines extending knowledge as seeing how things conform to the pattern one has in mind and attaining knowledge as becoming aware of the patterns as one sees them in things."[108]

The realization of this inherent cosmic pattern was not a sterile intellectual pursuit, but a pursuit that involved rigorous bodily training and the ordering of family, community, and society. Since only a return to the permanently ritualized society of the ancients would ensure the complete realization of the nature of things, Zhang Zai, the Cheng brothers, and the Lü brothers imposed on themselves a strict mental and physical discipline in accordance with ancient texts, in hopes of transforming those around them. Of Lü Dalin, author of *Investigations of Antiquity Illustrated*, several sources write that he "trained his body like the ancients."[109] *Assorted Sayings of Master Zhu* (*Zhuzi yulei*, 1270) quotes Zhu Xi, saying, "Yushu [i.e., Lü Dalin] also built a temple, and he used ancient vessels. But during sacrifice he would wear dark robes in ancient style, with wide sleeves and a black gown. That would be strange."[110] Similar anecdotes about the dedication to ancient ritual among members of this group depict them as practicing ritual straight from the canon, building a well with the "Record of Inspecting Public Works" (*Kaogong ji*) in hand, and winning the people's hearts for antiquity through a restored Community Wine Drinking ceremony.[111]

In dress and gesture these men signaled their break with contemporary society and their commitment to the restoration of antiquity. Like Chen Xiang and Sima Guang, Zhang Zai perceived the dangers of the embodiment of timeless ritual in the present:

> In general, in performing ritual one should take care not to frighten those who adhere to current customs. Those ignorant of ritual may find it strange and may object, and in the worst case they may grow angry and take offense. Therefore the restoration of ritual will have to proceed gradually. The performance of an occasional ritual already demands much from those who lack understanding. Nothing bars one from performing ritual behind one's gates, in one's own courtyard, but one should refrain from enforcing it upon others. As long as one realizes one's virtuous nature, others will transform of their own accord. Rectify thy self and the world will be rectified.[112]

And indeed, in the early twelfth century Cheng Yi's disciples inspired the rage of court officials because they dressed in "big hats and broad sleeves, and with lofty gaze walked in measured steps."[113]

If the ambitions and fears of this group resembled those of contemporary classicists, so did the hermeneutics that informed their commentaries and ritual manuals. Unfortunately, many of their writings have perished or survive only in part. Lü Dalin, for example, wrote not only *Investigations of Antiquity Illustrated* and commentaries on several canonical works, but he also compiled a manual on mourning ritual entitled *The Edited Rites* (*Bian li*), now lost.[114] Lü Dajun likewise wrote an extinct ritual manual on mourning, composed of passages from *Ceremonies and Rites* and the *Record of Ritual.*[115] Lü Dafang contributed to the drafting of archaic rites for the wedding of Emperor Zhezong in 1092.[116] The ritual manuals by Zhang Zai and Cheng Yi survive only in part: the rites for mourning and sacrifice by Zhang Zai, and the rites for weddings, burial, and sacrifice by Cheng Yi.[117]

Cheng Yi's protocol for wedding ritual is brief and terse, and appears to be incomplete. For Submission of the Choice, Asking the Name, Submission of the Auspicious Result, Submission of the Betrothal Gifts, and Requesting the Date, the present text provides only a brief explanation of the name of the ceremony and the words of the ritual dialogues between the host and the messenger. Under the caption Completion of the Wedding (*cheng hun*), Cheng Yi subsumes the canonical sequence stretching from Fetching the Bride through the groom's visit to the bride's parents two days later. In this sequence, Cheng Yi leaves the canonical structure largely intact, but he adds a visit by the groom to the bride's ancestral temple and to her relatives during Fetching the Bride. The mirror image of Sima Guang's inscription of Bowing to the Spirits of the Ancestors, Cheng Yi's addition similarly manipulates the symmetry of the wedding sequence to emphasize the continuation of the ancestral cult and the reproduction of the family as a ritual unit, and to decenter the consummation of the marriage.

The only comprehensive text to preserve the Lü brothers' views on family ritual is Lü Dajun's "Community Compact" (*Xiangyue*), the outline for a community of strict moral and ritual discipline based on the ritual scriptures: "The *Ritual Canon* suggests itself as the basis for those intent on reviving antiquity."[118] The placement of wedding ritual before capping in the section "Joyous Ritual" seems to imply an emphasis on weddings as the root of all ritual and on the sexual bodies that reproduce the ritual cycle, but Lü Dajun does not intend to restore greater visibility to sexual bodies in wedding ritual:

> Wedding ritual in antiquity was a most solemn occasion. The community was invited for food and wine so as to give weight to the differentiation instilled by the ceremony. The presentments at Fetching the Bride communicated respect. The absence of music and congratulations commemorated the role of weddings in the continuation of the ancestral cult. Sharing the Meal and Sharing the Nuptial Cup established affection [between the groom and the bride]. How could there be vulgar, lewd acts to insult and ridicule the couple!
>
> In recent custom, the Six Rites have largely been abandoned. Money and goods change hands, some grooms decorate their clothes and cap with flowers, and at some weddings the bride is led by musicians. Anything seems permitted in these crude ceremonies and vulgar practices. This is not the way to instill deference in the groom and the bride or to promote solemnity in the lineage temple. Although we may not be able to change everything instantaneously, we may at least consider

> [reviving] Fetching the Bride and Sharing the Meal. The common customs and harmful practices should, of course, be abandoned forthwith. Those intent on ritual can start from there.[119]

For Lü Dajun, wedding ritual as performed in antiquity inheres in the nature of things. After summing up its universal principles, he condemns various decontextualized contemporary practices for lacking in these principles. His vocabulary, his dichotomies, and his rhetorical techniques all resemble Sima Guang's.

What little survives of this group's writings on weddings emphasizes the solemnity of the occasion. Wedding ritual should instill respect between the groom and the bride, and a realization of their ritual obligations. Wedding ritual serves, again, to ensure the production of ritual bodies for the continuation of the ancestral cult.[120] Cheng Yi's manipulation of the structure of the canonical wedding sequence, like Sima Guang's, foregrounds the role of the groom and the bride within the family as a ritual unit and thereby diminishes the role of the groom and the bride as individual ritual actors.

While opponents of Wang Anshi retired from officialdom to attempt local reform, the court of Emperor Huizong revived Wang's legacy with grand imperial projects. The Ritual Revision Service (*Yili ju*), established in 1107, completed in 1113 the *New Ceremonies for the Five Rites of the Zhenghe Period* (*Zhenghe wuli xinyi*), in 220 fascicles. In his preface to this new ritual code, Huizong envisions a return to the ritualized society of antiquity in which the ritual embodiment of social distinctions ensures lasting order and peace. While he invokes the physical proximity of antiquity sensed by many scholars of the time, Huizong emphasizes that the continuity with antiquity can be established through precedent and current practice. Thus, he combines the rhetoric of current scholarship with the traditional hermeneutics of imperial ritual codes. He cites the changing rites of antiquity as precedent:

> It has been said, "We know in what ways the Shang modified ritual when they followed upon the Xia. We know in what ways the Zhou modified ritual when they followed upon the Shang. And hence we can foretell what the successors of the Zhou will be like, even supposing they do not appear till a hundred generations from now." The realm at present stands removed from the Zhou by more than a thousand years. Never has the Way been further obscured than it is now, and never

> have customs been so depraved or distinctions in rank so ill observed. Thus, imitating the government of the ancients, We have modified current custom according to the Way, and modified ritual for the present: We have acknowledged the change of a hundred generations since, while struggling to return to a hundred generations prior. Once a true king appears after a hundred generations, holding the fitting tally, the times return to the former standard. This is called, "succeeding the Zhou after a hundred generations."[121]

In the early years of his reign, Huizong sought to legitimize imperial rule with the casting of nine tripods of thick gold, the promulgation of new music, and the grand ceremonial presentation of eight auspicious, archaic imperial seals.[122] *New Rites of the Yuanfeng Period* (*Yuanfeng xinli*), however, begun under the direction of Su Song (1020–1101) and completed in 1107 in a prodigious 477 fascicles, did not pursue archaism but rather provided further adjustments to *Comprehensive Rites of the Kaibao Period* of 973.[123] *New Rites of the Yuanfeng Period* remained effective during a mere five years. Already in the year of its promulgation, Huizong established the Ritual Revision Service for a thorough reinvestigation of imperial ritual and ritual implements.

In its study and manufacture of ritual implements, the Ritual Revision Service relied on the ancient vessels in the imperial collection, on rubbings taken from private collections, and on vessels acquired through widespread excavations as well as through confiscation.[124] Within a few years, the Ritual Revision Service produced new manuals on auspicious ritual (*Jili*, 1109, in 231 fascicles) and on sacrifice and mourning (*Jifu zhidu*, 1109, in 16 fascicles).[125] The Service also compiled *Broad Researches in Antiquities of the Xuanhe Palace Illustrated* (*Xuanhedian bo gu tu*, 1107), a catalogue of the vessels in the imperial collection, in imitation of Lü Dalin's *Investigations of Antiquity Illustrated*.[126] *Broad Researches* at long last replaced the *Ritual Canon Illustrated* (*Sanli tu*), written in the early years of the dynasty by Nie Chongyi (tenth century). Based on transmitted drawings and textual research, the ritual implements displayed on the pages of the *Ritual Canon Illustrated* had long provided the models for the vessels cast in palace workshops for use in imperial ritual. But as the study of authentic ancient vessels developed in the eleventh century, many of the ritual implements drawn by Nie Chongyi had begun appear fantastic. Under Huizong, the Ritual

Revision Service changed imperial vessels, clothing, and musical instruments in accordance with the archaeological finds and hermeneutic insights of recent decades.[127]

Investigation of scriptures, antiquities, and precedent continued in preparation for a new comprehensive ritual code. Starting in 1112, a separate Ritual Regulations Service (*Lizhi ju*) assisted the Ritual Revision Service in "discussing the architecture, vehicles, clothing, and implements as well as weddings, cappings, and mourning of the past and the present."[128] The exchanges between the Ritual Revision Service and Emperor Huizong, included in an introductory fascicle of *New Ceremonies for the Five Rites of the Zhenghe Period*, debate matters of exegetical hermeneutics and material reconstruction, invigorated by the contemporary assumption of an unprecedented physical proximity to antiquity. But at the same time, the emperor and the Service maintain the fundamental correctness of precedent and current practice.[129] When the Service carefully explained, for example, that the Tang protocols had revised the ritual structures of Zhou, and that the *Comprehensive Code of the Kaibao Period* had adopted Tang protocol as a model, the emperor replied:

> Certain rituals instituted by the ancient kings cannot be changed, but other of their rituals cannot be followed. All one can say is that each case has its own proper principle. Ritual should be generated from its meaning; it need not be identical.[130]

The irresolvable contradiction between the hermeneutics of precedent and the hermeneutics of text proved productive rather than paralyzing. The refusal to acknowledge the contradiction between the two approaches necessitated the assumption of a principle inherent yet (of course) never explicated in either imperial protocol or in canonical texts. In the resulting absence of a clearly defined hermeneutical standard, the hermeneutical circle revolved unobstructed. The compilers of *New Ceremonies for the Five Rites* were able to support their hermeneutical decisions by reference to the letter of precedent, to the letter of the canon, or to the intention implicit in either—and also to invoke the rhetoric and imagery associated with both approaches:

> Following the essential principles of historical precedent we have prepared this ritual manual; after a detailed study of

> pertinent regulations we have compiled this ceremonial code. We have endeavored to produce a standard for our time; we have surpassed in one bound the eminence of the Three Kings.[131]

In the section on weddings (fascicles 166–179), too, the simultaneous commitment to canon and precedent results in hermeneutical inconsistency and tautologies. The memorials submitted on wedding ritual emphasize both the authenticity of material detail and the inference of ritual detail from general meaning, both the universality of ancient ritual and the preservation of timeless principles in current practice. General principles derived from scriptures justify not only changes in ceremonies, but condemnation of the texts themselves. When Emperor Huizong infers from the *Record of Ritual* that weddings, as the root of all ritual, should precede cappings, he concludes that *Ceremonies and Rites* cannot be an authentic ancient text since it places cappings before weddings.[132]

Despite this tension between canon and precedent, the hermeneutics of text has determined the very structure of *New Ceremonies for the Five Rites of the Zhenghe Period.* In contrast to *Rites of the Kaiyuan Period, New Ceremonies* arranges the ceremonies under the Five Rites first by ceremony (weddings, cappings, etc.) and then by rank (emperor, heir apparent, etc.). At the same time, it comprises a greater number of ranks, not only because it includes rites for commoners, but because it distinguishes between imperial kin and royal kin. It eliminates from the wedding sequence the gathering for the bride's relatives that *Rites of the Kaiyuan Period* added to the canonical sequence, but introduces a visit by the bride to the groom's ancestors prior to her meeting with her parents-in-law. *New Ceremonies* also inscribes the boxed engagement letter of contemporary practice into Submission of the Betrothal Gifts.[133]

The inclusion of ceremonies for commoners necessitates an unprecedented downward extrapolation from "Wedding Rites of an Ordinary Officer," which the compilers achieve through compression and reduction. A go-between replaces the messenger in a sequence that reduces the Six Rites to four by combining Submission of the Choice with Asking the Name, and Submission of the Betrothal Gifts with Requesting the Date. At the conclusion of these ceremonies, the host accompanies the go-between to the gate but does not offer a meal by way of reward.[134] The compilers also make allowances for buildings that do not face south, for the replacement of the goose with a pheasant or a turtle dove,[135] for gifts besides cloth and the letter, for performance of Fetching the Bride by the go-between "if necessary,"[136] and for the arrangement of ancestral tablets in a space other than a temple.[137]

*New Ceremonies for the Five Rites of the Zhenghe Period* remained merely a written representation of an ideal order. Huizong ordered the compilation of a digest of the *New Ceremonies* for commoners, to be distributed throughout the realm and to be enforced as law, and he appointed Ritual Duty Officials to answer ritual questions that commoners might submit. But even the digest proved too complex to implement, and in 1119 the digest was abolished, as were the Ritual Revision Service and the Ritual Regulations Service.[138] Although archaic projects continued at Huizong's court with the obsessive collection of bronzes, the recompilation of *Broad Researches of Antiquities Illustrated*, and the promulgation of new ritual implements and colors, these projects became embroiled in Huizong's preoccupation with Daoist ritual. Daoist experts now advised on the placement and ritual use of ancient and archaic vessels.[139] Scholars of the Southern Song looked upon Huizong's reign as a period of excess and corruption. His obsession with ancient vessels had not brought him closer to antiquity. Instead, it led him astray on a mad quest, his archaic rites and his storehouses of bells, beakers, and cauldrons increasingly grotesque and meaningless.[140]

## Toward a New Ritual Scripture: Zhu Xi's *Family Rituals*

Banished from the hallowed grounds of the ancient capitals and separated from the scattered remains of imperial and private collections of ancient vessels, epigraphists of the Southern Song had to rely almost entirely on notes and rubbings salvaged from the North, and on published reproductions.[141] But the reduction to the two dimensions of the page did not diminish the powerful physicality of ancient vessels. In his preface for *Record of the Collection of Antiquities* (*Jigu lu*, twelfth century) by Li Bing, Lü Zuqian (1137–1181) recounts,

> Since the events of 1126, records still abound of the plethora of works compiled in imitation of Ouyang Xiu, but the works themselves have not survived. My friend Mr. Li Bing, polite

name Zhongnan, of Shaowu, examined the remaining studies and collected fragmented compilations. Over the course of twenty years his reputation spread, and an increasing number of inscriptions were sent to him. His collection grew to a thousand scrolls, covering the entire period from the Xia through the Five Dynasties. . . .

Once I visited Li Bing during a bout of depression, with a heavy heart. He pulled out a few scrolls and carefully unrolled them. The magnificence of cauldrons and the splendor of seal script illumined the room, and my spirits lifted instantly. Such is the influence of the ancients, even if one does not speak with them face to face.[142]

If reproductions of ancient vessels and inscriptions could assert so powerful a presence, so could the words and intentions conveyed by scriptures. In the words of Li Jike (fl. 1157),

Whether it is possible to seek the words of the sages without understanding their meaning, I do not know. Ten thousand generations of honored teachers have not dared keep pace with the ancients, unable to turn with poise, to bow in perfect accord with ritual, unselfconscious. . . . *The Analects* concludes with the statement, "He who does not understand words cannot understand others."[143] But if one does understand the meaning of words, it is as though one meets face to face across a hundred generations. Conversely, one may talk an entire day to a person who does not understand the meaning of words, and still there will be things he will not have understood.[144]

To scholars of the Southern Song, as to scholars of the late Northern Song, the written page provided a timeless space where the past and the present conjoined, and where the physical reality of antiquity could be restored to the reader's living eye. In the twelfth and thirteenth centuries, the written space of the past and the lived space of the reader interpenetrated as illustrated, rearranged canonical texts grew increasingly similar to ritual manuals. Confident in their grasp of the cosmic principles conveyed by the words and rituals of the ancients, Southern Song scholars took unprecedented liberties with the scriptures. Both canonical commentaries and ritual manuals attempted to recover the physicality and materiality of antiquity. They differed merely in hermeneutical range: while authors of canonical commentaries confined themselves to scripture and ancient objects, authors of ritual manuals also sought cosmic patterns in contemporary practice and contemporary text.

In the late twelfth century, scholars resumed the study of *Ceremonies and Rites.* Zhang Chun (fl. 1172), acknowledged as the first to restore the text to the interest of his contemporaries, notes in the introduction to his philological *Explanation of Errors in Ceremonies and Rites* (*Yili shi wu*, ca. 1172) that he embarked on his analysis of textual variants after a friend complained to him that he wished to practice the ancient rites of mourning and sacrifice but failed to understand them.[145] Li Rugui (1193 *jinshi*) compiled a new commentary on *Ceremonies and Rites*, combining Zheng Xuan's Han-dynasty commentary with his own insights under the title *Collected Explanations of Ceremonies and Rites* (*Yili jishi*, ca. 1200). He wrote a separate *Analysis of Halls in Ceremonies and Rites* (*Yili shigong*, ca. 1190), a brief text that was long ascribed to Zhu Xi and that was included in the latter's collected writings.[146] In its preface, Li Rugui argues that a proper understanding of *Ceremonies and Rites* requires an embodied, four-dimensional reading of the text:

> Ritual texts abounded under the Zhou, but today their abundance is suggested only by *Ceremonies and Rites.* Because we are far removed from antiquity, however, and because the ritual canon is incomplete, those who read the *Rites* today are unable to examine the points of ascending and descending or the order of advancing and retreating, unless they first gain an understanding of the structure of the halls and chambers [of ancient buildings]. Those who wish to imagine their opulence and to bow, yield, and turn within their walls, will be unable to do so. Needless to say, they will never be able to fathom the meaning of the rites.[147]

Zhu Xi undertook the most ambitious exegetical project on the ritual scriptures: the *Comprehensive Explanations of the Scripture and Commentaries of Ceremonies and Rites* (*Yili jingzhuan tongjie*, 1217). He requested, and received, imperial funding for a reconstruction of the *Ritual Canon* (*Lijing*), an imaginary work of which *Ceremonies and Rites* conveyed the most accurate impression, but parts of which survived in the *Record of Ritual*, as well as in references in other scriptures, early commentaries, and the histories. The project—continued after Zhu Xi's death by Huang Gan (1152–1221), Chen Shijun (fl. 1200), and Yang Fu (fl. 1230)—involved a daring, hierarchical rearrangement of *Ceremonies and Rites*, from family ritual through community ceremonies to royal and imperial rites, as well as a reconstitution of the *Record of Ritual* according to Zhu Xi's ideas about the diverse origins of its parts.[148] Although similar to earlier imperial ritual compilations in its hermeneutical approach, Zhu Xi's project differed from its predecessors by its claim to canonical status: his was not merely a comprehensive protocol for the empire, it was itself a scripture, equal to the ancient canon.[149] Yang Fu later added maps of buildings and detailed choreographic diagrams to the *Comprehensive Explanations* and printed it as *Ceremonies and Rites Illustrated* (*Yili tu*, 1228).[150]

The architectural reconstructions in *Analysis of Halls in Ceremonies and Rites*, the exegetical manipulations of the *Comprehensive Explanations*, and the choreographic diagrams in *Ceremonies and Rites Illustrated* all presuppose a dialectic between the past and the present, predicated upon a shared, timeless truth. The general principles conveyed by text and cosmos allow the exegete to rearrange fragmented, corrupted scriptures and to make visible once more the performing bodies of the ancients. Ritual manuals, in their effort to allow the re-embodiment of the timeless ritual of the ancients, include in this hermeneutics the text of contemporary practice which, by the twelfth century, was already inscribed in a number of authoritative eleventh-century manuals.

Zhang Shi (1133–1180) edited and reprinted the Northern Song manuals by Sima Guang, Zhang Zai, and Cheng Yi, with a colophon by Zhu Xi. Zhu Xi published his own edition of these manuals, adding materials by Cheng Hao.[151] He also proposed to the court the compilation of an illustrated revision of *New Ceremonies for the Five Rites of the Zhenghe Period*, with digests for the local level, accompanied by a policy of enforcement.[152] (Zhu Xi must have intended a substantial revision, because elsewhere he condemns the *New Ceremonies* as a compilation produced "under the evil influence of its time, with arbitrary additions and omissions, unthorough and full of contradictions, and entirely lacking in understanding.")[153]

After Zhu Xi's death, a manual for family ritual surfaced that bore his name. His intellectual heirs Chen Chun (1159–1223), Huang Gan, and Yang Fu accepted it as authentic, writing colophons and commentaries for it, while correcting points that, they argued, Zhu Xi himself would have altered in recent years had he not lost the sole manuscript of this text in a monastery many years before his death. The story of the loss and recovery of the text—stolen by a Buddhist novice and returned as a copy in an unknown hand at Zhu Xi's funeral—reads like an apocryphal account designed to legitimize a forged text. Yet much of the contents of *Family Rituals* accords with ideas expressed in Zhu Xi's writings and in *Assorted Sayings*, with the occasional discrepancy that suggests the changes of mind alleged in the colophons by Chen Chun, Huang Gan, and Yang Fu. More important, the acceptance of the manual's authenticity by Zhu Xi's disciples and the embeddedness of the manual in the posthumous works edited by these same disciples renders identification of the historical authorship of *Family Rituals* both complicated and irrelevant. Nor is the concept of historical authorship pertinent to a text that came to be perceived as an objective embodiment of timeless truth, collapsing past and present, text and cosmos. As Huang Gan writes in his colophon of 1216:

> Once my late teacher [i.e., Zhu Xi] said, "Ritual is the patterned expression of the pattern of Heaven, the ceremonial principles for human affairs." When the ten thousand creatures first crawled between the lofty heavens and the subterranean realm, the structure of ritual already inhered among them. Of the Five Phases it is fire; of the four seasons it is summer; of the four virtues it is thoroughness: all natural, immutable manifestations of heavenly pattern. Since man is endowed with the five constancies at birth, ritual is embodied in him from the day he is born. Embodied in practice, it is respect and deference; embodied in writing, it is ceremony, volume, and measurements—again: the natural, immutable state of human affairs. The sages devised their rituals in accordance with human emotions, and hence in accordance with the correct heavenly pattern. . . . Mr. Zhu Hui'an [i.e., Zhu Xi] studied [the writings of former scholars] in their general purport and in their detail, yet retained certain doubts. Carefully weighing his additions and deletions, he composed his *Family Rituals*. . . . Scholars who study this work and who moreover dedicate themselves to Mr. Zhu's teachings will realize that this book is in complete accord with the natural pattern of Heaven and with the natural state of human affairs, and that one must practice it every day.[154]

Zhu Xi's *Family Rituals* consists of a preface, a section called "General Ritual," and four sections on family rituals: cappings (and pinnings), weddings, funerals, and sacrifice. The work largely follows Sima Guang's *Letters and Ceremonies*, often reproducing its literal text, but it also supplies abridgments, emendations, and additions.[155]

The preface outlines the strategy of the work. Zhu Xi writes that in preparing the manual he has attempted to find a balance between the fundamentals of ritual and its details, and between antiquity and the present, emending only slightly "the major structures that cannot be changed."[156] He expresses pity for the men of his day who have been unable to perform ritual (*li*) due to lack of means or due to lack of insight, exerting themselves in the performance of their own misguided adaptations of ancient ceremonies. Despite his tone of kindly pity and a certain modesty about his own scholarship, Zhu Xi asserts in this preface that he has grasped the essence of the ritual scriptures and that he alone is able to transpose the rites of the ancients to the present.

The section on "General Ritual" discusses the construction, management, and use of the offering hall; the make of the "long garment"; and the management of household affairs. All three expositions modify similar treatises in various parts of Sima Guang's *Letters and Ceremonies*. By placing these discussions in one introductory section and by stressing the need to exercise its stipulations daily, Zhu Xi foregrounds the importance of the permanent ritualization of the compound and its inhabitants. In this permanently ritualized space, cappings, weddings, mourning, and sacrifice will cause an intensification of ritual activity but not a rupture with the everyday, and the permanently ritualized bodies of the inhabitants will be well-conditioned to perform the ceremonies.[157] The "General Ritual" section represents the commentaries (*zhuan*), the separate injunctions and material details found mostly in the *Record of Ritual*, to support the scripture (*jing*) comprised by the remainder of the manual.[158]

Zhu Xi's wedding ritual (see fig. 1.5) distinguishes itself from Sima Guang's primarily by its pursuit of simplicity (*jian*) and by its consistent inscription of ritual primogeniture.[159] The apparent contradiction between simplicity and the demanding complexity of ritual primogeniture (or the descent-line heir system) resolves when simplicity is recognized as condensation, the proportionate reduction of canonical ritual.[160] The use of "between two and ten lengths of colored silk," as suggested in *Family Rituals*, may serve as an example. In *Assorted Sayings*, Zhu Xi discusses the difficulty of convincing his

## FIGURE 1.5. Schema of Wedding Ritual according to Zhu Xi's *Family Rituals*.

Submission of the Choice:

- Host of the groom's family prepares a letter

- Host announces wedding to the ancestors
  - Host dispatches the messenger
    - Host at bride's family receives the messenger
      - Messenger announces and presents the letter, host bows
        - Host presents the letter to the ancestors
      - Host presents the reply
    - Host rewards the messenger
  - Messenger reports to the host at the groom's family
- Host reports to the ancestors

Submission of the Betrothal Gifts:

- Preparation of gifts and letter by the groom's family

- Host at groom's family dispatches the messenger
  - Host at bride's family receives the messenger
    - Messenger presents letter and gifts
    - Messenger retreats
    - Host prepares a reply
    - Host presents the reply
  - Host rewards the messenger
- Messenger reports to the host at the groom's family

Fetching the Bride:

- Bride's family decorates the groom's chamber
  - Arrangement of vessels in the groom's chamber
    - Host reports to the ancestors
    - Host receives the groom; they ascend
      - Groom sacrifices, receives the host's command
    - Groom descends, exits, departs
    - Groom arrives
      - Bride's host reports to the ancestors
      - Host receives the bride and instructs her
        - Host receives the groom; they ascend
          - Groom presents the goose and bows
        - Groom and bride descend
      - Bride ascends the carriage
    - Groom and bride depart
    - Groom and bride arrive at the groom's house, enter
    - Groom and bride bow to each other, wash
      - Groom and bride sacrifice, eat, drink
    - Groom leaves the chamber
  - Followers remove vessels and consume leftovers
  - Groom re-enters the room
    - Groom and bride disrobe
  - Followers exit with candles
- Groom's parents reward the followers

The Bride Meets Her Parents-in-Law

The Bride Feeds Her Parents-in-Law

The Groom's Parents Receive the Bride

The Bride Visits the Temple

The Groom Meets the Bride's Parents

contemporaries to return to this ancient practice. When one of his students asks whether this presentment of five pairs of lengths of cloth would not be "difficult to practice due to its exceeding simplicity" (*tai jian nan xing*), Zhu Xi chastises him for speaking in terms of profit and adds: "If even we cannot set our sights on restoring antiquity, who then will reform current custom?"[161] Zhu Xi's commitment to simplicity is therefore not a matter of convenience or of accommodation of contemporary practice. Rather, it connotes a condensed representation of ancient ritual, a weighed reduction of the number of steps, not a compromise with the practices of his day.

The first ceremony of the wedding sequence, Submission of the Choice, incorporates Asking the Name. Patricia Ebrey observes that Zhu Xi makes the exchange of marriage documents "the center of the rite."[162] The host of the groom's family prepares the document on the day prior to the ritual, and a messenger conveys it to the host of the bride's family. After the latter has presented the document at the offering hall, the messenger receives a written reply prepared by the bride's family. The host of the groom's family reports this reply to the ancestors at the offering hall.

The merging of Submission of the Choice with Asking the Name hardly represents a radical departure from *Ceremonies and Rites*, where the two ceremonies are separated only by the messenger's brief egress from the host's compound. But Zhu Xi subsequently deletes divination (despite the central place of ancestors and the offering hall in his ceremonies) and the related Submission of the Auspicious Result, with reference to "simplicity and convenience" (*jianbian*), and he omits Requesting the Date without an explanation. Thus he condenses the Six Rites to three: Submission of the Choice, Submission of the Betrothal Gifts, and Fetching the Bride.

In Fetching the Bride, Zhu Xi largely follows Sima Guang's protocol, including the furnishing of the groom's chamber by the bride's family, the alternate bows of the groom and the bride prior to the nuptial meal, and the consumption of the leftovers by the followers prior to the ritual undressing. Still, small differences in wording and details, abridgments, and substitutions abound. The main differences lie in Zhu Xi's elaborations on ritual primogeniture and his silent omission of Sima Guang's Bowing to the Spirits of the Ancestors, with the concomitant reinstatement of the bride's Visit to the Temple after the wedding night and after her introduction to her parents-in-law.[163]

In devising the details of his wedding ritual, Zhu Xi employs the same hermeneutical techniques as Sima Guang, but to different results. Among Zhu Xi's interpretative choices, his elaboration of ritual primogeniture stands out by its impact and comprehensiveness.[164] He interprets the goose as an animal that follows yang and that never takes a second mate.[165] As substitutions Zhu Xi suggests chalk stripes where the offering hall lacks stairs, official robes (*mingfu*) as the current equivalent of opulent clothing, a sedan chair for the carriage, and unspecified presentments for the complex segregated foods that the bride offers to her parents-in-law at their first meeting. He further integrates the exchange of documents into Submission of the Choice, identifying this rite with the contemporary ceremony of Verbal Agreement (*yan ding*, a ceremony that Cheng Yi compares to Submission of the Auspicious Result).

In *Assorted Sayings*, Zhu Xi explicates a few important hermeneutical decisions that inform his wedding sequence. Arguing for the reinstatement of the Visit to the Temple, he explains that the bride in ancient times would have lacked a reason to visit the ancestral shrine if her parents-in-law were alive, because in the system of ritual primogeniture all ancestors would be enshrined in the temple of the great line. But because in his day all branches possess ancestral tablets, Zhu Xi has "therefore restored [this practice] through [investigation of] its meaning."[166] Zhu Xi also repeatedly criticizes Sima Guang and Cheng Yi for their disruption of the symmetry that he deems essential to ancient wedding ritual. The bride ought first to meet the groom, then her parents-in-law (whose libation mirrors that of her own parents), then the household (elders before juniors), until finally she faces the ancestors. The importance of this sequence demands that the bride wait to visit the ancestors until she has met her seniors, and thus the third day is acceptable.[167]

In *Family Rituals*, as in the *Comprehensive Explanations*, Zhu Xi takes astonishing liberties with the ritual scriptures. He reduces material details, entire ceremonies even, with a much more rigorous hand than does Sima Guang. Zhu Xi stated that he saw little use in regretting that one could not "bow and yield among the ancients," and in his manual made a daring departure from the literal archaism of the Northern Song.[168] Yet Zhu Xi did not deny the profound importance of "volume and measurements," the inherence of meaning in numbers. According to Yang Fu, Zhu Xi changed the design of his own long garment in the last years of his life. And despite his own advice to the contrary (cited in *Assorted Sayings*), he retained the archaic speech of the ritual dialogues in his *Family Rituals*.[169] But he was concerned to create the proper degree of ritualization and feared that excessive archaism would interfere with this aim: "The ancients were accustomed to these clothes, caps, and footwear by daily exposure, so that they were able to follow the rites without extensive deliberation."[170] The allowance of contemporary apparel and implements would therefore facilitate the realization of the ultimate objective of Zhu Xi and his predecessors: the return to a society in which every interaction, every movement accorded with ritual.

Whereas Sima Guang had attempted to produce a new ritual scripture by retaining as much as possible the material and narrative detail of the ancient *Ceremonies and Rites*, Zhu Xi's confidence in his superior understanding of the scriptures allowed him to eliminate details of canonical ritual without damaging its fundamental principles. The authority of his *Family Rituals*, when it surfaced after his death, rested on his disciples' belief that Zhu Xi had been a sage. In *Assorted Sayings*, these disciples arranged Zhu Xi's pronouncements on how a contemporary sage would pursue ritual reform in such a way that they reflect on *Family Rituals*.[171] First a surreptitious, heterodox conviction held by his disciples, this belief in the sagehood of Zhu Xi and other proponents of the Learning of the Way gradually gained acceptance, until Zhu Xi and his appointed predecessors were inducted into the Temple of Culture, as heirs to Kongzi.[172]

## CONCLUSION

The compilers of imperial protocol and ritual manuals in the Tang, the Five Dynasties, and the early Song attempted to reconcile precedent and current practice with canonical ritual. They reconfigured contemporary customs according to scriptural narratives and detail so that their time, in its turn, might preserve at imperial altars and in aristocratic courtyards the ancient ritual it had received across centuries of similar efforts. Imperial codes extrapolate the nuptial ceremonies of emperors and princes from the ancient "Wedding Rites of an Ordinary Officer" according to contemporary sumptuary distinctions in clothing, vehicles, and ritual space. Manuals of letters and ceremonies inscribe distinctly uncanonical practices (such as the chanting of bawdy songs and the removal of flowers from the bride's maiden head by means of a phallic tablet) into a distinctly canonical structure of interlocking symmetries that produces simultaneously the ritual bodies of husband and wife, and the sexual bodies of male and female.

Their awed studies of weathered inscriptions and patinated vessels convinced eleventh-century exegetes that the texts and rituals of the ancients enabled an immediate identity of the present and the past, unencumbered by centuries of compromising editions and adaptations. Rather than inscribing current precedent and custom into canonical structures, men such as Sima Guang, Zhang Zai, Cheng Yi, and Lü Dalin edited the fragmented ritual scriptures into seamless, detailed ritual narratives that allowed their performers to bow, yield, and turn among the ancients. Speaking ancient dialogue amid the walls and gates and vessels of symmetrical space and time, the groom and the bride acquire the solemn ritual bodies of husband and wife in a timeless fusion of canonical exegesis and ritual performance, reader and actor, present and antiquity.

With the loss of costly collections of tripods and rubbings to the invading Jurchen armies disappeared also the ponderous, bewildering archaism of the Northern Song. As scholars during the twelfth century took ever greater liberties with canonical texts, Zhu Xi wrote a ritual manual that reduced both the detail of ancient ritual and the jarring compromises with contemporary practice. With a daring, confident hand he condensed the Six Rites of canonical weddings to three and eliminated Sima Guang's Bowing to the Spirits of the Ancestors in order to restore the bride's Visit to the Temple and thereby the essential symmetry of ancient wedding ritual.

This bold reinscription of the ritual canon, this stunning attempt at the reincorporation of inherent cosmic patterns in a permanently ritualized domestic space, achieved the status of a new scripture by a latter-day sage. Later generations emended obsolete material details to prevent them from obstructing the performance of the rituals, but always maintained "the major structures that cannot be changed," the timeless truths that Zhu Xi had transposed from sacred texts to the living present. Thus, Qiu Jun (1421–1495) writes in the preface to his 1474 edition of *Family Rituals*:

> Ritual must needs always be present in the subcelestial realm. It is the possession of ritual that distinguishes the Middle Kingdom from the surrounding barbarians, that distinguishes man from beast. Ritual must needs always be present. . . .

> Mr. Wengong [i.e., Zhu Xi] wrote his *Family Rituals* based on Wengong's [i.e., Sima Guang's] *Letters and Ceremonies*, adding certain insights of Cheng [Yi] and Zhang [Zai]. It truly is a protocol that may be practiced by every family for a myriad generations. A few bores argue that this book was stolen upon completion, so that even Wengong himself never practiced it in its totality. Alas, because every gesture, every turn of Wengong's body accorded with ritual, he certainly needed not rely on this book during his life. But since he has passed away, those who are intent on practicing the rites of antiquity can only depend on this work.[173]

And more than two centuries later, in 1701, Wang Jian wrote in a colophon:

> Based on Wengong's original work I compiled *Family Rituals of the Wang Clan*. In the cappings of sons and grandsons, the divination of the guest, the divination of the date, the threefold surmounting, the completion of the attire, and the bestowal of a polite name to mark the conferral of the responsibilities of adulthood, each accords meticulously with ceremony. In weddings, all gifts must be sincere and all words must be beautiful. All ceremonies, from Submission of the Choice and Asking the Name through the revolutions of the wheels and the presentment of the goose, reflect antiquity and remain far from current custom. . . . Alas, Wengong wrote up in a book what was firmly rooted in his own embodied practice, as opposed to gentlemen of earlier generations who manifested in their actions what they had acquired from books. This makes Kaoting's [i.e., Zhu Xi's] footprints all the more distinct for later generations of students.[174]

Scholars of later centuries, in other words, reinscribed *Family Rituals* in order to reincorporate Zhu Xi's perfect ritual practice, just as scholars of the Northern and Southern Song had edited the ancient canon in order to re-embody the rites of antiquity. Zhu Xi's *Family Rituals* had become accepted as a new scripture by a latter-day sage.

The preconceived universalist frameworks of the secondary literature to date have obscured the discursive field of imperial protocols and ritual manuals of the Tang and Song dynasties, and have thereby condemned scholars in Mainland China, Taiwan, and the United States to unenlightening circular arguments. Zhou Yiliang and Zhao Heping have read the manuals of letters and ceremonies of the Tang and the Five Dynasties as desperate attempts of aristocrats to consolidate their privileged status and to halt their inevitable decline. Other Mainland scholars have interpreted the reductions and condensations of protocol in *Rites of the Kaiyuan Period*, the manuals of letters and ceremonies, Sima Guang's *Letters and Ceremonies*, *New Ceremonies for the Five Rites of the Zhenghe Period*, and Zhu Xi's *Family Rituals* as compromises with contemporary customs, designed to perpetuate oppressive feudal relations in changing times. Patricia Ebrey has argued that the manuals of Sima Guang and Zhu Xi constituted part of a broader attempt of a new elite to establish ritual hegemony in Song society. The presumed binary of the ruling class and the people, or elite and popular, and the anachronistic association of Song classicism and the Learning of the Way with a homogenous, conventional elite, disrupt the intricate coherence of the exegetical arguments of the manuals, ignore the dangerous eccentricity of the marginal group of possessed scholars who wrote them, and inspire unfortunate misreadings.

The assumption in Mainland historiography of an extended feudal period from the Zhou through the Qing creates a uniform elite whose every action was calculated to strengthen its ill-gained privileges. The simplification of ritual protocol in the Tang, the Five Dynasties, and the Song must therefore have been a sinister ploy to perpetuate feudal relations, an accommodation of incidental customs of the hapless commoners in order to preserve the hierarchical ritual of the oppressive ruling class. The preconceived Marxian categories, forcibly imposed on an alien discourse, revolve in endless circular argument and misreading, incapable of explaining any of the detail of ritual choreography. The feudal elite attempts to maintain its prerogatives by altering its rites and by accommodating custom, and therefore every alteration of the rites is an accommodation of custom designed to maintain feudal prerogatives. This argument accepts the rhetorical distinction between ritual (*li*) and custom (*su*) as descriptive of an historical, social difference in the practices of the ruling class and the people. It takes for granted the use of the ritual scriptures as the basis for Middle-Period protocol and assumes that the Six Rites of canonical weddings dominated nuptial practices throughout the feudal period. It ignores the fundamental transformation of customs in the process of their inscription as ritual. And it will never explain why Sima Guang insists on the use of a carriage or a wooden goose, or why Zhu Xi reinstates the Visit to the Temple, or why Sima Guang and Zhu Xi accepted Decking the Room out of uncounted hundreds of contemporary wedding practices.[175]

Patricia Ebrey, too, dismisses exegetical discourse on the strength of preconceived structuralist binaries. The linear time and space of the universal rite of passage (in which the ritual actor passes through a dark, threatening corridor between two safe, luminous spaces of established social identity) invalidates a priori the symmetrical time and space of exegetical discourse, in which a succession of stairs and doorways creates a stable, centered time and in which solemn ritualized bodies assume immediate ritual subject positions. The true, joyful customs of *A Dream of Hua* expose the cumbersome artifice of Sima Guang's *Letters and Ceremonies.*[176] The sole historical value of Song ritual manuals lies then in their documentation of an attempt at ritual hegemony by the new elite, created by the imperial examinations, and in their preservation of occasional popular customs.[177] An intermittent acknowledgment of the scriptural basis of the manuals and a consistent neglect of ritual narrative dissolve the intricate wedding sequences of Sima Guang and Zhu Xi into contrived collections of meaningless ceremonies and "rules."[178] Unerring circularity identifies the traces of popular practice: because Song scholars changed ritual protocol to accommodate popular custom, popular custom can be recognized by alterations of ritual protocol. Zhu Xi's *Family Rituals* achieves prominence not as an uncompromising, timeless scripture by a contemporary sage, but as the most permissive compromise with contemporary custom, whose "useful sketchiness" left "considerable room for maneuver" and many of whose details could be conveniently omitted.[179] The circular argument falters when Zhu Xi's modifications and adjustments overtly diverge from contemporary practice: "Despite his concern with making rituals easy to practice, Zhu Xi (or one of his students) did restructure Sima Guang's liturgies in terms of the descent-line heir system."[180] Such discrepancies, however, reveal the inadequacy of Song exegetes, not of the modern historian:

> The failure of Confucian scholars to achieve all of the reforms that they asserted were morally necessary could be attributed to their inability to understand their society adequately: they talked past the bulk of the population, telling them to give up meaningful ritual practices without offering satisfying substitutes.[181]

The tautological equation of modifications and adjustments with the accommodation of popular custom applies also to the revisions of *Family Rituals* by later generations of scholars, summarized in the final chapters of Ebrey's *Confucianism and Family Rituals* and meticulously listed in the footnotes to *Chu Hsi's Family Rituals*.[182] When the final pages of *Confucianism and Family Rituals* suggest the exegetical context of these centuries of debate, it is presented as the discovery of the modern historian:

> At another level, however, the debate in high intellectual circles unintentionally confirmed much of the Confucian discourse on family rituals. These debates were conducted within conservative parameters. Confucian scholars freely debated whether to adhere to the provisions of a text five hundred years old, one two thousand years old, or the very oldest ones available, not whether texts were relevant to establishing proper ritual practices. . . . These debates, therefore, by bracketing many of the most crucial cultural assumptions underlying Chinese family rituals may have in fact served to strengthen the capacity of family rituals to communicate basic social and cosmological principles.[183]

The placement of ritual manuals and imperial protocol among commentaries, epigraphic dictionaries, and catalogues of antiquities allows an archaic world to unfold in front of the text, where the present reader may see undaunted men in strange robes as they attempt to embody the ancient world of the scriptures. The hermeneutical circles of social history thus become the hermeneutical circles of canonical exegesis; the ritual theory of structuralist anthropologists becomes the ritual theory of structuralist literati; and the time, space, and bodies of the text become the time, space, and bodies of ritual. As reader and performer merge with antiquity through the written page, the text dissolves in a timeless embodiment of cosmic patterns. The ritual grammar of walls, gates, and stairs creates a temporal and spatial center where the solemn reader/performer achieves a physical and moral equilibrium at the assumption of a new subject position in the ritual hierarchies of family and society. Time and space are both symmetrical and porous, allowing the centered body to merge with the infinite pasts of timeless moral truth.[184] The time, space, and bodies prefigured in exegetical discourse, configured in ritual narratives, and refigured in reading or performance disprove the universalist assertions about liminality and rites of passage in structuralist anthropology, and reveal the radical doctrine of the Transmission of the Way (*Daotong*) to be merely one aspect of a more encompassing ambition of Song classicists to reinscribe and reincorporate antiquity. Writing can accommodate the cosmic choreographies of ritual because it shares its pattern (*wen*). The time of text is the time of ritual, and the time of ritual is the time of the text, transforming from the expanding, organic time of *Rites of Kaiyuan Period of the Great Tang* into the porous immediacy of *Family Rituals.*

# Chapter Two

## Wedding Correspondence and Nuptial Songs

### Writing as Cultural Capital and Text as Ritual Object

> In the Tang, fashions in writing changed three times, and under our august dynasty, too, writing has undergone several transformations. The style of parallel prose alone has changed time and again. Authors struggle for fame, desperately seeking a way to surpass others, so that they will practice writing long parallel sentences or compose an entire piece from ancient quotations, all to look "curious" (*qi*) or "tough" (*jue*). This goes against the proper spirit. Writing and words ought to flow with ease in order to facilitate recitation and reading. But nowadays a couplet may juxtapose several dozens of characters.
>
> —Lou Yao (1137–1213)[1]

> Proponents of ancient-style prose consider four-six parallel prose to be shallow to the extreme. Yet one encounters it throughout society, from the directives and decrees of the imperial court down to the missives and well-wishings exchanged among members of the local elite. Of course, in matching words and in juxtaposing allusions one should devise striking schemes, subtle and apt, so as to startle the reader and command his unflagging attention.
>
> —Hong Mai (1123–1202)[2]

After the demise of the hereditary aristocracy that maintained a firm grip on official appointments and landed wealth during the Northern and Southern Dynasties (386–589), Sui (581–618), and Tang, a struggle for cultural hegemony ensued during the Song.[3] Literati engaged the imperial court, and one another, in a battle for control over literary and artistic taste and for mastery over public space, including that of the painted surface and the printed page. Poetry and prose, and painting and calligraphy, provided the arenas for this cultural battle, fought with the brush. The struggle pitted parallel prose against ancient-style prose, court scenes against countryside themes, slanted-tip calligraphy against centered-tip calligraphy, the craftsmanship (*gong*) of skilled professionals against the clumsiness (*zhuo*) of feigned amateurs.[4]

The imperial examinations, an institution central to both the perpetuation of the imperium and the reproduction of literati culture, provided grounds for the fiercest battles. In academies, at court, and in print, the competing sides contested curricula and examination criteria, and at examination compounds disgruntled candidates erupted in violent protest demonstrations against perceived factionalism. Even literati who sought to establish themselves outside the political realm had to acquire legitimacy through participation in examination culture. And few could afford to forego official employment, since official appointments provided both the financial means and the political power necessary to further the cause of cultural claims.[5]

The champions of this cultural contest earned their distinction by the display of talent, erudition, and originality. Whether in prose, poetry, calligraphy, or painting, form and style mattered as much as contents. The act of cultural production became an aim in itself, as a distinctive mark of the unique hand that wielded the brush. The mode of representation became the object of representation.

Notebooks and collections of literary anecdotes (*shihua*, *siliu hua*), genres that originated in this milieu of cultural competition, record scores of instances of exceptional wit and clever phrases.[6] Literary production in general, but original turns of phrase in particular, functioned as cultural capital. The ability to combine elegant composition, erudite allusions, and mundane wit could yield concrete rewards: a promotion, a bride, release from prison, or a life-time career.[7] In the early thirteenth century, Ye Shi (1150–1223) complained:

> Excessive value has been accorded to four-six prose since the rise to prominence of the Erudite Literatus examinations. Yet this type of prose is debased and useless. Literati boast to each other about apt parallels and subtle allusions. It has even reached the point where a single well-crafted couplet can earn a man government employment for life.[8]

Four-six prose (*siliu*) became a favored vehicle for the display of erudition and originality.[9] Four-six prose is a technique rather than a genre. Its primary characteristics are those of the parallel prose developed under the Southern Dynasties, that is, couplets of irregular length that pair phrases with identical metrical, grammatical, and lexical structures, with optional use of euphonic and antiphonic effects. When parallel prose uses end rhyme, the irregular length of the couplets still sets parallel prose apart from poetry.[10] Traditional critics and present-day scholars trace the term four-six prose back to the late Tang, often to the work of Li Shangyin (813–858).[11] The four-six style of Song times distinguished itself from earlier varieties of parallel prose by the introduction of an archaic diction, freer metrical patterns, and the use of fillers and colloquialisms, all of which enabled the projection of a more distinct authorial voice. Other techniques, such as the insertion of full-length quotations into parallel structures or the composition of uncommonly long couplets, added to the opportunities for individual distinction through this style of prose.[12]

Between the tenth and fourteenth centuries, four-six prose dominated a broad range of genres of official communications and social correspondence.[13] The appropriation of the style and formats of memorials and other government documents for the conveyance of congratulations, compliments, seasonal greetings, and other matters of social intercourse deliberately blurred the line between literati culture and officialdom. The ability to write in the style and format of official documents confirmed an author's affiliation with examination culture and the imperium, while the display of exceptional command over the challenges of parallel prose afforded an opportunity for individual distinction. The fine stationery used in this manner of correspondence, and the refined accompanying gifts, hinted subtly at the financial means of the sender.

Yet, however great the power and prestige that accrued to four-six prose during those centuries, its dominance can barely be imagined today. The contested critical vocabulary of four-six prose, its incommensurable genealogies, and the diverging chronologies put forth by its proponents, prohibit the construction of a coherent narrative of evolving styles. More important, the proponents of ancient-style prose (*guwen*) wrote consistent, coherent indictments of parallel prose, and asserted a clear genealogy and a definite identity for themselves. This vocal minority in time obliterated the memory of their once dominant opponents. Secure in their association with imperial power, dedicated practitioners of parallel prose did not develop an articulate political or intellectual program. After the Yuan imperial court declared allegiance to the Learning of the Way and its ancient-style prose, the memory of four-six prose faded rapidly, preserved only in curious reference works and anthologies, verbose compositions in collected works, and an inextricable tangle of contradictory criticism and improbable literary genealogies.

The body of critical literature that took shape during the twelfth and thirteenth centuries explained and evaluated the characteristics of contemporary parallel prose and provided sample compositions by contemporary authors.[14] These works, however, apply the ill-defined terms of an ambiguous critical apparatus to confirm biased literary preferences rather than to explain them. Central evaluative terms such as curious (*qi*) or original (*xin*) do not refer to a particular style or technique and can be cited as either a positive or a negative attribute. The subjective terminology hence identifies the critic's particular taste rather than technical aspects of parallel-prose composition. Zhou Hui (b. 1127–d. after 1198), for example, cites a preface by Song Xiang (996–1066) that argues, "In writing prose, one's intention should be original, not eccentric; one's allusions should be appropriate, not far-fetched; one's words should be simple, not archaic; and one's allusions should be curious, not strange."[15]

Even where usage of critical terminology converges, in the uniform praise for the natural style of famous Northern Song authors, the critics of the Southern Song invoke the undisputed mastery of these men only to legitimize contemporary partisan preferences. All critics claim Ouyang Xiu or Su Shi (1036–1101), or both, as legitimate literary ancestors, accommodating them within widely different genealogies of Tang and Song prose that may also include Song Qi (998–1061) and Song Xiang, or Wang Anshi.

The works of these men are praised in terms that appear to preclude arbitrary judgment: all critics agree that good parallel prose looks effortless, as though composed of phrases that are naturally matched. The designation of a parallel couplet as natural (*ziran*), rather than well-crafted (*gong*) or clever (*qiao*), effaces the author's efforts as well as the critic's subjective assessment. Wang Zhi (fl. 1130), for example, praises Su Shi's early yet superb imitations of Ouyang Xiu with the words, "When four-six prose attains this level, it possesses the miraculous intention of cosmic creation."[16] And he asserts that Yuan Jiang's (1008–1083) perfect matches of elegant citations from authors past and present cause "even metal and rocks to split spontaneously."[17] The highest standard of four-six prose thus denies the act of creation as well as the complex cultural convictions that inform its evaluation. This standard Southern Song critics then transpose to their own time, where they designate a select group of men as the true heirs to the Northern

Song masters, who perpetuate the effortless style of these masters in a time of general literary decline.[18]

The vocal opposition to parallel prose by advocates of ancient-style prose further encumbers any attempt at a reconstruction of the dominance of four-six prose. Not only did proponents of ancient-style prose challenge the literary antecedents of four-six prose with their own, more legitimate, claims to Ouyang Xiu and Su Shi as their literary forebears, but they denounced parallel prose as an ephemeral vestige of bygone times. While critics and anthologists of parallel prose devised competing genealogies and disputed critical terminology, advocates of ancient-style prose declared that parallel prose belonged to the past, practiced merely by men of superficial talent and shallow morals.[19] Subsequent generations of critics, from the Ming through recent decades, have misrecognized polemical taunts as historical description and have dismissed four-six prose as a marginal phenomenon confined to certain inconsequential circles of Northern Song literati.[20]

Although the competing claims and contentious vocabularies of Song and Yuan literati have forever overwritten a history of evolving literary fashions, one may still recognize these zealous partisan discourses themselves as history, as traces of a furious struggle for cultural hegemony and individual distinction. And one should recognize that four-six parallel prose was once a dominant literary style: not a peripheral phenomenon of the eleventh century, but a pervasive, prestigious, powerful practice of literati culture in the twelfth and thirteenth centuries. The narrative of this chapter on wedding correspondence and nuptial songs thus complements the preceding chapter on ritual manuals: the writings of the small minority that advocated archaic ritual and ancient-style prose were carefully preserved and reproduced—first by dedicated followers, later also by the Yuan and Ming imperial courts—while the voluminous, stunning compositions in parallel prose in time were neglected until their importance was no longer understood.

## Cultural Capital and the Inscription of Ritual Time in Wedding Correspondence

The earliest examples of the inclusion of formal letters in wedding exchanges date from the Eastern Han. The *Classified Compendium of Arts and Letters* (*Yiwen leiju*, seventh century) preserves an elegant engagement letter by Cui Yin (d. 92 CE), and the *Comprehensive*

*Records* (*Tongdian*, 801 CE) cites the elaborate stipulations for wedding presentments from *Words to the Six Rites for the Imperium* (*Baiguan liuli ci*) by Zheng Zhong (fl. 58–76 CE): "The letters for all of the Six Rites should be folded in envelopes: first in a sheet of paper, then in black cloth, and this should in turn be placed inside a wooden box. . . . The letter should be accompanied by thirty different gifts."[21] Another early engagement letter, written by the famous calligrapher Wang Xizhi (321–379) on behalf of his son Wang Xianzhi (344–388), survives in the *Collected Works by One Hundred and Three Authors of the Han, Wei, and Six Dynasties* (*Han Wei Liuchao baisan jia ji*, ca. 1641).[22]

These materials from the first and fourth centuries bear a strong resemblance to the model letters and ritual formats found in Tang-dynasty manuals of letters and ceremonies. These eighth- and ninth-century manuals contain descriptions of wooden encasings reminiscent of the box suggested by Zheng Zhong, letters that display a preference for refined four-character phrases similar to those composed by Cui Yin, and formats for summary family genealogies in the manner of Wang Xizhi's marriage proposal.[23] The model engagement letters in these manuals (*tonghunshu* by the groom's family, *dahunshu* by the bride's family) appear among other forms of family correspondence, using the same formats and the same formulaic language as letters to grandparents, siblings, affinal kin, and other relatives.

The sprawling wedding correspondence of the Song abandons the polite formulas of private missives of earlier times. The variety of letters exchanged between the groom's family, the bride's family, and the go-between, as well as wedding invitations and congratulatory notes, display the wit and erudition of four-six parallel prose, in the public space of social correspondence and in the public format of official communications. The earliest surviving examples of Song wedding correspondence, dating from the mid-eleventh century, already encompass a range of literary styles, from the simple, archaic prose of Cheng Yi to the intricate virtuosity of Su Shi and Huang Tingjian (1045–1105).[24]

The Tang genre of the manual of letters and ceremonies did not withstand the forces of the struggle for cultural hegemony in the Northern Song. While Sima Guang appropriated the genre of the letters and ceremonies for his unprecedented hermeneutics of archaic ritual, the new formats and style of wedding correspondence required a virtuosity that formulaic manuals could not provide. Only in the thirteenth century did manuals appear that contained neutral sample letters as well as phrases and couplets that allowed the user of the manual to compose wedding letters of moderate originality, to suit individual occasions. But, from the eleventh century through the gradual demise of wedding correspondence during the Yuan, the composition of dazzling letters that vanquished the challenges of four-six prose (with erudite allusions to nuptial rites in the literary canon and with inventive suggestions of historical ties between the two families joined in marriage) remained the undisputed domain of the most gifted literati. Hundreds such letters survive in collected works, literary anthologies, and writing manuals.

Weddings, in other words, became one site for the display of cultural capital. More prestige may have accrued to other genres and to other occasions of literary composition, but the demonstration of literary mastery in wedding correspondence, if less important, was nonetheless compulsory. The cultural capital displayed in engagement letters, invitations, and other prenuptial correspondence confirmed the worth of one's family and the value of the alliance. As Yu Yan wrote, reflecting on the characteristics of the engagement letter and on its place within four-six prose around the turn of the fourteenth century:

> Matching the fours and pairing the sixes; picking yellow and juxtaposing it to white: there starts the study of every family, the exercises at the northern window. Every examination candidate untiringly attempts to master it. But it is true that in practice, too, one cannot always avoid writing four-six prose. . . .
>
> When my youngest daughter was betrothed to the nephew of Route Commander Shu Jingzhai, my reply to Jingzhai's engagement letter included the couplet, "Tall trees, dense so dense, fondly I remember the gardens and forests of old; young blossoms, bright so bright, happily a boy and a girl marry in time." These lines may not be well-crafted [*gong*], but the Shu family lives in my old homestead. Therefore I tell my students, "The greatest concern in applied composition should be aptness. What good is a well-crafted phrase if it is not apt?" This holds true also for the composition of poetry.[25]

As in so many literary genres of imperial times, the challenge of wedding correspondence lay in the achievement of original effects within strict boundaries of generic convention. Although wedding correspondence comprised a number of different formats (exchanges with the go-between, invitations and congratulations, and letters by the families of the groom and the bride for a number of different ceremonies), letters in all these formats make use of the same structural device: the resolution of a tension between unworthiness and compatibility. The author's presumption of equality to the recipient would lack in deference, yet his consistent self-deprecation would hardly compliment the recipient to whom he will soon be allied by marriage. The resolution of this tension is achieved through the standard narrative of wedding letters, through wit and allusions, and through the material and ritual context in which these letters were exchanged. An extensive analysis of two early examples will demonstrate this.

Seeking a match for my son Guo [1072–1123], by Su Shi

> When I venture to discuss marital ties, perhaps I ought to turn to the dregs of this hamlet; but I choose to neglect proper status and seek an alliance based on a compatibility of spirit. Since divination has been auspicious, the ancestors must be pleased. Your honorable son's second daughter is the most elegant of your blessed women's quarters: surely not only the Honorable Wei possessed five desirable qualities; my third son has little literary skill with his dull wit: perhaps he emulated Nan Rong and his third repetition. With respectful haste I bear these lackluster gifts, to bind us forever in unremitting joy. Of the worries that beat in my breast, I cannot fully account.[26]

Reply to the engagement letter of the Yang family, by Huang Tingjian

> Our reputation lacks every substance; our house is of no consequence. As I guard a region of oranges and grapefruits on the southern waters, how remote seems my presence among the caps and robes of the northern capitals. I remember with fondness our former collegiality; and I receive with embarrassment your grave ceremony. Immature is this granddaughter of mine: she awaits the pinning ritual. Your son the Court Gentleman for Fasting: the cap clasp and official tablet rest naturally in the folds of his robe; the purple fungus and noble orchid flourish gracefully in the doorway of his courtyard. When we divined and prognosticated at the ancestral temple, we were enjoined to seek out a great family. Without merit we

> have imposed on distant kinship with its ties and bonds; I fear that we have not yet mastered the elementary tasks of sweeping and sprinkling. We confirm this tight alliance which we shall not renege without good cause; we hasten to express our gratitude which we shall match with respectful obedience.[27]

These two engagement letters, among the earliest surviving examples of the format, well illustrate the standard narrative as inscribed in thousands such letters during the ensuing centuries. The average engagement letter opens with a couplet that posits an embarrassing disparity between the family of the sender and the family of the recipient, often represented in spatial terms (the recipient's imposing residence overshadowing the sender's lowly hut, and so forth). The second couplet cites outside forces that have mitigated this inequality, be they invisible (ancestral approval, geomantic forces, fate), natural (geographical proximity, children of matching marriageable ages), or social (kinship ties, prior acquaintance, intellectual affiliation, mediation by a skilled go-between). The third couplet introduces the groom and the bride as an ill-matched pair, the sender's preposterous descendant being unworthy of the recipient's virtuous, talented offspring. The fourth couplet reiterates the inequality of the two families but assures the recipient of the gratitude, joy, or sincerity of the sender's family. The final couplet makes a material or emotional offering, referring to accompanying gifts, promising the observance of proper ritual, or pronouncing the family's high hopes of the match.[28]

The letters by Su Shi and Huang Tingjian follow this narrative with minor variations. Su Shi defends his proposal by reference to compatibility and ancestral approval, and Huang Tingjian cites previous ties of employment and kinship to justify his positive response to the Yang family. The juxtaposition of the groom and the bride takes a different form in these two letters. While Su Shi matches the groom and the bride in one brilliant couplet, Huang Tingjian enhances the divide between his granddaughter and the prospective groom by relegating each to a separate couplet. Like all such couplets, these lines identify proper, prestigious male and female pursuits rather than attempting an accurate description of individual proclivities. Although ostensibly denying important qualifications, the couplets in fact confirm cultural competence through denial, pointing to specific, legitimate holdings of symbolic capital. Su Guo, though dismissed by his father as a dullard, admittedly does practice composition and memorization.

This internal resolution of narrative tension, however, amounts to little more than a compositional conceit. The actual resolution proceeds through style and allusions—of which the ironic self-representation is in fact itself an instance. The association of the format and its four-six prose with examination culture and the imperium endows the engagement letter with a fund of cultural capital that redeems any social disparity asserted in the contents of the letter. In other words, the very language in which the narrative tension is phrased denies its reality. The narrative tension is a mere excuse for a display of erudition and wit, and thereby becomes itself an instance of wit.[29]

Apart from their archaic diction, with phrases borrowed from texts such as *Mr. Zuo's Commentary on the Spring and Autumn Annals*, the *Book of Songs*, and *Selections of Refined Literature* (*Wenxuan*), the engagement letters by Su Shi and Huang Tingjian contain specific literary allusions. Su Shi juxtaposes the "five desirables of the Honorable Wei" (*Wei gong zhi wu chang*) to the "three repetitions of Nan Rong" (*Nan Rong zhi san fu*). The former phrase refers to an episode in the *History of the Jin* (*Jinshu*) in which Emperor Wu (r. 265–290) argues with his spouse, Empress Yuan, about an appropriate bride for the heir apparent. Although the emperor asserts that "The Honorable Wei has five desirable qualities, and the Honorable Jia has five undesirable qualities," he allows himself to be persuaded into an alliance with the ambitious, scheming Jia family, with disastrous consequences.[30] The "three repetitions of Nan Rong" convinced Kongzi to marry a niece to this disciple: "Nan Rong in reciting the 'Yi' Song repeated the verse about the sceptre of white jade three times. (In consequence of which) Master Kong gave him his elder brother's daughter to marry."[31] In this couplet, Su Shi manages not only an apposite pairing of two disparate allusions to historical marriages, but the allusions develop the motif of inequality. Su Shi compares the recipient of the letter (Su Guo's bride was the granddaughter of the prominent, incorruptible statesman Fan Zhongyan [989–1052]) to Wei Guan and to Kongzi, while likening himself to the flawed Emperor Wu, and his son to Nan Rong. Su Shi forestalls the appearance of presumption in the latter comparison by implying that his son in his studies repeated a phrase three times not due to virtue, but due to stupidity. This pretended misinterpretation of the passage from *The Analects* in turn makes Su Shi the equal of his dull-witted son. The clever pretense of obtuseness creates a witty paradox.

The central allusions in Huang Tingjian's letter occur in the lines dedicated to the groom and the bride, as they do in Su Shi's letter, but to a different effect. "The cap clasp and official tablet rest naturally in the folds of his robe" is a direct quote from "Parallel Couplets on the Region South of Chang'an, in One Hundred Fifty Rhymes" (*Chengnan lianju yibai wushi yun*) by Han Yu, revered ancestor of the ancient-style prose movement and a prominent literary model for Huang Tingjian.[32] The purple fungus and the orchid that Huang plants in the courtyard of the groom are metaphors for virtue, uprooted from the biography of Xie Xuan (343–388) in the *History of the Jin*.[33] Huang Tingjian's allusions do not pertain to historical weddings but instead proclaim his intellectual affiliation and his concern with courageous virtue, and thereby enhance the bitterness that permeates the text. Huang composed the letter during his exile in Yizhou (in present Guangxi province), where he died a year and a half after arrival, in 1105.[34]

In such allusions resides the most valuable cultural capital. In these lies the author's chief distinction, whether in the flawless display of rare virtuosity or in the earnest confession to ideological commitment. The virtuoso takes stock in the originality, obscurity, aptness, and specificity of his allusions. Allusions that suggest historical ties, especially prior marital ties, between the two families joined in marriage, combine these qualities and therefore fetch the highest symbolic yield.[35] Statements of ideological commitment, by contrast, narrow the scope of allusions and value literary homogeneity. Proponents of the Learning of the Way such as Cheng Yi, for example, eschewed engagement of the full range of the literary canon and instead confined their allusions to the scriptures and to the writings of their appointed predecessors. Devout followers in the thirteenth and fourteenth centuries openly refer to "our faction" (*wudang*) in their wedding correspondence, allude to the surnames of the leading figures of their movement and to the titles of its founding texts, and excoriate contemporary practices that violate ancient ritual.[36]

The materiality of the letter and the ritual context within which the letter was conveyed further mitigated the artificial tension construed by the narrative of wedding letters. Not a single original such letter has survived, and the reduction of these calligraphed writs on costly paper to the uniform, printed texts of collected works and anthologies has transformed the letters from ritual objects into stark literary compositions, devoid even of their standard opening and closing formulas. Yet many of these bare texts inscribe their own materiality, with references to their ink and their paper, to additional sheets and accompanying gifts. And writing manuals on their printed pages mimic for the benefit of the reader the proper format of the handwritten letter, including the additional formal notes, the standard introductory and concluding phrases, and the honorific elevations omitted from anthologies and collected works.

*Wedding Ritual: A New Edition* (*Hunli xinbian*, ca. 1200) reproduces Su Shi's letter for his son Guo in its original format (though perhaps with adjustments to conventions of the early thirteenth century). An editorial comment indicates that this engagement letter was accompanied by two polite introductory notes of six lines each (hence: the twelve-line letter format [*shi'er hang qishi*]). A different text results:

> Submission of the betrothal gifts (the first sheet and the second sheet as stipulated above), by Mr. Dongpo
>
> The humble kinsman (surname, given name), in imperial employ.
>
> The above-named submits the following. Humbly I take the liberty to discuss the matrimonial alliance between the daughter of honorable official so-and-so of
>
> Your esteemed family to my son so-and-so.
>
> When I venture to discuss marital ties, perhaps I ought to turn to the dregs of
>
> This hamlet; but I choose to neglect
>
> Proper status and seek an alliance based on a compatibility of spirit. Since divination has been auspicious, the ancestors must be pleased. Humbly:
>
> Your honorable son's second daughter is the most elegant of your blessed women's quarters: surely not only the Honorable Wei possessed five desirable qualities; my third son has little literary skill with his dull wit: perhaps he emulated Nan Rong and his third repetition. With respectful haste I bear these lackluster gifts, to bind us forever in unremitting joy. Of the worries that beat in my breast, I cannot fully account. Respectfully I submit this letter for
>
> Your perusal. I humbly beg

> You, sir, to examine it and to make a pronouncement. Respectfully, (Month, day), your humble kinsman (surname, given name), in imperial employ.[37]

Hereafter, *Wedding Ritual: A New Edition* provides an illustration of the tube in which the sender is to enclose the three sheets of the engagement letter, with a specification of the proper format for the addresses of the sender and the recipient.

Internal references in letters and instructions in writing manuals not only recreate the materiality of the wedding letter as a ritual object, but they place the wedding letter among other ritual objects of exchange. Su Shi, for example, alludes to "these lackluster gifts" that accompany his missive, and other engagement letters refer to a separate inventory of presentments: "Our lackluster ceremonial gifts are all listed on a separate form."[38]

These allusions to an accompanying display of material wealth explicate the function of the engagement letter as cultural capital to a point where cultural and financial capital almost merge. Although wrapped in a respectable allusion ("lackluster" [*bu tian*] invokes an injunction in the *Record of Ritual* about words and gifts proper for weddings[39]), the reference to the letter's material context implies an equivalence between the two kinds of capital exchanged. The delicate relationship between cultural and financial capital inevitably becomes yet another occasion for literary play. Many authors draw attention to the parallel by juxtaposing, in a couplet, a reflexive reference to their letter with a reference to the betrothal gifts.[40] Some authors resolutely deny any material display, pretending that only intellectual and personal compatibilities have inspired the engagement.[41] But more daring authors indulge in shameless hyperbole, generating cultural capital by a bold, ironic exaggeration of mercenary motivations. Having secured a match with a recent imperial graduate, Liu Gong (1122–1178) alleges poverty as well as bad taste, stating that only a lack of funds prevents him from emphasizing monetary transactions: "Being a poor family from the wrong side of the road we are embarrassed about a contract that discusses wealth; having found an eminent groom on the eastern couch we hope that they will live to old age together."[42]

The sequence of ceremonies that occasioned wedding correspondence interacted with the text of the letters in a similar manner. The conceit of self-deprecation is readily discerned in the letters of Su Shi and Huang Tingjian, both men of towering fame in their own day, and well acquainted with the recipients of their letters. But engagement letters in general present as precarious what oral agreements and signed contracts had already ordained. The engagement letter does not provide unfamiliar facts or new contractual stipulations; it confirms prior knowledge and a prior agreement by its performance. The format, the narrative, the style, the allusions, and the materiality of wedding correspondence lend substance to the factual information exchanged through other, prior venues. The inimitable erudition and wit of parallel prose composition confirms the author's inalienable membership of the most rarefied circles of the literati elite.

In wedding correspondence, writing is a ritual practice, and the letter is a ritual object. The composition of the letters proceeded along with the sequence of ceremonies, inscribing the bodies and objects that the letters accompanied as well as the ritual time and space in which the letters were exchanged. Each act of writing, however, preceded other forms of ceremonial performance. While the letter as an object, enclosed in its box or tube, achieved a prominent place in the ceremonial exchanges, the text borne by the letter created a parallel ritual time and space, inhabited by parallel bodies and objects. Wedding correspondence as it survives today—imprinted in reduced formats on the generic pages of collected works and writing manuals—represents only this parallel time and space, with their allusive bodies and immaterial gifts.

Any attempt at the reconstruction of ritual time from wedding correspondence is encumbered not only by the incompleteness of the record (inconsistencies in collected works suggest that compilers did not necessarily include all of an author's compositions for one wedding), but also by the bewildering array of ceremonies for which the letters are named, which moreover appear in different sequences. For instance, oftentimes *ding* (confirmation) and *nabi* (submission of the betrothal gifts) both denote an engagement, but some collected works include both a *dinghunshu* and a *nabishu* for the same wedding.[43] An inventory of all the various names in use for letters of betrothal, letters announcing wedding dates, and so forth would make for dreary, unedifying reading. The multifarious names and formats of wedding correspondence are better understood as yet another example of individual distinction within the conventions of a shared practice, in other words: as a function of the practice of the text rather than a function of the practice of ritual.

The remove between the practice of the text and the practice of ritual becomes especially important in the gendered aspect of wedding correspondence. In the practice of wedding correspondence, the representative of the groom's family assumes the masculine role, and the representative of the bride's family assumes the feminine role.[44] This informs the phrasing of the letters, since distinct sets of appropriate allusions exist for the two sides, but it especially informs the timing of the exchanges. In the practice of wedding correspondence, a letter from the family of the groom must precede a letter from the family of the bride. And because wedding correspondence takes place in a parallel time, it can overwrite ritual practice and inscribe masculine initiative in negotiations and ceremonies in which the family of the bride has taken the first step. The manual *Wedding Ritual: A New Edition*, for example, contains a category labeled "Female Precedes Male" (*nü xian nan*), whose letters allude to the pursuit of the groom by the bride's family. Yet in the correspondence itself the groom's family has regained the initiative.[45] In letters for the ceremony Sending Off the Phoenix (*song luan*), too, the family of the groom forestalls in writing the precedence of the bride in ritual practice. In Sending Off the Phoenix, the bride's family delivered the bride to the groom's compound, but in the accompanying correspondence the groom's family extends the invitation, requesting the bride's family to deliver the bride to its residence. Hereupon the bride's family sends a reply, inviting members of the groom's family to its house for the occasion.[46]

The variety of formats and styles visible already in the earliest examples of Song wedding correspondence only increased over time. By the thirteenth century, two centuries of accomplished writers had exhausted many of the possibilities of nuptial allusions and witty self-deprecation. The anthologies and writing manuals that collected the finest examples of wedding correspondence added to the burden of thirteenth-century literati, not only by reproducing the daunting store of masterly compositions, but by allowing men of lesser skill to participate in the practice of wedding correspondence. While some literati chose to desist from writing wedding letters altogether, those who persisted in the practice composed letters of increasing intricacy and length, replete with obscure allusions. Allusions that established historical or literary connections between the surnames to be joined in matrimony became especially prevalent, functioning not only as a mark of literary ability, but as a mark of authenticity, a guarantee that a letter had been composed for one specific occasion and not copied from a writing manual. Thirteenth-century literati further distinguished themselves from predecessors and contemporaries by appropriating new, demanding formats such as the *zha* (a memorial comprising five or seven sections, certain of these in parallel prose), and by constantly changing the preferred sizes and colors of paper, numbers of sheets, and ceremonial sequences.[47]

## Social Boundaries and Symbolic Capital in Writing Manuals

Among the anthologies and writing aids that survive from the twelfth and thirteenth centuries, two manuals are dedicated in their entirety to wedding correspondence: *Wedding Ritual: A New Edition*, already mentioned above, and *A New Book for the Old Man under the Moon: A Comprehensive Guide for Wedding Ritual, New Edition* (*Xinbian hunli beiyong yuelao xinshu*, ca. 1260).[48] As historical objects, these two manuals reveal a complex culture of literary composition and ritual performance in which commercial printers could earn profits by allowing families of lesser accomplishment limited access to the practices of the most erudite circles of the literati elite. As collections of individual texts, the manuals constitute broad, ambiguous spaces whose materials are arranged to construe hierarchies of literary production and matrimonial strategy.

Although many of the eighty-odd authors, senders, and recipients of wedding correspondence collected in the twenty fascicles of *Wedding Ritual: A New Edition* defy identification, a significant number of those known from other sources lived in northwestern Fujian and affiliated themselves with the Learning of the Way. The compiler of the manual, Ding Shengzhi, is otherwise unknown, but the manual identifies him as a man of Wuyi, a mountainous area near the centers of the Fujian commercial printing industry and the site of the Wuyi Retreat where, in 1183, Zhu Xi began lecturing students.[49] The contents of *Wedding Ritual* exhibit clear traces of affiliation with the Learning of the Way besides the compiler's inclusion of compositions by students of Zhu Xi. The manual opens with the archaic wedding ritual from Sima Guang's *Letters and Ceremonies*, with a few insertions from Cheng Yi's ritual manual. In its selection of letters and allusions the manual echoes the injunctions of these authors against child marriage, mercenary marriage, and the remarriage of widows, as well as their concern with proper ritual and the virtue of the bride.[50] (Given the manual's intellectual affiliation, the reproduction of Sima Guang's wedding sequence suggests that Ding Shengzhi compiled his *Wedding Ritual* before the recovery of Zhu Xi's *Family Rituals* in the 1210s. The identification of Chen Zonggui as District Defender sets the *terminus post quem* firmly at 1193.)[51]

The structure of *Wedding Ritual* combines ritual narratives with hierarchies of matrimonial strategy and moral conduct. The first fascicle contains Sima Guang's wedding sequence, followed by a comprehensive sample of written materials arranged in chronological order of use: formats for proposals and brief genealogies, for soliciting a go-between, for engagement letters, for notes accompanying betrothal gifts, and for thanking the go-between. The remainder of the manual provides materials to assist the reader in the composition of the more demanding of the formats listed in the first fascicle: annotated examples of intricate engagement letters and letters for Requesting the Date (fascicles 2–10), and a thesaurus of nuptial allusions (fascicles 11–20).

The amplitude of letters and allusions in fascicles two through twenty requires an additional ordering device beyond ritual chronology. A moral hierarchy of matrimonial strategy affords such a secondary organizing principle. The topical arrangement of the engagement letters ranges from generic letters through various forms of intermarriage (repeated intermarriage, intermittent intermarriage, initiative of the bride's family, cross-cousin marriage, parallel-cousin marriage, teacher and student, child marriage), to marriage defined by social status (imperial kin, commoners), and inauspicious or unprestigious forms of marriage (widower remarriage, uxorilocal marriage, concubinage, marriage to a courtesan). The allusions in the thesaurus similarly deteriorate from generic, auspicious allusions in the initial fascicles to euphemisms for the less reputable practices that comprise the later categories, such as sororate marriage, widow remarriage, and political alliances.

Such hierarchies, however, are not absolute. Not only does the overall chronological arrangement interfere with attempts to impose a strict moral hierarchy on the materials, but the reduction of complex matrimonial strategies to the timeless two-dimensional space of the printed page results in the conception of arbitrary, overlapping categories and in awkward choices such as the pairing of marriage to imperial kin and marriage among commoners in the ninth fascicle. The moral universalism of *Wedding Ritual* ill accommodates the strategic practice of wedding correspondence—and the analysis of *A New Book for the*

*Old Man under the Moon*, below, will reveal further tensions between literary strategies and matrimonial practice.[52] Nor is *Wedding Ritual* everywhere consistent in its moral judgment. The first fascicle, for example, prints a sample of the very kind of mercenary contract that Sima Guang condemns a few pages earlier.[53]

Its unwieldiness as a work of reference and the literary intricacy of its examples render *Wedding Ritual: A New Edition* useless to all but the very skilled among writers. The first fascicle describes only those aspects of social correspondence specific to weddings, assuming the reader's familiarity with its standard conventions. The annotations of the sample engagement letters identify the sources of allusions but do not explain them. And the allusions listed in the second half of the manual remain to be worked into striking couplets by an experienced hand. Literati already proficient in other formats and genres of parallel-prose composition would be able to gain from *Wedding Ritual* current formats and suitable allusions required for participation in the practice of wedding correspondence, but the manual's arrangement as an anthology rather than a work of reference, prohibits its effective use by the less accomplished. In its format and careful, erudite editing as well as its reliance on the works of a small group of prestigious authors for the majority of its sample compositions, *Wedding Ritual: A New Edition* resembles writing manuals and anthologies such as *A Comprehensive Anthology of the Pervasive Refinement of Five Hundred Famous Worthies of the Sacred Song Dynasty* (*Sheng Song mingxian wubai jia bofang daquan wencui*, 1190), *Brocade Valley of a Myriad Flowers* (*Jinxiu wanhua gu*, 1230s [1188]), and Li Liu's (1208 *jinshi*) *Standard for Four–Six Prose* (*Siliu biaozhun*).[54]

The boastful advertising language of *A New Book for the Old Man under the Moon*, its thesaurus of surname allusions, its ready-made parallel phrases and couplets, and its lengthy section of engagement letters for commoners indicate that its anonymous compiler intended this manual for an audience different from that of *Wedding Ritual: A New Edition*. Where the use of the latter manual requires a rigorous prior command of parallel-prose composition, *A New Book for the Old Man under the Moon* supplies materials that allow a lesser craftsman to cobble together wedding letters of moderate originality.

But while *A New Book* may thus appear to suspend the social boundaries of the practice of wedding correspondence, it in fact confirms such boundaries through both external markers (social and moral hierarchies of matrimonial strategy) and internal markers (stylistic differences between letters for literati and letters for commoners). The cultural capital of wedding correspondence remains the inalienable possession of literati and never stands in danger of appropriation by others. The wedding letters for commoners derive their value from the letters of the elite. Their relative lack of originality renders them mere auspicious tokens, objects bought to represent hopes of social advancement and wealth. Purchased with hard cash, the letters for commoners represent symbolic capital by alluding to the cultural capital produced by literati.

Particularities of its physical appearance as well as the incompleteness of its contents suggest that the sole surviving imprint of *A New Book for the Old Man under the Moon* is a pirate edition published for a competitive market.[55] In this uneven imprint, blotted pages alternate with clearly printed ones, and in various places splinters in the coarse paper make characters illegible. The narrow characters, at times irregularly spaced, include many simplified forms. Discrepancies between the table of contents and the main text indicate that this imprint did not belong to the original edition.[56] The clearest evidence of this circumstance presents the final page of the work, where a printed caption announces the end of the fascicle, whereas the table of contents lists additional letters of thanks, prayer texts, and wedding addresses. The surviving imprint thus appears to be a cheap, pirated reprint of a damaged manual that fell into the hands of an unscrupulous commercial printer.

Its editorial notes, advertising language, convenient reference, and emphatic punctuation suggest the attractions of this manual for an audience beyond the most rarefied literary spheres. Editorial notes promise to inform the reader of the latest fashions in elite weddings: "This is the ritual as it is practiced by the official families and literati of Our Dynasty," notes the anonymous compiler after describing the elaborate beribboned and sealed box for the conveyance of wedding correspondence, "In recent times commoners have used a simpler version of it."[57] And elsewhere: "Today there are also literati families who have eliminated the two seasonal sheets from their wedding rites and who use instead only a single-sheet engagement letter, and a single-sheet form to list the gifts."[58] Captions likewise emphasize the currency and sophistication of the contents of *A New Book*. The sections of parallel phrases boast of "paired gems" and "startling couplets," while sample letters demonstrate "new genres" and "new formats."[59] And not only do the several fascicles of parallel phrases and ready-made couplets provide materials that the user of the manual may combine into letters appropriate to the circumstances, but in the sample letters by famous authors, too, the printer has identified noteworthy couplets by means of emphatic punctuation—cuts through the vertical rules between lines of text that thereby come to resemble the jots with which readers mark, in red ink, passages of special interest.

The awed references to elite practice, the convenience of use, and the overt commercialism of *A New Book for the Old Man under the Moon* do not warrant, however, an identification of this manual as popular. However cheaply made, a book in twenty-four fascicles still commanded a forbidding price. The specialized contents of these fascicles would moreover have made the purchase of this work a wanton expense for most families, since few would have many occasions to use it. Nor should one underestimate the literacy required for the effective use of these volumes, or overestimate the number of those who possessed such literacy.[60] The dozens of letters for commoners included in *A New Book for the Old Man under the Moon* do not therefore identify commoners as the intended buyers of the work. Rather, the purchase of this manual would have been a useful investment for scriveners—persons who rented their skills in composition and calligraphy to those who wished to be inscribed into the practices of the elite.[61]

*A New Book for the Old Man under the Moon* thus suspends the strict social boundaries of literary production only to reaffirm them. The value of wedding correspondence lay not so much in the finished text of a letter as in its production, since the act of its composition represented prolonged, costly education and participation in examination culture and officialdom. Prestigious connections could substitute for literary ability, and families of the very highest prestige could confirm their status by commissioning an engagement letter from one of the acclaimed authors of their time.[62] But a manual such as *A New Book* could offer only purchased texts or, with its ready-made couplets and thesaurus of allusions, an adumbrated version of the writing process. Instead of the cultural capital of writing, it offers the symbolic capital of the finished text, a configuration of signs that refers to a world from which the user of the manual is ipso facto excluded. The structure of *A New Book for the Old Man under the Moon* as well as stylistic differences between letters for literati and letters for commoners confirm that the manual excludes commoners through inclusion.

*A New Book for the Old Man under the Moon* consists of two installments of twelve fascicles each. The first installment opens with the wedding sequence from Zhu Xi's *Family Rituals* and a section entitled "Admonitions by Sages and Worthies" (fascicle 1), followed by a thesaurus of surname allusions (fascicles 2–6), full citations of nuptial stories and anecdotes (each summed up in four-character titles that could be used in parallel prose; fascicles 7–9), a thesaurus of literary allusions to different ages (from five through eighty; fascicle 10), and short parallel phrases for matched surnames, for generic opening lines of engagement letters, and for couplets about the bride (fascicles 11–12). The second installment offers a section of ready-made couplets (fascicle 2), but in the main comprises integral sample compositions arranged, as in *Wedding Ritual: A New Edition*, in order of use: a comprehensive summary of all current formats, from the draft contract and the engagement letter to the complex *zha* and an inventory of the bride's trousseau (fascicle 1), followed by more extensive selections of letters for soliciting a go-between, for suggesting the conduct of wedding correspondence, and for Asking the Name (fascicle 3), engagement letters (fascicles 4–11), letters for Requesting the Date (fascicle 11), and, finally, compositions pertaining to the day of the wedding itself (letters for Sending Off the Phoenix and for Fetching the Bride, letters of thanks, prayers for the ancestral temple, and wedding addresses; fascicle 12).

Like *Wedding Ritual*, *A New Book for the Old Man under the Moon* introduces a moral hierarchy of matrimonial strategy as a secondary organizing principle in the longer sections. But unlike the former manual, *A New Book* combines this moral hierarchy with a hierarchy of occupational classes. Its expansive selection of engagement letters opens with generic letters and letters with intricate surname allusions (fascicle 4), but then follow sections with letters suitable for particular classes and their proper matrimonial strategies: officials and scholars (*guanru*: officials, imperial kin, examination graduates, examination candidates, and scholarly families; fascicle 5), literati and elites (*shishu*: intermarriage between student and teacher, between friends, between fellow townsmen, and between families of different regions, and letters that dismiss slanderous rumors; fascicle 6), intermarriage (*qinjuan*: long-standing intermarriage, intermarriage with affines, cross-cousin marriage, exchange marriage [i.e., two families each marrying a daughter to the other family's son], sororate marriage, marriage of multiple daughters to the same family, and parallel-cousin marriage, and letters for marriages arranged by siblings and cousins, initiative of the bride's family, child marriage, marriage at an advanced age, and uxorilocal marriage; fascicles 7 and 8), farmers and craftsmen (*nonggong*: marriage among farmers, merchants, and craftsmen; fascicle 9), widower remarriage and widow remarriage (fascicle 10), marriage to a courtesan, and the adoption of a son as the future groom for his stepsister (fascicle 11).[63]

In this intricate hierarchical scheme, the pitiful marriage of commoners ranks between the undesirable practice of uxorilocal marriage (marked as an embarrassed appendix in the text) and the inauspicious and shameful practices of remarriage, marriage to a courtesan, and the marriage of an adopted son to his stepsister. The sequence of categories charts a depletion of symbolic capital, as the social status of the groom declines and his degree of kinship with the family of the bride increases. A groom who has secured an official post has achieved his full worth and therefore commands higher prestige (and a larger dowry) than a student who may yet fail, and therefore occupies the foremost position in the manual's hierarchy.[64] (The anomalous position of the imperial family is explained by the gendered order of *A New Book* in which the letters of the groom's family precede those of the bride's family; the manual does not presume to provide model letters for the marriage of imperial princes.)[65] Contemporary sources (as well as current anthropological literature) document the strategic disadvantages of practices such as uxorilocal marriage, endogamy, and infant marriage, and the engagement letters cited for these practices in *A New Book* themselves mark the loss of symbolic capital by added humility of expression, an increased narrative tension, and an explicit defense of their matrimonial negotiations.[66] The first letter in the category "Two Aunts" (that is, marriage of maternal cousins) thus opens with the lines:

> If our ways seem familiar, it is because we grew up as sisters in the same house; since our fates match, we will renew our alliance for another hundred years. Our old ties should not be forgotten; and a new marriage ought to be attempted. Some may question whether the marriage of maternal cousins does not offend the rites; but since they issue from different mothers how can it harm propriety?[67]

And one of the letters for uxorilocal marriage begins:

> An alliance between two families must depend on marriage; all men within the four seas are bound in brotherhood. This

> custom of uxorilocal residence is a remnant of warlike times. Yet principled men never object to it; therefore this venerable practice still obtains among them.[68]

The categorical hierarchies in *A New Book for the Old Man under the Moon* create an idealized social space in which commoners are segregated from literati and are marked as socially and morally inferior. The literati occupy positions of power and prestige, and their marital practices span a wide variety of alliances and ceremonies. Their shared literary abilities supersede ideological differences. The manual collects compositions by authors of inimical intellectual affiliations and arranges them in a generic ritual sequence that similarly combines incommensurable ceremonies. *A New Book* opens, for example, with the wedding sequence from Zhu Xi's *Family Rituals*, but it does not offer sample letters for Submission of the Choice and Asking the Name, a ceremony for which Zhu Xi's manual explicitly prescribes the use of a written document. Instead, the materials in *A New Book* are weighted toward betrothal. The ceremony of Sending Off the Phoenix, in which the parents of the bride deliver their daughter to the groom's family, offends the core principles of Zhu Xi's wedding ritual. *A New Book*, in other words, subordinates ideological differences between literati to their common distinction through the act of writing.

The anonymous, indiscriminate engagement letters for commoners stand in sharp contrast with the variegated samples of literati correspondence. In the idealized social space of *A New Book*, literati and commoners do not intermarry, nor do literati pursue the trades or commerce. The manual establishes this segregation of literati and commoners not only through the external markers of its social and moral hierarchy, but also through stylistic characteristics of the letters themselves. Both the external markers and the internal markers set commoners apart from literati as lowly, vulgar, and laughable.

The same literary allusions that in the wedding correspondence of literati function simultaneously as auspicious metaphors and as cultural capital, in the letters for commoners are used as puns on their professions. This reduces metaphor to metonym, and wit to humor. The dependence of commoners on the writing of others reduces their engagement letters to symbolic capital, auspicious objects bought to mimic the prestigious practices of literati. But the humorous metonymic use of allusions in these purchased letters diminishes even the symbolic value of the letters and, by referring constantly to the professions of the sender and the recipient, further emphasizes the exclusion of commoners from literati culture. Crude talk of money, cloddish dismissal of cultured pursuits, and inappropriate sexual innuendo augment the humiliating effect.[69]

The first entry in the category "Betrothal of Farmers and Artisans" well bears out these characteristics:

> A farmer son marries a farmer bride (using colloquial language)
>
> Although our fields lie in different villages, we can hear each other's roosters and dogs; because we share a common manner, we betroth a son and a daughter. Their bond was predestined by fate; but it was confirmed by the go-between. What use has my son for reading?—deep furrows and shallow sowing are his art; a woman's worth lies not in her appearance—fine thread and thick yarn are her craft. Verily, between partners there should be no envy, and I send you half a catty and eight taels; in betrothals there should be agreement from the outset, I fix one string at two thousand cash.[70]

Despite the title's claim, the language of this letter is not, strictly speaking, colloquial. The author merely adds a few colloquial phrases for flavor, but otherwise creates a rustic tone through conventional literary language and imagery. After the insulting juxtaposition of the groom and the bride with roosters and dogs (from *The Way and Its Power* [*Daodejing*]) in the opening couplet follow more explicit denials of the attributes of literati identity: literacy, beauty, delicacy about financial dealings, and sexual modesty (plowing and sowing being metaphors for sexual intercourse). The letters written on behalf of other professions use the same devices:

> A dyer's son marries the daughter of a silk merchant
>
> My son is not one warped by learning, he can barely tell black from white; now that we join two surnames in marriage, I am glad that we are bound by silken cords. Although we have measured each other up several times already, eventually it is fate that ties us together. We have not yet discussed the splendors of choosing purple, of picking black; and I dare not bring up the fortune of emulating the Reds, of honoring the Whites. Before offering these five lengths of plain cloth I labored as

though tailoring silk were my profession; in presenting this length of text I regret that I cannot add to its substance with clouds of dye.[71]

A boatman's son marries a broker's daughter

As you sell your services on the roads and thoroughfares, your runaway reputation keeps pace with your ability to please your customers; as I leave my traces on rivers and lakes, my navigation skills cannot compare to the marvelous swiftness of the gods. But you, old man, know the valuable from the worthless; while my son recognizes the shallow and the profound. Long ago I learned that one buys when the price is right; now, too, I set sail while the wind is favorable. Your daughter has found fulfillment on Chu Terrace in dreams of evening rain and morning clouds; my son is ready to step onto the willow bank for the daytime breeze and the slanting moon. Marrying off a daughter is like aiming for profit: one has to choose the right moment; marriage for a son is like crossing a river: he has to reach the other side. I hope to contract a joyful alliance for a hundred years, and to join these mortal lives like floating leaves.[72]

To say that the above letters are empty of cultural capital is misleading, because they show unexpected, often brilliant uses of conventional nuptial imagery. But the commoners for whom these letters were composed and copied, received no share of these rich stores. The cultural capital rested solidly in the hand of the writer, who, by means of pun and metonym, ensured that none of this value accrued to the finished text. The third letter, for the unfortunate oarsman, best exemplifies the discrepancy between writing and text, between author and user. The author has produced a gem, but its precious virtuosity becomes worthless in the possession of the boatman. Not only does the letter draw attention to the humble status of the boatman and the broker through the relentless use of puns, and address inappropriate matters such as the financial strategy of weddings and the sexual desires of the bride and the groom, but the first line describes the broker's trade in such a way that he (and, by implication, his daughter) sounds like a whore.

The fanciful proliferation of matches between members of different professions raises the suspicion that the composition of engagement letters for commoners may also have been a frivolous literati pastime, suitable perhaps for drinking games.[73] In *A New Book*, the engagement letters for commoners range from matches between farmers, and between generic tradesmen, to a marriage between a pearl-craftsman and a tailor, or a boatman and a hairdresser: "Sailing my million-gallon ship I have long indulged in the joys of this floating life; extracting one hair for profit I now dare aim for an alliance between our surnames."[74] A later manual, *A Complete Book of the Art of Writing with Classified Allusions and Compositions of Past and Present, New Edition* (*Xinbian gujin shiwen leiju hanmo quanshu*, 1307), contains the following extreme example:

> Marriage of two ugly people: A dark-skinned man surnamed Huang [Yellow] marries a spotty girl surnamed Zhu [Red]
>
> Behold that beauty, yonder: like a true leopard one recognizes her by her spots! This elegant groom, now: he embarrasses the very crows on the roof! So subtle are the workings of predestination in this universe, evidence that no one is without a match in this world. Truly, this is an eminent couple, all due to a skilled go-between. Your beloved daughter's virtue is perfect though her appearance is not radiant, and when she wears a motley dress one can't tell where her face is; our son's martial skills are abundant though his literacy is poor, and when he sits in a pool of mud it is difficult to make out his body.[75]

Not all engagement letters for commoners use metaphors as metonyms, and not all are anonymous.[76] But the above examples show that literati, by definition, hold a monopoly on the prestigious practice of wedding correspondence and that they determine to whom they allow participation, in which capacity. The apparent fluidity of social boundaries brought about by writing manuals such as *A New Book for the Old Man under the Moon* was in fact always contained and immediately recongealed. Commoners were excluded through inclusion, and their attempt at participation afforded literati additional opportunities for the display of their wit: bright pearls that turned to dust as soon as they were touched by commoners.

The question whether commoners allowed themselves to be thus inscribed into the social and moral hierarchy of *A New Book for the Old Man under the Moon* raises broader questions about the relationship between the manual's hierarchy and late Southern Song matrimonial practice. With its chronological and hierarchical arrangement the manual suggests a representation of ritual practice that closer consideration proves to be misleading. Not only does the manual combine, within its chronological framework, ceremonies that are incommensurable, but the two-dimensional space of the text necessarily creates a linear moral hierarchy of symbolic capital that denies strategic uses of practical time. As Pierre Bourdieu argues,

> . . . every matrimonial transaction can only be understood as a stage in a series of material and symbolic exchanges, since the economic and symbolic capital that a family is able to commit to the marriage of one of its children is largely dependent on the position this exchange occupies in the entire matrimonial history of the family and the balance-sheet of these exchanges.[77]

In other words, the social and moral hierarchy in *A New Book for the Old Man under the Moon* not only creates an idealized social space, but also assumes that this space is absolute and timeless.

A consideration of the gendered aspects of wedding correspondence reveals immediately the discrepancy between the static timelessness of *A New Book* and the strategic timeliness of matrimonial practice. The classification of marital alliances from the perspective of the groom's family obscures the gender asymmetry that obtains in many of the alliances as well as the shifting position of most families over time, between taker and giver of brides. Although endogamous marriage or widow remarriage may cause both parties to lose face, the loss of symbolic capital incurred by the groom's family in an uxorilocal marriage equals the gain of the bride's family.[78] (A consideration of practical time also suggests, however, that the loss of symbolic capital suffered by the groom's family in uxorilocal marriage is temporary, and that it is in fact an expenditure that will increase the symbolic capital of the next generation.) Selections of wedding letters in the collected works of Song and Yuan authors correct the reifying hierarchy of bride-takers and bride-givers, presenting instead a balance-sheet (be it usually an incomplete one) of a family's matrimonial strategy through one or two generations. The textual environment of collected works preserves practical time and shows a family moving laterally through a series of alliances that writing manuals such as *Wedding Ritual: A New Edition* and *A New Book for the Old Man under the Moon* can only present as a linear hierarchy.[79]

The moral hierarchy of these writing manuals thus resembles the narrative tension in the letters that comprise their main contents. Just as in wedding letters the cultural capital of the act of writing (the ability to write elegant parallel prose with apt allusions), as well as the ritual and material context of its display, redeems all conventional claims to unworthiness; so in writing manuals the inscription of undesirable alliances into the shared formats and language of wedding correspondence by the same prestigious authors (especially notable in *Wedding Ritual: A New Edition*) and the practical time of matrimonial strategy mitigate the loss of symbolic capital. This mitigation does not pertain, of course, to the letters for commoners collected in these manuals, since their language and literary techniques set them forever apart.

The act of writing and the space of the text create their own ritual time and ritual space, parallel to the time and space of ritual practice. The composition of a wedding letter is a ritual act, producing the ritual object that is the finished wedding letter. But ritual practice is not reducible to the wedding letter. In much the same way, *Wedding Ritual* and *A New Book* as texts create an ideal, timeless social and ritual space that collapses the social space and ritual time in which these manuals circulated as historical objects. A similar creation of ritual time and space occurs in wedding addresses and wedding poems, intricate compositions in which the written bodies of the groom and the bride move through a literary time and space.

## Ritual Time and Sexual Metaphors in Wedding Addresses, Poems, and Jokes

The table of contents to the second installment of *A New Book for the Old Man under the Moon* lists three addresses (*zhiyu*) as the final segment of the book:

> Format for the Address at the Prostration of the Bride at the Ancestral Hall; Address at the Prostration of the Bride at the Ancestral Hall (pastiche of song titles); Format for the Address at Scattering the Curtain of a Hundred Sons (pastiche of song titles).[80]

The extant imprint of *A New Book* does not contain the texts of these addresses, but a number of collected works, writing manuals, and encyclopedias from the twelfth through fourteenth centuries offer examples of such wedding addresses, as well as cycles of poems that inscribe a related ritual narrative through similar literary imagery.

These addresses and cycles of poems inscribe a ritual narrative in which the groom and the bride meet for the first time in a bedroom at the house of the groom's family. In this narrative, the bride arrives at the groom's house, visits the groom's ancestral shrine, pays her respects to the groom's living relatives, and retires to the bedroom, decked in flowers, to await the groom. The groom attends a banquet, receives a flower crown, then sets out for the bedroom. Accompanied by the guests, or by a master of ceremonies, he overcomes the challenges put before him, enters the bedchamber, and raises the curtains of the bedstead to meet his bride. After stepping down from the bed together, the groom and the bride perform a number of ceremonies (given in variable order): they bow to each other; the groom picks a flower from the bride's hair; they loosen the fold of each other's clothes; and they drink from nuptial cups. Then they retreat to the bedstead, where the guests scatter grain at them.[81]

This sequence represents, of course, a public defloration. Crowned with a symbol of abundant seminal fertility, the groom personifies a penis, slowly penetrating the doorways and draperies that are the bride's labia and vagina, until he plucks the flower of her virginity. The sexual urge inscribed on the groom and the bride lends a strong forward thrust to the narrative. The guests actively participate in the groom's journey, helping him in forcing the bedroom door, penetrating the curtains with their gaze, and finally strewing symbolic semen around the bedstead.[82] This written narrative of public defloration prefigures the ritual narrative of consummation, with which it interlocks.

Modern scholars have been eager to read these performance texts as traces of popular practice, ignoring their literary intricacy and misconstruing their precise allusive imagery as the expression of a natural sexuality of which only the lower classes are deemed capable.[83] But rather than a function of class, the erotic imagery is a function of ritual time. Not only in these addresses and poems, but in letters, invitations, and congratulatory notes composed around the wedding day, the representation of the ritual time of the wedding suspends conventional standards of propriety and allows allusions to things otherwise unmentionable. The written space and time of writing manuals and encyclopedias reproduce the ritual time and space of weddings and therefore allow the preservation of these compositions, while few compilers of solemn, posthumous collected works have deemed them suitable for inclusion.[84] Jokes and anecdotes about weddings similarly replicate nuptial time and space, thus providing a setting in which characters of conventional modesty such as brides and clerics can be made to speak of immodest matters. To insist on reading the sexual imagery in wedding addresses and poems as a function of class rather than a function of ritual time is to propose an unhelpful homology of literati society and popular culture.

The language and imagery of the addresses and poems derive in part from the poetic tradition and in part from miracle tales and unofficial histories. To composers of these performance texts the prose-poem (*fu*) furnished tempting goddesses of immortal beauty, and the lyric (*ci*) procured languishing beauties in lush boudoirs. Miracle tales and unofficial histories, as well as the poetic tradition, provided narratives of a male quest consummated by sexual union, such as the visit of Hou Yi of the Sun to the Moon Goddess, Chang'e; King Huan's encounter with the spirit of Wu Mountain (also known as Yang Terrace or Gaotang); Emperor Wu's journey to the Queen Mother of the West; the reunion of the Cowherd and the Weaving Maiden across the bridge of magpies; the lost fisherman's entrance into the hidden world of the cave at Peach Blossom Spring; and the unwitting discovery by woodsmen Liu and Ruan of a community of immortal maidens in distant, unknown mountains.[85]

The address as a literary form is defined by the public occasion of its performance as much as by its literary conventions. Wedding addresses consist of descriptive passages and well-wishings in four-six parallel prose and a rhymed or recitative section. The parallel prose (*zhiyu* or *zhici*) inscribes an ideal gathering of lively guests in an opulent space and the immortal presence of the bride or the groom. The rhymed or recitative section may either conclude the composition, summing up the scene described in parallel prose with a brief modern-style poem (a *jueju* or a *lüshi* called the *kouhao*), or it may occur between a descriptive passage and the pronouncement of blessings (commonly in the Address at the Prostration of the Bride and the Address at Scattering the Curtain).[86]

Although few anthologies and collected works of the Song and Yuan include wedding addresses, a great many contain compositions in these same literary forms. The elaborate parallel-prose composition followed by a brief poem enjoyed considerable popularity at banquets during the Northern and Southern Song, and commonly appears in anthologies and collected works under the name of Musical Words (*yueyu*).[87] The Address at Scattering the Curtain is identical in form to the Composition at Hoisting the Ridgepole (*shangliang wen*), written by many prestigious authors for the consecration of new buildings.[88] As a genre of parallel-prose composition associated with examination banquets, officialdom, and court life, the address therefore belongs to the same culture of literati display as wedding correspondence.[89]

The wedding addresses and the cycles of poems form a unified ritual sequence. Instead of dividing them by genre, writing manuals alternate addresses and cycles of poems in a coherent narrative, sometimes providing an address and poems for the same ceremony, such as the obstruction of the gate at the bride's arrival, or the groom's banquet. But for the Prostration of the Bride and Scattering the Grain only addresses exist, while the groom's quest is inscribed entirely in poems. Since only minor variations in sequence distinguish the ritual narratives for the wedding night in extant writing manuals, nothing prohibits a judicious combination of the materials collected in *A Complete Book of the Art of Writing with Classified Allusions and Compositions of Past and Present, New Edition* (*Xinbian shiwen leiju hanmo quanshu*, 1307), *A Household Necessity* (*Jujia biyong*, fourteenth century), *Amassed Riches for Letters and Writs with Classified Allusions and Compositions, New Edition* (*Xinbian shiwen leiyao qizha qingqian*, 1324), and *A More Comprehensive Record of A Forest of Facts Digested and Classified, New Edition* (*Xinbian qunshu leiyao shilin guangji*, 1333 and 1699 [1315]).

The ritual narrative of public defloration, inscribed as an allusive male quest for a remote female goddess, requires that the groom's house be presented as the bride's dwelling: her Moon Palace, her Peach Blossom Cave. The poems and addresses for Blocking the Gate, the first stage in this ritual sequence, therefore present the bride's arrival as a return:

Poem at Blocking the Gate

The crowd at the gate is armed with flutes and songs,
Happy to receive the immortal descending from Pengying.
It is well known that Nongyu expects her Xiao Shi,
Surely she will bestow abundant baskets of bribes?[90]

Reply

To my cave they have all come, standing in the crack,
Why do I suffer this blockade in front of my gate?

The bribes they seek are exorbitant,
How could I retreat, yet how may I advance?[91]

Her impendent encounter with the groom compels the bride to seek entry, rendering her powerless against the demands for bribes.[92] The innuendo written into the bride's reply (the predicament over advancing and retreating in front of a crevice), implies, however, that her sense of urgency is not inspired by a polite concern about being late, but by sexual desire. This inscribed yearning of the bride and the groom is the motif of the entire sequence, inspiring them to vanquish all obstacles put in the way of their union.

The "Composition for Obstructing the Gate" (*lanmen wen*) by Dai Yi (1223 *jinshi*), printed in *Amassed Riches*, uses similar devices in a lengthy piece of parallel prose. After inscribing the assembled guests and the arrival of the radiant, immortal bride (and likening himself to an immortal guest at a banquet on Mount Gaoyang), Dai Yi writes, "I offer this one mad piece to block the fragrant wheels that carry a hundred riches; she should scatter ten thousand pearls to buy a romance of the Five Lakes."[93]

The Address at the Prostration of the Bride (*changbai zhiyu* or *baitang zhiyu*) sustains the erotic narrative. The compositions for this solemn occasion first expound in parallel prose the weighty significance of the ceremony, then enjoin the bride to bow to the deities, ancestors, and living relatives of her new household, and close with the pronouncement of blessings for a lasting, harmonious, and fertile marriage. The precepts for public conduct and conjugal obligations draw on different literary registers, enfolding stern moral injunctions in the red glow of the wedding chamber and allowing underneath the layered canonical references a glimpse of the bride's bound feet. In the ritual time of the wedding night, consummation and procreation are moral imperatives.[94]

*The Art of Writing* preserves an address for the bride's religious induction of the kind announced in the table of contents of *A New Book for the Old Man under the Moon*: a pastiche of song titles. Its parallel prose exploits the erotic implications of these titles (italicized and capitalized in the translation) while inscribing the Prostration of the Bride into the ritual narrative of the wedding night:

A trembling shimmer betrays the arrival of *Spring in the Painted Chamber*; rolled up, the *Precious Pearl Curtain* reveals its red sheen. The distant woman in the window resembles the moon over *Jasper Terrace*; *The Tibetan Traveler* becomes *The Immortal of the Magpie Bridge*. *Grateful for the Imperial Grace* we *Congratulate the Groom*; with *Her Inebriating Beauty* the bride will *Welcome the Immortal Guest*. She already knows that *Something Good Is Near*; she is not obstructed by *A Small Mountain Range*. *The Romantic Gallant* has not yet arrived to make her acquaintance; *Seventh Maiden* first should prostrate herself.

Let the bride prostrate herself before the God of Heaven, the Spirit of the Earth, the King Father of the East, and the Queen Mother of the West. Second prostration. Third prostration.

Let the bride prostrate herself before the taboos of this household, the Dragon God, the Well, the Stove, and the Guardians of the Gate. Second prostration. Third prostration.

Let the bride prostrate herself before all the gods whom this household serves and honors with incense. Second prostration. Third prostration.

Let the bride prostrate herself before the great-great-grandfather and great-great-grandmother, the great-grandfather and great-grandmother, and the grandfather and grandmother. Second prostration. Third prostration.

(After the prostrations to the gods, please remove the incense table.)

Let the bride prostrate herself before her father-in-law, her mother-in-law, their family and in-laws, and the elderly, as they are present in the hall.

(She should bow to them in order of rank, from high to low. After the prostrations, all should assume their original position.)[95]

*One Branch of Blossoms* conveys *Spring in the Garden of the Heart*, swaying wildly from the immortal's pendant; ten rolls of brocade are displayed on the *Table of Green Jade*, to join forever their *United Hearts*. The *Burner of Incense* has come out to burn incense; the porter [?] has come especially to chant injunctions. The *Barbarian Bodhisattva* and the *Son of the River God* beckon you from beyond *Zhuying Terrace*; *The Immortal Lord An* and the Immortal Madame Gu invite you into the brocade-windowed pavilion. *Seventh Maiden* has been ushered in to perform the rites; *Mister Ruan Returns* and she has to await their union. Please enter the *Palace of Nocturnal Travels*, before the arrival of a *Morning under Frosty Heavens*.[96]

The groom's quest for this retired goddess begins at the banquet. Most of the cycles of poems that inscribe this quest are too long to allow a full translation, comprising more than twenty poems in *The Art of Writing* and in the various editions of *A Forest of Facts*.[97] But a brief cycle of six lyrics in an early edition of *A Forest of Facts* interweaves lush literary textures with the tense linearity of the ritual narrative, to yield an elegant miniature that well represents the longer sequences. Where the latter cycles are composed of modern-style four-line poems (*jueju*), this short cycle consists of lyrics of two strophes each, to the melody "Welcoming the Immortal Guest" (*Ying xian ke*).[98]

Welcoming the Immortal Guest: Entering the Banquet

The Minor Examination,
An auspicious occasion,
We are gathered in joy, all radiant faces.
Be drunk and sing,
And clap your hands,
And I ask everyone,
To join in chanting Welcoming the Immortal Guest.

The smell of musk and orchids,
The bedside of silk and gauze,
Red candles flicker beneath the blue-white moon.
Lead along the groom,
Away from his silken seat,
Into Peach Blossom Spring,
To seek the abode of the divine immortal.

Welcoming the Immortal Guest: Leaving the Banquet

This human realm,
A land of pleasure,
Hawksbill seats, pearls crowded on three thousand shoes.
The sound of voices resonates,
The music of Shun suspended,
Clap your hands and sing loudly,
Let us all chant: lalala.

The young groom,
Falters when rising,
Flushed with wine, his underwear too tight, his eyes radiant with joy.
Honor stature and ceremony,
Indulge in elegance and beauty:
Two rows of red candles,
Lead into the realm of Penghu.

### Welcoming the Immortal Guest: Opening the Door

Embroidered curtains are suspended,
Where united hearts are joined,
Thick clouds of auspicious smoke obscure the immortal gate.
Sound out the sweet music,
Rely on your skilled tongue:
A crowd armed with flutes and song,
All guests push at the doors.

Please open the door,
We will not remain outside,
Mister Liu approaches on joyful feet.
This boy's light heart,
This boy's hot [character missing]:
Between the layers of silk,
He will exhaust his cunning prowess.

### Welcoming the Guest: The Door Opened

The door has opened,
But where do we head?
Colored mist and auspicious clouds obscure the red curtains.
One should know,
Not to be rueful:
A mere light wind,
Will open a prospect of a thousand miles.

The Immortal Lad approaches,
Brave is he, and strong,
Now that he has glimpsed Chang'e he wishes to embrace her.
Both tortured and comforted,
They do not let go:
Their eyes dart back and forth,
Their expressions change without cease.

Welcoming the Immortal Guest: Opening the Curtain

Mandarin ducks with necks entwined,
A phoenix pair engaged in a ritual dance,
Embroidered hibiscuses cover the red gauze curtain.
Her cloud-like hair uncoils,
The hazy mist grows thick,
But with an intent gaze,
One can discern the Peach Blossom Cave.

This good groom,
Truly stands out,
*The Jade Butterfly* yearns for the *Swaying Flower Heart.*
Before he lowers his body,
His eyes take her in:
A joyful union through a gaze,
Countless dreams of King Huan.

Welcoming the Immortal Guest: Stepping Down from the Bedstead

The night is deep,
The water clock pushes on,
Yet the groom outside the curtain can only wait.
The lover joins his maiden,
He helps the charming beauty,
To lower herself gently from the majestic bed,
Stepping carefully on her delicate golden lotuses.

Her shoes are curved,
Exposed by her dress,
This bride truly takes your breath away.
Walking jade,
A smiling flower,
This must be a perfected consort,
Alighting from the island of Penglai.[99]

The enchanting realms of miracle tales and the perfumed curtains of boudoir poetry provide a hazy, voluptuous setting for the groom's inebriated quest. The lyrics inscribe a festive crowd that accompanies a yearning groom through sumptuous chambers, assisting him in forcing open the door, and penetrating the Peach Blossom Cave with their gaze.

The longer cycles of poems ("Wedding Poems of the Silken Seat," *jiaqi qixi shi*) likewise use the literary imagery of the male quest to create a ritual narrative of public defloration. These cycles encompass a more extensive ritual sequence, however, beginning before the banquet that opens "Welcoming the Immortal Guest" and continuing after the groom and the bride have descended from the bedstead. The cycles of poems also employ multiple perspectives, giving a voice not only to the guests and the groom, but also to the bride and a master of ceremonies. More than "Welcoming the Immortal Guest," moreover, the short poems, and their titles, suggest a series of well-defined ceremonies of which the chanting of the poems constituted part: Blocking the Gate, Inviting the Master of Ceremonies, The Groom Bows to the Guests, Forcing the Groom to Drink, and so forth. Driven by sexual desire, the yearning bride and the eager groom pay bribes and meet challenges while the basin of the water clock rises toward the disenchanting hour of dawn:

Demanding Bribes from the Groom

The charming Star Maiden awaits the Immortal Lad,
Don't trust the water clock to last the journey.
We seek red gauze and also bribes:
Only then may he return to the cave where the phoenix pair will form.[100]

Ridiculing the Groom for Finding the Door Closed

The Immortal of the Moon Palace has descended into the orchid chamber.
Her eyes entreating, her heart expecting, she awaits the Jade Lad.
Now that he has reached the entrance to the cave, he finds it closed,
Who possesses an iron heart that can resist the yearning?[101]

The poems that follow upon the couple's descent from the bedstead color canonical ceremonies with suggestive detail:

Poem to Request the Toast with the Nuptial Cups

The Jade Maiden's vermilion lips drink half an inch,
The side of the cup reveals a small unfired speck.
The Immortal Lad leaves some drops on purpose,
Unwilling to swallow their cherished fragrance.[102]

Poem to Request Loosening the Folds

The Dipper turns, the stars move, the night is deep,
The Immortal Lad and the Jade Girl long with ardor.
The mandarin curtains will soon enclose their dalliance,
Why don't her slender hands loosen his fold?[103]

After the metaphoric penetration of the bedstead and the fondling scrutiny of the bride, the rite of public defloration reaches its climax with the Address at Scattering the Curtain. Like the Address at the Prostration of the Bride, the Address at Scattering the Curtain consists of a series of ceremonial injunctions, enclosed by elaborate compositions in parallel prose.[104] The prose introductions to Scattering the Grain inscribe the wedding chamber with a dense eroticism, drawing on literary imagery (especially in the pastiches of song titles: "Within *The Tibetan Curtain* they entwine their necks like mandarin ducks; amid *The Incense at the Silken Seat* they merge in joy *Like Fish in the Water*")[105] but also on canonical texts:

> From this day forward, the husband will lead and the wife will follow; from this moment on, she will receive what he provides. At Sharing the Nuptial Cup they realize the mutual needs of their united bodies; with the Mutual Bows they solemnize the true beginning of the Great Relationship.[106]

With the rhymed ceremonial injunctions, the ritual narrative moves forward to the consummation of the marriage. The symbolism of the scattered grain hardly requires explanation:

Scatter grain to the east,
A cloud of incense rises when they strike the curtain,
Their joined hearts and jade tips pressed against each other,
Rubbing the blossoming branch leaves drops of red.

Scatter grain to the west,
Within the bulging gauze curtains, the soft sound of teasing,
On both pillows, dreams of butterflies,
The tip of the branch drips under the red-beaked cuckoo.

Scatter grain to the south,
Too eager, they have not awaited the wishes for many sons,
The white jade is already sowing in the furrows,
The bright pearl moves to receive the bee's load.

Scatter grain to the north,
Ajiao has moved into the Yellow-golden Palace,
On the Terrace of the Purple Flute the phoenix pair has
come to roost,
Deep in red softness bathe the mandarin ducks.[107]

Other rhymes, though perhaps less graphic, invoke the same explicit imagery: dripping sweat and rising temperatures, clouds around Wu Mountain, Chang'e permitting her guest to pick her blossoming cinnamon branch.[108] Written time rushes ahead of ritual time as the couple, while seated on the bed under a hail of grains, is imagined to be engaged in insatiable sexual intercourse toward the approaching dawn:

The gallant scatters grain to the left,
Like a butterfly the powdered groom yearns for the flower bud.
Worn out by frantic movement, they trim the wick,
As the water clock presses, they mourn the night's end.[109]

The well-wishings that follow proceed further in time to depict a harmonious, fecund marriage.

This disjunction between written time and ritual time reveals once again the remove between text and ritual performance. The time, space, and bodies inscribed in these addresses and poems are not the ritual time, the ritual space, or the ritual bodies of an historical wedding. Nor could they be, since the composition of these accomplished pieces preceded the weddings themselves. The relationship between the performance of the texts and the performance of ritual also remains unclear. The performativity of the form and contents of the addresses and poems suggests that they were chanted in the manner inscribed in the texts themselves. But whether the users of these manuals adopted the compositions offered in their printed sequence, whether they performed these ceremonies in the spaces and times inscribed in the texts, whether they changed the words and added poems of their own, and so forth, must remain a matter of speculation.

One may, however, see the composition of these addresses and poems itself as a ritual act, construing a parallel ritual time. This ritual act and this parallel ritual time, fixed on the page, are the ever manifest traces, not of the ritual performance of weddings, but of the ritual practice of writing. The canonical quotes, the poetic allusions, the intricate parallel prose, the immaculate prosody, and the deft pastiches convey in their surface meaning the writer's hopes of a lasting, prolific marriage while as the products of an accomplished act of writing they confirm the elevated status of all those who participate in the wedding: the families of the groom and the bride as well as the guests. These merged hopes of biological and social reproduction allow, within the ritual time of weddings, the composition of texts with strong erotic overtones.

Congratulatory poems and letters, and an occasional wedding invitation, confirm that conventional standards of propriety were suspended during the auspicious period that surrounded weddings. While in the staid formality of engagement letters and other correspondence pertaining to prenuptial ceremonies erotic imagery would appear highly inappropriate (as indeed it does in the engagement letters for commoners), in a few wedding invitations the use of such imagery extends the groom's quest backward in time, to the travels of the guests toward the site of the wedding.[110] Congratulatory letters and poems to the groom abound in speculation about conjugal relations and other sexual innuendo. Six congratulatory *shi* poems in *The Art of Writing* project the imagery of spring onto the wedding chamber, with wishes for a harmonious marriage and plentiful progeny.[111] Congratulatory letters in parallel prose, too, invoke the erotic imagery common in wedding addresses and poems:

> After concluding a propitious match, you have now encountered the Divine Maiden of Yang Terrace; so let us hear the good stories: please recount of the Immortal Lad of Liu's cave.[112]
>
> The hibiscuses on the embroidered coverlets quicken the joyful spirits of the proud gallant; the motley candles in the cave chamber flatter the divine immortal in the dazzling room.[113]

Congratulatory lyrics, too, resemble wedding addresses and poems.[114] Not only do they combine the motif of the male quest with the voluptuous imagery of the boudoir, but they employ the same literary techniques, including the pastiche of song titles.[115] Two strophes may serve as an illustration:

Melody: Bu suanzi (groom surnamed Peng)

The parting petals of the jade plum in spring,
A small gathering of golden lotuses and candles.

He engages in romantic play, this roving Lad,
And finds his way straight to Yang Terrace.[116]

Melody: Xijiang yue

The disposition of blossoms seems to suit the pleasure of man,
How to compare the aroma of wine to laden passion?
As slumber approaches in the still of the night, the
pomegranate blossoms:
Frantic, the mounted phoenix hen, the riding phoenix rooster.[117]

Literary anecdotes about the composition of poems during weddings illustrate this conjunction of educated wit and ritual time. Just as the engagement letter for commoners allows literati to explore humorous metonymic uses of conventional metaphors, so the wedding poem provides a rare legitimate occasion for sexual innuendo. The staid pages of posthumous collected works may exclude such lubricious poems, but notebooks and specialized collections of literary anecdotes—genres that preserve writings without a proper place in other genres—readily accommodate them. Many of these anecdotes appear to be spurious: several poems are attributed to multiple authors and to different occasions, and the general exclusion of such compositions from collected works lent a generous opportunity to forgers of jocular or malicious intent. But the combination of brilliance and marginality that characterizes the textual environment of notebooks and collections of literary anecdotes reproduces the liminal wit of the wedding poem and thereby authenticates these wedding poems, not as historical documents, but as illustrations of an historical practice. In his *New Records from Taozhu* (*Taozhu xinlu*), for example, Ma Chun (fl. 1160s) describes how Wang Ang (b. 1090), the top graduate of the 1118 imperial examinations, was forced by the parents of his bride to improvise a "lyric to hasten the bride's adornment" (*cuizhuang ci*). Wang obliged and "without lifting his brush from the paper composed a lyric on the melody *Haoshi jin* [Something Good Is Near]":

In a joyful spirit we gather at the door,
A shimmering light reveals a fragrant path through
resplendent gauze.
As I arrive and gaze up at the faint red blossoms,
I realize that I am not an ordinary guest.

One does not rouge or powder natural perfection,
Lest one overdo its blush or palor.
I stay to pluck stray hairs of the blackened eyebrows,
And to paint a spring scene at the Terrace of Splendor.[118]

Where literary anecdotes preserve clever compositions by men, often famous, whose exceptional talent is given extended rein in the ritual time of a wedding (and in the textual environment of the notebook or collection of literary anecdotes), jokes about weddings invent hapless, usually anonymous, grooms, brides, and guests who transgress even the expanded boundaries of propriety by using images that are too explicit, or language that is too crass.[119] Jokes, as a genre, suspend boundaries of propriety, allowing a circumscribed space for the discussion of topics sensitive or forbidden in other genres of speech or writing. Song- and Yuan-dynasty joke books exemplify this generic suspension by printing all kinds of jokes (puns, anecdotes, scatological humor, etc.) without any particular order or imposed categories.[120] Wedding jokes, therefore, whether told in person or printed in joke books, reproduce the ritual time of weddings. But the boundaries of propriety in this indecorous genre are wider than those of the wedding night, containing even the transgressions of their blundering stock characters. The less seemly it is for a person to speak about sex in everyday life, and the more explicit the language, the funnier the joke.

A joke recorded in Zhou Hui's *Miscellaneous Jottings of Qingbo Gate* (*Qingbo zazhi*, 1192) celebrates the quick wit of a groom who suffers from an excessive growth of facial hair. The mother of his bride bewails that her "bodhisattva-like daughter is marrying this hairy monster" and demands that he improvise a poem in recompense. The groom promptly writes a quatrain that shames his mother-in-law by transposing her images, inverted, to the genitalia:

In this world one bed never unites two attractive people,
How can an attractive girl ever get a decent man?
When I roll up high the red curtain, my candle alight,
I'll make the bodhisattva look at the hairy monster.[121]

In *The Records of Yi Jian* (*Yi Jian zhi*), an expansive collection of miracle tales recorded by Hong Mai, a government official expresses his fear of undertaking a daunting task by identifying himself with the nervous bride in a wedding joke:

> Have you heard the one about the fox who married a tiger? A fox had a daughter and he found her a tiger for a groom. During the wedding night, the master of ceremonies pronounced the wish that she might soon bear five sons and two daughters. The fox bride bowed and said, "I dare not hope for five sons and two daughters. I would be lucky enough just to save my wretched life!"[122]

In *A Collection of Laughter Worth a Thousand Pieces of Gold* (*Xiaoyuan qian jin*), finally, four men of local prominence jointly compose a poem at a village wedding, each contributing a line appropriate to his profession. The clerk, the doctor, and the student manage suggestive yet appropriate lines, but the shaman falters with clumsy vulgarity:

> The section clerk said, "Everyday he stands on guard, erect at his proper station." The doctor said, "Medicine knows of ruler and subject, of hot, cold, and wet." The degree-holder said, "In the still of the night, the bride displays her skill with brush and makeup." The shaman said, "When the amulet arrives she receives it and sets to work, faster, faster, faster."[123]

## Conclusion

The practice of wedding correspondence in parallel prose originated in the eleventh century among the literati elite. Its couplets, allusions, letters, poems, and addresses circulated in the public space created by that new elite—whether calligraphed on fine paper and encased in elaborate boxes, composed on behalf of patrons for substantial remuneration, declaimed at brilliant banquets, printed in collected works and anthologies, or cited in literary anecdotes. Like countless similar exchanges of refined compositions and elegant gifts at other social occasions—birthdays, seasonal festivities, promotions—the practitioners of wedding correspondence appropriated the language and formats of official communications to confirm their membership of the most privileged social strata of the empire. Their literary ambitions inspired an unremitting pursuit of individual distinction, limited only by a self-imposed restriction to a particular range of allusions or the observance of certain rare ceremonies, as an expression of intellectual affiliation.

The writing manuals of the thirteenth and fourteenth centuries construct by means of editorial remarks and categorical imperatives a social and ritual space that allows a fuller view of the practice of wedding correspondence than is afforded by collected works and anthologies. Not only do these manuals, with their thesauruses and their ready-made couplets, accommodate the less proficient writer and extend even toward the inclusion of commoners, but in their selection and arrangement of sample compositions they encompass a range of contrary positions among the literati. *Wedding Ritual: A New Edition* presents a narrow range of authors and formats for a limited audience: accomplished writers, familiar with the conventions of social correspondence and committed to the moral precepts of the Learning of the Way. By contrast, *A New Book for the Old Man under the Moon* comprises a wide range of authors and formats for a broad audience. While the manual opens with the wedding sequence from Zhu Xi's *Family Rituals*, lists Zhu Xi as the only Southern Song person in its thesaurus of surname allusions, and includes sample compositions that profess affiliation with the Learning of the Way (and convictions even more staunchly archaic), *A New Book* abounds in variegated allusions and incommensurable ceremonies of uncanonical provenance, and through motley literary variety identifies the act of writing as the defining practice of the literati elite.[124] The compiler of *A New Book for the Old Man under the Moon*, in other words, inscribes wedding correspondence as a practice through which literati distinguished themselves as a class. His inclusion of the archaic practices and restrained allusions of the Learning of the Way as merely another mode of literary distinction attenuates, within the fascicles of his manual, the exclusivity of that movement.[125]

This ideological contest—between the narrow definitions of writing and ritual propounded by the Learning of the Way, and the unbound, fashionable practices of those in search of individual distinction—has left its most marked traces on the pages of successive editions and extant imprints of *The Art of Writing*. In his 1307 preface to *The Art of Writing*, Xiong He (1253–1312), citing Zhu Xi, remonstrates with his contemporaries for violating the immutable genres of antiquity by their appropriation of the formats of court memorials for private, frivolous use, and chides booksellers for promoting this deplorable trend.[126] Although the section on wedding correspondence of the 1307 edition of *The Art of Writing* does not survive, the editorial remarks that punctuate the fascicles dedicated to wedding correspondence in extant imprints of *A Complete Book of the Art of Writing* and *The Great Compendium of the Art of Writing* similarly protest the vain pursuit of distinction through parallel prose and promote the return to a simple style and to ancient ritual:

Submission of the Betrothal Gifts

(i.e., what is presently called "the engagement letter")

> In the ritual sequence extending from Submission of the Choice to Requesting the Date, the exchange of betrothal gifts is the most important ceremony. Therefore, in antiquity, "the betrothal gifts invariably expressed sincerity, and the words were always well chosen." Previous generations wrote simple engagement letters, emphasizing a correct style. They did not boast of high status and famous officials [in their family] or discuss their genealogy and the great surnames. Therefore the compositions of previous generations head this section, under the rubric "For General Use." Then follow [letters that address particularities] such as status and descent, alliance by contract, and marriage between affinal kin, from the literati down to artisans, merchants, and the various crafts, each in its own category. Although it is impossible to avoid the ingrained habit of parallel prose, [this selection] largely expresses a concern with sincerity and well-chosen words, while much of the bragging and vulgarity has been excised.[127]

The author of this despairing statement sets out to reduce the practice of wedding correspondence to archaic ritual and to the sober conventions of ancient-style prose, but he is not able to sustain this effort for more than a few sentences: the pernicious attributes he unwisely conjures in his description of ephemeral generations of recent virtue proliferate at the bottom of the paragraph and become the ineradicable substance of the section on engagement letters. The separation of allusions and sample compositions into categories labeled "proper" and "vulgar," the pruning of immodest phrases, and the prominent display of virtuous compositions by proponents of the Learning of the Way, in these seven fascicles of *The Art of Writing*, cannot expurgate the playful spirit that is the essence of the practice of wedding correspondence.[128] Contemporary readers, not surprisingly, disregarded the editors' injunctions. Their emphatic red jots and underlines betray a particular interest in the sections most disparaged by the compilers:

the addresses, the poetic cycles, and the congratulatory poems and lyrics.[129] Later editions of *The Art of Writing* lack the trenchant ideology of Xiong He and Liu Yingli, whose grim warnings were rewritten or deleted by unauthorized commercial printers.[130]

These ideological debates surrounding wedding correspondence have not received proper attention from modern scholars in China or the United States, who have insisted instead on reading engagement letters and wedding addresses as spontaneous effluences of popular culture. Positing a simple binary of elite culture and popular culture, and having identified the ritual manuals of Sima Guang, Zhu Xi, and the imperial court as texts associated with the elite, these scholars have embraced all other materials as evidence of a monolithic popular practice. This ill-advised dichotomy accepts the rhetorical categories of the Learning of the Way (ritual versus custom, canonical versus vulgar, and so forth) as descriptive of a real, social divide, while reversing their moral implication: the secondary literature praises the perceived natural expression of the addresses and poems, and derides the oppressive, archaic ceremonies of the ritual manuals as contrived efforts that disregard the true nature of ritual.

The mistaken preconception of the social origins of these intricate compositions results in unfortunate misreadings. The poems, the lyrics, and the rhymes of Addresses at Scattering the Curtain all become "songs," products of a vague, unexamined oral culture that allow facile interpretations and that obviate the need for careful formal analysis. The voluminous Chinese literature on premodern weddings and marriage has consistently disregarded all parallel prose, ignoring the many hundreds of wedding letters and removing the accomplished prose compositions from the addresses to enhance their likeness to popular songs:

> *A Forest of Facts* and *The Art of Writing* both record Addresses at Scattering the Curtain and blessings that were commonly chanted at wedding banquets during the late Song and the early Yuan. The Addresses at Scattering the Curtain are rather long, and consist entirely of common expressions and suggestive language.[131]

In *The Inner Quarters*, the only work to examine wedding correspondence, Patricia Ebrey cites the letters for commoners in *A New Book for the Old Man under the Moon* as evidence of the popular origins of this practice, and then observes that literati in the eleventh and twelfth centuries wrote letters that resembled those of commoners. The characterization of the erudite literary allusions in these letters as semiconscious images allows her to remove the letters from their rarefied surroundings and to present them as repositories of common folk notions.[132]

Inspired by a reductive social binary, these misreadings are legitimated by an untenable notion of text. An examination of literary form and textual environment reveals the association of wedding letters with the parallel prose of the imperial examinations, official communications, and the elegant social correspondence of literati, and establishes the identity of the nuptial addresses with the Musical Words recited at official banquets, and with the Composition at Hoisting the Ridgepole found in numerous collected works and anthologies. Of course, one could argue that the composition of a text does not determine its use, and that commoners may have adapted letters and addresses composed by literati into any form and in a ritual context that defied all of the inscribed narratives. But social historians do not propose such a postmodernist severance of text from history. To the contrary, they regard text as an immediate transcription of historical reality. The ascription of the addresses and wedding letters to popular culture, especially, allows a disregard of authorship and a denial of text, and therewith the illusion of an unmediated view of past events. The authorless text, however, possesses a dread power common to other beheaded beings. The indiscriminate transformation of surface narrative into historical fact not only raises imaginary trains of revelers engaged in colorful ceremonies, but it breathes demonic life into literary abstractions: the categories of wedding letters in writing manuals become "people [who] wished to recognize the particularities of their ties to the other family," and the yearning immortal bride of the poems and addresses becomes an ambivalent young woman who "also had to worry about whether she could please her mother-in-law and avoid provoking the others in the house."[133]

Only the recognition that text is connected to history by the historical act of writing, will exorcise these unwholesome ghouls, reducing them to the written traces of an historical world. The dull-witted grooms, immature brides, lackluster gifts, illiterate farmers, immodest boatmen, lively wedding guests, and luxurious wedding chambers exist on the written surface of the page where, in their two dimensions, they fulfill important functions in the social traffic of those who created them by the tracings of their brush. The historical uses of the finished text one can often merely surmise—from the marks of readers, from the state of the physical page, more often only from the text itself—but as a trace of the act of writing, that particular cultural practice with its constricting generic conventions, a text preserves the memory of an educated hand, long years of recitation and composition exercises, association with hopeful students and demanding patrons, an official career, evenings of erudite banter, a lifetime of practice in calligraphy and the crafting of poetry and parallel couplets.

When considered as written traces and printed objects, wedding letters, wedding poems, and wedding addresses reveal their historical function as cultural capital and as inscribed ritual time. As genres of parallel prose, wedding letters and addresses belonged to the culture of the examinations and officialdom, and thereby confirmed the elevated status of both the author and his audience. When literary fashions changed in the fourteenth century and parallel prose lost its prestige, the practice of wedding correspondence ceased, its glamorous legacy disparaged and neglected by subsequent generations. But one may still, at present, recognize them, not only as boastful assertions of social privilege, but as the palpable remnants of historical weddings. Though stripped of their mandatory formulas and reduced to the uniform script and rigid format of the printed page, the parallel couplets of wedding letters preserve in their intricacy the ritual time of weddings as well as reflexive references to the letter as a ritual object. The suspension of conventional boundaries of propriety in addresses and poems replicates in writing the ritual time that allowed their composition. Only by recognizing the lush textures of these addresses and poems as the rich textual layers of literary allusions, written time, and inscribed sexuality, can one understand the witty poem allegedly composed by Ouyang Xiu on the occasion of the second marriage of his old friend Liu Chang, with its mischievous fusion of written time and ritual time, of page and body, of brush and penis:

> Putting the brush to paper, who will finish first?
> On the couch a poem is completed destined to be spread far
> and wide.
> Paper will be dear in the capital tomorrow:
> When one opens the curtain and pushes away the bride's
> fan, one will find a brand-new composition.[134]

# Chapter Three

## Calendars, Almanacs, Miracle Tales, and Medical Texts

### Cosmic Cycles and the Liminal Affairs of Man

> Wedding books [*hunshu*] have always been extremely numerous, yet the bibliographical section of the *History of the Tang* mentions only one such work, and the *Catalogue of the Chongwen Library* lists no more than one fascicle. The *Catalogue of Missing Books of the Four Repositories* records none at all.
>
> —Zheng Qiao (1104–1160)[1]

> In general, when making a match, one should first assess whether the fateful years of birth are compatible, and then one should examine whether the characters of the full horoscopes stand in a relation of mutual generation. Alternatively, one may apply the method of "Increasing Wealth and Decreasing Wealth" to judge whether the Awesome Gate, the Six Harms, the Orphan Deity, or the Widow's Chamber exert their noxious influences over the match; conflict means "decreasing wealth." Or again, if the fate of the match corresponds to a noble deity, nothing can obstruct it. In sum, no comprehensive system exists for marriage.
>
> —*A Household Necessity* (14th century)[2]

In 835, Feng Su (792 *jinshi*), Military Commissioner of Dongchuan, Sichuan province, memorialized to the throne to obtain an imperial edict prohibiting the publication of illicit calendars. The edict was granted forthwith, for not only in the Jiannan region where Feng Su presided, but also "in Huainan Circuit [present Jiangsu and Anhui provinces] were printed calendars offered for sale on the market. Every year, before the Bureau of Astronomy had handed down the new calendar, these printed calendars already flooded the empire."[3] But the prohibition failed to deter commercial printers:

> When Emperor Xizong [r. 874–889] arrived in Sichuan [in 881, fleeing the armies of Huang Chao (d. 884)], the calendar of the Director of the Astrological Service had not yet spread south of the Yangzi River. But there were printers on the market who detected discrepancies between the first and last days of the month in each others' calendars, and this led them to contest with one another the correct days of the seasonal changes until they were embroiled in an irreconcilable dispute. A community elder apprehended them and sent them to the official. "Isn't it true," said the official, "that you are merely debating whether a month has twenty-nine or thirty days? As long as your calendars keep pace with the celestial movements, a day's or half a day's difference is but a trifle," and he dismissed them with a scolding. He ignored, however, that such yinyang calendars, with their selection of auspicious and inauspicious days, mislead the people on many an occasion.[4]

Throughout history, the imperial court maintained a monopoly on time. For the duration of its reign, the imperial house of Li inscribed its dynastic title of "The Great Tang" on both the territorial and the temporal extent of its rule: from the founding of the Tang in 618 to its fall in 907, its name was calligraphed on imperial insignia—banners, seals, plaques, monuments—and thereon carried to the very boundaries of the realm. The emperors of the Tang, like their predecessors, chose reign titles to name periods within their rule, changing these titles to commemorate auspicious events or to counteract disasters. When, on his flight from Huang Chao's armies, Emperor Xizong arrived in Chengdu on August 10, 881, he promulgated the reign title "Peace in the Central Plains" (Zhonghe), and upon his return to Chang'an in April 885, he marked the restoration of order by the inauguration of the reign title "Brilliant New Beginning" (Guangqi).[5] From the present, time stretched backward as a continuous series of lofty reign names, solemn posthumous titles, and proud dynastic houses. Whoever attempted to reckon the present time without reference to the ruling house thereby either rebelled—as did Huang Chao in 881, when he founded the Great Qi and promulgated the reign title of Jintong—or remained ignorant of the actual date—as the reclusive immortal Xing Hepu complained to Mr. Li, a strayed traveler:

> "I have experienced no difficulty counting the individual days according to the sexagenary cycle. Only my ignorance of the name of the dynastic house and its reign titles prevents me from knowing what day it is." Li thereupon told him that the current reign title was Xining [1068–1078], and informed him of the imperial surname and dynastic title, and of the succession of years and months.[6]

The emperor asserted this monopoly on time as the Son of Heaven, as the representative of Man in his triad with Heaven and Earth. In this capacity, he performed the Grand Sacrifices at the solstices and equinoxes as well as other cyclic rites, inaugurating the successive seasons and thereby manifesting the heavenly patterns in the human realm.[7] The cosmic responsibility of his rule placed the emperor in a privileged relationship with the soil and the skies. The plains, mountains, and streams of the empire, as well as the sun, the moon, and the stars above it, produced omens and prodigies in response to the actions of the imperial house. Imperial officials apprised the throne of earthquakes, anomalous births, and rare plants and beasts that appeared in the land, and court astronomers recorded eclipses, comets, and other celestial irregularities.[8]

The imperial calendar inscribed the subjects of the realm into this numinous universe. The Directorate of Astronomy (*Sitian jian*, or the Bureau of Astronomy [*Sitian tai*]) compiled this annual calendar, computing not only the length of the lunar months and the dates of festivals and seasonal changes, but also the auspiciousness of a variety of human undertakings. Many of the calendrical calculations were based on mathematical cycles, abstracted from celestial movements, rather than on astronomical observation.[9] The calendrical spirits of the year, the months, and the days, and the plethora of imaginary stars did not correspond to identifiable celestial bodies but instead occurred in relation to a series of cycles that revolved throughout the calendar: the sexagenary cycle composed of the Ten Heavenly Stems and the Twelve Earthly Branches (*jiazi*, *yichou*, *bingyin*, and so forth); the *nayin* (Matching Tone) cycle that attached the sexagenary signs to the Five Phases (earth, metal, water, wood, and fire); and the twelve stages of the *jianchu* (Foundation-Elimination) cycle (*jian*, *chu*, *man*, *ping*, and so forth).[10] The revolving combinations of these various cycles conjured calendrical spirits and baleful stars, and determined in conjunction with these the auspiciousness and inauspiciousness of "the hundred affairs" (*bai shi*) of man.[11] Thus, for the twenty-ninth day of the second month in the fourth year of the Baoyou reign of the Song dynasty (March 27, 1256), the calculations of the court astronomers produced the following entry:

> Twenty-ninth day, [sexagenary cycle:] *xinmao*, [*nayin* cycle:] wood phase, [*jianchu* cycle:] *jian*, [constellation:] *zhang*.
>
> [Baleful stars:] Little Hour, Celestial Fire, Celestial Demon, Terrestrial Bureau, Prominent Swagger, Counter-Demon, Ninefold Ugliness, Double Sun.
>
> One should not: roof or build a dwelling or shed, move soil, travel by boat, file a legal suit, plant sprouts, dig a well, construct a chamber, marry, change residence, stray far from home, look for something.[12]

"In antiquity, emperors and kings ruled the world primarily by providing the true pitches and an accurate calendar," and the annual promulgation of the new calendar remained in the Tang and the Song a solemn occasion of great ritual importance, because the calendar brought the empire and its subjects in accord with cosmic patterns to ensure a lasting order.[13] The issue of printed calendars, beginning in 805, added quantitative weight to this imperial prerogative, as every year thousands, perhaps tens of thousands, of uniform calendars spread across the empire.[14]

Yet the imperial calendar failed to substantiate its claims to cosmic order. Although the imperial court attempted to recruit men of uncommon mathematical skill for the compilation of its calendars, court astronomers continued to be surprised by unforeseen solar and lunar eclipses and at times even failed to predict correctly the days of the new moon.[15] Such embarrassing errors invited humbling corrections from officials and commoners, and inspired an unremitting series of calendrical reforms, none of which achieved lasting improvement.[16]

The proliferation of cosmological ephemera on the commercial market further reduced the stature of the imperial calendar. Early printers applied their novel art to the multiplication of cosmological tracts rather than to the distribution of the more lasting printed book.[17]

Besides the illegal private calendars that appeared in Huainan, Chengdu, Dunhuang, and even in the capital Chang'an itself, a bewildering array of almanacs and calendrical works became available throughout the late Tang and Song empires.[18] Such manuals, many not longer than one fascicle, propounded divinatory systems that shared the cosmological principles of the imperial calendar and pertained to the same human affairs:

> For entry into office and for weddings, for the construction of dwellings and sheds, for breaking ground and burial, for the construction of Buddhist and Daoist monasteries, platforms and pagodas, altars and temples, and bridges and roof beams, for departures and homeward journeys, for travel by boat and transport of goods, and for all various purposes, this work records in separate categories all essential methods for the selection of auspicious days.[19]

In these printed ephemera, diviners competed with one another and with the imperial court. The titles recorded in the bibliographical section of *Comprehensive Treatises* (*Tongzhi*, 1161) suggest the multifariousness of the divinatory technologies that informed the prognostication in these works and hint at the prodigious number of pamphlets in circulation: seventy-one works on the *dunjia* system, forty-eight on the *taiyi* system, eighteen on the Nine Halls system, eighty-two on the *liuren* system, twenty-two on the *shijing* system, and so forth.[20] At times, the imperial court handed down an extensive, learned almanac intended to abolish illicit practices and to realign cosmological calculation with the canon. In 641, for example, Lü Cai (ca. 600–665) completed at imperial behest his academic *Book of Yin and Yang* (*Yinyang shu*) in fifty-three fascicles, and in the 1050s, Wang Zhu (997–1057) compiled a similar scholarly work for the Song imperial government, entitled *A New Book on Geomancy* (*Dili xinshu*), in fifteen fascicles. But in due time, commercial printers pilfered sections from these extensive works and published them with unmarked revisions, or they merely impressed the prestigious names of these able men on the pamphlets of others.[21] A more successful instance of imperial interference with printed ephemera occurred under Song Taizu (r. 960–976), who rendered worthless the countless copies of a proscribed work on omens by introducing into circulation a large number of forgeries.[22]

The transmitted titles of almanacs represent a mere fraction of the many thousands of works in circulation, and these published tracts in turn constituted but a small part of a cosmological discourse that was conveyed through oral transmission and secret manuscripts, and through traceless objects and transient practices, plied at countless, immemorial market stalls throughout the empire:

> Signs advertising a miscellany of divinatory arts appear everywhere in profusion: *wuxing*, *liuren*, *yanqin*, *sanming*, *guixi*, *taiyi*, *dongwei*, *ziwei*, *taisu*, *dunjia* . . . Every man fancies himself a Yan Junping, every stallholder imagines himself a Sima Jizhu—one more vulgar than the next.[23]

A limited number of shared assumptions underlay the technologies set forth in thousands of competing tracts and deployed at a myriad stalls.[24] The hundred affairs prognosticated in calendars and almanacs range from events of great social importance, such as burial or the submission of a legal suit, to matters of private preoccupation, such as cutting one's hair or nails, or sweeping the floor. Not their social importance, therefore, defines these activities, but their liminal quality: the incipient transformation of bodies (biological, social, spatial) through manipulation or transgression. Most prominent in almanacs and calendars ranks construction in all its stages: moving soil, raising pillars and hoisting ridgepoles, erecting walls, and so forth—activities that transform physical space in the process of creating social space. Events such as weddings and burials, travel and entrance into office, disrupt enduring social entities by the addition or subtraction of persons. The liminal spaces that acquire prominence in such transformations—a gate or doorway opened in the smooth surface of a wall, a grave dug in mute rock or soil—resemble the bodily orifices through which dissipate vital breath and blood. Because hair and nails grow through the skin, they are permanently liminal and dangerous (offensive to deities, the matter of sorcery), as is blood that breaks through the skin during acupuncture, menstruation, or childbirth.[25]

Over these liminal spaces and these liminal times—a body weakened by loss of blood, a family adjusting to the departure of one of its members, the exposed frame of a house—cosmic cycles exert their influence. The liminal affairs of man create gaps in the continuity of time and space, and thereby expose him to the influence of cosmic forces that revolve in continuous, blind, amoral transformation. Time, like Heaven, is circular, and with the sun, the moon, and the stars that move its hours, days, months, seasons, and years, rotate at individual velocities the cycles of the Ten Heavenly Stems and the Twelve Earthly

Branches (separately, or joined in the sexagenary cycle), the Five Phases, the Five Tones, the Five Colors, the Nine Halls, and a multitude of stars, deities, and spirits. Earthly space is square, but by the movement of the celestial bodies over its surface, its five directions (east, west, north, south, and center) correspond to the same stems and branches, phases and tones, colors and numbers, stars and deities. All these various cycles enable the diviner, who fathoms cosmic forces by means of numinous objects, to transpose pertinent constellations into calculable signs, and from these in turn he derives his prognostications.[26] The multiplicity of these cycles allows an infinite number of divinatory calculations, complicated further by the introduction of arbitrary stars and spirits that defy regular computation.

Yet the fragmentary evidence yields only dim, intermittent views of these awesome cycles and their manifold calculations. Extant almanacs assume a culture of divinatory and ritual practice long forgotten so that their dense formulations often pose grave difficulties to the present reader.[27] The mnemonic rhymes cited in these almanacs, moreover, hint at an oral culture in which the written word assumed but a subsidiary function, an impression strengthened by the many poems (*fu*), ditties (*jue*), and other verse forms mentioned in the titles preserved in contemporary bibliographies. Indeed, according to Zhou Mi (1232–1308), such rhymes aided even Deng Zongwen of the Astrological Service at the imperial court in his rough calculation of the first day of spring, intercalary months, and major festivals: "He knew mnemonic songs for the calculation of new moons and full moons, and of long and short months. Unfortunately I cannot remember all of them."[28] And in the end, the efficacy of prognostication depended not on the divinatory method or material aids, but on the interpretation by the diviner of the results obtained:

> In Fengzhou [Shaanxi province] lived a soldier named Li Wenhe. Originally he had been a monk, but he had committed a crime for which he was condemned to be a tattooed serviceman. He was able to tell people's fortunes by reading their pulse according to the *taisu* method. In this manner he could fathom even the subtlest depths of their hearts and minds. . . . I later obtained his book [which explains that the basis of his method consists in] pairing the twelve arteries with the twelve branches, like the division into halls used by specialists in the Five Phases. It also explains the various methods for

> determining fate and fortunes. The days are counted by the twelve branches, which in turn correspond to the revolving pulse, and thereby one may perceive in exact detail approaching blessings and disasters. . . . Thereafter I have often seen, in the capital and all across the empire, diviners who had achieved a reputation for reading the pulse by the *taisu* method, but none could compare to Li Wenhe.[29]

Throughout history, the limited function of text and writing in the divinatory arts has resulted in oblivion. Written characters, in this discourse, serve only in an intermediary stage between the manifestation of cosmic patterns and prognostication. They transcribe the cosmic order into legible signs, to be interpreted by the diviner. They may also aid the diviner's memory by recording elaborate systems and mnemonic rhymes. But writing is not an aim in itself, and thus the written instantiations of this discourse remained outside the established culture of the printed book. Calendars lost their usefulness after one year. The systems expounded in almanacs possessed a more enduring value, but their owners rarely included them in their libraries and seldom reprinted them in lasting collectanea. The draft calculations in the personal archives of diviners held little interest for others and were unlikely to survive their compiler.[30] It is therefore significant that most of the Tang and Song calendars and almanacs to survive into the present century were preserved, not in the grand collectanea and famous libraries of the eastern provinces, but in the arid sands of Turfan and among the discarded papers in the hidden caves of Dunhuang.[31]

Medical texts were deemed worthy of inclusion in prestigious libraries, and some fine Song and Yuan imprints of extensive manuals are extant today. This mode of transmission, however, has reduced the range of medical treatises, as it has preferred the large print of imperial editions and the learned tracts of literati practitioners to the cheap pamphlets of professional doctors and diviners. From the pages of surviving manuals emerges a cosmology of forces and fluids whose circulation corresponds to the revolution of cosmic cycles. Obstruction of the flows of blood, breath, and energy causes surface symptoms of ill-health that the expert doctor recognizes and diagnoses, just as wise officials trace meteors and floods to ailments in the imperial government. The texts of medicine resemble calendars and almanacs not only in their cosmological assumptions, but also in the imperfect inscription of the knowledge of its practitioners.[32]

Literati confine their discussions of cosmological discourse to their notebooks and collections of miracle tales, and in these marginal genres profess a mere amateurish interest, an ignorant curiosity.[33] Or else they affect, in expositions on divinatory systems in their notebooks, or in philosophical analyses of the supernatural in their miracle tales, a distant academic attitude that matches their portrayals of their detached ambulation among the stalls of diviners and storytellers in the marketplace.[34] Only divinatory technologies that they deem to preserve ancient knowledge receive their undivided attention, and in such essays they offer an occasional keen observation about the disjunction between writing and divinatory practice, and about the resulting obliteration of practices once most prestigious:

> The ancients accorded great importance to divination, and the refinement of their art allowed them to communicate with the divine. Divination by means of the tortoise shell was called "plastromancy" [*bu*], and the manipulation of milfoil stalks was known as "achillomancy" [*shi*]. . . . When Shun issued his command to Yu, when King Wu undertook his campaign against King Zhou, "when the Duke of Shao sited his residence and the Duke of Zhou walled Chengzhou," these sagely men without exception "committed their charge to the numinous tortoise" and examined with utmost care the cracks obtained. Since the tortoise was held in higher esteem than milfoil stalks, plastromancy exceeded in prestige even divination by the *Book of Changes*. The *Seven Treatises* by Liu Xiang [ca. 77–6 BCE], as preserved in the bibliographical section of the *History of the Han*, lists a *Book of the Tortoise*, *The Tortoise of Xia*, and other works, combining to a total of four hundred and one fascicles by fifteen authors. Subsequent generations failed to transmit these works. Many of those who divine by milfoil stalks today still follow in the footsteps of their illustrious predecessors, but only the measliest of stallholders practice the art known as tortoise divination. They receive but a few coins for their services, and literati never bother to consult them.[35]

Thus with this chapter. The almanacs and calendars that appeared on the early market for printed materials outnumbered, by thousands of titles and millions of copies, rarefied, expensive works such as canonical commentaries, ritual handbooks, collected works, and writing manuals. As a practical discourse, divination in all its forms affected the lives of anonymous millions at all levels of society. Its basic principles were familiar to all. Yet the instrumental function of writing in this discourse left its knowledge imperfectly inscribed and deprived its pamphlets of the prestige that secured the transmission of more restricted bodies of texts. And very few scholars show any interest in cosmological texts today.

The fragmentary materials pertaining to the divination of weddings illustrate by their disparate complexity the shared principles of this cosmological discourse and by their sorry paucity the ephemerality of its texts. The transfer of the bride at betrothals and weddings causes a traumatic reconfiguration of social and physical space both in her old and in her new household, and thereby opens a gap in cosmic time and space. If the parties to this ominous occasion manage to avoid offending the stars, deities, and spirits that hover above the gates, the doorways, and other pregnable spaces during these liminal times, the groom and the bride will raise their bright, plentiful offspring in prosperity and robust health. But any transgression of harmful hours or proscribed space will create young widows and sickly orphans, scavenging around the crumbling walls of their extinct household.

As firmly as calendars, almanacs, miracle tales, and medical texts agree on the blessings and dangers of weddings, so widely do they differ in their calculations of auspicious times and directions. And in this, the divination of weddings illustrates also the unrelenting competition between diviners of all times:

> Emperor Wu of Han [r. 140–87 BCE] "summoned his diviners and asked them whether a certain day was acceptable for taking a wife. The specialists in the Five Phases said that the day was acceptable; the specialists in the *kanyu* method said that it was not acceptable; the *jianchu* experts said that it was not auspicious; the *congchen* experts said that it was greatly inauspicious; the calendrical experts said that it was moderately inauspicious; the *tianren* experts said that it was moderately auspicious; and the *taiyi* experts said that it was greatly auspicious. They debated without end, each stating his arguments, until an edict resolved that 'the Five Phases are the most important in avoiding mortal taboos.'" Thus it may be seen that the different results obtained by all the various calendrical and divinatory methods are not a recent phenomenon.[36]

## PATTERNS OF AUSPICIOUS AND INAUSPICIOUS TIME IN CALENDARS

During the seventeenth and eighteenth centuries, the earliest calendars at the disposal of scholars interested in the history of calendrical techniques dated to the Southern Song and the Jin (1115–1234): a slightly damaged manuscript of the *Fully Annotated Huitian Eternal Calendar of the Fourth Year of the Baoyou Reign [1256] of the Great Song* (*Da Song Baoyou sinian bingchen sui Huitian wannian juzhu li*) and a *Calendar of Great Luminance* (*Daming li*) of the Jin dynasty.[37] Only around 1900 did this meager stock increase with the three dozen calendars found among the strange trove of handwritten and printed materials at Dunhuang, the earliest a Northern Wei calendar for the years 450–451, the remainder dating to the ninth and tenth centuries. More recent excavations at Turfan have uncovered additional calendars from the fifth through seventh centuries, while in tombs throughout the People's Republic of China archaeologists have unearthed calendars of even earlier periods.[38]

The Dunhuang calendars, most of them handwritten fragments, few of them complete, offer rare, confounding glimpses of the diverse calendrical systems in use during the late Tang, Five Dynasties, and early Song. Imperial astronomers compiled at most two of these calendars, and even these two, the calendars of 877 (S-P6) and 978 (S0612), may have falsely invoked an imperial provenance to advertise their unofficial calculations. All others are without doubt illicit calendars: a calendar of 882 printed in Chengdu (S-P10), a calendar of unknown date printed in Chang'an (S-P12), the rest calculated by reputable men of the remote town of Dunhuang itself.[39] The fragmented remains of these calendars allow only intermittent views of the logic of their computation. The damage wrought by neglectful use and neglectful time, and the individual practices of copyists have compromised the coherence of the original documents. Stretches of days fill empty spaces in divinatory works and sutras, while more solid patches of months appear on the reverse of ritual manuals, scriptures, and other texts.[40] Some copyists satisfied themselves with the reproduction of a calendrical preface or a few select months, while others copied complete calendars from which they omitted information they did not require.[41] Only the calendar of 986 (P3403) is both complete and unabridged. The idiosyncratic, fallible hand of the copyist has in many cases created a new text, distinct from the calendars prepared by astronomers and diviners.

From these uneven documents emerge the uncertain patterns of auspicious days for betrothals (*jiehun*) and weddings (*jiaqu*). The prefaces and almanacs attached to some of the surviving calendars identify baleful stars especially pernicious to weddings, and a few provide tables for the determination of marital horoscopes, but none explains the principles of the selection of favorable days for betrothals or weddings.[42] The inference of such principles from the patterns of auspicious days is encumbered not only by the fragmentary state of many of the calendars—and by omissions and possible errors of copyists—but also by evident yet unexplained changes in methods of computation over time. "Introducing a wife into one's household" (*nafu*), for example, appears a total of six times among the activities in the calendars of 834, 858, and 864, all on the cyclical dates *jisi*, *renwu*, and *guiwei* in the first or second month of the year, with a preference for *ping* days of the *jianchu* cycle. The category vanishes when, starting with the calendar of 877, *ping* and *shou* days permanently lodge the *gang* and *kui* spirits of the *liuren* cycle and thereby become uniformly inauspicious for all undertakings.[43]

Unlike the favorable days for many other prognosticated activities, the 386 auspicious days for weddings and the sixty-four auspicious days for betrothals in the Dunhuang calendars do not correspond to particular calendrical spirits. Instead, they are determined by combinations of the sexagenary cycle, the *jianchu* cycle, and the number of the month.[44] The Non-infringement System (*bujiang zhi fa*) accounts for 207 of the auspicious wedding dates and for eighteen of the auspicious betrothal dates. On such days, the Dunhuang calendars often, but not always, list Non-infringement (*bujiang*) or Non-infringement of Yin and Yang (*yinyang bujiang*) among the calendrical spirits. The Non-infringement System (fig. 3.1) intersperses in one circle the twelve branches and the ten stems, both arranged clockwise. The Lunar Demon (*yueyan*) moves counterclockwise along the branches, from *xu* in the first month to *hai* in the twelfth month. On the cyclical dates composed of the four stems to the right of the Lunar Demon and the five branches to its left, yin (represented by the branches) and yang (represented by the stems) during that month "are not infringed upon," which renders these dates auspicious for weddings (and, to a lesser extent, for betrothals). This system, typical in its strict elaboration of arbitrary parameters, yields irregular patterns of cyclical dates: some cyclical dates, such as *jiazi* or *yichou*, are never Non-infringement days while other cyclical dates, such as *jichou* or *gengyin*, are Non-infringement days for as many as five consecutive months.[45]

**FIGURE 3.1. The Non-Infringement System.**

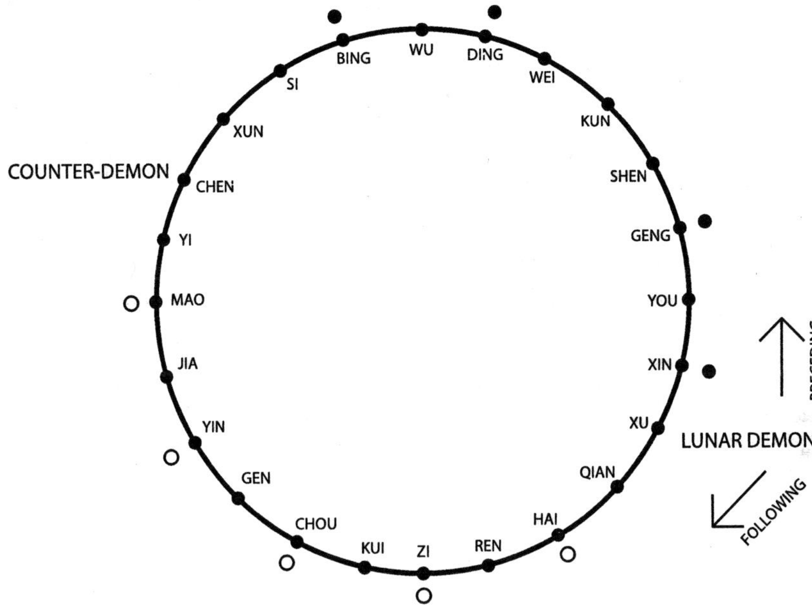


Complications arise in the calendrical application of this system due to interference by the *jianchu* cycle and by baleful stars, and due to occasional wanderings of the Non-infringement System in the guise of a calendrical spirit. Many Non-infringement dates are not auspicious for weddings or betrothals when they coincide with a *po* day in the *jianchu* cycle, for example, but other days in the *jianchu* cycle, too, harbor their particular conflicts with select cyclical dates. Around 900, moreover, a divinatory shift of unrevealed origin eliminated some of these conflicts and created new ones. Ninth-century calendars, for example, do not list weddings or betrothals as an auspicious activity on *jiashen*, a Non-infringement date from the fifth through the eighth month, when it falls on a *man* day, but tenth-century calendars ignore this prohibition. By contrast, in tenth-century calendars *cheng* and *wei* days in the *jianchu* cycle counteract the auspiciousness of *wuzi* during the third and fourth months, a restriction that does not obtain in ninth-century calendars. When Non-infringement operates as a calendrical spirit rather than as a computational system, it blesses weddings or betrothals on days that strict application of the Non-infringement System would exclude, extending even to cyclical dates that are never

Non-infringement dates, such as *jiazi*, *yimao*, and *dingsi*.[46] The calendar of 858 records the first of thirty such untimely appearances, but they become more common in calendars since 897. The calendars of 900, 933, and 982 mark all auspicious wedding dates as Non-infringement dates, both those that accord with the system and those that do not.

Non-infringement as a calendrical spirit does not roam indiscriminately, but largely settles its blessings on two groups of cyclical dates that Dunhuang calendars frequently designate as auspicious for weddings and betrothals. One group (*jiazi*, *renshen*, *jiaxu*, *yihai*, *renwu*, *guiwei*, *yiyou*, *yisi*, *xinhai*, and *guihai*) comprises cyclical dates that become auspicious in conjunction with specific stages of the *jianchu* cycle or in particular months. *Jiazi*, for example, is consistently auspicious for weddings when it coincides with a *wei* day (always in a third or fourth month), and on such days the calendars of 897 and 956 include Non-infringement among its calendrical spirits. The other group (*bingzi*, *jimao*, *gengyin*, *xinmao*, *renyin*, *guimao*, *renzi*, *jiayin*, *yimao*, and *wuwu*) consists of cyclical dates that are more generally auspicious for weddings and betrothals, irrespective of the month, and reduced only by select conflicts with the *jianchu* cycle. In most calendars, for example, *bingzi* days are always auspicious for weddings or betrothals except on *zhi* and *po* days (and, of course, *ping* and *shou*), and on a number of such auspicious days Non-infringement appears among the calendrical spirits in the calendars of 905, 933, and 989. The first group accounts for fifty-one auspicious wedding dates, three betrothal dates, and thirteen appearances of Non-infringement as a calendrical spirit; the second group for 108 auspicious wedding dates, thirty-six betrothal dates, and fourteen untimely appearances of Non-infringement. These ten restricted and ten less restricted dates combine with regular Non-infringement days for 366 of the 386 auspicious wedding dates and fifty-seven of the sixty-four auspicious betrothal dates. The remaining days diviners may have selected by individual, untraceable means.[47]

The proliferation of baleful stars in divination during the Song dynasty decimated the number of auspicious wedding dates and increased the prominence of Non-infringement dates. The *Fully Annotated Huitian Eternal Calendar of the Great Song* of 1256 marks as Non-infringement days all thirteen of its auspicious days for weddings (*jiaqu*, *xingjia*, *yingqu*).[48] Of these thirteen days, eleven accord with the Non-infringement System, and two (*jiazi* and *jiaxu*, both in the fourth month) belong to the restricted group of auspicious wedding dates in the Dunhuang calendars. The specific lists of inauspicious activities in the calendar of 1256, on days when noxious influences dispel all beneficent forces, suggest that baleful stars caused particular harm at weddings. Where the thirty-two auspicious betrothal dates amount to more than double the thirteen auspicious wedding dates (a reversal of the ratio in Dunhuang calendars), inauspicious dates for weddings outnumber inauspicious dates for betrothals by fifty-two to twenty-five.[49]

*Composite Essentials of the Three Calendrical Systems* (*Sanli cuoyao*), an undated almanac extant in an immaculate Southern Song imprint, explicates the importance of Non-infringement under the fearsome baleful stars of the Southern Song. *Composite Essentials* is not a calendar for one particular year but comprises lists of generic cyclical dates auspicious for twenty-two distinct activities (weddings, betrothals, travel, construction, moving, burial, filing a legal suit, and so forth) for every month of the year, followed by expositions on some of the divinatory systems mentioned in its pages. As in the calendar of 1256, the great majority of auspicious wedding dates are Non-infringement dates (fourteen of seventeen), and the number of auspicious betrothal dates (*qiuhun*) greatly exceeds the number of auspicious wedding dates (*jiaqu*), by fifty to seventeen.[50] The qualifications attached to eleven of the wedding dates enlarge this discrepancy between betrothal and wedding dates. Of the seventeen auspicious wedding dates, the compiler of *Composite Essentials* marks six as emergency dates, two as dates subject to curtailed use, and three as otherwise restricted. No such qualifications pertain to betrothal dates. The compiler also dismisses twenty wedding dates (against five betrothal dates) put forth as auspicious by compilers of earlier calendars, citing conflicts the latter did not recognize. The comments explaining the compiler's considerations in these matters set forth the dangers attending to weddings, unacknowledged in the calendars of the ninth and tenth centuries:

> Third month. Auspicious days for weddings: *jiazi*. One day only, from the *Huiyao Calendar*. Although this date conflicts with the Return Taboo, it is an acceptable date because of its many propitious stars. Previous calendars listed *dinghai* and *yihai*, but these are days of death according to the *Wantong Calendar*. Although *bingzi* is a Non-infringement day in this month, its conflict with the Return Taboo renders it unusable.[51]

> Eleventh month. Auspicious days for weddings: *dingchou*. Only this one date is a true wedding date. Yet because it conflicts with the Great Killer's entrance into the Central Hall and because the music habitually played at weddings enhances the force of baleful deities, one should avoid this day by all means. The dates *xinsi* and *xinchou*, from the *Fully Annotated Eternal Calendar*, are both Non-infringement days and are both advantageous, but the *Hundred Taboos Calendar* does not include them. *Bingzi*, *renzi*, *dingmao*, *xinmao*, *jimao*, and *yimao* conflict with the branch of the month [*zi*] or coincide with *kui*, *gang*, Lunar Punishment, or other baleful stars and should not be used.[52]

## THE CALCULATION OF COSMIC BLESSINGS AND DANGERS IN ALMANACS

As Zheng Qiao observes in the first epigraph to this chapter, the numerous wedding books of his time circulated outside the legitimate culture of the printed book as it was inscribed in imperial bibliographies and catalogues. As a result, nearly all the books that could have revealed the principles behind the calendrical computations of auspicious days for betrothals and weddings have perished. Only the titles of vanished books in old bibliographies, a sporadic anecdote, and a few fragments of such almanacs suggest today the multiplicity of complex divinatory systems put forth by diviners to secure the rich blessings of betrothals and to ward off the lethal dangers of weddings.

In the bibliographical section of his *Comprehensive Treatises*, under the rubric of "The Five Phases," Zheng Qiao lists twelve titles of wedding books:

> *The Scripture of Weddings* (*Hunqu jing*), 4 fascicles; *The Yinyang Book of Weddings* (*Yinyang jiaqu shu*), 4 fascicles; *Book of Weddings* (*Hunjia shu*), 2 fascicles; *Laws of the Yellow Records for Weddings* (*Hunjia huangji ke*), 1 fascicle; *Liuhe Wedding Calendar* (*Liuhe hunjia li*), 1 fascicle; *Book of Weddings according to the Liuhe System, With Diagrams* (*Liuhe hunjia shu ji tu*), 2 fascicles; *Book for the Wedding Day* (*Jiaquying shu*), 4 fascicles; *Yinyang Diagrams for Weddings* (*Jiaqu yinyang tu*), 2 fascicles; *Miscellaneous Diagrams and Techniques for Weddings and the*

> *Bedroom* (*Za jiaqu fangnei tushu*), 4 fascicles; *Nine Heavens Wedding Diagrams* (*Jiutian jiaqu tu*), 1 fascicle; *Wedding Book* (*Hunshu*), 1 fascicle; *The Yao and Chen Book for Wedding Negotiations* (*Yao Chen yihun shu*), 1 fascicle.
>
> Above: Weddings, 12 titles, 27 fascicles.[53]

The first ten of these titles Zheng Qiao recovered from the seventh-century *History of the Sui*.[54] Of these ten titles, one (the *Book of Weddings* in two fascicles) also appears in the bibliographical sections of the *Old History of the Tang* and the *New History of the Tang*.[55] The final two entries, however, the first copied from the *Catalogue of the Chongwen Library* and the second unique to *Comprehensive Treatises*, confirm that wedding books remained an identifiable genre in Song.[56] Two entries in the Five Phases section of the bibliographical treatise of the *History of the Song* lend additional support to this assumption:

> *Jing Fang's Wedding Book, Corrected Edition* (*Jiaoding Jing Fang hunshu*), 3 fascicles; . . . *Book of Wedding Divination* (*Zhanhun shu*), 1 fascicle.[57]

The tantalizing titles of these works reveal little about their precious contents. The Celestial General *liuhe*, mentioned in two of the titles, presides over auspicious wedding days in the *liuren* system.[58] Jing Fang (77–37 BCE), a famous diviner and a scholar of the *Book of Changes*, belonged to a group of illustrious men whose names diviners and commercial printers attached freely to apocryphal divinatory systems so that his appearance in the title of a wedding book betrays nothing of its method. But the arrangement of sections and titles in these bibliographies reconstitutes at a remove the familiar context of liminal activities, placing the titles of wedding books amid texts on childbirth, the construction of houses, and the siting of tombs.

*A New Book on Geomancy*, the learned imperial almanac compiled during the 1050s, introduces a mention of a wedding book in the same broad divinatory context. A section on divination by means of the Five Surnames (*wuxing*) criticizes the pedigree of the various systems derived from this method that were current in contemporary texts and practice:

> The method of the Five Surnames does not date back to antiquity, yet today all literati use it. But I suppose that it is not

> the task of yinyang books to instill universal order in society, and I assume that few literati understand the calculations of the auspicious and the inauspicious in these books.

The section concludes that the method may be employed for burial, the construction of houses, or weddings, as long as it does not conflict with any stipulation in the ritual scriptures: "According to a passage in a *Book of Weddings* [*Hunshu*], 'A girl born in a *zi* or *wu* year is advantageous, and she should marry in a sixth or a twelfth month. If her surname belongs to the *shang* or the *jiao* tone, she should be received with a banquet.' This ignores ritual."[59]

An entry in Zhu Yu's (fl. 1080s) *Talking Matter* (*Ke tan*) describes a book that similarly extrapolates marital fortunes from surnames:

> When during my youth I traveled with my mother's family to Changzhou [in present Zhejiang province], a student surnamed Qian once showed us a book with diagrams. If one knew the surnames of three generations of a boy's family, one could discover the last name of his [future] wife, and if one knew the surnames in a girl's family, one could find her husband's name. It never failed.
>
> Of my three older sisters the eldest married into the Wu family and the second eldest married a Shen. When Qian checked his book, he found that both husbands should be surnamed Wu. At the time, we wondered how he could be wrong. But after a few years the sister married to a Shen was divorced, returned to the lineage, and was married off to Wu Kuan. Her husband did not know about the book. The chances were a hundred thousand to one, and still it worked out. How can that be? How can these few volumes of written characters encompass in their entirety the expansive masses of mankind?[60]

Besides these titles and references, only a few substantial fragments survive from almanacs dedicated entirely or in great part to the divination of betrothals and weddings: a handful of passages in Dunhuang divination texts, the incomplete *Scripture on Taiyi* (*Taiyi jing*), and a section contained in the chapter on cappings and weddings in *A Household Necessity*. Already these few intermittent, incomplete texts display a remarkable variety of divinatory methods, and a striking diversity of objects of calculation.

Dunhuang documents P2905, S2729v, P3288, P4680, S4282, and Dx00098v offer propitious and unpropitious marital horoscopes as well as a number of methods for calculating auspicious months and days for weddings. The horoscopes of grooms and brides are variously determined by the Five Phases, the Five Phases combined with the sexagenary cycle and the Five Emperors (Green, Red, White, Black, and Yellow), the twelve branches combined with the Six Dragons, or the twelve branches combined with Hook, Connection, and Destruction: "*zi* hooks to *mao*, *mao* connects to *you*, *you* destroys *wu*."[61] Likewise, auspicious and inauspicious dates for weddings may be determined by means of a bewildering array of incompatible diagrams and calculatory systems. The reverse of document S2729, for example, contains a passage that divides the thirty days of the lunar month into four (incomplete) cycles of eight days, dominated by the Deities of the Four Directions: the Vermilion Bird of the South; the head, side, and legs of the White Tiger of the West; the Dark Warrior of the North; and the head, side, and legs of the Green Dragon of the East. These Four Deities determine the distant future of all marriages:

> If one has a wedding on a day dominated by the side of the White Tiger, the husband and wife will become noble, their marriage will be peaceful, and they will be blessed with many children and grandchildren, five sons and two daughters: very auspicious.[62]

Document P2905, by contrast, attributes decisive influence over wedding days to the *jianchu* cycle, to six-day cycles revolving from Great Yang to the Heavenly King, and to the Round Hall. Although many of these divinatory texts are fragmentary or partly illegible, they suggest, sometimes even within one document, the innumerable, incommensurable systems that existed during the ninth century for the prognostication of weddings.

The *Scripture on Taiyi* survives in the Ming-dynasty collectaneum *Ramparts of Talk* (*Shuofu*), which ascribes the authorship of the scripture to the Dark Maiden, a goddess in the Daoist pantheon, and includes it in a fascicle of texts on construction, geomancy, agricultural production, sexual intercourse, divination, chronomancy, the stove, and miscellaneous records of the miraculous. Like most texts in *Ramparts of Talk*, this *Scripture on Taiyi* is an excerpt from a longer text already rare in the compilers' time and now lost. The *Daoist Canon* (*Daozang*) also includes this incomplete almanac, under the title *Scripture of the Dark Maiden, Bestowed by the Yellow Emperor on the Three Masters* (*Huangdi shou sanzi Xuannü jing*).[63] Marc Kalinowski dates the text to the Six Dynasties, citing certain characteristics of its technical vocabulary, and its use of a formula also found on a pre-Sui divination board in the Shanghai Museum.[64]

The text opens with a general exposition on the movement of Taiyi along the *liuren* cycle, where it assumes twenty different positions within one ten-day cycle, measured by the ten stems (see fig. 3.2.1). After a brief explanation of the use of the *liuren* cycle for the divination of proper times for travel and visits, the remainder of the fragment elaborates its various applications for the divination of auspicious days and hours for weddings.

The formulas proffered by the *Scripture on Taiyi* assist the reader in mapping the mortal dangers that attend weddings. The cosmic discontinuity caused by such occasions invites the noxious influences of baleful stars and traveling deities, and lends lethal force to conflicts between time and space:

FIGURE 3.2.1. **The *liuren* Cycle.**

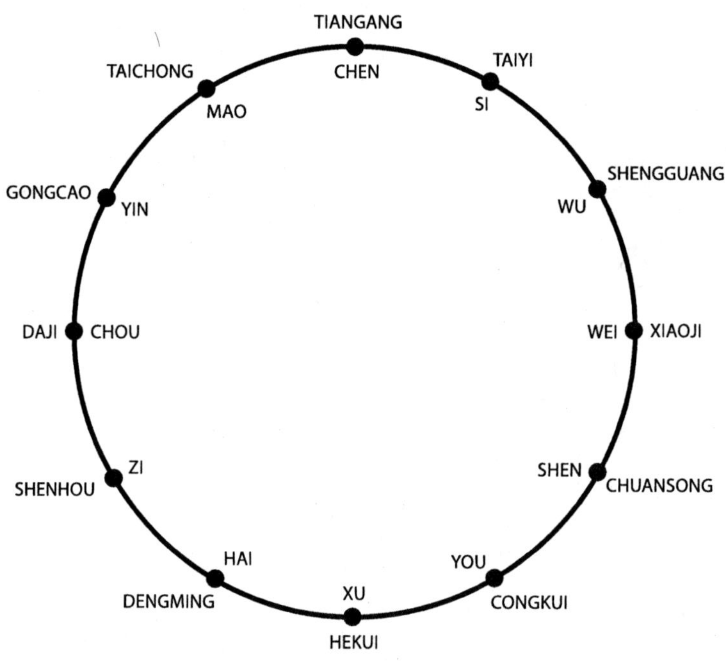

> Whenever one wishes to take a wife or marry off a daughter, one should record the day of the original betrothal to serve as the root. At the time of the wedding, one should conspicuously avoid conflict with the day and the hour of the betrothal. Conflict with its day harms the father-in-law, and conflict with its hour harms the mother-in-law. ("Father-in-law" and "mother-in-law" are the father and the mother of the groom.) All conflicting days and hours cause ill fortune to the entire family.[65]

Proper use of the *liuren* cycle identifies all such conflicts and determines the positions of the baleful stars and deities. The avoidance of the inauspicious days and hours thus established ensures the safe passage of the groom, the bride, and their families through the liminal times and liminal spaces of wedding ritual. The computation of a possible conflict between the bride's horoscope and the orientation of the groom's house illustrates both the variety of dangers and the dense complexity of the calculations in the *Scripture on Taiyi* (see fig. 3.2.1, and 3.2.2):

> Do not let the gate of the husband's family harm the wife's date of birth, or the wife will suffer immediate disaster. Given: an *yiwei* day during the second month at a *si* hour [9–11 a.m.]. *Tiangang* is set at *si*. If the branch of the wife's year of birth corresponds with *congkui* and the gate of the husband's house faces *zi* territory, corresponding with *taiyi*, or the gate faces *chou*, corresponding with *shengguang*, then the gate of the husband's house in both cases harms the wife's horoscope. That is to say, the Fire Deity on the gate of the husband's house consumes the Metal Deity on the gate of the wife's house. If the husband's gate faces *you*, corresponding with *gongcao*, and the wife arrives from the east (*mao*) at the west (*you*) and enters at *gongcao*, she comes to immediate harm. All other cases follow these principles.[66]

The diagrams and calculations in *A Household Necessity* assume the same cosmic dangers that overshadow weddings in the *Scripture on Taiyi*. They appear in an untitled divinatory section, toward the end of a chapter on "The Ceremonies of Cappings and Weddings," in the ninth installment of this fourteenth-century reference work.[67] The

**FIGURE 3.2.2. The Gate of the Husband's Family Harms the Wife's Date of Birth.**

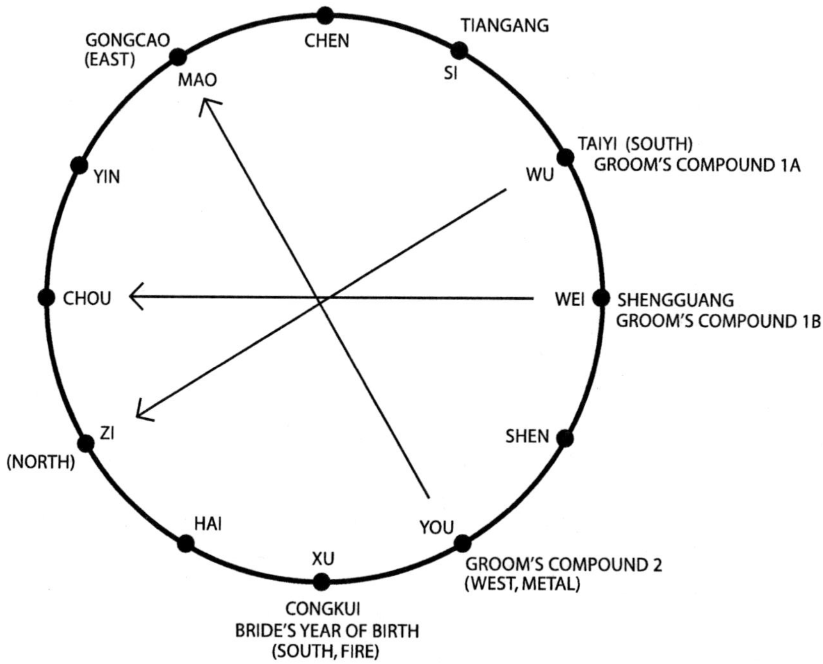


technical and colloquial language of the section contrasts sharply with the language of the preceding sections: the outline of Zhu Xi's archaic wedding ceremonies from *Family Rituals*, contract formats, wedding addresses and poems, and legal stipulations promulgated by the Yuan imperial court. The succession of these unintegrated ceremonial elements, with their incompatible discourses and styles, suggests that the compiler of *A Household Necessity* copied each from an independent work. The divinatory section reproduces part of an almanac, perhaps of a lost wedding book.

The introduction to the divinatory section, translated in part in the second epigraph to this chapter, informs the reader that "no comprehensive system exists for marriage," and it characterizes the materials treated in the section as "the standard elements." The thirteen parts that the section comprises range from the initial negotiations of a match to the entrance of the bride into the groom's compound: five entries on horoscopes, one entry on "Increasing Wealth and Decreasing

Wealth," six entries on auspicious dates for betrothals and weddings, and one on the entrance of the bride into the groom's compound. As the introduction explains, these thirteen parts do not only offer alternative ceremonies for the same ritual stage, such as the determination of horoscopes and the method of Increasing Wealth in the initial negotiations, but they encompass a number of alternative, incompatible methods of calculation.

The five horoscopic tables base their lists of auspicious and inauspicious matches severally on the twelve branches, the Five Surnames, or a combination of the twelve branches, the twelve months, and the Five Phases. The first table, entitled "Nine Auspicious Matches," lists nine categories of auspicious combinations of branches, each category characterized with a two-character phrase: "Of the Same Category: This means that *zi* faces *zi*, *chou* faces *chou*, and so forth." The second table, "Nine Inauspicious Matches," operates in the same way, with categories such as "The Six Harms" ("*zi* and *wei*, *chou* and *wu*, *yin* and *si*, *mao* and *chen*, *shen* and *hai*, and *you* and *xu*") and "The Four Defeats" ("*zi* and *mao*, *you* and *zi*, *mao* and *wu*, and *wu* and *you*"). The third table, however, assesses the compatibility of prospective grooms and brides by means of their surnames, spelling out auspicious and inauspicious combinations of the Five Tones (into which all surnames are divided) as well as the phases, branches, and months taboo for each surname:

> The *gong* tone: Marriage with the *shang* and *zheng* tones is auspicious, the others are inauspicious; ought not marry a girl associated at birth with the wood phase or with the branches *shen*, *you*, *chen*, or *xu*, or born in the third or ninth month.[68]

Like the first and second horoscopic tables, the fourth and fifth tables are complementary, but their "Methods for Matching Branches and Stems for Males" and "Methods for Matching Branches and Stems for Females" introduce sexual difference and baleful stars into their computations:

> A male born in a *zi* year should marry a girl born in a *zi*, *chou*, *si*, *chen*, or *shen* year; the first month [of these years] occupies the Orphan Position, and the sixth month brings the Six Harms. He should not marry a girl born in a *wu*,

> *mao*, *you*, or *wei* year; the ninth month [of these years] is the Widow's Chamber.
>
> For a female born in a *zi* year, *si* is the auspicious branch for a male. The sixth month brings the Six Harms, the seventh month the Benefiting Husband, and the first month Orphan Obstruction. If her father-in-law is born in a *chou* year or her mother-in-law is born in a *wei* year, the first and second months are the Murdered Husband, and the ninth month is Widowhood.[69]

The sixth entry in the divinatory section of *A Household Necessity*, "Sample Calculation for Decreasing Wealth and Increasing Wealth Based on the Female's Horoscope," opens with a mnemonic verse that links the Five Phases to certain signs of the zodiac. A commentary explains how the poem's concise diction summarizes the principles of this prognostic method:

> The poem says:
>
> Water and fire leave with the goat,
> Wood grows upward, following the hare.
> When metal ascends, the ox is its companion.
> The earthen female travels with the pig.
>
> The above poem looks at the month of birth in the female's horoscope. If the female horoscope is dominated by the water or the fire phase and she was born in the sixth month [with the *wei* branch and hence associated with the goat], then the wealth of the husband's family will increase. This method uses only periods of half a year. If the female is born half a year after the month that brings an increase in wealth, the husband will suffer the contrary fate. Thus, if the female is born in the twelfth month [of a water or fire year], the wealth of the husband's family will decrease. The other lines of the poem work the same way.[70]

Entries seven through twelve concern auspicious days for betrothals and weddings, providing four lists of generic auspicious dates and diagrammatic explanations of the Non-infringement System and "Weddings according to the Round Hall." "Auspicious Days for Requesting Marriage," "Auspicious Days for Sending the Betrothal

Gifts," "The Ten Completely and Greatly Auspicious Days for Weddings," and "Secondary Auspicious Days for Weddings" (entries seven, eight, ten, and eleven) offer from eight to eleven generic cyclical dates, with a few dates recurring for different ceremonies.[71] Of the "Ten Completely and Greatly Auspicious Days" (*bingzi*, *jimao*, *gengyin*, *xinmao*, *renyin*, *guimao*, *renzi*, *jiayin*, *yimao*, and *wuwu*), five coincide with dates in the second group of auspicious dates identified in the Dunhuang calendars, above, and one with a date in the first Dunhuang group. Of the eight "Secondary Auspicious Days for Weddings" (*jichou*, *gengyin*, *bingchen*, *guisi*, *renwu*, *yiwei*, *xinyou*, and *xinhai*), two coincide with dates in the first Dunhuang group, and one with a date in the second group. Three of the eighteen wedding dates in *A Household Necessity*, however, are never once auspicious in the Dunhuang calendars (namely, *yichou*, *bingchen*, and *xinyou*), suggesting a measure of historical change.

The explanation of the Non-infringement System (the ninth entry) paraphrases *Composite Essentials of the Three Calendrical Systems* and cites another, unknown work on the mantic importance of the method:

> The *Zong'e* says: "Infringement upon yin results in the death of the female. Infringement upon yang leads to the death of the male. Only when there is no infringement upon yin or yang does great auspiciousness result." And *Composite Essentials* remarks: "If a prospective wedding date is not a Non-infringement day, one cannot use it, even if it should have auspicious stars such as Celestial Virtue or Lunar Virtue."[72]

In the final two entries of this divinatory section, the numinous sites of the groom's household determine auspicious times and spaces for the wedding day. The first of these, "Weddings according to the Round Hall" (*zhoutang jiaqu*; see fig. 3.3), presents the four central persons and the four central sites of wedding ritual in a circle: the groom, the bride, the kitchen, the stove, the residence, the groom's father, the ancestral hall, and the groom's mother. To determine whether a chosen day is auspicious, one counts off its number around the circle, counting clockwise from the groom in long months and counterclockwise from the bride in short months. Days that correspond to the kitchen, the stove, the residence, or the ancestral hall are greatly auspicious.[73]

**FIGURE 3.3. Weddings according to the Round Hall.**

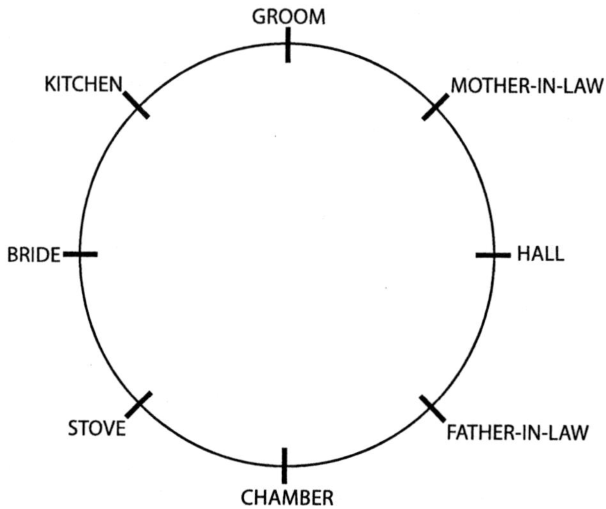


TABLE 3.1
The Celestial Dog

| | *head* | *tail* | *back* | *belly* | *front paws* | *hind paws* |
|---|---|---|---|---|---|---|
| spring | you | mao | zi | wu | wu | chen |
| summer | wu | zi | you | mao | wei | chou |
| autumn | mao | you | wu | zi | chen + wei | chou + you |
| winter | zi | wu | mao | you | chou + hai | wei + shen |

The final entry, "Taboo on Treading on the Directions of the Celestial Dog at Entering the Gate," lays out in a table the positions of the head, tail, back, belly, and front and hind paws of the Celestial Dog, a baleful star, as they shift during the four seasons (see table 3.1). The head, tail, back, and belly correspond to perpendicular directions, as of a dog lying on its side. The head moves counterclockwise from *you* in spring to *zi* in winter. The positions of the paws vary. The table specifies one position for the front paws and one for the hind paws in spring and summer (one position up from the head and one up from the tail), but gives separate and more divergent positions for left and right paws in autumn and winter. The explanation reads:

> Whenever a bride enters the gate [of the groom's compound] she should enter from the back, the paws, or the belly of the Celestial Dog. In this manner she will soon conceive a son, and all is auspicious. Under no condition can she tread on the Celestial Dog's head or tail, or the head of the household will be killed, her husband will come to harm, and her parents-in-law will remain without an heir for the rest of their lives. Nor can she step on the directions that correspond to the horoscopes of the husband or the wife, the Year Star, the branch of the month of the wedding, or the Official's Tally. If the bride upon descending from the carriage first bows to the west, [the couple will enjoy] wealth and status; this is very auspicious. When the bride enters the gate, her parents-in-law are seated in the hall. Her feet do not touch the ground, and she faces away from them. Only after the bride has entered the chamber can her parents-in-law descend from the hall and walk around.[74]

The array of materials collected and preserved in the divinatory section of *A Household Necessity* exemplifies both the enduring continuity of the basic elements of cosmological discourse and the overwhelming diversity of their applications. The stems, the branches, the Five Tones, and the zodiac turn clockwise or counterclockwise to combine with the Five Phases, the nine directions, the *liuren* cycle, baleful stars, gates, halls, years, seasons, months, hours. This fragmented evidence of the divination of weddings and betrothals still conveys an impression of the competition among diviners, commercial printers, and the imperial court, vying to sell their authoritative methods to an audience convinced of the mortal dangers inherent in all liminal activity. Yet, the multiple cycles that enable this variety also ensure continuity. Five of the "Ten Completely and Greatly Auspicious Days for Weddings" in the fourteenth-century *Household Necessity* occur in the same capacity in the calendars of ninth- and tenth-century Dunhuang. At least one of the nine sets of auspicious marital horoscopes ("The Eight Correspondences") in *A Household Necessity* is identical in name and contents to one of the eight sets of auspicious marital horoscopes in the almanac attached to the calendar of 877.[75] And the diagram and explanation of "Weddings according to the Round Hall" in *A Household Necessity* differ only slightly from similar diagrams and captions in the 877 calendar and in P2905.[76]

## The Blessings and Dangers of Weddings in Miracle Tales

Miracle tales bear out the promises of prosperity and the warnings of misfortune that accompany the computations in calendars and almanacs. Few of these tales offer examples of the blessings flowing from the effective divination of an auspicious wedding date or of the harm caused by a willful offense to baleful stars.[77] Such fleeting causes of changing fortunes do not provide the solid ground that miracle tales require for their arguments about the supernatural. But a proper match, like a well-sited tomb, exerts a lasting influence over the fortunes of a family, and stories about such matches abound.

Like calendars and almanacs, miracle tales belong to an oral literature of cosmological knowledge and religious practice, and, like calendars and almanacs, their written transmission preserves but a partial, distorted record of that knowledge and that practice. Miracle tales from the late Tang and Song take the form of plain, brief accounts of the strange (*yi* or *guai*).[78] In simple classical language they recount experiences that transcend the everyday—sometimes the author's own experiences, more often those of others—gathered by the author, his friends, and other informants.[79] This translation of a diverse oral literature into a written discourse was not an innocent one. Inscribing stories from divergent traditions and regions into a generic discourse on "the strange," literati rewrote proselytizing accounts of Buddhist monks, Daoist priests, practicing laymen, and devotees of local cults, or refashioned older written collections of miracle tales to suit their own interests. Whether they searched for one universal explanation of supernatural phenomena; or collected divergent tales to argue that no single tradition could claim an all-encompassing truth; or sought to support the ancient view of Heaven as a source of unfailing justice; or subjected truth and falsity to closer scrutiny; or provided light entertainment and conversation matter, literati manipulated oral discourses to accommodate their own interests and their own audience.[80]

In miracle tales, fate determines marriage as it determines man's station at birth, his success or failure in the imperial examinations, the length and distinction of his career, the number of his offspring, and the hour and circumstances of his death. The name or the appearance of his future wife is conveyed through divination, predictions, poems, dreams, physiognomy, or omens.[81] Submission to the fate thus revealed ensures a long, prosperous marriage and a prodigious number of successful sons. Marriage to the wrong spouse results in infertility, divorce, or untimely death.[82] The following story from *Miscellaneous Notes from the Black Box* (*Qingxiang zaji*, 1087), by Wu Chuhou (1053 *jinshi*), illustrates the consequences of both auspicious and inauspicious matches:

> Before Mr. Liu Hua [968–1029] of the Dragon Diagram Hall had passed the examinations he married the eldest daughter of Minister Zhao Huang. When she died at an early age, there were still two younger sisters who had not married. By the time Mr. Liu obtained his degree, Zhao Huang had already passed away, but his widow wanted to provide Liu with another wife, and sent a matchmaker to convey her intentions.
>
> Mr. Liu replied, "If this regards the virtues possessed by King Wu, I dare not accept a marital bond; but if it concerns the continents separated by Emperor Yu, I gladly follow the orders."[83] Apparently Mr. Liu wrote these words because he did not want to marry Seventh Aunt, but much preferred to negotiate about Ninth Aunt. Mistress Zhao chided him, "The saying goes, 'Pancakes are eaten from the top of the pile down.' Since you have only recently passed the examinations, you are not in a position to order other people's daughters at your whim." But Mr. Liu countered, "I should not dare claim a choice but for the cold and thin physiognomy of Seventh Aunt's bones which shows that she is not my match. Ninth Aunt, however, is my true match."
>
> He subsequently married Ninth Aunt, and their marriage produced seven sons, each of whom had a serious disposition, and each of whom rose to high office. Seventh Aunt later married student Guan, who never passed the examinations and remained unemployed, leaving them cold and hungry. In later years, the Liu household supported them for the rest of their lives.[84]

A bride such as Ninth Aunt was said to be "advantageous" (*li*), like a geomantic site, bringing good fortune due to a quality other than intelligence or character. *Talking Matter* describes how two households in the ardently mobile cultural periphery that was Fujian province during the Northern Song meet disparate fates. While the daughters of the Hu household all possess "extreme advantageousness" (*shen li*), as evidenced by the sudden rise of all husbands from obscurity to high office, Lü Jifu harvests nothing but worthless sons-in-law.[85] The *Record of Grace and Virtue* (*Houde lu*, eleventh century) cites a verdict by the humane official Cao Bin (931–999), in which Cao condemns a yamen runner to strokes on the back but postpones the execution of the punishment for one year. Asked for the reason, he explains:

> I learnt that this man has recently married. If I were to subject him to a beating now, the woman's parents-in-law would suspect her of bringing bad luck [*bu li*] and bear a grudge against her. They would whip and scold her day and night until she would barely be able to sustain herself. Now I delay the case without, however, extending a pardon.[86]

In the second marriage of Liu Hua and in the advantageous matches of the Hu sisters, the workings of cosmological forces extend beyond the bond of husband and wife to affect the public life of the protagonists and of their progeny. Fate, similarly, does not realize its objects severally, but establishes firm connections between birth, marriage, examinations, career, and prestige.[87] Successful marital strategy depends on fate, and divination and dreams will bear out the vision of the perspicacious patriarch:

> The Dream of Assistant Magistrate Zheng
>
> In the year 1180, Zheng Jingshi of Putian [Fujian province] followed his fellow townsman Chancellor Chen, Duke of Wei [Chen Junqing, 1113–1186], to Jiankang [present Nanjing]. His son Yue, although only six *sui* [ca. five years] old at the time, already showed eminent promise. Duke Chen invited them to his office and when he saw that this boy indeed possessed extraordinary talent, a strong character, and advanced reading skills, he realized that this was no common vessel. He said to the father, "Some day he will come to my family as a bridegroom." Zheng humbly expressed his gratitude, but paid no further heed.
>
> In 1188, Zheng served in the private secretariat of Commander Xiang. His son, who had come along to assist him, said one day, "Last night I dreamt that I arrived at the compound of Chancellor Chen. A splendid banquet was laid out.

> The women and concubines pulled a girl to the front, lavishly dressed and coiffed. A master of ceremonies pulled down my arms to make me bow. Shortly afterward I woke up. What kind of omen could this be?" His older sister laughed, "Don't get any funny ideas! Just you concentrate on your studies. Once you have a degree and an official post, some family will take you as a groom."
>
> After another three years [in 1190], when Zheng served as Office Manager at the Accounting Office, the youngest son of the Duke of Wei visited Zheng and announced, "Burdened by my wish to carry out the will of the late Duke, I have come with the horoscopic data [*gengjia*] of both my younger sister and a niece in order to attempt a match." When they asked a diviner for advice, the match with the niece turned out to be auspicious. The proper negotiations through a matchmaker had not yet been concluded when, in 1193, Yue passed the examinations at his first try, being only nineteen *sui* old. He was appointed Assistant Magistrate of Jian'an [present Jian'ou, Fujian province] and subsequently married according to his ambitions. The girl's father was Acting Director of the Ministry of Works.[88]

Manifestations of fate bear out the prediction of a farsighted man, who perceives with the naked eye what diviners establish by means of numinous objects and calculations. Hong Mai, the author of this tale, emphasizes the uncommon insight of the Duke of Wei by drawing the reader's attention to the passage of time. Thirteen years pass, the protagonists travel, the Duke dies, but fate runs its inevitable course.

The grinding cycles of destiny revolve relentlessly, and only the small-minded extend a puny hand in an ill-conceived effort to stay them:

> Zhang Han, of Jiangling [in Hubei province], pursued the degree of Presented Scholar. His father's late wife had borne three sons, but Han was a child of his father's second wife, Ms. Dou. Since Ms. Dou's date and hour of birth had not been advantageous to Zhang's father, her family had fabricated an auspicious date by reducing her age by one year and had thus married her off to Mr. Zhang. Soon after the wedding, she went with her husband to pray for an heir at the Temple of the

Three Purities in the Original State Monastery. The prayer reported her reduced age.

After they had borne several sons, Han's father passed away. Around that time, a fire caused heavy damage at the Original State Monastery. Ms. Dou secretly gave one of the Daoist priests five hundred thousand cash for the restoration of its halls. Not long after, Ms. Dou also died.

Several years later, Han was suddenly possessed by a deity. Holding his topknot he bowed and said, "Hark these sacred words: Ms. Dou has insulted the highest among immortals by reporting a false year of birth. Moreover, she has illicitly used family assets without consulting her sons. These matters have been subject to investigation in the offices of the underworld and have now been reported through this divine manifestation."

Both these matters had been conducted in secret, more than once, unknown to anyone. Now everyone in Jiangling heard about it. Alas! To change the age of a girl in order to contract a profitable marriage may be a small transgression, but to report this falsified age to the gods is a grave crime. The appropriation of family funds for the construction of sacred buildings, without the knowledge of one's sons, inflames even greater wrath in the gods. And it defeats its purpose![89]

## The Vulnerable and Dangerous Body of the Bride in Miracle Tales and Medical Texts

Miracle tales do not only substantiate the blessings of well-matched horoscopes that almanacs and calendars promise, but they explicate the grim dangers that descend upon the vulnerable hour of the wedding. On the wedding day, the bride becomes the epitome of yin, at once vulnerable to evil forces and dangerous to the groom's family and its deities. Suspended between households, between adolescence and womanhood, between virginity and defloration, the bride is carried through the openings in time that are the auspicious days and hours, and through the openings in space that are the safe gates and doorways, veiled and swathed both to shield her orifices from baleful penetration and to protect her new household and its benevolent gods from her harmful emanations:

> In recent wedding ritual, prior to receiving the bride, the groom's family fills its mortar with three bushels of grain, covers its well with a mat, blocks its windows with three pounds of male nettle-hemp, and places three arrows above its door. After the bride has boarded the carriage, the groom rides around it three times on his horse. . . . When the bride is about to step into the carriage, she covers her face with a kneepad. As she enters the gate, everyone in the groom's household, from the parents-in-law downward, leave through the informal gate and re-enter through the main gate, supposedly "to tread in the bride's footsteps." Also: when the bride enters the gate, she first bows to the pigsty and to the stove. When the groom and the bride bow to one another during the wedding, sometimes they wear a mirror suspended from a cord.[90]

Despite its distortion of the meaningful coherence of contemporary practices, this disdainfully disjointed list in Duan Chengshi's (d. 863) *Variegated Banquet from the Youyang Mountain Library* (*Youyang zazu*) preserves rare evidence of ceremonies that presume a fear of penetration and permeability on the wedding day. The rites focus on vital pregnable sites (the mortar, the well, the windows, the door, the stove), protecting them with yang objects (grain, nettle-hemp, and arrows) in the yang number of three. A kneepad and a mirror protect the bride. Since the taboos of ritual practice implied in such scattered passages have carried over into writing, a deductive combination of miracle tales, medical texts, and an occasional custumal can only suggest the unmentionable sources of ritual fear: the penetrability of the bride's body, and the polluting blood of defloration.[91]

No strict line divided medicine from the pursuit of immortality or doctors from diviners in the late Tang, Song, or Yuan, and medical texts of that era display the traces of this "medical pluralism and eclecticism."[92] Doctors, diviners, literati, and the imperial court published medical manuals that legitimized their enterprise by a wide array of citations from ancient texts and Daoist hagiographies. Yet, from clinical collections of prescriptions to alchemical tracts on the preservation of the life force, medical texts share the assumption that the human body is a microcosm whose health depends on the unobstructed circulation of balanced fluids and forces. Discursive continuity in Song and Yuan manuals is further enhanced by their preponderant reliance on Sun Simiao's (ca. 581–682) *Methods Worth a Thousand Pieces of Gold*

(*Qian jin fang*, 652) and *Additional Methods Worth a Thousand Pieces of Gold* (*Qian jin yi fang*, ca. 682), whose treatises and prescriptions they quote at length.[93] The vital matter of their contents allows medical texts to discuss body parts, processes, and substances that are subject to strict taboos in other genres of writing. Although medical manuals inscribe their bodies with gendered and reproductive ideologies, their bodies are real, universal (sometimes individual), and classless.

Blood defines the female body, just as energy (*qi*) defines the male body, but unlike the strong, ordering force of yang that favors man, the yin substance that is blood causes the mental and physical health of woman to be precarious.[94] The dominance of blood asserts itself in the fourteenth year of a woman's life with her first menstruation, and from that moment her diseases become "ten times more difficult to cure" than those of men.[95] Virulent desires and emotions compound the prevalence of fluids to render the female body both vulnerable to illness and resistant to treatment.[96] Nuns, widows, and virgins suffer most severely from these weaknesses, since their unwholesome fluids and unheeded desires collect in dark, clogging pools that are never drained.[97] Whereas sexual abstinence contributes to man's longevity by containing his vital force, sexual deprivation leads to deficient health in women, who depend on borrowed yang for the healthy circulation of their blood and for resistance against polluting substances and possession by spirits.[98] "Truly, yin collects abundantly in woman."[99]

Demons, spirits, and deities of all varieties invade the receptive female body in miracle tales. Men seduced by fox spirits and other female demons are depleted of their semen at repeated visits, sometimes leading to their death. The demonic possession of the female mind and body differs from such momentary delusions by beguiling beings. Although in miracle tales any woman may fall victim to possession by a powerful evil spirit, especially when weakened by ill health or lascivious thoughts, adolescent virgins appear particularly vulnerable to incubuses.[100] Stories about such cases frequently note that the girl had reached puberty (*jiji*, had attained the age of the pinning ceremony), but that she had not yet married or was about to be married. Gods and demons take possession of these yin bodies through the vagina and the uterus, such as the "toad the size of a bowl" that a shaman finds lodged in the vagina of a possessed girl.[101] When incubation results in pregnancy, the womb proves an accommodative reproductive space that may produce tree roots, cubs, or other inhuman births.[102]

The numinous, liminal time of weddings exposes the young bride to a multitude of deities and spirits, and danger of possession looms darkly during that uncertain time, in the unfamiliar spaces of her new household:

The Spirit of Leqiao

> The daughter of a family of Leqiao, Pingjiang county, was harassed by a spirit during the nights after her wedding. Her mother, gravely concerned, decided to share her daughter's bed in order to investigate the matter. Immediately after sunset, a man jumped out from the floor, two topknots of beautiful red gauze hanging down his back. He emerged with the deafening sound of a thunderclap, and the ground closed beneath him. This happened several nights in a row. When they told the husband, he started digging a pit in the floor and at a mere two feet below the surface found a bronze bell with red cords attached. Only then did he remember that he had buried this bell during a strictly enforced copper embargo that the imperial court had promulgated many years ago. In time he had forgotten about the bell. He instantly smashed it and threw away the pieces. The girl's illness was thereby cured.[103]

The yin forces emanating from the bride's body attract evil spirits and offend benevolent deities, but her amassed blood, spilled in the nuptial bed, possesses an especial, unspeakable power. However important the first menstruation in women's medicine, it is defloration that establishes the crucial medical distinction between girl/virgin (*shinü*) and adult woman/sexually active woman (*furen*). The putrid stains of virginal blood that mark this social and biological transition add to the ordinary pollution of sexual intercourse and possess the traumatic contamination of childbirth.

*Nurturing Health, Arranged by Category* (*Yangsheng leizuan*), citing the *Record of the Infinitesimal* (*Suosui lu*), establishes the connection between weddings and the pollution of sexual intercourse:

> Bedroom activities are taboo on the cyclical days *jiazi* and *gengshen*, and on one's own birthday. Transgression of these taboos reduces one's life span by two years. Intercourse on the day of a new moon reduces the life span by a dozen years. The day of a full moon: minus ten years. The two foundational

> days: minus five years. The first day of the four seasons, the vernal and autumnal equinoxes, the summer and winter solstices, and the day of sacrifice to the Earth God: minus four years each. The third and fourth *geng* days after the summer solstice, the first *geng* day after the beginning of autumn, and a solar eclipse: minus one year. On these days and hours a special taboo is also in force for wedding ritual.[104]

Apart from the clinical entries on "wedding pain" (*jiatong*), a term for postdefloration pains and bleeding, medical texts do not discuss virginal blood.[105] They do, however, provide elaborate, diagrammed discussions of the pollution and dangers of childbirth. Like the blood of defloration, the polluting blood of childbirth flows in a ritualized domestic setting, with complex associations of life, reproduction, and death.

> A woman in labor is polluted [*hui'e*], but neither when the contractions of childbirth start nor at any time before or after the delivery is it permissible to let her die in her polluted state [*wuhui*]. If family members come to watch, complications will arise. If they arrive after the delivery, they will harm the child.
>
> The month whose number is contrary to the branch [of the year?] is taboo for women giving birth. If a delivery should occur during such a month, the woman should be placed on an oxhide. If she gives birth on the bare ground, do not allow any water, blood, or polluted matter [*e'wu*] to touch the ground, for it will kill people. And the clothes should all be washed in amply filled vessels. These precautions should not be suspended until the taboo month has passed.
>
> If during childbirth one does not use delivery charts to avoid transgressions and offenses, both mother and child will die afterward, and if they do not die, both will fall ill, and many unpleasant things will occur. If, with the aid of the charts, one is able to avoid transgressions and offenses, the mother will avoid all illness and the child will be easy to raise. . . .
>
> Whenever a woman is about to give birth, one should first take off one's regular clothes and cover the top and the front of the stove as densely as possible with baskets. This will facilitate the delivery.[106]

Concern with cosmic time and space connects this passage to the cosmology of weddings in calendars, almanacs, and miracle tales, while the injunction to cover the stove with baskets is reminiscent of the ritual precautions noted by Duan Chengshi. The advice to launder polluted clothes in amply filled vessels, avoiding open bodies of water, ties these medical paragraphs to a miracle tale about the pollution of brides.[107]

The Student from Kuaiji

When Zhang Guobi of Kuaiji studied at the prefectural school, he had a classmate who liked to wander. As a habit, this student would climb over the wall at midnight and climb back in by the fifth watch [3 a.m.–5 a.m.].

One night he returned early, during the first double-hour [11 p.m.–1 a.m.], because he had to participate in sacrifices the next day. Half-way, he heard a sweeping sound and hid in an alley overhung by eaves. He saw four men dressed in tight purple garments, their heads turbaned and their feet wound in cloth. They carried red lanterns. Between them they held a woman, dressed in red, headless, mounted on a horse. The student was frightened out of his wits. He waited for them to disappear, but they seemed to follow the same road as he. When they had arrived at the plain in front of the school, they entered an overgrown garden, several dozens of yards diagonally across from the school. There, the men with the candles formed a square in whose center the woman performed a kind of mourning dance. After a long time they vanished.

When the student returned to the school and told his housemates, none would believe him. The next morning he visited the garden, where he found a large well. He asked the gardener whether there was anything unusual about it. The gardener replied, "Several days ago, the daughter of some folks in the outskirts of town got married. On the way back to her mother's house, she washed her clothes at this well. Then she suddenly suffocated and lost consciousness, and she had to be carried back to the groom's house. They called a shaman to put things back in order. He said that the bride had offended the body of a girl that lay in the well and had done harm to her ghost. On a sheet of paper he drew four men in purple

> clothes, with lanterns, and he cut out a dress from dry red paper. Then he prepared wine and rice, and burnt it as a sacrifice to them. I heard that the girl recovered when the whole thing ended, after the third watch [11 p.m.–1 a.m.] last night." When the student asked where the girl's family lived, the gardener said she was from Huilan Bridge—exactly in the direction from which the student had come.[108]

Like the copper bell buried during an obsolete copper embargo, the body in the well had faded from memory, until the polluted bridal garb touched the water in the well and stirred its wronged ghost.

The vulnerability of the bride to demonic possession explains the efforts in calendars and almanacs to calculate days and hours when baleful stars and deities are few, and to determine directions whence the bride may safely enter the groom's compound. This vulnerability fails to explain, however, the danger that the bride presents to her environment. Only the fragmentary evidence of the horrid pollution of amassed virginal blood suggests why an unseen, unseeing bride is carried past a covered well and blinded windows in *Variegated Banquet from the Youyang Mountain Library*, or lifted from the ground and borne past her parents-in-law, her face invisible, in *A Household Necessity*.

## Conclusion

The argument about the pollution of virginal blood, formulated in the final section of this chapter, depends on the coherence of cosmological discourse demonstrated in the pages that precede it. Above calendars, almanacs, miracle tales, and medical texts revolve the same cosmic cycles, exerting their amoral influence over the same liminal spaces, times, and actions. These cosmic cycles become manifest on the tables of diviners and on the written page, through numinous objects and cosmological graphs, prognosticated in a shared vocabulary of stems and branches and tones and phases. In this discourse, their common liminality associates betrothals and weddings not only with childbirth and burial, but with travel, commercial transactions, and the construction of houses and tombs. By their sudden transformation of social relations and social space, and by their transgression of social and physical boundaries, the bride's entrance into the groom's compound and the consummation that inaugurates her into the reproductive life of adulthood tear asunder the continuity of cosmic time and space, and thereby invite the influences of stars and deities. The coherence of cosmological discourse allows reference to delivery charts for a better understanding of the lethal dangers of weddings.

Not the remove between the practice of the text and the practice of ritual requires this more episodic argument (proceeding by connected patches of translation rather than by a strong causal narrative), but a remove within the practice of the text itself, between writing and transmission. The exegetical discourse laid out in the first chapter, and the literary discourse discussed in the second chapter, are both eminently written discourses. Although the authors of ritual manuals envisioned the re-embodiment of ancient ritual in the present, and although the authors of engagement letters harbored worldly designs on fame and fortune, all inscribed themselves into solid textual traditions wherein, moreover, writing and text achieved the status of ritual performance. The victory of ancient-style prose over parallel prose in late imperial times, ensured the careful preservation of its literary achievements through the continuous reprinting of its founding texts, while reducing the legacy of four-six prose. The loss of collections of refined social correspondence, however, does not compare to the obliteration of the tens of thousands of calendars, manuals, tracts, and pamphlets that competitive printers once offered for sale on the bustling markets of the Tang and Song empires. And these printed materials, in turn, set forth only a modest share of the innumerable divinatory technologies transmitted in a sprawling culture of practice, oral texts, and ephemeral manuscripts.

The limited role of text and writing in cosmological discourse should not be mistaken for a sign that this was a "popular" discourse. Rather, from the Astronomical Bureau at the imperial court down to the diviners' stalls at the village market, professional experts and lay practitioners contested with one another the efficacy and authority of an array of divinatory technologies that in their endless variety all drew on a limited number of shared cosmological assumptions. The calendars prepared by court astronomers sustained the imperial monopoly on time. Literati examined divinatory systems for traces of the all-penetrating mathematical and cosmological knowledge of the ancients. Professional doctors and diviners asserted a unique insight into the flows of energy through the human body and into the workings of fate. The designation of such disparate claims as "popular" ignores important distinctions in both the contents and the context of surviving cosmological texts. Indeed, current knowledge of this discourse relies disproportionately on almanacs and medical texts compiled and printed at the imperial court, and on divinatory manuals included in expensive, illustrated compendia. Many such texts consciously inscribe divinatory and medical knowledge into a textual environment of authoritative quotations from ancient masters and canonical texts, which places them at a remove from the realm of unlettered popular practice.

The identification of all forms of divination as traces of popular practice would, once more, reproduce and endorse the rhetorical categories of proponents of the Learning of the Way and other archaist scholars who denounced as uncanonical or vulgar any reading or practice that did not conform to their narrow construction of ancient texts. Those denunciations are misleading, not only because divination was practiced in all reaches of Middle-Period society, but also because the canonical claims of cosmological treatises and medical handbooks have indisputable merit. Just as exegetical analysis of the wedding ceremonies in Tang ritual manuals in the first chapter reveals a legitimate hermeneutics of canonical wedding choreography discarded by Sima Guang and Zhu Xi, and just as literary analysis in the second chapter identifies wedding correspondence and addresses as part of a dominant practice among the literati elite of the twelfth and thirteenth centuries, maligned and forgotten in later centuries, so a serious consideration of the canonical claims in divinatory manuals and medical texts restores configurations and readings of the canon that later generations did not recognize.

In the first decades of the twentieth century an early generation of European sinologists proposed a fundamental reinvestigation of canonical texts, circumventing the received wisdom of Han, Song, and Qing commentators in search of a new antiquity. In his pioneering work, Marcel Granet asserted that traditional scholarship had purified ancient myths, beginning in the Zhou and Han dynasties but perpetuated by literati throughout imperial times. By sifting, rewriting, and misrecognizing ancient beliefs and practices, Granet argued, traditional scholars had fashioned ancient narrative myths into history.[109] In the *Book of Songs*, Granet perceived a cosmology that integrated sexual activity into a regulated universe, and he discerned, in the textual traces of ancient mating dances and wedding rituals, attempts at mitigating the dangers of sexual intercourse.[110] Bernard Karlgren saw fertility and fecundity as central concerns in ancient ritual. He recognized phallic symbols in ritual objects (such as ancestral tablets) and in the written signs for important ritual concepts.[111] According to Robert van Gulik, Song scholars consistently misread references to sexual techniques, numerology, and pollution in ancient texts.[112] During the second half of the twentieth century, however, when the products of the wealthy American area studies came to dominate the field of Chinese history (a field of study in fact invented at that time), the valuable insights of these early sinologists were forgotten, and the traditional reified notions of the canon were safely reinstated for several decades.

The canon as constituted by Song scholars, however, still includes passages more reminiscent of the wedding ceremonies in almanacs than of the rites devised by Sima Guang and Zhu Xi. The chapter "Monthly Injunctions" (*Yueling*) in the *Record of Ritual*, for example, marks the second month as taboo for sexual intercourse because children conceived during its frequent thunderstorms would suffer birth defects.[113] The *Record of Ritual* also expounds on numerological convictions that regulate sexual intercourse in the women's quarters of the aristocracy and the royal court.[114] The chapter "The Meaning of Weddings" departs in its final section from a close exposition on wedding ritual to address the cosmological patterns that determine intercourse in the royal bed, as if to argue that wedding ritual creates a privileged cosmic site that bestows on the groom and the bride a ritual responsibility habitually carried by the king and the queen.[115]

When scholarly diviners cite canonical precedents for their practices, they do not, therefore, couch a contemporary popular discourse in an inappropriate, prestigious language. Rather, they formulate a substantial claim to a remote ancestry, legitimated by a hermeneutics that Song and Qing literati have taught modern scholars to misrecognize and to dismiss. The cosmological interpretation of the canonical ages for marriage (thirty for males, twenty for females) as absolute numbers and the insistence on the divination of the wedding date offer examples of legitimate exegetical decisions that rival those of Sima Guang, who takes the canonical ages of marriage as upper limits, and Zhu Xi, who excised divination from his wedding sequence. Liu Xun (1240–1319), among others, explains how the twelve branches, the sexagenary cycle, and the Five Phases each suggest the age of thirty for males and the age of twenty for females as the most favorable for conception. In the cycle of the twelve branches, he states, creation starts at *zi*. After yang has moved thirty places clockwise and yin has traveled twenty places counterclockwise, representing male and female genital development, both are ready for reproduction at *si*. After the ten-month gestation period, the male stands at *yin*, or "three yang," and the female at *shen*, or "three yin."[116] Diviners who based their calculations of wedding dates on the *Book of Changes* certainly held a firmer claim to canonical precedent than Zhu Xi did when he deleted divination from his wedding rites.[117]

This is not to argue that cosmological discourse did not encompass vast ranges of popular practice, but it is to illustrate that due to imperfect inscription and selective transmission the realm of popular practice can be inferred only from sporadic anecdotes, from fortuitous fragments found at Turfan and Dunhuang, and, most important, from the broadly shared cosmological assumptions and divinatory practices that establish such firm links between all surviving instantiations of this discourse.

The calculation of the blessings of betrothals and the dangers of weddings provided one occasion for the fevered competition in this shared discourse. Imperial calendars and commercial almanacs, diviners and go-betweens, exorcists and geomancers all vied to offer auspicious stretches of time and safe tracts of space to families engaged in marital negotiations. The discontinuous time and space of these cosmological calculations, and their horoscoped bodies, are therefore the time, space, and bodies of wedding ritual. But if the very few extant texts preserve only a feeble trace of the remarkable variety of divinatory technologies for weddings, they preserve even less of the wedding ceremonies they superscribe. The exorcist rituals and veiled brides glimpsed in these fragments remain dim blurs, faintly discernable across the distance between text and ritual practice. In the next chapter, a culture of regional wedding practices remains at a tantalizing distance as the remove between the practice of the text and the practice of ritual increases further.

# Chapter Four

## Legal Codes, Verdicts, and Contracts

### Universal Order and Local Practice

When the Ruler of man establishes the laws, he promulgates what he has received from Heaven. He who knows to serve the Ruler, knows to serve Heaven. In honoring the Ruler and in honoring Heaven, he cannot but honor the laws.

—Ouyang Xuan (1283–1357)[1]

The great majority of the farmers in the fields and villages have never set a foot inside the court of a Prefect or a Magistrate, or set an eye on the face of a clerk. Their tongues are ill-trained in argument and their hands are unaccustomed to the brush.

—Hu Ying (1232 *jinshi*)[2]

In 650, Emperor Gaozong (r. 649–683) ordered Zhangsun Wuji and other high officials to edit all the numerous legal materials promulgated under the previous two reigns and to excise from these materials everything that caused unnecessary complication. Emperor Gaozu (r. 618–626) had attempted, in 624, to "restore the codes that have lapsed for a thousand years and to redress the harmful legacy of a hundred kings."[3] He enacted a revision of the lenient *Sui Code* (*Suilü*) compiled under Emperor Wendi (r. 581–604) of the Sui dynasty. Emperor Taizong (r. 626–649), however, deemed the laws he received still too severe. He reduced the number of crimes subject to the death penalty and abolished mutilation as too cruel a punishment. The code handed down during his reign, comprising five hundred articles in twelve fascicles, greatly diminished the penal measure of Sui-dynasty laws: "Countless were the complications cut, the harms eliminated, and the severe penalties reduced."[4] A compendium of 1,590 ordinances in thirty fascicles and a compilation of seven hundred regulations in eighteen fascicles followed the promulgation of this compact code, as well as edicts about matters such as ritual limitations to the death penalty, the administration of pardons, and the standard sizes and weights of cangues, manacles, clamps, locks, and the heavy and the light rod. It was this archive that Emperor Gaozong commanded to be ordered. The efforts of Zhangsun Wuji and his assistants resulted in the *Annotated Tang Code* (*Tanglü shuyi*), in thirty fascicles, promulgated in 653.[5]

The *Annotated Tang Code* devised a transparent hierarchical structure in which official rank, degree of kinship, and age determined the rights and obligations of all imperial subjects. Transgression of these rights and neglect of these obligations warranted punishment in proportion to the crime, reckoned by "the five punishments" (*wuxing*) in their twenty careful gradations: blows with the light rod (ten, twenty, thirty, forty, or fifty strokes), blows with the heavy rod (sixty, seventy, eighty, ninety, or one hundred strokes), penal servitude (one, one and a half, two, two and a half, or three years), exile (1,000, 1,250, or 1,500 kilometers), and the death penalty (strangulation or decapitation).[6] A system of deliberations, petitions, reductions, and commutations allowed those of privileged rank and those of proven virtue or accomplishment to obtain lesser punishment or to convert physical pain and deprivation into a fine.[7] The Ten Abominations (*shi'e*) alone, forbade recourse to this system, being outrages against the cosmic order: rebellion, destruction of imperial temples and palaces, treason, battery and murder of close kin, violation of the Way (multiple homicide, mutilation, sorcery), sacrilege (destruction of sacred objects, forgery or violation of imperial insignia), unfiliality (crimes against close kin), unkindness (crimes against removed kin), insubordination (crimes against superiors), and inner disorder (fornication with close kin).[8]

During the years following the promulgation of this code, several officials had occasion to remind Gaozong of the immutability of this representation of universal order, among them Di Renjie (607–700):

> Your Majesty has made the laws and suspended them from the imperial watchtowers [i.e., made them public]. Penal servitude, exile, and the death penalty each have their ranked gradations. How can there be a crime without its appropriate punishment,

> meriting an especial grant of the death penalty? If the law is not constant, the realm "loses its hold and footing."[9]

But Gaozong himself, too, insisted on the completeness and transparency of the imperial laws. When, in 677, he received a copy of Zhao Renben's *Legal Precedents* (*Fali*), a brief manual composed to aid officials in reaching verdicts, he found it unsatisfactory. Praised abroad for its fairness, the work appeared to Gaozong confusing since it interfered with the comprehension he and his predecessors had achieved:

> The laws, ordinances, regulations, and specifications provide the common standard for the realm. Not I, incompetent, forged this structure. During the Wude reign period [618–626] and in the Zhenguan years [627–649], imperial intentions were identified, debated in extensive detail, and offered up in complete articles and paragraphs. Together they form a luminous track that will prove inexhaustible to all who proceed by it as every case requires. What need can there be for records of precedents? They will only cause confusion by tangling the thread.[10]

Although Gaozong's successors supplemented this code with a continuous flow of edicts, and although subsequent dynasties promulgated their own legal codes, the *Annotated Tang Code* provided an enduring legal structure, its laws emended but its categories unchanged.[11] The emperor's word was law and "all officially enacted law . . . derived its force from the emperor, even if it had not been handed down directly by him."[12] The decrees dispensed in the routine course of government therefore amended the legal code and required regular compilation into ordered volumes that apprised officials throughout the realm of the law that was "the latest relevant expression of the imperial will."[13] Such amendments, however, concerned crimes not yet codified or details of punishment, and did not alter the fundamental structure laid down by Taizong and Gaozong.[14] Even if certain laws in the *Annotated Tang Code* had become outdated, its plain text, unencumbered by detailed modifications, afforded a clear view of a timeless, sacred legal order. As Liu Yun wrote in his preface to a 1327 reprint of the Tang code:

> That the current version of the code counts thirty fascicles [instead of the twelve promulgated by Taizong] proves that its contents had already accrued by the time Zhangsun composed

> his commentary—even though he began his commentary in 650, when the Zhenguan reign had only just ended. The ordinances enacted, the regulations trimmed, the specifications compiled in the years since have reduced and enhanced the code according to the needs of the times. Yet these stipulations have no merit, for they derive almost without exception from the laws.
>
> Therefore, although the laws were established in the Tang, they possess a quality that penetrates and exhausts the unstable configurations of human circumstances and legal principles, and that quality has not perished with the Tang. The present dynastic house has firmly established the cosmic patterns. It has attained to virtue and treads the Way. When compared to recent eras, its structure most resembles that of the Tang. . . . This reliance on the Tang is inevitable, since the Tang fathomed the Way and found its middle course. Any addition will overstep it; any subtraction will come short of it; "and both will be equally amiss." Indeed! The code of the legal specialists resembles the scriptures of the classicists. The Five Scriptures instantiate the Way to extend it to a myriad generations; the twelve categories of the code set forth the law to rectify the people's hearts.[15]

Although created in recent times by fallible men, imperial law conformed to heavenly patterns and therefore matched the timeless truth of the ancient scriptures. It had attained the mean, that metaphoric center through which run the straight, upright lines of morality and justice: "At the mean lies indeed the most perfect virtue. That it is but rarely found among the common people is a fact long admitted."[16] Just as the scriptures allowed the scholar to recover the Way of the ancients and to embody their moral rectitude, so the "luminous track" of imperial law allowed officials to attain universal justice and thereby protect the centered hierarchy that reached down from the imperial temple to the ancestral altars of filial subjects.

Through hereditary privilege, recommendation, and layered examinations, the emperors of the Tang and Song dynasties recruited officials capable of interpreting the imperial will. Their descent from meritorious officials, the recognition of their talents and virtue by trusted members of the imperium, or the command of canon and composition they displayed in the examination halls, ensured that the selected men possessed the ability to speak in the emperor's voice and to perform the rituals of local government as extensions of the imperial body. They were vessels, clad in imperial robes, infused with the impartiality of imperial government, and placed in the ritualized seats of government and on the altars of Soil and Grain throughout the empire. On these men the imperial court relied to uphold the universal distinctions codified in its laws.[17]

Handbooks for local government printed between the eleventh and fourteenth centuries, advise the inexperienced Magistrate that he may attain peace and justice by contemplating the source of universal order: "He should embody the heart-mind of Heaven and Earth in their creation of the ten thousand beings."[18] Through industry, the official may become impartial, upright, pure, transparent, effacing all traces of personal dispositions.[19]

Frugality Breeds Honesty

> . . . Truly, when a man of extravagant habits one morning finds himself destitute, he will not bear it. His mind will turn to secrecy and theft. Cunning clerks will aid him in covering up his intentions and then plot their own schemes. And one day everything will come out. Such a man will lose his position and blemish his private person [*shen*: body]. Regret will come too late. Therefore, the best way to breed honesty is to calculate incoming funds and to be frugal in spending. Even if one passes the days in bland thrift, dressed in coarse clothes and nourished with simple food, one's actions, at least, will not be encumbered by shame. When one is at rest, one is at peace. When one moves, everything follows one's pace. One's mind achieves utter calm. Surely there is joy in this, too?[20]

The official's private person should remain unimpeachable, even if he should err in his public office: "Public crimes are inevitable; private crimes are inexcusable."[21]

Just as private desires should not soil the official's public robes, so the official residence should remain impregnable. The Magistrate should maintain his impartiality by being impervious to the words of lesser men and protect his reputation by avoiding their company. For the same reasons he should scrutinize all who seek to enter his compound. He should refuse men and women of suspicious trades who could insinuate themselves into his private quarters and there either upset the domestic order or obtain details for malicious rumors about his private circumstances.[22] Similarly, he should refrain from bringing a personal doctor, diviner, monk, priest, personal slaves, or concubines to his post, lest these succumb to the temptation of selling knowledge of his private matters, or plain lies, to the local populace.[23] The forbidding gates should shield his blameless household as the robes of office enfold his sober body.

This severity of bearings and circumstances not only eliminates occasion for embarrassment and disgrace, but it makes the official receptive to truth. Government handbooks as well as casebooks and forensic manuals assert with confidence that impartiality, combined with diligence, will ever reveal the sincerity of plaints and confessions:[24]

> Truly, when probing deception one must sometimes pay attention only to the faces [of the suspects]. At other times one must also pay attention to their words. If there is something irregular about their faces or something different about their words, it must be a case of deception. The only thing one cannot do is to harbor suspicion beforehand. One has to discern something different, something irregular, and only then should one investigate it. . . . This method has never failed.[25]

The violence of torture destroys the subtle traces of this evident yet fragile truth, while anger, inebriation, and the interference of unscrupulous men blind and deafen the official to this truth by distorting his senses:[26]

> To prevent oneself from being deluded in one's perceptions, one should keep the unscrupulous at a distance. The clerks and runners who serve prefectures and counties are egregious in their unscrupulousness. They handle the documents in the office and exert themselves daily in planning crimes and evil deeds so as to confuse the clarity of their superior's perceptions and to abuse their authority in his jurisdiction. . . . Among the senses, the eyes have charge of sight, and the ears have charge of hearing. He who cannot see properly is called undiscerning. He who does not hear accurately is undiscriminating. Therefore, consort with true [*zheng*: straight, upright] men, study with true teachers, contemplate the true Way, and listen to true words. Do not lend your eyes and ears to the unscrupulous, and do not allow them to distort your sight or hearing.[27]

The clerks, with their family ties and selfish interests, belong to local networks of power whose members vie to appropriate imperial resources for private ends. While the clerks embezzle public funds and abuse imperial insignia for schemes of illicit gain, local strongmen tug at the official's robes to divest him of his impartiality and to enfold his corrupt, naked power into the regime of terror they have established by means of money, violence, and litigation: "Evil, perverse commoners earn a living by intimidation and theft, making common cause with the clerks and regarding the official residence as a private household, utterly shameless in their abuses."[28] If the official does not resist their efforts, they will usurp his financial and symbolic resources to bolster their private wealth and power. Tax exemptions will fill the coffers of the rich and increase the burdens of the poor. Public trials will degenerate into one more means at the disposal of the powerful to torture and extort the resourceless. Only discipline and impartiality protect justice against such infractions:

The Rich and Powerful

> . . . If I have failed to discipline myself and have failed to be impartial in my decisions, even a common man may file a suit against me at my first lapse. But if I act with sincerity and respect, and treat all in accordance with ritual, will they, even if they be wealthy and powerful, dare to disrupt my governance? Therefore I advise that although one certainly should not bend and strain to meet the demands of the rich and powerful, neither should one put on airs to distinguish oneself. Be plain in interactions. If by accident one offends someone with a joke in an informal setting, he may still dismiss it as an aberration, since one has achieved a certain reputation.[29]

Empty of desires, sober of habit, the imperial official becomes a ritual vessel—balanced, upright, and receptive to truth. He instantiates the imperial presence at the temple of the City God, at the altar of Soil and Grain, and on the bench of his court of law. His voice and his bearings project the awesome, remote authority of the Son of Heaven as he enforces the transparent stipulations of the imperial code. The official residence represents the imperial center, established as a source of universal order and civilization beyond the capital.[30] There, the official confronts the feuds induced by jealousy and greed, the victims of intimidation and deception, the perversion of local customs, the violence of the periphery.

Verdicts are the written traces of this confrontation between the still imperial center and the disorderly margins. But through the allusive prose of extant verdicts one does not descry a raucous court of law or discern the rustic speech of plaintiffs or defendants. For on the written page, the author of a verdict has arranged the pertinent facts, impressions, and laws into a graceful essay, rendering uncertain colloquial action into meticulous classical prose. This translation of local practices into the universal terms of imperial law distorts regional conceptions of morality and justice, quite often resulting in the condemnation of a plaintiff, or in sentences for a crime unsuspected by either the defendant or the plaintiff. The verdict, in other words, is a trace of legal practice through which local circumstances are only dimly visible.[31]

But even legal practice is remote. If the practice of legal writing places local practice at a remove, the practice of textual transmission has preserved but a small, uneven selection of legal writing from the eighth through the fourteenth century. "A circuit such as Fujian comprises two commanderies, six prefectures, and forty-five counties, administered by a hundred and eighty officials. The number of legal cases amounts to several thousands each year," wrote Chen Xiang in the 1040s, and Hu Taichu (1200–1260) warned that rampant litigation threatened to confine the County Magistrate to his courtroom every single day of his tenure.[32] Yet of the millions of plaints, verdicts, petitions, appeals, memorials, and edicts none survives that was not printed. The earliest extant imperial archive dates to the late Ming dynasty, the earliest extant county archive to the late Qing. Large compilations such as *Collected Data for a Continuation of the Comprehensive Mirror for Aid in Government* (*Xu Zizhi tongjian changbian*, 1183), the digests of imperial documents (*Tang huiyao*, *Song huiyao*), and the dynastic histories, preserve occasional legal texts. The *Annotated Tang Code* and the *Song Penal Code* (*Song xingtong*, 963) survive, but only part of the Yuan code, *Comprehensive Institutions of the Great Yuan* (*Da Yuan tongzhi*, 1323). The incomplete *Classified Laws of the Qingyuan Period* (*Qingyuan tiaofa shilei*, 1202) offers the only example of an imperial supplement to these codes. All extant verdicts were printed as literary models, whether in collected works or in *A Collection of Pure and Lucid Verdicts by Famous Authors* (*Minggong shupan qingmingji*, 1261, 1569), an anthology transmitted in two different editions. From the Yuan survive two legal compendia, *Imperial Canon of the Sacred Governance of the Great Yuan* (*Da Yuan shengzheng guochao dianzhang*, 1317) and its

1322 supplement, as well as twenty-two fascicles of *Comprehensive Institutions of the Great Yuan* and miscellaneous fragments, to suggest important changes in legislation and legal ideology during that period.[33]

The small number of these texts prohibits an understanding of general legal practice, while their incommensurability disallows comparison across time. The transmission of texts, not their composition, determines the historical narrative formed by these intermittent compendia. Middle-Period bibliographies and anecdotal evidence suggest a greater continuity in legal writing than is borne out by present remains. Unrevealing of the daily practice of the law, the legal texts of the Tang, Song, and Yuan preserve attempts at the creation of a universal order, devised by emperors and interpreted by officials.

Weddings, in this discourse, reconfigure boundaries of kinship and therewith alter rights and obligations between persons: rights to property and sexual intercourse, enhanced and reduced punishments for criminal offenses against kin, the status of offspring, and obligations of mourning, burial, and sacrifice. The codes of the Tang and Song define the stages that inaugurate these rights and obligations, as well as the stages by which they become obsolete upon divorce or death. Yuan legal texts, preoccupied with the definition of restrictive ethnic boundaries, interfere with the ritual practice of weddings, by means of ethnic ritual protocols and sumptuary regulations, and prohibitions against customs deemed to deviate from proper ethnic practice. Verdicts from the Southern Song and precedents from the Yuan, prompted by infractions upon these laws, suggest that local practice upheld different definitions of marriage and divorce, informed by divergent understandings of ritual, marriage, and boundaries of kinship. The translation of these cultures of local practice into the categories of written law, however, always already distorts local marital strategies and nuptial customs: the universalist practice of the legal text overwrites local ritual practice.

## MARRIAGE AND THE UNIVERSAL ORDER: THE *ANNOTATED TANG CODE* AND THE *SONG PENAL CODE*

Marriage laws occupy between a half and a third of the "Family and Marriage" (*huhun*) sections of the *Annotated Tang Code* and the *Song Penal Code*.[34] Their precise definitions of the stages of marriage negotiations (*hunyin*) chart the shifts in legal boundaries occasioned by betrothals and weddings, and stipulate the punishments for those who transgress them. The sharp definitions of these changing boundaries were intended in part to contain the endless litigation that attended marriage negotiations in all quarters of the realm.[35] The substance of the marriage laws, however, does not concern the restitution of betrothal sums or the punishment of fraudulent promises, but the continuity of the universal order envisioned by the Tang and Song codes, in which the legal rights and obligations of all subjects are at all times determined.

The betrothal and the wedding divide marriage negotiations into three stages: the period prior to legal engagement (*wei ding*, not yet engaged), the period from the legal engagement to the wedding day ([*yi*] *ding*, [already] engaged, or *wei cheng*, not yet completed), and legal marriage (*yi cheng*, already completed). The submission of a wedding contract by the bride's family to the groom's family or the acceptance by the bride's family of the betrothal sum marks a binding engagement:

> Whoever suddenly reneges on marrying off a female after having returned a wedding contract and having achieved a personal understanding ("understanding" refers to prior information about the age and health of the groom and, if he be adopted or be not a son of a principal wife, about his status) receives sixty blows of the heavy rod. (If the groom's family themselves regret the agreement they are not liable to prosecution, but they forfeit the betrothal sum.) If a written wedding contract is lacking, the acceptance [by the bride's family] of the betrothal sum is considered its equivalent. (There are no upper or lower limits for betrothal sums. Wine and food do not qualify as a betrothal sum, unless it is specified that wine and food are used as betrothal gifts, in which case they are the equivalent of a betrothal sum.)[36]

Although the submission of a contract or the acceptance of the betrothal sum by the bride's family makes the agreement legally enforceable, it does not yet alter the boundaries of kinship. The two families are held to arrange a wedding in due time, but otherwise they remain strangers (*fanren*):[37]

> The ritual scriptures distinguish three stages in their definition of a "husband": the period following the bride's visit to the ancestral temple in the third month of marriage, the period

> prior to the bride's visit to the ancestral temple, and the day of the wedding. This coincides with the legal understanding of a "husband." Those who have selected a prospective groom or an auspicious day for the wedding are only held to observe the contract and are prohibited from marrying the prospective bride to someone else. For all other crimes the two families may perpetrate against one another, they will be tried as strangers.[38]

The wedding (*jiaqu*, *chengqin*) introduces the bride (and to a lesser extent the groom) into new mourning circles, and this change of ritual status bears with it new rights and obligations. The clearest definition of these rights and obligations in the *Annotated Tang Code* and the *Song Penal Code* occurs in contrast to the rights and obligations of concubines and servants. Whereas the rites of the wedding inaugurate the bride into the groom's ancestral cult, concubines and servants remain marginal to this cult, although they may bear children who become part of it.[39] Her membership in her husband's ancestral cult obliges the legal wife to assist in its perpetuation, and obliges her husband and his family to mourn her death, to bury her corpse, and to sacrifice to her ancestral tablet.[40] Marriage also extends rights to property that concubines and servants do not possess.[41] But the wife's obligations to her husband's ancestral cult also involve enhanced punishment for acts by which she threatens its continuity: verbal abuse, battery, and murder of her husband and his family fall under the Ten Abominations and carry higher penalties than the perpetration of these same crimes against the same victims by a stranger. By contrast, a husband who injures his wife (and a wife who injures a concubine or a servant) receives a punishment two degrees lower than would a stranger.[42] The wedding, in other words, introduces the bride into a ritual hierarchy whose intricate patrilineal gradations determine her legal rights and obligations.[43]

The dissolution of a marriage, whether by divorce or by her husband's death, disengages the wife from the mourning circles of her husband's ancestral cult. The preparation of official documents for divorce or the fulfillment of her mourning obligations toward her deceased spouse make her a stranger once more and allow her to remarry.[44] Only one law remains to tie her to her former mourning circles, demanding particular punishment for the murder of a parent or grandparent of her former husband.[45]

The reconfiguration of mourning circles by marriage is contingent upon the observation of more encompassing boundaries of ritual obligation, kinship, class, and law that circumscribe imperial subjects. Transgression of these boundaries, even if unintentional, voids the marriage and warrants immediate separation. Should a man and a woman continue their cohabitation in defiance of the compulsory separation, they are liable to prosecution for fornication, since the unlawfulness of their union has left them strangers.[46] The *Annotated Tang Code* and the *Song Penal Code* condemn as void the elevation of a concubine or servant to the status of a wife; a marriage consummated during a period of mourning for a parent or a husband, or during the incarceration of a parent or a grandparent; a marriage to close kin or to a former wife of close kin, and a marriage between persons of the same surname; a marriage to an escaped convict; a marriage contracted by an official within his jurisdiction; a marriage to a man or woman already betrothed or married, or improperly divorced; a marriage across the rigid social boundaries between officials and commoners, and between commoners and slaves or the dishonorable occupations (unless the commoner willingly and knowingly consents to such a marriage); and a marriage preceded by any form of violence or intimidation by the go-between, the guarantors, or members of either family.[47]

These stipulations constrain marriage by universalist boundaries of ritual and morality that extend the patrilineal hierarchy of the family to the order of the empire, demanding the observance of due ceremony as well as the proper segregation of bodies bound by kinship or separated by hereditary class.[48] The prohibition against marriage between persons of the same surname represents an extreme instance of this androcentric definition of marriage and kinship, but the asymmetrical law against marriage to close kin also excludes a range of patrilineal kin that far exceeds the range of proscribed matrilineal kin.[49] For their enforcement, too, the marriage laws rely on the ritual hierarchy of the family, according more extensive rights but also graver responsibilities to parents and grandparents in the arrangement of marriages. Only they possess the legal authority to remarry a widowed daughter or granddaughter against her will, and only they bear the responsibility for an illegal marriage in which they have acted as a guarantor (*zhuhun*).[50] The inherence of the ritual and legal boundaries of marriage in the very bodies of bigamous grooms and incestuous brides prevents unlawful unions from being eligible for imperial pardon.

Fraud, robbery, and murder may be forgiven, but not the transgression of the boundaries of human relations (*renlun*).[51]

Combining canonical exegesis with the examination of legal precedents, the compilers of the *Annotated Tang Code* and the *Song Penal Code* devised a legal structure that protected the cosmic order of the empire by meting out appropriate punishment for the transgression of eternal, universal, inherent boundaries:

> Where the rites do not provide, there serve the laws; they tend toward leniency, but combat the cruel. A hundred kings improved upon one another by deletions and additions; all within the Four Seas now find herein their spirit-level and plumb-line.[52]

Within this universal order, weddings accord to females their necessary place in an ancestral cult and ensure the proper reproduction of the boundaries of kinship and class. Within the patrilineal hierarchy of the family, the sharp gradations of the mourning circles determine rights to financial support, to property, to the use of violence, and to burial and sacrifice. The insistence on the immediacy of boundaries, however, leaves undefined the rites that inaugurate the change of status of the legal wife. The careful definition of betrothals in the Tang and Song codes contrasts with the generic references to the Six Rites, the wedding day (*jiuhun*), and the bride's visit to the ancestral temple in their definitions of legal husbands and wives. This failure to circumscribe the rites of marriage implies a reliance on established custom that verdicts prove to be unwise.

## UNIVERSAL LAW AND LOCAL PRACTICE: *A COLLECTION OF PURE AND LUCID VERDICTS*

All historical verdicts from the period between the eighth and fourteenth centuries that survive into present times date to the Southern Song, preserved in the 1261 and 1569 editions of *A Collection of Pure and Lucid Verdicts by Famous Authors* and in the collected works of Huang Gan and Liu Kezhuang (1187–1269).[53] During the Tang and the early Northern Song, verdicts (*shupan*) belonged to the genres tested in the imperial examinations, and anthologies and collected works from that period offer exemplary exercises in this form. Although historical cases may have prompted the composition of some of the verdicts in the works of Bai Juyi (772–846) and Yu Jing (1000–1064), in Zhang Zhuo's (675 *jinshi*) *Verdicts Stirring with Dragon Sinews and Phoenix Marrow* (*Longjin fengsui pan*), and in anthologies such as *Splendors from the Garden of Writing* (*Wenyuan yinghua*, 986) and *A Mirror of Contemporary Writing* (*Huangchao wenjian*, twelfth century), most authors introduce their generic protagonists A, B, and C (*jia*, *yi*, *bing*) as abstractions, dislodged from time and space, who commit their infractions in the title, to be subjected to the author's legal reasoning in the hermetic prose of his brilliant essay.[54] If in these verdicts the author seeks to impress his peers with his literary ability, the "ornamental verdicts" (*huapan*) of the Southern Song and Yuan aim to amuse, condensing the summary of a case and the verdict into a pointed, witty poem, replete with recondite allusions:[55]

Judge Huang's Verdict on Ms. Dai's Plaint
against Her Husband

> Examination candidate Wang went to take the Metropolitan Examinations and in the capital married Ms. Dai, promising to take her home as his wife. When they arrived at his house, Dai realized that Wang was already well supplied with a wife and children, and she filed a plaint with the County Magistrate. My ornamental verdict reads,
>
> Ms. Dai of Shanyin lived in sorry poverty,
> But she kindled a new love in Student Wang.
> He merely asked the girl to sign a paper slip,
> Without a scribe or broker to assist her.
> Upon his return he had another change of heart,
> "My lord goes to the clear streams of the Xiang, I to Yue."
> The urge of Student Wang had wasted and he returned,
> His boat now carrying only the moon's bright luster.[56]

Casebooks reduce not defendants and plaintiffs but judges to generic figures. The poised, undaunted officials who solve mystifying cases and pass enlightened sentences in *A Collection of Difficult Cases* (*Yiyu ji*, tenth century), *A Magic Mirror for Solving Cases* (*Zheyu guijian*, twelfth century), and *Parallel Cases from Under the Pear Tree* (*Tangyin bishi*, 1211) have been copied from hagiography and transcribed from legend, to exemplify timeless ideals of law and truth.[57] The unfailing justice of the casebooks and the literary prowess of examination verdicts belonged to an enduring, historical repertoire of legal practice—as their continuous reproduction attests—but a legal practice whose self-referential textuality precludes infringement by a disorderly world.[58]

Huang Gan, Liu Kezhuang, and the authors anthologized in *A Collection of Pure and Lucid Verdicts* attempt in their judgments to reduce the entangled feuds of their jurisdiction to the transparent order of imperial law, but unrepentant litigants, brutal clerks, incompetent and conniving officials, indomitable strongmen, and ignorant commoners driven by vulgar greed intrude everywhere upon the precarious order of the written page. Although collected as examples of admirable legal writing, these verdicts have not been trimmed of the references to attached documents, to earlier verdicts, to unfamiliar circumstances and persons, or other untidy fringes to which still adheres, as it were, the soil of the counties and prefectures of the Southern Song from which these verdicts were gathered. In those counties and in those prefectures, local networks of power and local customs contested the universal authority of imperial law and the moral imperative of the ancient scriptures.[59]

In many of the marital cases, defendants have willfully disobeyed the law, relying on violence and false promises to obtain forcible advantages which they feebly protect in court with lies and contradictory depositions.[60] The impecunious Jiang Baisan (who has sold his betrothed daughter to become a servant), the ambitious Instructor Qiu (who forced his impoverished son-in-law to divorce his daughter when his own fortunes improved), the eager Wei Ruji (who acted as his own guarantor in his marriage to a courtesan), the mendacious Ms. Zhang (who seeks to divorce her husband with the assertion that he is a paraplegic), the lowly Zheng Yingzhen (who dressed up as a scholar to seduce with a false marriage contract a girl of imperial ancestry)—all betray their ill faith by their reliance on deception.[61] In such cases, it remains for the judge "merely to sort out the crooked and the straight," exposing the falsehoods that amply emerge from the evidence and from the defendant's own inconsistencies, "and to identify and impose the relevant law":[62]

A Man Falsely Accuses Others of Seizing His Mother and Abducting His Sister; by Weng Fu [1226 *jinshi*]

In the fifth month of last year, Zhu Qiansan filed a written plaint at the official residence of the county, in which he accused Zhu Qian'er and Zhu Wanwu of seizing his mother, Ms. Sun, of abducting his sister Shouniang, and of being responsible for the death of his father, Zhu Yuanyi, who succumbed to his anger about these acts. The unusual nature of these accusations startled everyone who heard of them. After a year had lapsed, the case was still open.

Now, Xu Nianqi, Zhu Wanwu, Ye Jiyi, and others involved in this matter have been brought to this court, and I have obtained the contract by which Zhu Yuanyi divorced his wife. Examination of this document reveals that Ms. Sun was married off to Zhu Qian'er; she was not seized. Shouniang was married off to Zheng Nianjiu, and subsequently to Zhu Wanwu; she was not abducted. Her father, Zhu Yuanyi, died from spitting blood, not due to any crime committed by Zhu Qian'er or Zhu Wanwu. By the time Zhu Yuanyi died, his wife, Ms. Sun, had already taken up residence in the household of Zhu Shisan [a relative of her husband]. Even when Shouniang married a third time, to Ye Jiyi, Zhu Qiansan did not file a plaint. What basis has he now for bothering the authorities with this evil, fabricated suit?

The contract proves clearly and beyond doubt that Zhu Qiansan's accusations are groundless and false. This cannot be lightly forgiven. The most severe punishment for this crime is penal servitude beyond the prefectural boundaries; the lightest punishment would still require that he be tattooed with circles and incarcerated. Considering that Ms. Sun in her old age has only one son to support her and that prosecution to the full extent of the law would inevitably reduce her to homelessness and starvation, I have no choice but to impose the lighter penalty. Since Zhu Qiansan has been previously tattooed for robbery, I condemn him to a hundred blows of the heavy rod and to the redrawing of his old tattooed circles; he thereby avoids imprisonment. All others go free. Those who have not yet come to court will not be prosecuted.[63]

In other verdicts, however, a rift becomes visible between imperial law and local customs. The townsmen or villagers who have gone to court to seek adjudication in a tenacious disagreement find that the presiding official, citing imperial law, redistributes their property and rearranges their families in ways that defy all claims of the disputing parties. Accepted negotiation practices and established forms of intermarriage prove offensive to the universal norms of law and scripture, resulting in forcible separation and an unfamiliar allocation of rights and obligations. Conversely, the universality of imperial law is compromised by unburied bodies and contested lands which cannot be rightfully assigned to any party, and especially by marital conflicts in which enforcement of the relevant law would lead to battery, suicide, or murder:

> Litigation about marriage negotiations differs from other kinds of suits, since in such cases the disputes and accusations between two families will not be brought to an end overnight. And if one forces them to share the nuptial cup, one merely plants the seeds of disaster.[64]

From judgments in *A Collection of Pure and Lucid Verdicts* it appears that local practice imposed fewer restrictions on matrimonial strategy than did imperial law, an impression that occasional entries in notebooks confirm. The cancellation of the betrothal of a daughter by marrying her off to another family appears to have been common, as does the practice of divorcing a wife by marrying her off to another man. But imperial officials voided such marriages when made aware of them:

> A Wife-giver and a Wife-taker
> Both at Variance with the Law; by Weng Fu
>
> According to the law, "Whoever consents to marrying another man's wife or marries off another man's wife is liable to two years of penal servitude. This law also applies to a husband who marries off his own wife. This voids both marriages."[65] . . . Ye Si was married to Ms. Shao, but he was unable to support her. He himself wrote a divorce contract and a receipt, signed them by tracing the shape of his hand, and married off Ms. Shao to Lü Yuanwu. Lü Yuanwu and his father paid him three hundred strings of cash in official bank notes and owed another two hundred strings in bank notes to the family of Ye Wanliu. After signing the contract and paying the money, he moreover filed a complaint with the authorities [against Ye Si, who had come to regret his divorce]. To allow such a marriage is to allow the whimsical sale of wives. . . .

> In accordance with the law, all three persons are convicted to penal servitude and will be submitted to a hundred blows of the heavy rod in this county. Also in accordance with the law, both marriages are annulled. Neither Ye Si nor Lü Yuanwu has rights to his wife. After Ms. Shao has served her sentence, a broker will be commissioned to marry her off. . . . The illicit money will be confiscated. . . .[66]

Ye Si's contract, Lü Yuanwu's ungrudging commitment of a large sum of money, and especially Lü Yuanwu's confident reliance on the assistance of the Magistrate for the enforcement of the agreement suggest that this divorce and remarriage of Ms. Shao proceeded according to established custom. Only the invitation of official arbitration disrupts the common course by allowing Weng Fu to impose the terms of imperial law. His verdict reconfigures bodies and property by inscribing them in unexpected legal categories. From the very first sentence, the verdict treats not of Ye Si's poverty or his ambivalent divorce, or of Lü Yuanwu's contractual rights, but of bigamy—a severe legal and moral offense.[67]

A few suggestive cases provide insufficient evidence to argue that the legal restrictions against marriage during a mourning period or marriage across social boundaries conflicted with local custom.[68] But strong evidence exists that imperial law prohibited as incestuous marital ties not regarded thus in local practice. Wu Qian'er, for example, married a woman who shared his surname and only later married her off, for fear of prosecution. The judge annuls both marriages, the first because of the shared surname, the second because Wu Qian'er, as a stranger, did not have the right to arrange a second marriage for Ms. Wu.[69] Weng Fu in one verdict voids posthumously a marriage between maternal cousins, although he condones such a marriage elsewhere.[70] In a third verdict, a feud of several years affords Weng Fu the opportunity to dissolve a marriage between a widow and her late husband's brother, abhorrent to him but hardly of concern to the disputing parties:

> The Wife of a Younger Brother Fornicates with
> His Older Brother, Expels His Children,
> and Sells His Property; by Weng Fu
>
> According to the law, "Whoever fornicates with the wife of a relative of the lowest degree of mourning and above is liable to three years of penal servitude."[71]

Yang Zizhi is the older brother of Yang Zicheng. Zicheng married Ms. Shao and had three children with her before he died. If Ms. Shao had been possessed of eminent wifely virtue, she would have been aggrieved at his death and have taken pity on those who survived him, plowing her late husband's fields, sacrificing to him, and raising his orphans. This would have earned her a resplendent reputation for her sense of duty. Even an armed villain could not rob her of such a possession.

But it was not thus. Already during the wake for her deceased husband she began to dally with her brother-in-law, Yang Zizhi. Acting no different from an animal, Zizhi indulged his perversion to the fullest and then swallowed her whole, taking her home to be his wife. Those who heard of it were grieved and enraged by this subversion of natural principle, this ravage of human relations. But this was only the second of their crimes. Their greatest outrage was that, upon the consummation of their incestuous relations, Zizhi and Ms. Shao expelled all of the children she and her husband had raised, and sold illicitly all the land and property she and her husband had acquired. To destroy a man's household, to disperse his children, to cut off his sacrifice—such acts would not be tolerated of a man who had previously followed the Way, much less of Zizhi and Ms. Shao! Horrid crimes of this sort are reported to Heaven!

Their close relative Yang Zida filed a plaint in 1241, now three years ago, but the case was never solved. If the dead are conscious, Yang Zicheng must be writhing in anger below in the Nine Springs. The present plaint submitted by Ms. Lu, the mother of Ms. Shao, finally presents me, as the responsible official, with the opportunity to investigate this matter to the smallest detail. Ms. Lu is not concerned with lending a voice to Zicheng's grievances but apparently has conspired with her daughter to request that the authorities restore the proper meaning to words and divorce her from Zizhi merely because he has squandered everything, to the last coin, leaving Ms. Shao without any support. She abandons her own and thrusts herself upon another for money, but when the money is spent, she rejects once more what she has and casts about for something new—such is Ms. Shao's inhuman calculation.

> All that remains for the authorities is to disentangle this matter according to the best of their abilities. First, the crimes of Zizhi and Ms. Shao must be rectified. Zicheng's infant son must be retrieved from Wang Bingyi and his kin, and returned to his own lineage, so that he may succeed to his father's sacrifice. Of the six plots of Zicheng's land illicitly sold by Zizhi, the plot he gave to his son Shaoseng will remain outside consideration. The other five plots, however, have been traded in defiance of the law, and the original contracts of these mortgages and sales must be retrieved from the middlemen, and destroyed. . . . Yang Zizhi escapes inspection of ill-gained goods, but he will be led under escort to the prefectural boundaries of Chuzhou [Zhejiang province]. After Ms. Shao has suffered her sentence, she will be placed under supervision of Ms. Lu. Lu Zicheng and all others go free.[72]

These paragraphs inscribe the patrilineal family of imperial law into the moral structure of Heaven and the underworld, and into the nature of things. The relations of Yang Zizhi and Ms. Shao transgress these natural boundaries and thereby void the very meaning of words: Yang Zizhi is not a brother, Ms. Shao is not a mother, not a wife. Yet the plaint of Ms. Lu, not filed until four years after the marriage, indicates that Weng Fu's universal boundaries exist only vaguely besides other boundaries that inform local practice. Like Qu Tianyou, who intended to use his knowledge of the impropriety of his niece's marriage to a maternal cousin merely to lay hands on her dowry, Ms. Lu invokes the boundaries of imperial law only to have dissolved a marriage that has become hateful to her for other reasons. The inherent patrilineal structure perceived by Weng Fu exists for Qu Tianyou and Ms. Lu only as a set of rules to which they may turn for the enforcement, by means of manacles and penal servitude, of their selfish advantage.

The strict, inherent boundaries of the patriline that Weng Fu recognizes in the *Song Penal Code* and in the cosmos are extended beyond the law in other verdicts—verdicts that cite the scriptures, not the laws, as their authority. Such verdicts define the patrilineal family by more forbidding lines, notably to impede the remarriage of widows. A redoubtable denunciation of a remarrying widow does not in all cases deprive her of her legal rights:

> There can be no doubt that Ms. Qu, a woman who has changed husbands three times, has severely compromised her chastity.

> But this by no means gives Li Xiaode, who was merely her brother-in-law, the right to determine her fate. If he hates her because she turned her back on his brother, he should have voiced his misgivings about her transgression when she remarried to Li Conglong, and conveyed them to the authorities. Then, his words would have possessed their proper meaning, and his statements would have suited the context. . . . After Li Conglong died, Ms. Qu herself had the right to decide whether she was to remarry or not. What concern was it of Li Xiaode?[73]

But other verdicts defy both law and local practice to enforce the judge's stern moral views. Weng Fu and Huang Gan assert, contrary to law, that "the trousseau and dowry lands brought into a marriage by the wife are a gift from her parents to her husband's family."[74] Hu Ying in three separate verdicts denies a married woman the right to sue her father-in-law for sexual assault, arguing that such plaints subvert the hierarchical relations of the family, especially when the allegations are true, and that this deed of unfiliality always exceeds any wrongdoing by the pater familias.[75] In such verdicts, the general patrilineal structure of the law hardens into a rigid hierarchy that defines not only the rights and obligations, but the speech and movements of its immutable members in the language and detail of the scriptures.

Yet at times the encompassing structure of law and canon fails. The universal boundaries cannot accommodate the endless variety of local practice, and the angry, suffering men and women who appear in court resist the places assigned to them by the *Song Penal Code*. Judges realize that the plaintiff who insists on the marriage of his daughter to a reluctant groom will in the end be ill served by the enforcement of his claim, however firmly supported by the law.[76] Similarly, judges recognize the need to grant a divorce even to those who seek it with false accusations, as the wronged spouse, too, could hardly desire a forcible reunion.[77] In a few verdicts, the judge is forced to seek an expedient solution for a case that exceeds the foresight of the laws. Liu Kezhuang decides to recognize the third of Ms. Wu's three illegal marriages since its annulment would lead to endless litigation about the child she has conceived in her last union.[78] Huang Gan entrusts the corpse and the property of Ms. Zhou, twice divorced and once abandoned, to the family of her first husband who have given her shelter after the cruel abandonment by her third spouse.[79] And a property dispute forces judge Ye Wuzi (fl. thirteenth century) to admit that he does not know whether Ms. Hu Wujie was legally married to the late Weng Tai:

> As far as Hu Wujie is concerned, we need to investigate who originally served as guarantor, who as matchmaker; which valuables constituted the betrothal gift and which valuables were presented in reply; who wrote the wedding contract, and when the rites were completed; which family members gathered at the wedding night, which members of the local community were invited, and whose kitchen was used for the preparation of the banquet and the beverages. If this was indeed a ritual wedding [*lihun*], then Hu Wujie will be allowed the management of the property that Weng Tai had not yet sold off by the time of his death. . . . But if she was never married, it is incumbent upon her parents not to waste any more time in arranging a timely marriage for her.[80]

The disorder of local practice that the legal codes, the examination verdicts, and the casebooks exclude from their hermetic pages (except as remote hypotheses and faceless abstractions), ever impinges upon the feeble written order of the verdict. With the aid of rhetorical and literary devices, Huang Gan, Liu Kezhuang, and the authors anthologized in *A Collection of Pure and Lucid Verdicts* attempt to reduce the greed, the violence, and the disturbing customs they encounter in their courts and prisons to the universal categories of imperial law. Yet in the margins of their angry, moralizing judgments become briefly, dimly visible fathers, widows, husbands, brothers, brides, uncles, whose silent understanding of the rights and obligations of kinship belong to unknown, unwritten cultures of practice.

Literary merit, not legal accomplishment, has protected these few hundred Southern Song verdicts from oblivion. The commercial printers of *A Collection of Pure and Lucid Verdicts* and of the collected works of Huang Gan and Liu Kezhuang, have thereby preserved a more erratic selection of judgments than would have imperial editors concerned with the illustration of legal technicalities. The brief, mute glimpses of local society afforded by these Southern Song verdicts therefore differ from those offered by the precedents collected in the imperial compendia issued by the Yuan court. The gradual regeneration, during that period, of a legal code through ad hoc decisions and a new concern with the regulation of customs bring into view practices not seen in the sources of Tang and Song. The shifting perspective reveals new customs, but local practice remains at the same inscrutable distance.

## INTERFERENCE WITH RITUAL PRACTICE: *IMPERIAL CANON OF SACRED GOVERNANCE* AND *COMPREHENSIVE INSTITUTIONS*

During the years prior to the promulgation of the Yuan dynasty in 1272, the court of Khubilai (r. 1260–1294) anticipated with a protracted series of new laws the abolition of the *Taihe Code* (*Taihe lü*) that the Mongol rulers had adopted in 1234 from the defeated Jin dynasty.[81] This period of intense legal deliberation yielded a mere outline, however, leaving the Yuan empire at its founding without a comprehensive code of law. The Yuan court continued to consult the codes of the Tang, Song, and Jin dynasties while compiling an ever-increasing, ill-ordered archive of laws, ordinances, and precedents toward a new code.[82] Not the *New Statutes of the Zhiyuan Reign* (*Zhiyuan xin'ge*) of 1291, not the *Laws and Ordinances of the Dade Reign* (*Dade lüling*) of 1299, but the *Comprehensive Institutions of the Great Yuan* (*Da Yuan tongzhi*) of 1323 organized in one authoritative compendium the miscellaneous laws of past decades:

> By lack of a code, laws were first established through individual cases. With the passing of long years, the number of laws grew beyond proportion, until Emperor Yingzong [r. 1321–1324] for the first time ordered the Secretariat to compile them in the *Comprehensive Institutions*, and to distribute this work throughout the realm, there to be honored by the officials and clerks.[83]

The *Regulations of the Zhizheng Reign* (*Zhizheng tiaoge*) of 1346 supplemented the *Comprehensive Institutions* with new laws and precedents. During its preparation of the *Comprehensive Institutions*, moreover, the Yuan imperial court issued two temporary, practical compendia to assist officials and clerks in deciding legal cases: *Imperial Canon of the Sacred Governance of the Great Yuan* (*Da Yuan shengzheng guochao dianzhang*, 1317) and *Precedents of the Zhizhi Reign: A New Collection of the Imperial Canon of the Sacred Governance of the Great Yuan* (*Da Yuan shengzheng dianzhang xinji Zhizhi tiaoli*, 1322). A similar compilation,

*Great, Comprehensive Legal Compendium for Ordering the World* (*Jingshi dadian xiandian*, 1331), assisted members of the imperium in the enforcement of the *Comprehensive Institutions* after its completion.

Of these numerous compilations only the *Imperial Canon of Sacred Governance* and its supplement survive complete, in a splendid 1322 imprint. Of the *Comprehensive Institutions*, proud accomplishment of Yuan law, remain only twenty-two discontinuous fascicles of precedents in an early Ming manuscript, and a condensed rendition of its laws in the 1333 and 1340 editions of *A More Comprehensive Record of A Forest of Facts.*[84] Of the other compendia exist only prefaces and occasional fragments.[85] The very format of the *Imperial Canon of Sacred Governance* identifies it as a work of convenient reference: the tabular summary of the main terms, pertinent laws, and punishments on the first page of each section; the arrangement within each section of the laws in their full original wording, all followed by successive precedents that illustrate their most complex applications; and the layout of the printed page, with its subheadings in bold lettering, titles in contrast, bullets, and indentions.[86] The drab, incomplete fourteenth-century manuscript of the *Comprehensive Institutions* not only lacks the lucid format of the *Imperial Canon of Sacred Governance*, but its arrangement of cases and laws does not follow a clear order. The current text of the *Comprehensive Institutions* therefore does not bear out the judgment of contemporary literati who praised its nature and substance while they disparaged the *Imperial Canon of Sacred Governance.* Especially their stylistic criticism of the latter work is not readily understandable today, as the writing in the extant fascicles of the *Comprehensive Institutions* is markedly inferior and many of its documents are not cited in full.[87]

The nature of the sources, being precedents selected to illustrate the origins and application of imperial law, prohibits an accurate assessment of the local practice of law. While the lack of a code during the first fifty years of its rule may have given the Yuan imperial court unprecedented influence over legal decisions in every corner of its expansive realm, the unremitting stream of appeals for ad hoc decisions may also have overburdened the court and its Ministries, possibly resulting in chaos in the central offices and prolonged uncertainty in the counties and prefectures.[88] The clear, tight organization of the *Imperial Canon of Sacred Governance* instantiates the transparent order praised in the extant prefaces to Yuan legal compendia.[89] But the *Comprehensive Institutions*, though likened by Su Tianjue (1294–1352) to "one swift horizontal stroke," contains many a case that suggests undue, stultifying appeals to the highest authorities, such as a verdict by the Ministry of Rites, dated as late as 1305, that allows a family to remarry a daughter whose prospective groom was exiled for a severe crime before the betrothal sum was paid.[90]

The laws and precedents pertaining to weddings and marriage exemplify the marked characteristics of Yuan law: the gradual re-enactment through ad hoc decisions of stipulations from the codes of previous dynasties, and the attempt to inscribe imperial subjects into a rigid hierarchy of segregated classes and ethnic groups. The often unadorned prose of the precedents, intended to inform higher authorities of local circumstances, contrasts with the literary, moralizing verdicts of *A Collection of Pure and Lucid Verdicts*. Although less detailed in their brief, summary statements of legal disputes, the precedents do at times identify with some precision conflicts between imperial law and local practice that the surviving verdicts of the Southern Song represent as conflicts between universal morality and ignorant perversion. The effort to maintain a segregated hierarchy of ethnic groups (Mongols, miscellaneous aliens, and Han) accorded a new importance to weddings as occasions where ethnic difference was performed and reproduced. The prescription of proper ethnic custom constituted part, however, of a larger attempt by the Yuan imperial court to exert unprecedented power over the bodies of its subjects. The ethnic differentiation of law and morality under Yuan rule obliterated the universal claims of the laws adopted from the Tang and Song codes, leaving their intricate patrilineal boundaries arbitrary lines for the circumscription of Han subjects. The fixed protocol for Han weddings, the sumptuary laws, the attempt to create semiofficial go-betweens, and other marital regulations, served as means to mark those cynical boundaries and thereby to reduce litigation.[91]

The Yuan court gradually adopted most of the familiar marital laws of Tang and Song. A signed contract or the acceptance of the betrothal sum constituted a binding engagement, to be consummated within five years.[92] The wedding rites introduced the bride into a patrilineal grid that determined her rights and obligations in life and in death, unless a valid divorce or remarriage (upon completed mourning for her late husband) extricated her from these.[93] The Yuan court also enacted laws declaring void a marriage contracted or consummated during a period of mourning for parents, grandparents, or a deceased husband; a marriage to close kin, to a wife of close kin, or to a person of the same surname; a marriage contracted by an official within his jurisdiction; a bigamous marriage; a marriage across class boundaries; and a marriage arranged by an unauthorized person.[94]

The exemption of Mongols and miscellaneous aliens from the laws against bigamy and marriage during mourning periods, and the prohibition of the practice of levirate marriage among the Han, evince that Yuan rulers regarded the marital laws, not as instantiations of inherent moral boundaries, but as means to establish and perpetuate a hierarchical society divided by lines of essentialist ethnicity.[95] Although some of its officials invoked the scriptural rhetoric of sacred bonds and moral obligations, the Yuan court itself designed its detailed regulations and prohibitions to eliminate causes for protracted litigation.[96] It therefore extended its laws to areas that the codes of Tang and Song had left uncharted, such as the regulation of uxorilocal marriage, the rights to the betrothal sum in case of the death of one of the betrothed, the procurement of wives for officials serving far from their native region, and the remarriage of wives bereaved or abandoned in the military garrisons.[97] In familiar areas of controversy, such as the remarriage of widows, the Yuan court narrowed its laws to reduce occasions for plaints, transferring the right to remarry widows from parents and grandparents to the parents-in-law, and tersely prohibiting, in 1303, remarrying widows (and divorcées) from taking their dowry into a second marriage.[98]

The transformation of the universal, moral boundaries of Tang and Song law into cynical regulations for an ethnic social order did not diminish the conflict between law and local practice. Officials throughout the realm reported with dismay on accepted customs that filled their courts with irreconcilable plaintiffs. Route Commander Shi Jiayi in 1313 called for strict enforcement of the Tang-dynasty stipulation on binding betrothals in the persecution of guarantors who lightly broke wedding contracts and remarried their betrothed daughters—a common strategy for obtaining the largest possible betrothal sum.[99] Cases dated 1278, 1290, 1292, 1295, and 1302 assert that by established practice husbands in Shandong, Anhui, Jiangsu, Zhejiang, and Jiangxi rent out their wives to serve other men as a wife, concubine, or servant, for a period of three to five years. A Surveillance Commissioner in Zhejiang writes of this custom, "unheard of even among poor people in the Central Plain":

> According to the official laws [*guanfa*], a man who consents to his wife's adultery in exchange for money is liable to severe

> punishment. The ignorant people of the South openly accept money in renting out their wives to others for several years, allowing them to live as man and wife. This should of course require a heavier punishment than forcing one's wife to violate the law a single time. I propose that the rental of married women be prohibited. If a husband and a wife rent themselves out together, without separating, they should be permitted to do so.[100]

Officials in Shaanxi, Hubei, Hunan, Guangdong, and Guangxi denounce the widespread practice of divorce by sale (*maixiu*) or marriage by sale (*jiamai*), in which men divorce their wives by marrying them off for a betrothal sum.[101] An edict dated 1309 responds to reports from many regions about the betrothal of widows during the mourning period for their late husband, "remarrying on their own initiative."[102] Officials writing in 1286, 1295, 1306, and 1321 express their horror about weddings that do not only violate mourning obligations, but take place in the presence of a corpse. Wang Zhang of Suzhou stored away his mother's body during his son's wedding banquet, to bury her a few days later, but other defendants openly displayed the deceased relative during wedding ceremonies in which the groom and the bride "crossed the threshold, bowed to the spirit, and consummated the marriage."[103]

Despite its stated commitment to the preservation of ethnic custom, the Yuan court forbids the above practices and annuls most of the resulting marriages. Different from the verdicts surviving from the Southern Song, Yuan precedents recognize unlawful marital strategies as coherent, meaningful practices. Covetous negotiation tactics, the rental of wives, divorce by sale, the immediate remarriage of widows, and "bowing to the corpse" appear not as individual aberrations of perverse minds, but as widespread, established regional customs. Although some of the officials condemn these practices as violations of universal, sacred bonds of marriage, the Yuan court prohibits them because they result in litigation.

In some cases, however, the concern with order and the prevention of unending suits results in the acceptance of an illegal marriage or divorce. Like certain authors in *A Collection of Pure and Lucid Verdicts*, the Yuan court reasons that a marriage with children should not be disbanded to honor a binding betrothal belatedly remembered by a prior party, and that a husband's mere accusation of adultery voids a marriage, even when false.[104] In several cases, moreover, it confiscates the betrothal sum of a marriage contracted during a mourning period or through divorce by sale but declares the match itself to be valid.[105]

The unprecedented regulations of ritual protocol, too, were intended in large part to reduce litigation. The sumptuary laws subjected officials and Han commoners to graded limits of expenditure in order to prohibit them from emulating the lavish feasts of Mongols and miscellaneous aliens, but they also cite concerns with the miserable bankruptcies that led to frequent postponements of weddings and to ceaseless litigation. Even the standard protocol for Han weddings—arbitrarily adapted from the archaic ceremonies in Zhu Xi's *Family Rituals*—was aimed at the reduction of the number of legal suits by its prescription of simple, frugal ceremonies, to replace the violence and prodigality of current practices. Compulsory marriage contracts and the appointment of registered go-betweens with a knowledge of marital law were to eliminate causes for irresolvable disagreements, by fixing uncertain oral agreements in writing and by replacing mercenary matchmakers with respectable public persons. Yet even on the pages of the *Imperial Canon of Sacred Governance* and the *Comprehensive Institutions* this transparent order of compulsory ceremony is beset by inflation, illiteracy, ineradicable customs, and hopeless amendments.

The legislative authorities formulated their first sumptuary laws in response to a report from Taiyuan Route (Shanxi province), dated May 1270, that described how the copious wedding banquets of that region lasted deep into the night and often ended in fisticuffs and litigation. To prevent such "needless waste," the Secretariat and the Ministries ruled that banquets could take place only by daylight, until curfew, and they imposed limits on the number of dishes that could be served at such occasions. They ordered that these restrictions be promulgated throughout Taiyuan Route, written on boards and pasted on walls.[106] An edict handed down in March or April 1271 extended similar restrictions to the entire realm, adding sumptuary regulations for the betrothal gifts of ranked officials and the three ranks of commoner households (upper, middle, and lower).[107] In August of that same year, the Secretariat and the Ministry of Revenue designed additional sumptuary laws for uxorilocal marriage and imposed restrictions on matchmakers' fees.[108] In October 1284, the Secretariat and the Ministry of Rites confirmed the existing sumptuary laws in response to a report from the Censorate about the penury caused by weddings and funerals in Handong circuit, Shaanxi province.[109]

According to Hu Qiyu (1227–1295), the ambiguity of a crucial phrase in the edict of 1271 and the rapid inflation following its promulgation rendered the law ineffective almost instantaneously. Rich households readily interpreted the phrase "Those who wish to set their own [sum] are free to do so" to mean that sumptuary laws did not apply to those who could afford to break them. A sudden bout of rapid inflation, moreover, led to almost automatic violation of the 1271 sumptuary laws, as the price of a length of cloth increased from one string to eight strings of cash, and prices in general increased eight- to tenfold.[110] In accordance with these trends, the legislative authorities, in February 1304, allowed a significant rise in the upper limit of spending and abandoned the conversion of betrothal gifts into strings of cash, instead laying down their restrictions in stable bullion of gold and silver as well as in lengths of cloth. The law condemns once more the irresponsible spending that has led to widespread bankruptcy, postponement of weddings, and litigation.[111]

The formulation of a standard protocol for Han weddings proceeded in the same years as the promulgation of the first sumptuary laws, informed by similar circumstances. A 1268 prohibition of a custom called Blocking the Bride's Carriage or Invitation to the Railing expresses concern that "roving hoodlums and idlers, undeterred by the public laws [*gongfa*], gather crowds on wedding days to block the bride's carriage." With demands of food, drink, and other gifts, these crowds disrupt the wedding procession and cause the bride to miss the auspicious hour of her arrival, often causing violence and injury. The authorities prohibit the practice throughout the empire, citing as instructive instance a case from Ji'nan route, Shandong province, that cost the lives of two men.[112] The concern, in October 1271, with another wasteful ceremony prompted the Department of State Affairs and the Ministry of Rites to propose to the throne the definition of Han wedding ritual:

> In the Way of human relations, marriage occupies the preeminent position. Laws already exist for betrothal sums and banquets. Item: The ceremony of Bowing at the Gate [*bai men*] is a Jurchen custom. It should be eliminated everywhere. Item: For the original protocol of Han weddings one may examine the wedding ritual in Zhu Wengong's [i.e., Zhu Xi's] *Family Rituals*. The items listed below were designed with the rationale of preserving the ancient while accommodating the present.[113]

Drafted by the Department of State Affairs, revised by the Hanlin and Historiography Academy, and further simplified by the Secretariat, the protocol for Han weddings follows a bare, broken outline of Zhu Xi's wedding ritual. Where Zhu Xi envisioned a re-embodiment of antiquity through the permanent ritualization of dress, movement, speech, and domestic space, the Yuan legislative authorities turned to his *Family Rituals* only to obtain a sequence of authentic Han wedding ceremonies. Removed from the ritual context of the obsolete capping ceremony, archaic burials, daily sacrifice, and ritual primogeniture, the wedding ceremonies become arbitrary choreographies, imposed on incongruous spaces and unfitted bodies. The authors of the protocol further reduced this hollow outline by eliminating horses and carriages and the offering hall, and rewrote entirely the ceremony for the Submission of the Betrothal Gifts to allow a banquet at the bride's house, with a public display of betrothal gifts outside the gate. A curt note at the end of the protocol briefly addresses uxorilocal marriage, "although this is not an ancient rite," stating that it ought "to be performed according to the rituals that obtain in present custom."[114]

The only surviving case to refer to the 1271 protocol confirms its purpose as an arbitrary ethnic guideline designed to prevent litigation. In response to a report submitted in May or June 1297 by the Surveillance Commission of Hanzhong circuit (present Nanzheng county, Shaanxi province), the Censorate determines that certain customs in Shaanxi cannot be accepted as Han ceremonies because they invite legal suits:

> In the popular customs of Shaanxi, families that seek to marry invite matchmakers to find out about betrothal gifts. Prior to any agreement they already present them with dried goat meat. One household has not yet finished, before another already asserts itself. Not only are these customs insubstantial, but they actually encumber the marriage process.
>
> I propose to observe the stipulations regarding the negotiation of marriage, Submission of the Choice, and so forth, as laid down for the Han by the Ministry of Rites. I also refer to the imperial decree of 1271 that regulates betrothal, marriage, and betrothal gifts among commoners, and so forth.
>
> The Censorate concurred: "If miscellaneous aliens marry among themselves, they follow their own customs and laws. If

> miscellaneous aliens intermarry, [the ethnicity of] the groom's family takes precedence. Mongols are excluded from these stipulations."[115] Moreover, there are laws already in existence that demand that commoners who negotiate a marriage should write up a clear wedding contract. Although the ceremony of the dried goat meat is a local custom of Shaanxi, it should be prohibited by analogy with the stipulation about Bowing at the Gate, in hopes of preventing litigation.
>
> The Ministry of Rites drafted the following after review: Eternal rites exist for each marriage between a male and a female. In the case of the customs of Shaanxi, here under review, we endorse the prohibition proposed by the Censorate.
>
> The Department of State Affairs endorsed this.[116]

Unlike the inherent universal rituals of Zhu Xi, the eternal rites invoked by the Ministry of Rites are distinguished by ethnicity and class, and derive their durability, not from an inherent truth, but from the dynastic house that has promulgated them.

With laws prescribing the use of contracts and with attempts to reform the institution of the go-between, the Mongol court created a structure by which it might enforce its marital laws. In April 1269, the Secretariat and the Ministry of Revenue described the legal complications caused by oral agreements and unreliable matchmakers:

> In the Way of human relations, marriage between males and females occupies the pre-eminent position.
>
> By our observation, the rites and ceremonies as they are performed today differ widely. Some draw up wedding contracts, but others fail to record the original agreement in writing, relying solely on a go-between in their negotiations. If the slightest violation occurs after all has been settled—if the groom's family takes advantage of the lack of a contract to ignore the original agreement and to raise or lower the betrothal sum arbitrarily, or if an uxorilocal son-in-law claims that he is temporary rather than pensionary and they bring their suits to court, and if the people involved state their opinions [instead of the facts], and the go-between and others are biased in favor of one of the two parties, then the official who has to confront the endless litigation, relying entirely on oral depositions, finds himself in a very awkward position.[117]

In response to this proposal, the Secretariat passed a law that commanded the use of wedding contracts throughout the realm, requiring the exact stipulation of betrothal sums and of the terms of uxorilocal marriages.[118] A law promulgated in May 1269 prohibits prenatal engagements on the grounds that one cannot write up a specific contract for such matches.[119] A law of 1273 requires clear contracts to enforce the distinction between wives and concubines.[120] In 1303, the Yuan court ruled that no divorce was legal without a contract.[121] The 1333 and 1340 editions of *A Forest of Facts* cite the detailed law on wedding contracts from the *Comprehensive Institutions*:

> In wedding contracts, stipulate clearly the betrothal sum and other gifts. The guarantor and the matchmaker both sign their names. The contract returned by the bride's family records in addition the amount and number of betrothal gifts received. The guarantor and matchmaker of the bride's family also sign their names. Then in large characters write "contract" on the reverse of the two completed betrothal contracts. Both families receive one half of each. Whoever comes to court in a litigation case with a wedding contract composed in common, vulgar words or in ornamental parallel prose, and with the characters "contract" drawn on it despite its vague terms, will be prosecuted for fraud.[122]

The attempt of the Yuan court to appropriate the institution of the go-between for the enforcement of its laws appears to have been as novel as its protocol for Han weddings. Sources from the Song era forward include matchmakers among the women who ought to be barred from entering a decent house, and the *Imperial Canon of Sacred Governance* contains a case, dated October 1266, in which a go-between arranges the secret meetings of two illicit lovers.[123] This disreputable institution the legislative authorities superscribed in a clause to the law on uxorilocal marriage, of August 1271:

> Item: Set regulations for the betrothal gifts of both regular and uxorilocal marriage now exist. From the present, go-betweens should be recommended and chosen from among trustworthy women, and guaranteed by officials, community heads, block heads, elders, and others. Officials are responsible for keeping a register of their family names and given names, and for the

imposition of severe restrictions on the exorbitant fees that go-betweens have demanded till now. Violators will be prosecuted.[124]

The Surveillance Commission of Dongxi circuit, Shandong province, in May 1282 repeated these obligations of officials, community heads, and go-betweens, adding that the matchmakers should be older women with a knowledge of "the edicts" (i.e., of the relevant laws), and that they are prohibited from "demanding ten percent [of the betrothal gifts] as a matchmaker's fee."[125] A stipulation in *New Statutes of the Zhiyuan Period* of 1291 places go-betweens on a par with brokers, and requires that they understand the pertinent prohibitions so as to be of service in the reduction of the number of litigation suits.[126]

There is no evidence that the protocol for Han weddings ever extended beyond the written page or that appointed, registered go-betweens ever materialized from the hopeful words of edicts and legal compendia. Nor do the sources confirm that the sumptuary laws curtailed wedding expenses or that a sudden proliferation of contracts reduced litigation. Although the 1271 law on Han weddings orders that the protocol must be "promulgated as designed and implemented as outlined above," it neither indicates how this implementation should proceed, nor even specifies a punishment for the disregard of proper ethnic ceremony.[127] Verdicts in the *Imperial Canon of Sacred Governance* and in the *Comprehensive Institutions* repeat time and again the injunction to employ go-betweens and to secure wedding contracts, suggesting both insistence and failure. When determining the status of a disputed betrothal or marriage, verdicts assess the amount of the betrothal sum, its acceptance by the bride's family, and the consummation of the marriage; sometimes they name a go-between, rarely a contract.[128] Two cases preserved in the *Comprehensive Institutions* suggest the hopelessness of enforcing marital law, accusing in 1278 and 1303 members of the imperium of enticing with forged contracts women and girls in their jurisdiction, with the aim of either selling them as slaves or taking them into their own household for the duration of their tenure:

When traveling officials arrive at their post, they [often] deceive the commoners in their jurisdiction. They ask around about girls and women, then write up void wedding contracts,

> trump up a betrothal sum, and take them as wives or concubines. This truly harms the Sacred Transformation.[129]

Like the universal boundaries of Tang and Song law, the intricate structure of Yuan marital regulations does not represent ritual practice, nor even legal practice, but the practice of the legal text, with its vision of a hierarchical society ordered by perfect laws.

## CONCLUSION

The remove, in legal discourse, between text and ritual yields vague, distorted glimpses of unknown, unwritten cultures of local practice. The text/performance of ritual manuals, the composition of wedding correspondence, and the calculation of auspicious hours belong themselves to the repertoires of wedding practices they inscribe. There, writing is a ritual practice, the author is a ritual actor, and the text is a ritual object. The judge, by contrast, is not a ritual actor in the marital cases he adjudicates. He gathers contracts and hears depositions of ceremonies past, and in his verdict determines whether the rites and negotiations as performed in unfamiliar houses and distant streets conformed to the imperial order he represents. The verdict mediates between the transparent structure of imperial law and the disorderly variety of local practices, and becomes thereby a written trace of the position of the local official—the rhetoric and allusions his robes, the citations of the code and the final sentence his prisons and his instruments of sanctioned violence. In the ritualized space of the county seat, the judge translates local practice into the solemn language of the imperial order. In the margins of his verdict, at the fingertips that hold the official's brush (the extremities of imperial power), become visible the lavish banquets of wedding nights, the violence of interrupted bridal processions, the marriage of cousins and other forbidden kin, the rental and sale of wives, and grooms and brides bowing to a corpse.

Only in contracts do legal writing and wedding ritual coincide. A two-part Southern Song "ceremonial confirmation document" (*huiding yizhuang*), drawn up by Zheng Yuande and copied by Ye Sheng (1420–1474) into his *Daily Records Written East of the River* (*Shuidong riji*), inscribes itself into the profuse exchanges between two prominent families.[130] In the first part, dated March 16, 1260, the bride's family conjures in its compulsory genealogical information the splendor of a long record of official service. Although residing in Kunshan county, Pingjiang prefecture (Jiangsu province), the family identifies Kaifeng as its place of origin—the lost capital where the early emperors of the Song convened with their most trusted officials. The bride's maternal kinship also extends to that noble city: "Her mother, Ms. Wang, is a granddaughter of the late Recorder of the Directorate for Armaments Wang Zhongshi, and a descendant of Wang Wenzheng, Duke of Yi [i.e., Wang Ceng, 978–1038]." Between this summation of cultural capital and the display of the financial wealth of the dowry, the bride is presented and given away, and all is enfolded in costly envelopes:

> My eldest daughter, Qingyi, aged fourteen *sui* and born between 9 and 11 in the morning on the eleventh day of the twelfth month [January 8, 1248?], is hereby married to County Magistrate Pan Wanba, polite name Xin'en, of the household of Pan Shaoqing, with dowry lands to the amount of 500 *mu*; dowry funds to the amount of 100,000 strings of cash, to be paid in seventeen installments; and a betrothal sum of 5,000 strings of cash, also in seventeen installments. . . . Bowing in respectful devotion I offer for your kind acceptance my household's three ceremonial letters in envelopes with double-goldfish design.[131]

The second part of this contract, dated April or May 1262, lists the gifts carried to the groom's household on the day of the wedding: an array of textiles, thirty branches of tea leaves wrapped in patterned red silk, four kinds of fruit, and two jugs of wine—as well as four lengths of striped gold-lump gauze and a thousand strings of cash in official bank notes for the go-between.

The wealth conveyed by this document stands in stark contrast with the war-stricken poverty of a 1365 "greatly auspicious wedding contract," excavated in 1983 at Alashan Meng, Inner Mongolia, in which military serviceman Toghon marries off his late brother's widow Badma to Wu Kharabaatai for some ninety-five liters each of white polished rice, wheat, and barley: "In these days of massive conscription and incessant levies, of military unrest, of days spent in the saddle, of meager income, one cannot see a point of light." The contract describes Badma's miserable condition upon the death of her husband and confirms Toghon's reception of the betrothal sum. It concludes with clauses designed to prevent future litigation:

> If in marrying off his younger brother's wife, Badma, Toghon has not told the complete truth and is marrying her off under false pretenses while her former husband is still alive, the resulting complications will not affect Wu Zizhong, but will be due to the lack of prior warning by Toghon and his witnesses. If Kharabaatai does not elevate this wife to the position of legal spouse, he will be fined ninety-five liters of wheat. If Badma refuses to serve her husband or does anything untoward, the main guarantor [Toghon] will be fined ninety-five liters of white polished rice for official expenses. This greatly auspicious wedding contract has been written up for future reference.[132]

In the running script of this contract, writing and ritual practice concur. The written marks below the names of the bride, of the guarantors, and of the witness are physical traces of the ritual actors; the ink is congealed ritual time. Although the contract of 1262 survives only in a printed Ming-dynasty notebook (just as three divorce contracts found at Dunhuang survive only as copies, written among other documents), the reduced format of its text still preserves the ritual moment of its writing and the inscribed traces of the materiality of the original document.[133]

Although in these contracts writing coincides with the ritual practice of weddings, their paucity prohibits an accurate assessment of their historical significance, just as the incommensurable codes, verdicts, and precedents impede a proper comparison of the practice of legal writing across the centuries. How tempting it is to perceive in the Southern Song verdicts the beginnings of the Ming dominance of the Learning of the Way, to read the 1262 contract as an omen of the imminent collapse of the decadent southern empire, and to see in the clauses of the 1365 contract and in the sorry remains of the *Comprehensive Institutions* the traces of a short-lived, trustless, violent dynasty![134] But one need only imagine a complete local archive of a few decades of decrees, verdicts, and contracts (as indeed exist in certain European cities) to realize how scattered and uneven the legal sources for these long centuries are, and how false the narratives they suggest.

Not the practice of legal writing has forged these narratives, but the practice of transmission. The prestige of the Tang and the Song, and the prominence of the Learning of the Way ensured the reproduction by Ming printers of the Tang and Song codes, of a work such as *A Collection of Pure and Lucid Verdicts*, and of the collected writings of Huang Gan, a son-in-law to Zhu Xi. By contrast, the violent scorn for the defeated Mongols placed all remnants of the Yuan dynasty in danger of destruction. Generic contract formats survive, printed in durable reference works, but individual manuscript contracts were obliterated, unless preserved by chance underground.[135] And local and imperial archives perished, of Tang, of Song, of Yuan, as they had in all of imperial history.

The secondary literature to date, however, has failed to distinguish between the ritual practice of Middle-Period weddings and the ritual practice of the legal text, and it has mistaken the narrative created by the transmission of codes and verdicts for an historical narrative of legal practice. "Marriage was . . . a legal institution, for laws promulgated by the state recognized only certain sorts of unions as valid," writes Patricia Ebrey in *The Inner Quarters*.[136] If not a tautology, this statement must assume either that imperial officials effectively oversaw marital practice in their jurisdiction or that imperial subjects themselves obeyed marital law for fear that their illicit marriages be reported and annulled. The sources support neither assumption. Local officials heard only cases brought to their court, and these already amounted to such a burden as to prevent officials from setting out in search of unlawful unions. The verdicts surviving from the Southern Song, moreover, suggest an uneven knowledge of marriage law among commoners. Some plaintiffs act in accordance with the law, others seem misinformed about crucial details or entirely ignorant of wrongdoing, or invoke imperial law merely for selfish gain. In Song verdicts, and in Yuan precedents, the negotiation and consummation of marriage appears to accord with local practices that observe customs and kinship boundaries distinctly different from those inscribed in imperial law.

In *Women, Property, and Confucian Reaction in Sung and Yüan China (960–1368)*, Bettine Birge similarly collapses the practice of the legal text with the practice of law, and thence equates legal text with social practice. The introduction to the book conjures the familiar three-dimensional past of social history, of education and the new elite, of the economic revolution and technological progress. This prediscursive, materialist past reduces the Middle-Period text to a source of interchangeable fragments that readily accommodate preconceived meanings and narratives. Although Birge recognizes ideological difference, social complexity, and historical change, these rarely surmount the limiting confines of binaries: philosophical ideal versus historical reality, brideprice versus dowry, the Chinese versus the Mongols, the improvement of women's property rights versus their deterioration. In the opening chapters of the book, the materialist past and the objectivist binaries hide a gradual, subtle narrowing of sources: the tension between the strict patrilineal rhetoric of "Confucian" texts and the evidence of inheritance by daughters in legal texts identifies the latter as truthful, transparent documents, and this in turn allows the construction of a broad historical narrative based almost entirely on legal texts, while obviating the need for a critical examination of the historical practice of the composition and transmission of such texts.

As is common in social history, the neglect of the practice of the text results in an equation of text with the past, the unevenness and incompleteness of the text suggesting a false sense of historical change. *Women, Property, and Confucian Reaction* charts a trajectory from "a high point for women's property rights" in the Song to "a re-Confucianization of the law and a swing back toward patrilineal principles that deprived women of their property rights and reduced their legal and economic autonomy" during the Ming and Qing dynasties.[137] The linear, though tortuous, path of the argument leads from the guaranteed rights to an inalienable dowry, in the *Song Penal Code*, to the encroachment on these rights by proponents of the Learning of the Way in *A Collection of Pure and Lucid Verdicts*, and thence to stipulations on levirate marriage and widow chastity in the *Imperial Canon of Sacred Governance*.[138] In the 1260s, "Mongol and other steppe customs were beginning to exert a creeping influence on the Chinese" who were "willing to negotiate the new customs they saw around them and use non-Chinese laws to their advantage."[139] The brief, violent exposure to the unaccustomed practice of levirate marriage "made possible a change in the marriage and property regime that had dominated Chinese society until that time. . . . New laws in the early fourteenth century stripped women of their property rights and their freedom to remarry."[140] The Mongol institution of levirate marriage, in other words, accomplished the reactionary goals of the Learning of the Way. The succession of brothers to the same bride had suggested the permanent appropriation of the dowry by the husband's family, while the life-long chastity of widows had gained in attraction and prestige as the only alternative to levirate marriage or the loss of the dowry.

This narrative derives its coherence from the assumption that the height of women's property rights during the Northern Song must be connected to the depths of the cruel cult of widow chastity during the Ming and Qing dynasties by a single, straight, descending line, and that this historical slant may be extrapolated from the fragmentary sources. The paucity of legal texts facilitates this reduction of history to the shortest distance between two points. Sufficient evidence exists, however, to disprove the resulting linear narrative and to show that its intermittent segments belong to horizontal, diachronic lines of legal writing and marital practice. First, if by Chen Xiang's estimate the courts of Fujian province adjudicated several thousand cases per year during the 1040s, the few hundred decisions in *A Collection of Pure and Lucid Verdicts* should not be taken to represent the whole of legal practice in the latter decades of the Southern Song (when even the province of Fujian itself was more densely populated than it was in Chen Xiang's day). Moreover, although the individual verdicts in the collection demonstrate certain aspects of the practice of the legal text in Southern Song, the lack of any comparable collection from an earlier period prohibits an assessment of the relative prominence of the ideology of the Learning of the Way in Song legal decisions. The disparate judgments of the famous case of Ms. Yun, for example, from its occurrence in 1068 through commentaries on the case written in the Ming, show that patrilineal fundamentalism found expression in eleventh-century legal discourse and that there still existed opposition to it in the fifteenth century.[141]

Second, the transition from the southern disputes about dowries in *A Collection of Pure and Lucid Verdicts* to the cases of levirate marriage in the *Imperial Canon of Sacred Governance* silently elides some 150 years of Jurchen and Mongol rule in the lands north of the Yangzi. If the subjects of the Jin dynasty, or indeed of the Liao dynasty (916–1125), had not noticed the practice of levirate marriage among the Jurchen and the Qidan, it is not clear why they should have noticed it among the Mongols in the 1260s.[142] More important, the identification of a brief spell of levirate marriage among the Han as an awkward stage in a trend toward the dispossession of widows mistakes the greater visibility of a phenomenon in extant sources for the historical origin and prominence of that phenomenon. The codification of levirate marriage by the Mongol court created a separate category for this practice in Yuan legal texts. In the Tang and Song codes, marriage to a brother's widow falls under inner disorder (*neiluan*), a severe transgression of the laws against marriage to close kin. An instance of levirate marriage duly appears in *A Collection of Pure and Lucid Verdicts* as one of four verdicts under that category (translated above). A second instance occurs elsewhere in the collection, as one among many egregious deeds of a corrupt clerk.[143] In the legal sources of both Song and Yuan, therefore, the practice of levirate marriage marks a discrepancy between the universal boundaries of imperial law (moral in Song, ethnic in Yuan) and local practice. However few the examples, they disallow the argument that Mongol custom inspired Han families to attempt a clumsy imitation of this practice.

Third, the Yuan cases of levirate marriage make no mention of dowries, and a consideration of marriage payments in the Song and Yuan suggests that the widows in these cases may not have possessed one.[144] Instead, the connection between levirate marriage, dowries, and the promotion of widow chastity depends on an extrapolation of the canonical rhetoric against female property from Southern Song verdicts into the Yuan.[145] The 1303 law that prohibits widows from taking their dowry into a second marriage provides one of only four mentions of dowries in extant Yuan legal texts.[146] While dowries appear much more frequently in the surviving Southern Song verdicts than betrothal sums, dowries are almost absent from surviving Yuan marital cases.[147] In the Yuan precedents (as in the Tang and Song codes), betrothal sums define a legal marriage, and betrothal sums are the subject of litigation. This marked discrepancy between the Southern Song verdicts and Yuan precedents likely does not signify an historical shift in marriage payments, and is rather a function of the practice of legal texts and their transmission. But the unimportance of dowries in extant Yuan legal texts disallows the citation of litigation about dowries as an important factor in an historical trend toward the dispossession of widows. The current text of the 1303 law, moreover, is devoid of the rhetoric of the Learning of the Way. It even lacks the statement that "in the Way of human relations, marriage occupies the preeminent position," a perfunctory phrase that introduces several Yuan marital laws.

Although *Women, Property, and Confucian Reaction* offers perceptive readings of *A Collection of Pure and Lucid Verdicts*, and although its proposed collusion of the Yuan government with the Learning of the Way seems probable, its narrative and argument about the dispossession of widows is based on an invalid equation of legal text with social practice. Not only does the book mistake shifts in the writing and transmission of legal texts for changes in marital practice, but it assumes that Song and Yuan officials enforced imperial law effectively and universally.[148] Only when the more abundant transmitted texts of the Ming and Qing reveal the discrepancy between local custom and the practice of the legal text does Birge admit that "changes in the law did not necessarily transform practice."[149]

Changes in the practice of legal writing and the uneven transmission of legal texts bring into view a shifting array of local practices. In the two editions of *A Collection of Pure and Lucid Verdicts* and in the collected works of Huang Gan and Liu Kezhuang, literary merit has preserved routine judgments against local violence and greed. The ad hoc decisions of the Yuan imperial court and its unprecedented ambition of a hierarchical ethnic order have yielded terse descriptions of unlawful regional practices. The changing legal categories and the incommensurability of the sources create a false sense of movement. Divorce by sale, rental of wives, marriage to close kin, levirate marriage, mercenary negotiation strategies, and other unlawful practices belonged to enduring repertoires of unwritten local practices—not unchanging, perhaps, but independent of the changes in imperial law and legal practice. The distance between the legal text and local practice is the distance Liu Kezhuang remembers of surveys of losses caused by droughts:

> Whenever I have witnessed, in the counties and prefectures where I have served, an official investigation into damage done by a drought, the officials and clerks would visit with the rich and powerful wherever they went. All exemptions would be awarded to formidable families of means, while the poor and downtrodden would rarely share in their beneficence. In every township and in every village, moreover, there are evil, unscrupulous persons who share their deceitful schemes with the clerks and accountants dispatched by the officials. Even worthy officials of discriminating intelligence are rarely able to perceive their fraud. If one adds to this the consideration that even the landowners and local elders are sometimes unable to identify with certainty which of the countless plots of land—stretching as far as the eye can see—had poor yields, which abundant, one may imagine the unlikelihood that the

responsible official, unfamiliar with local customs, will assess the situation accurately with one quick glance. He merely sits in his sedan chair, dependent entirely on the oral reports of his runners and the village clerks, which he then writes up in his documents.[150]

# Conclusion

## Texts and Tombs, Ritual and History

> Material culture patterning characteristically consists of sentences and texts within texts. For example, a series of pots in a grave may form a sentence constituting part of the text of a cemetery.
>
> —Christopher Tilley (1991)[1]

> Between the sentences—and I am thinking of very ancient books which were first recited—in the interval separating them, there still remains today as in an inviolate burial chamber, filling the interstices, a silence centuries old.
>
> —Marcel Proust (1906)[2]

Between 1972 and 1979, the Gansu Provincial Museum and the Zhang County Cultural Office conducted a few brief salvage excavations at Xujiaping, two and a half kilometers southeast of the Zhang county seat in southern Gansu.[3] On a gradual slope stretching southward from the Zhang River stood the delapidated remains of more than a hundred and twenty burial mounds, flanked in the east by a small stream and an imposing hillside. There, in a plot measuring two hundred by a hundred and fifty meters, the descendants of Wang Shixian (1195–1243) had buried their dead for fourteen generations, from 1243 to 1616, from the early years of Mongol rule through the late Ming dynasty. As a reward for his military exploits, the Mongol court posthumously enfeoffed Wang Shixian as Prince of Longyou, the area in southern Gansu where in 1235 this Jurchen commander had first joined the Mongol forces in their conquest of the Jin empire. Many of his warlike sons and loyal grandsons in turn received prestigious appointments and posthumous titles, and throughout their centuries of prominence the Wang retained their feudal prerogatives to this ancestral seat.[4] Although in the course of neglectful time grave robbers and natural decay dimmed the former luster of the Wang cemetery, the historical eminence of this local family persuaded the Cultural Office and the Provincial Museum in 1972 to clean up (*qingli*) twenty-seven of the remaining grave mounds as the area was converted into farmland.

One of the excavated tombs belonged to Wang Maochang, a great-grandson of Wang Shixian, who had died on the sixteenth day of the third month (April 15) in the year 1329, at the age of 38, and was buried a month and a half later (on June 1).[5] The tomb also shielded the skeletons of his wife, Ms. Yila, and of a young daughter. A sloping ramp, two and a half meters long and a little more than a meter wide, descended westward to the entrance of the tomb. The four straight walls of the square brick chamber supported an octagonal corbeled dome, from whose square capstone a bronze mirror was once suspended. Carved bricks set in the walls enlivened the burial chamber with blossoms, vines, animals, and scenes of famous deeds of filial devotion. At the top of the walls, at the base of the dome, projecting bricks mimicked the corbels and brackets of a timber-frame structure. On the tiled floor lay the remains of three simple wooden coffins, with traces of carved and painted decorations, placed parallel with their headboards facing the eastern wall.

Between the coffins, toward the rear wall, stood three small earthenware tables bearing sacrificial vessels. Apart from five regular jars and a vase, all pottery imitated ancient bronzes: two *gu*-shaped candleholders; two *ding*-shaped incense burners and a patterned *ding*-shaped tripod decorated with the eight trigrams and with legs in the shape of animal heads; a patterned *jue*-shaped vessel on a round tray; two *he*-shaped vessels and a *zun*-shaped vessel with lids capped by a small likeness of a tortoise; and two *dou*-shaped vessels. The jars and the *he*-shaped vessels contained traces of offerings of cereals and meat. A round bronze mirror, fallen from the dome, mimicked the style of Han-dynasty mirrors. The inscription on its outer rim read:

> A mirror like a noble canopy must have an inscription,
> It bars evil and avails the ancestral remains.
> The lasting protection of parents benefits grandsons,
> Who will become long-lived officers and high officials.[6]

On the waist of the male skeleton lay draped a yellow silk belt with a jade belt hook, and by his side were found two bronze *vajras*, or thunderbolts, ritual objects of esoteric Buddhism. The remains of a cap with four carved stone ornaments (three plum blossoms and a bird in flight) clung to the daughter's skull. Besides these objects, the tomb contained a *dharani sutra* (a Buddhist scripture with magical spells) copied on silk, two small silk pouches, a silk kerchief, a pair of women's shoes of yellow satin, a goat-leather cap, and a funerary inscription with cover, but the perfunctory site report fails to specify their location.

Wang Maochang's funerary inscription follows a standard format. The caption identifies the tomb occupant by his surname and titles. The inscription lists his illustrious pedigree, mentions his precocious intelligence and his youthful dedication to his studies, sums up his career and achievements, and records the date of his death, the date of his burial, and the position of his tomb: "He was buried in the ancestral cemetery by the Zhang River, one generation below Lord Xuanzhong [i.e., his father, Wang Weiqin], as ritual requires." Thereafter, the inscription names the wife of the deceased, with a brief pedigree, and their children, to conclude with a brief eulogy of this worthy descendant of a distinguished family.

In this tomb, exegetical, literary, and cosmological discourses, so strictly segregated in printed texts, converge in ritual time and space to amplify the unifying, interlocking themes of filiality, immortality, and reproduction. The capstone mirror coordinates these themes in its inscription. "The lasting protection of parents benefits the grandsons," reads its third line. The mirror itself, with its magical reflection, protects the deceased parents from evil demons. The suspension of this inscribed mirror by the descendants of the deceased is therefore a deed of filial concern, deserving of retribution. The rewards, however, extend not directly to the filial sons themselves but to their offspring, whose prestigious offices and certain longevity will enable them to support their parents in life and in death. The filial man thus performs the rites of burial and sacrifice as both son and father, as both benefactor and beneficiary.[7] This natural proliferation of referents makes filiality the "reproductive virtue par excellence."[8]

The text of the funerary inscription, the filiality scenes on the walls, the mimicry of a wooden structure in brick, and the generational position of the tomb within the ancestral graveyard all bear out these same themes of filial devotion, immortality, and reproduction. The funerary inscription not only praises Wang Maochang as a worthy son and grandson, but recounts his life and career as the realization of his filial duties, connecting the illustrious ancestors of the opening lines to his own son in the concluding sentences. The filiality scenes refer both to the exemplary deceased and to their descendants, who commissioned the construction of an enduring tomb. The simulation of wood architecture in undecaying brick converts the temporary dwellings of the living (*yangzhai*) into the permanent dwellings of the dead (*yinzhai*), thereby transforming death into immortality.[9] The location of the tomb in the ancestral cemetery replicates the generational order of ancestral tablets (*zhaomu*), its mound the physical evidence of the ritual continuity of a prominent, wealthy, virtuous family—and of the transformation of this Jurchen military family into a civilian, educated Han lineage.[10] During the Yuan and Ming, grave trees may have grown on the cemetery, casting beneficent shade on the tombs and signifying by their prosperous girth and expansive branches the healthy proliferation of filial descendants.[11] The eastward orientation of the tombs on this sloping southern river bank may have held geomantic significance, and thereby may have been intended to contribute to the continued eminence of the family, but the lack of a specific mention in the funerary inscriptions, the inevitable changes in the landscape, and the endless variety of geomantic theories prohibit confirmation of this possibility.[12]

The materiality of these funereal metaphors collapses sign and referent, and thereby enables the convergence of incompatible discourses in ritual time and space. The mirror inscribes the filial deed that the object itself proclaims, purchased and hung by filial sons. The filiality scenes, too, represent the virtue that created them. The apt grave goods, the solemn funerary inscription, the durable tomb, and the extensive cemetery are each evidence of substantial expenditure and ritual performance, and are therefore each an instantiation of the reproductive filiality they represent. Their shared reference to the ritual, social, and biological continuity of the lineage creates an equivalence between the objects that cancels their discursive incompatibility. Wang Maochang's simple funerary inscription, the archaist vessels, and the generational arrangement of the cemetery assert a desire to return to the ritualized order of the ancient sages.[13] The *vajras* and the *dharani sutra* bespeak hopes of an enlightened awareness and a magical power in the multiplying, illusory universes of esoteric Buddhism.[14] And the eastward orientation of the tomb and the corpses likely aims to ensure the worldly wealth and well-being of the descendants by harmonizing the surname of the family, or the hour of death, or the day of burial, or any other cosmological coordinates, with the surrounding landscape, in the more concrete universe of geomantic calculation. Yet, together these deathless traces of burial create a monument to filiality and reproduction—perhaps intended for the family and the community, perhaps for the deceased and the underworld, but perhaps also intended as an inherently meaningful space of material metaphors in which signs eternally produce their referent, namely the filial devotion that created them.[15]

Such discursive synergy is not only achieved by the juxtaposition of miscellaneous objects in a shared ritual time and space, but it occurs even in single objects, such as the slabs of dark stone that are funerary inscriptions. The text of Wang Maochang's inscription accords with the staid format proposed in Zhu Xi's *Family Rituals*, yet its cover is hewn in the shape of a truncated pyramid, the powerful cosmological form of divination boards and imperial tumuli.[16] The cover of the funerary inscription of Wang Yuanchang, a cousin of Wang Maochang, assumes the same cosmic shape, but its sloping sides are carved with peonies, lotuses, chrysanthemums, and plum blossoms, symbols of elegant prosperity.[17] Carved signs of the zodiac, the deities of the four directions, or the eight trigrams on the covers of other Middle-Period inscriptions explicate their likeness to divination boards.[18] Underneath such portentous covers, the texts of the inscriptions juxtapose classicist virtues, literary refinement, conspicuous display, and cosmological calculation. Their grim association with rigid death did not exclude tomb inscriptions from the vigorous cultural competition among Song and Yuan literati. While proponents of ancient-style prose and the Learning of the Way studied corroded stones and epigraphic collections in search of sober, authoritative models, others vied in composing striking, unconventional epitaphs.[19] Patrons offered pounds of gold and bolts of silk to prominent writers in hopes of securing literary immortality for their ancestors, and they sought out skilled craftsmen who would preserve in stone the prized calligraphy of the drafted compositions.[20] Thus, the descendants of Liu Runeng (988–1043), a minor official, postponed his burial for more than thirty years, until in 1175 they could afford a proper burial in a brick tomb of several chambers, and a stunning funerary inscription, whose text was composed by Gentleman for Court Audiences and Probationary Minister Xin Ziyan. The inscription begins:

> I had already inscribed the tombs of the late Mr. Liu Tunwei and the late Mr. [Liu] Wensi when I received another request from my lord's [i.e., Liu Runeng's] son, Zhongfu. He said, "The virtue of my grand ancestor and uncle you have already

> unforgettably inscribed. Yet if the various achievements of my late father will not have been carved in stone by the time of his funeral, it will be as though he has been left unburied. Could you be interested in this matter? If not, we orphans will have to forgo even this small consolation in our boundless sorrow." One of my brothers is a son-in-law of the Liu family. When he said that such a composition could propagate the proper facts to others, I no longer dared refuse.
>
> My lord's personal name was Runeng; his polite name was Chuyue. He came from Kaifeng. His eminent ancestry I have already detailed in the funerary inscription of the late Mr. [Liu] Tunwei. . . .[21]

This bold opening draws attention away from the deceased to focus it upon the writer and upon the inscription itself, an effect enhanced by the meticulous reproduction on the stone of the author's graceful running script. Through the references to his earlier epitaphs, moreover, the continuity of the lineage becomes entwined with the continuity of Xin Ziyan's own literary achievements.[22] Although sumptuary laws forbade those without official rank from being buried with a funerary inscription, commoners, too, were drawn into this economy of cultural capital. Many commoners satisfied themselves with a modest tomb contract that mimicked an epitaph, but an occasional brazen merchant purchased the illicit posthumous prestige of an actual funerary inscription.[23]

The essential polysemy of funerary inscriptions disappears when their texts are committed to print. The cosmic shape of the cover, the carved blossoms or signs of the zodiac, and the costly skill of the workmanship are not transferred to the printed page. From a complex, multivalent object in a complex, multivalent ritual space, the funerary inscription is reduced to a stark literary composition. The conventions of printing transform even the text itself, as these public, circulating versions of funerary inscriptions often omit the date and hour of death and the place of burial, thereby eliminating what limited cosmological connotations the abstracted text might have preserved.[24] In the pages of collected works or anthologies, a funerary inscription represents foremost the literary achievements and the social networks of its author. It is a trace of the act of writing, and points to literary fashions and intellectual debates at the time of its composition, rather than to the tomb and burial rites of its subject. Although its patron may have hoped that the author's fame would preserve his ancestor's reputation in the illustrious company of such a transcendent literary circle, this vicarious immortality in the printed realm was only one among several diverse strategies to ensure the enduring remembrance of his kinsman.

The monumental traces of burial enable a comparison between the practice of the text and original ritual space, and between printed, generic texts and original written objects. Such comparisons are not possible for wedding ritual. The courtyards and carriages of Sima Guang, the ribboned boxes and banquet tables of wedding letters and wedding songs, the covered wells and dreadful thresholds of almanacs and calendars have all vanished. An equivalent of a funerary inscription discovered in the corridor of an undisturbed tomb does not exist: a set of cue cards with archaist ritual dialogue found in an abandoned ancestral temple, with all vessels and foods in place; an original wedding letter in its tube, accompanied by its various gifts and bearers; or a sedan chair with a magic mirror and cosmological graphs, stranded by a residential gate. Just as it would not be feasible to build an authentic Middle-Period tomb, let alone to stage an accurate Middle-Period funeral, based merely on surviving texts, it is impossible to reconstruct an historical Middle-Period wedding sequence. The material remains of joint burials of husbands and wives suggest that a unifying theme of reproduction may have allowed incompatible discourses to converge in weddings as they do in the ritual time and space of tombs. But the proper coordination of such a convergence in an authentic nuptial ceremony would require a sense of ritual that cannot be inscribed in texts and that as a consequence has been irretrievably lost.

"Historical texts illustrate discourse under minimal conditions, because of the vast amount that can never be known of the context," writes William Hanks, "and this makes it all the more necessary to be explicit about how we read."[25] In the determinate, generic texts of the Middle Period, wedding ritual survives where the text is a ritual object and where writing is a ritual practice. These incomplete configurations of wedding ritual on the written page allow an understanding of the prefigured notions of time, space, bodies, and writing that inform the distinct discourses of ritual manuals, wedding letters, calendars and almanacs, and legal texts, but they prohibit knowledge of their refiguration in ritual performance. Although the material traces of joint burial suggest that incompatible discourses may have converged in the ritual practice of weddings, this convergence is imaginable only as unknown configurations of prefigured discourses enabled by an embodied, individuating sense of ritual, not as a refiguration of the immutable, segregated configurations of the ceremonies inscribed in texts (with the possible exception of a perfect performance of the meticulous choreographies in Sima Guang's *Letters and Ceremonies* or Zhu Xi's *Family Rituals*, whose very detail marks their remove from living practice and their restraint of the performer's contemporary sense of ritual). The historian's engagement with a living, meaningful past, in other words, requires an admission of loss. The denial of text by structuralist historians has led, ironically, to an unqualified equation of their dead, completed past with text.[26] The recognition of texts as historical objects (their constellation transformed by transmission and obliteration) and the understanding of writing as a cultural practice (distinct from human expression in material culture or embodied practice) restores the essential incompleteness, contingency, and coherence of texts, and demonstrates the need for a valid historical hermeneutics. For only a critical, dialectical, reflexive hermeneutics will allow the unfolding of the proposed worlds of the text and the unrealized potentialities of a living past in the changeful present.

## THE PRACTICE OF THE TOMB: MATERIAL TRACES OF RITUAL

If joint burials in the Middle Period resembled weddings, they did so most closely at the moment of interment, when the bodies of a husband and a wife were reunited in the ritual space of the tomb, amid ritual objects and ritual choreographies, in the ritual time of the funeral:

> We rejoice that in the tomb she joins her phoenix rooster,
> Though we mourn the tender age of this phoenix hen.[27]

Although single burial, too, aimed to convert death into immortality and to ensure the ritual and biological continuity of the family, only the filial offspring who brought their parents or grandparents together in death built veritable monuments to the fecundity of their ancestors. Allowing a few particular exceptions, only joint burial tombs mimic timber-frame structures in brick or stone, as metaphors of the lasting houses founded by the deceased, and only joint burial tombs are decorated with filiality scenes, those emblems of reproductive virtue. The simulated corbels of brick and the panels of filial devotion, however, are often the sole remains of joint burial, after the mourners have dispersed, and after the bodies and grave goods have suffered the destruction of natural decay, the greed of grave robbery, and the carelessness of salvage archaeology.

A tomb is in the first place the material trace of a funeral. At the moment of burial, the descendants and the ritual experts place the deceased in the tomb with grave goods and offerings, amid choreographies of sounds and smells and movements such as they deem proper and satisfactory. The tomb at its closure is a diminished but intentional trace of that ritual (a circumstance that distinguishes tombs from many other archaeological sites, such as fallow fields, waste pits, or abandoned cities). Then, gradually, the forces of decay begin to change the careful configuration of this ordered space. Paper and textiles decompose first, then wood and bones. Rising groundwater or a flooding river fills the tomb with mud and dissolves the painted plaster. A collapsing wall breaks vases and figurines. Forgetful centuries fell the grave trees, level the mound, and build roads and suburbs in the geomantic landscape. The descendants may have foreseen, possibly even intended, the decay of their ancestors' bodies, and of the paper houses and the spirit money.[28] Limited means may have forced a reluctant choice of wooden figurines instead of more durable earthenware statues; pious wealth may have allowed filiality scenes to be carved in stone rather than traced in paint. But natural decay is indiscriminate: a blind, mute, amoral force that disrupts the discursive coherence of the tomb and its surroundings.

Grave robbery, by contrast, is a discriminate (and immoral) act. In the flickering light of the robber's torch, grave goods transform into a collection of vulnerable commodities whose monetary value is still recognized in the worldly market from which the tomb attempted to exclude them.[29] The scope of grave robbery changes with the whims of that market, expanding with time from jewelry, precious metals, and fine porcelain to encompass at present the entire tomb.[30] Grave robbers disrupt the discursive space of the tomb not only by their selective removal of valuable objects, but also by breaking into the tomb through the roof or a wall rather than through its entrance, and by scrambling the bones of the dead in hopes of warding off vindictive ghosts.[31] Grave robbery, in other words, disturbs the coherence of the tomb by rearranging its contents according to a violent alternative discourse, a perverted ritual:

> The grave robber said, "My wife and I have been looting tombs for a living for more than ten years now. Whenever we set out to plunder a tomb, we take wine and a heater. After our gang has opened the tomb and we get to the coffin, my wife and I pour out the wine in turns. First I drink a cup and say, 'The guest wants a cup.' Then I drip wine into the mouth of the deceased and say, 'The host drinks a cup.' Then my wife drinks a cup in her turn. Then I say, 'Who's paying for the wine?' and my wife answers, 'The host pays for the wine.' And then we take his clothes and valuables."[32]

Archaeologists, of course, perform their own peculiar rituals and incantations. After the leaders of the Chinese Communist Party founded the People's Republic of China in 1949, they availed themselves of the vast expanse of the newly conquered soil to substantiate the linear narrative of Marxian historiography.[33] In the 1950s and early 1960s, archaeologists ("under the leadership of the Communist Party") engaged in vigorous debates about the precise dates of the transitions from matriarchy to patriarchy and from slave society to feudal society, and showed only a tepid interest in Middle-Period tombs.[34] In the 1970s, when archaeological publications resumed after an extended suspension during the early years of the Cultural Revolution, Middle-Period tombs ("the congealed blood and tears of the laboring masses") afforded evidence of protracted feudal oppression, endemic class struggle, and the lasting scientific and artistic achievements of workers and peasants.[35] Murals and artifacts in Qidan, Jurchen, and Mongol tombs proved the early assimilation of these nomadic peoples to Han culture, and thereby confirmed the enduring, inviolable boundaries of the "unified, multi-national fatherland," in the face of encroachment by "Soviet revisionist traitors" and unspoken political instability.[36] Since 1978, under the policies of the Four Modernizations and "socialism with Chinese characteristics," Middle-Period tombs have demonstrated a long, unique history of rapid technological development and vibrant commercial activity. The tombs of the "minority nationalities" (*shaoshu minzu*) of the Liao, Jin, and Yuan empires retained their political importance: before 1989, to illustrate an extended history of regional and ethnic diversity (in a socialist country with a market economy and with profitable ethnic tourism); after 1989, to illustrate an extended history of regional and ethnic unity (in one of few socialist states able to resist political change and the forces of nationalist separatism).[37]

Although the politics of archaeology cannot guide archaeological discovery, politics do determine which sites receive funding for careful excavation and which sites are abandoned to brief salvage digs, which sites are extensively documented in monographs and which are given a page or two in an archaeological journal, or none at all. Within archaeological publications there exists a further hierarchy of color plates, black and white plates, halftone reproductions in the text, line drawings, detailed description, cursory mention, and omission. The general preference in Chinese archaeology for sites that supplement the historical record or contribute to a detailed time line of technological and artistic development has yielded monographs on imperial and royal cemeteries, and on tombs with pristine murals, extensive architectural detail, or rare grave goods.[38] Site reports of Middle-Period tombs in archaeological journals, too, emphasize tomb structures, dates and other historical facts, murals, unusual objects, and examples of technological accomplishment in porcelain and textile manufacturing. This nationalist, Marxist, and antiquarian disposition renders site reports into an almost exact reversal of burials, both in the order and in the importance of events: the descendants place the deceased in the grave, arrange the grave goods, and close the tomb; the site report describes the tomb, analyzes the grave goods, and in the conclusion makes brief mention, if any, of the number of persons buried. The disinclination to consider the tomb as a trace of burial is explained not only by the overbearing materialist interests of Chinese archaeology, but also by the relative unimportance of Middle-Period tombs, which condemns many such tombs to salvage excavations by local cultural offices. These offices generally lack the means and the skills required for a proper determination of forms of burial, including the number and the sex of bodies. The average site report of a Middle-Period tomb, in other words, records but a trace of a trace: a selective written rendition of a complex material site already diminished by natural decay, grave robbery, and salvage excavation.

Table 5.1 intimates both the frustrations and the thrills that attend the perusal of Chinese archaeological journals. Although the archaeological disinterest in Middle-Period burial forms has doubtless swelled the number of instances in which the form of burial is unknown or simply not recorded, this same disinterest enhances the credibility of the correlations the table establishes between joint burial and filiality scenes, and between joint burial and the mimicry of timber-frame structures, since neither correlation is sought by the archaeologists.[39]

TABLE 5.1
Correlations between Filiality Scenes, Mimicry of Timber-Frame Structures, and Joint Burial

| | *Joint burial* | *Single burial* | *Unknown/Unstated* | *Total* |
|---|---|---|---|---|
| Total number of tombs | 269 (+15?) | 119 (+6?) | 534 | 961 |
| Filiality scenes | 22 | 0 | 13 | 35 |
| Mimicry of woodwork | 99 (+11?) | 12 (+4?) | 47 | 175 |
| Partial mimicry | 5 (+6?) | 3 (+1?) | 6 | 21 |
| Mimicry of woodwork and filiality scenes | 16 | 0 | 9 | 25 |
| Parallel chambers | 63 (+1?) | 2 | 10 | 76 |

Table 5.1 tabulates a total of 961 tombs from the Tang, Five Dynasties, Liao, Song, Jin, and Yuan, based on 382 site reports. In order to avoid undue imbalance, the statistics exclude the 849 tombs in the Northern Song charitable graveyard at Sanmenxia, Henan province, described in an extensive publication by the Archaeological Team of Sanmenxia City. Of the 1,037 tombs in the Northern Song imperial cemetery at Gongyi (also in Henan province), the table includes only the two that had been excavated by 1997, when the Henan Provincial Institute of Cultural Relics and Archaeology published its monograph about the site. Although an occasional indulgence of an impatient desire to pursue a tempting reference may have weighted the numbers slightly toward joint burial, by far the greater share of these statistics tabulates the findings of indiscriminate perusal of archaeological journals, notably entire years of *Kaogu* and *Wenwu*, supplemented with stray issues of the regional periodicals and the few available monographs.

The table shows that filiality scenes adorn only the walls of tombs that enshrine fecund couples. Funerary inscriptions may praise the filiality of those buried without a spouse, and filiality scenes may even decorate the stone coffin of a single burial (just as some stone coffins mimic elements of residential architecture), but filiality scenes carved or painted on the walls, or represented by figurines on the floor, appear to be exclusive to joint burial.[40] The table suggests a weaker correlation between joint burial and the mimicry of timber-frame structures, but examination of the twelve to sixteen exceptions reveals particularities that explain their apparent deviation. Six or seven of the exceptions in fact confirm rather than contradict the correlation between the mimicry of woodwork and joint burial, two being special forms of imperial burial, three or four being the tombs of Buddhist monks, and one the tomb of a Daoist priest.[41] Although monks and monastic priests led celibate lives, their community created its own continuity of generations and descendants, perpetuated by a filial transmission of teachings from master to disciple. The contributions of deceased monks to the perpetuation of their monastic lineage were commemorated by simulated wood architecture not only in tombs, but also in the crypts of pagodas.[42] The remaining six to ten exceptions may be explained by particular burial practices of the early Liao aristocracy, by archaeological oversight, or by incomplete burial.[43] The latter possibility is suggested by the two lonely exceptions to the firm correlation between joint burial and parallel-chamber tombs (table 5.1). In both these tombs, a deceased husband vainly awaited the burial of his widow in the adjoining, undecorated, unused chamber.[44] It seems reasonable to assume that the mimicry of timber-frame structures in single-chamber domeshaped tombs in some cases also anticipated a joint burial that never took place, due to the remarriage of the widow or due to other reasons, especially because most of the single remains found in such tombs appear to be male.

Simulated timber-frame structures, filiality scenes, and other material metaphors create complex, polysemous spaces in which may converge incompatible notions of time, space, bodies, text, and death, reconciled by their common reference to filial devotion, reproduction, and immortality. Excavated tombs instantiate this flexible metaphoric repertoire in a variety of materials, in a variety of structures, from the late Tang through the Yuan, from Heilongjiang to Sichuan and from Fujian to Gansu, in the joint burials of wealthy merchants, ranked officials, and imperial princes. A summary description of a few select tombs may illustrate the discursive variety enabled by a broadly shared funereal repertoire.

In May 1984, construction at the state-owned Huai-Hai Machinery Plant on the outskirts of Changzhi City, in southeast Shanxi province, uncovered a dome-shaped brick tomb.[45] When members of the provincial archaeological institute and the local museum arrived, they found that several objects had already been removed from the inundated tomb and that its structure had been damaged in several places. Closer scrutiny revealed a rectangular, single-chamber tomb, measuring 2.1 meters from its arched southern entrance to the rear northern wall, 2.66 meters from the western to the eastern wall, and 3.2 meters from the floor to the domed ceiling. Doorways in the eastern and western walls, now collapsed, once gave onto two small side chambers. A coffin platform stretched across the full breadth of the northern wall, decorated with auspicious *qilin* (chimeras) of carved brick. Above the platform, in the northern wall, stood a red, double-panel false door (its posts, architrave, and brasswork carefully mimicked in brick), guarded by a pair of lions and flanked by a symmetrical pair of lattice windows. Above the door, elaborate bracket sets rose as if to support the dome, as did identical sets at the top of the other walls. In both the eastern and the western wall were set two false lattice windows, along with carved bricks depicting scenes of filial devotion or domestic work (women by a well, women by a grindstone, women by a stove), each framed within the contours of a magic *ruyi* (as you wish) cloud. Another pair of filiality scenes appeared under the false windows in the northern wall. Apart from a porcelain pillow, a plate, a lamp, a jug, and an earthenware female figurine, the tomb contained a funerary inscription. This inscription, composed in 1081 by a certain Liu Cigong of Pengcheng (present Xuzhou, Jiangsu province) and carved with blossoms and vines, coordinates the motifs of the tomb:

> Funerary Inscription of Mr. Ma Yuxiu of Shangdang
>
> My lord Mr. Ma of this township has reached the blessed age of seventy-two. On the twenty-second day of the second month of this year [April 3, 1081], his wife, Ms. Chen, passed away at the age of sixty-four. Ms. Chen was by nature intelligent and able. She excelled at serving her parents-in-law. She never tarried in fetching water or preparing food, whether early in the morning or late at night, whether in the cold of winter or the heat of summer. My lord Mr. Ma was a precocious youth, and he served his parents with utmost filiality. He was a merchant by trade. His readings in Buddhist texts gave him a considerable understanding of their principles. In addition, he had a talent for construction, having mastered the craft of carpenters without ever having apprenticed with them. The coffins in this tomb were indeed made by my lord himself [? character illegible]. Although his household was always poor, these coffins are as sturdy and as lavish as those of wealthy households. Upon his wife's death [? several characters illegible], he began planning the tomb and arranged a funeral that did not overlook the smallest detail. He had five sons . . . three daughters . . . grandsons . . . granddaughters . . . and a great-granddaughter . . . On the seventeenth or *gengwu* day of the tenth or *jiayin* month, in the fourth or *xinyou* year of the Yuanfeng reign [November 20, 1081], he was buried one mile south of Pucheng. To the east, the tomb looks out on the Temple of the Two Immortals; to the west, on Mafang Village; to the south, on the Five Dragon Mountains; and to the north on the battlements of the city wall. The eulogy:

Life invariably ends in death,
It has been thus of old.
The place whither Yuxiu returns—
Who can compare with my lord?

Alas! this, too, may be called an ability to understand the principles.

As in *A Dream of Hua*, the ignorance of literary conventions in this unusual inscription reproduces the horizontality of practical space, and therewith recreates the juxtapositions of the diverse funereal motifs in the tomb. Ma Yuxiu's filial devotion, his study of Buddhist texts, and his skills in carpentry follow upon one another in a disjointed list. The clumsy adverbial phrase "in addition" cannot mask the contradiction between Buddhist insights and the geomantic connotations of carpentry. The flat surface of the inscription, unshaped by the hierarchies of determinate conventions, thus accommodates classicist filiality, Buddhist devotion, the magical skills of carpentry and the geomantic location of the tomb, and the conspicuous display of its coffins and structure.[46] The text transcribes thereby the tomb, with its images of filial devotion and domestic obedience, its geomantic site, and the conspicuous display of its size, workmanship, and bracket sets, and indeed of the illicit funerary inscription itself. However contradictory the understandings of life and death connoted by these juxtaposed objects, together they create a coherent space that transforms death into immortality, aided by metaphoric emblems of filiality, production, and reproduction.

The difference between the tomb of the merchant Ma Yuxiu and the tomb of Zhao Jun, Prince of Wei, is largely a matter of scale. Built thirteen years later, in 1094, the tomb of Zhao Jun, Prince of Wei, and Ms. Wang, Lady Wei and Yue, stood 150 kilometers south of Ma Yuxiu's tomb, in the Song imperial cemetery at Gongyi, Henan province.[47] Of the spirit road remained only the statues of a tiger, two rams, and a military official, found underground in 1985, twenty-four years after the original excavation in 1961. A ramp 5.52 meters wide descended across 13.5 meters to the southward entrance of the tomb: an arched gate of brick and stone slabs, 3.08 meters wide and 2.36 meters tall, carved and painted to simulate a gatehouse with bracketed eaves. Inside the gate, a corridor gave onto two shallow, vaulted side chambers in the walls and onto the vaulted doorway, 3.2 meters wide and 4.8 meters high, to the main chamber. The round, domeshaped tomb chamber measured 6.54 meters in diameter, and 6.48 meters from its flagged floor to the center of its dome. Across the centuries, grave robbers had broken into the tomb on at least four occasions, leaving yawning holes in the walls and the roof, and depleting whatever riches the tomb once held. Meanwhile, a thick layer of mud corroded all traces of coffins and bodies. Some fourteen shards were the sole remains of a set of variously glazed porcelain vessels, and an engraved stone box was the only remnant of the stringed jade tablets that once proclaimed the investiture of Zhao Jun as Prince of Wei. Only two large funerary inscriptions, placed upright at the entrance to the tomb chamber, remained in place: the inscription of the Prince of Wei, standing in the southwest corner of the tomb chamber, and the inscription of Lady Wei and Yue, standing in the southeast corner.

The prince's inscription consisted of a cover in the shape of a truncated pyramid, with the deities of the four directions carved into its sloping sides, and the inscription proper, adorned on its ample edge with the twelve signs of the zodiac in the guise of civil officials. The accomplished masonry of these impressive stones is matched by the literary refinement of the inscription, composed by the famous Fan Zuyu (1041–1098). Its introduction intertwines the imperial genealogy of the deceased with a celebration of its proud tradition of filiality and brotherly love, which it likens to the hallowed virtues of the founders of the Zhou dynasty. A summary list of the many investitures he received as the fourth son of Emperor Yingzong and as a younger brother of Emperor Shenzong, ends with a detailed account of his illness and death in 1088 at the age of 33, followed by his temporary burial at a Buddhist shrine. The inscription then praises the prince's appearance and bearing, his accomplishments in classical studies and calligraphy, his ritual performance and sagacity, and his frugality and virtues, and it makes brief mention of his sophisticated dabblings in Buddhist, Daoist, and medical texts before listing the names and titles of his ten sons and seven daughters. Thereafter the inscription renders an account of the prince's burial in the imperial cemetery, in 1094, north of his father's imperial tumulus, and concludes with a eulogy of the prince's exemplary contribution to the virtuous continuity of the imperial house.

The cover and funerary inscription of Ms. Wang, Lady Wei and Yue, assumed the same shape as those of the Prince of Wei, if at slighter proportions and without carved decorations. The text of the inscription, too, composed by the illustrious Zheng Juzhong (1059–1123), accords with the same conventional structure: genealogy, enfeoffments as spouse and widow of the prince, death (in 1103, at age forty-seven), accomplishments and virtues as a daughter, a wife, a widow, and a mother (culminating in a faintly miraculous death on her birthday), temporary burial, the names and titles of her seventeen children and some of her twenty-eight grandchildren, the final coburial in 1107, an assessment of her character, and a rhymed eulogy. The account of the rites of joint burial in the inscription emphasizes their chronomantic aspect:

> In the first year of the Daguan reign period [1107], after the Grand Astrologer had divined an auspicious date, he received an edict commanding him, under escort of E, Minister of Rites, and Guan, Commissioner of the Palace Visitors Bureau, to open the tomb on the eleventh day of the third month, and to cobury her on the twenty-ninth or *yimao* day, in the tomb of the late Prince in Yong'an County, in Henan.

The virtue enshrined in this imperial tomb—the ensurance of the continued supremacy of the imperial house by classicist virtue and ritual, by filial, brotherly, and wifely devotion, by unusual fecundity, by geomantic precautions, and by unmatched conspicuous display—was broadcast at a tremendous scale by the tumuli, temples, and monuments of the imperial cemetery that stretched southward and upward from the grave of the Prince of Wei and Lady Wei and Yue. The prince's tomb stood in the precinct of the Tumulus of Eternal Grace (Yonghouling), the tomb of his father, Emperor Yingzong, together with the tombs of Empress Gao (1032–1093), of his brother Zhao Hao, Prince of Yan, and of his nephew Zhao Jun, Prince of Yan (d. 1077).[48] The cemetery comprised eight such imperial precincts, as well as two graveyards for imperial kinsmen.[49] The tumuli arose in a mountainous landscape of 12 by 13 kilometers, in strict obedience of geomantic principles. Because according to the Five Tones system the imperial surname of Zhao belongs to the *jiao* pitch and therefore to the wood phase of the Five Phases, the burial grounds must slope downward from the southeast to the northwest, and a river must flow west of the cemetery in a southward direction.[50] The imperial tumuli and their satellite tombs were therefore built in four sites with the same properties: mountains to the east and to the south, affording a downward northwestern slope on which were set in succession the ritual precincts and tombs of emperors, empresses, and close imperial kin, laid out from the south to the north according to rank, and from the southeast to the northwest in chronological order of death.

Within this numinous site stood also the sacrificial halls of classicist ritual, Buddhist monasteries of continuous prayer, and a temple where statues of the deceased emperors were once enshrined. In front of the tumulus of each emperor and each empress, within the enclosure of the spirit wall, or upper palace (*shanggong*), once arose a temple for the performance of rare, elaborate sacrifices.[51] Everyday sacrifices for the deceased emperors were conducted at the temple of the lower palace (*xiagong*). At the four Buddhist monasteries, one at each of the four imperial burial sites, especially appointed monks offered uninterrupted prayers for the well-being of the deceased emperors:

> Emperor Shenzong ruled the subcelestial realm by means of filiality, and all the most venerable ceremonies by which his day sacrificed to its ancestors he offered without fail. In 1068, he decreed that at the Tumulus of Eternal Brilliance [of Emperor Renzong, r. 1022–1063] and the Tumulus of Eternal Grace [of Emperor Yingzong] there be erected a residence for Buddhist monks so as to secure their holy blessings. When the work was completed in 1072, he bestowed on it the name "Monastery of Luminous Filiality" and calligraphed the plaque in his own imperial hand.[52]

On a tall plateau above the northern bank of the Yiluo river are still discernable the foundations of a hall where once the immortal statues of eight deceased emperors commanded a view of the vast cemetery.

Imagine this site in its imperial splendor! The mountain ridges to the east and the south, the remote tumuli rising beyond imposing gates and long spirit roads lined with tall silent statues, the bright paint and blazing tiles of the sacrificial halls, the robed monks in their rich monasteries and the robed officials at the cemetery's county seat, the monumental steles and the imperial kilns, and across the shimmering river the Hall of Assembled Sages with its imperial statues. The entire, expansive site held the grandest accomplishments in geomantic planning, architecture, stonework, engineering, classicist ritual, Buddhist worship, literary composition, and calligraphy, and reconciled them by making them subservient one and all to the eternal glory of the imperial house of Zhao.

Although the parallel-chamber tombs of the South and the Southwest differ in structure from the domeshaped tombs of the North, they use a similar repertoire of funereal metaphors to amplify the same themes of filiality, reproduction, and immortality. A twelfth- or thirteenth-century tomb excavated in March 1959 in the Zhongliang Mountains outside Chongqing serves as an example.[53] Built with slabs of local sandstone inside a hillock, the tomb consisted of two symmetrical chambers, each with its own entrance, but connected within by two corridors. The two entrances, facing east-southeast at 113°, measured 1.60 meters in height and 1.28 meters in width, and assumed the aspect of small gatehouses, with double-panel stone-slab doors, pointed stone-slab roofs, and a protective gargoyle glaring from the ridgepole. The chambers each were 3.60 meters deep, 1.28 meters wide, and 3 meters high. Above the burial platforms, and inside the two corridors, projected the mimicked shapes of pillars, tiebeams, and bracket sets, carved out of the stone panels, while corbeled stone slabs suggested light wells in the front and back of each of the two chambers. These feigned architectural elements framed a profusion of decorated panels. Inside the front light well of each chamber, the carved shapes of the Green Dragon of the East, the Vermilion Bird of the South, the White Tiger of the West, and the Dark Warrior of the North corrected the awkward orientation of the tomb by creating an imaginary space laid out along an ideal south-north axis. Between the carved pillars and tiebeams of the chambers and the corridors were set four panels with auspicious flowers, eleven panels with filiality scenes (depicting both classical and Buddhist tales), five emblems of immortality (a grazing deer and a crane, an immortal mule, a monkey stealing peaches, and, on the capstones of the front light wells, the legends "eternity" [*yanchang*] and "longevity" [*fushou*]). In the rear wall of each chamber (the ideal north) stood a false double-panel lattice door decorated with blossoms and auspicious clouds. Although natural decay and grave robbers had reduced the contents of the tomb to some broken pottery and a handful of coins, the solid sandstone walls and ceilings perpetuated the immortal filiality of the couple they once protected, and of the descendants who built them.

A 1230 funerary inscription, finally, explicates similar motifs, in a similar structure, in a tomb on the northern outskirts of Dexing City, in northeast Jiangxi, more than a thousand kilometers east of Chongqing.[54] In a hollow in the White Lake Mountains, archaeologists of the Dexing County Museum found a brick tomb comprised of two parallel barrelvaulted chambers, facing eastward. Local villagers had already removed the stone slabs that sealed the tomb and had taken out most of the grave goods. On the paved floors of the tomb chambers, discolored earth, rusted nails, and chips of black lacquer still indicated the outlines of two decomposed coffins: the coffins of Lan Wenwei and his wife who were buried there in the tenth month of 1230. In addition, the archaeologists retrieved thirty-nine figurines that had stood around the coffins: a seated old man, a civil clerk, an armed warrior, a little boy, two broken figurines of dancers, twenty robed figurines with animal heads representing two incomplete sets of the zodiac, seven figurines representing two incomplete sets of the deities of the four directions, a prone figurine and a supine figurine, two roosters and a dog, and one fish. The tomb also yielded fragments of a porcelain vase clutched by a coiling dragon, and eight coins.

Although incomplete and disrupted, the pictorial program may yet be reconstructed in part. The figurines of the zodiac and the deities of the four directions must have stood around the coffins or along the walls of the two chambers to reorient them along the desired south-north axis.[55] The prone and supine figurines, the golden rooster of the east, and the jade dog of the west contributed to the protection of this ideal, cosmic space.[56] The civil clerk and the armed guard confirmed the official rank of the deceased. The fish (*yu*), a familiar visual pun, conjured prosperity (also *yu*), while the dancers provided posthumous entertainment.[57] Thus the descendants attempted to ensure the lasting peace and happiness of their reunited ancestors:

The Tomb of Lord Lan, Late Court Gentleman
for Ceremonial Service, of the Song

> My lord's personal name was Wenwei, his polite name was Yanzhang. He was from Lake Mountain, Hualong village, Jinjie township, Dexing county, Raozhou prefecture. My lord was born between 9:00 and 11:00 at night on the twenty-seventh day of the second month in the *maochen* year of the Shaoxing reign period [March 19, 1148]. He married Ms. Wang of the same village. They have six sons . . . one daughter . . . ten grandsons . . . ten granddaughters, two great-grandsons . . . and six great-granddaughters. Lady Wang predeceased my lord by three years. On that occasion, a plot was divined in a valley outside the village and there a pair of vaults was constructed. On the twenty-sixth day of the third month in the

*gengyin* year of the Shaoding reign period [May 10, 1230] my lord suddenly dreamt that he changed his clothes, stepped into a coffin, and closed it. When he awoke, he reflected that he would not dwell much longer in the world of men. On the ninth day of the ninth month [October 16] he rose with a sense of foreboding. He summoned the household and announced, "I am eighty-three years old. This is my allotted span." Then he sat up straight, recited a few words from a Buddhist scripture, and expired. On the third or *xinyou* day of the tenth month [November 9] of the same year, his orphaned descendants buried his coffin next to that of Lady Wang, in accordance with his will.

I am the same age as my lord's youngest son, Jianzao. The latter sent a missive posthaste, requesting a eulogy. Since obligation did not allow me to refuse, I composed the following:

> In these valleyed mountains,
> The phoenix pair dance and soar.
> Now that my lord has taken up his abode,
> His descendants will prosper.

Respectfully composed in the ninth month of the third year of the Shaoding reign [October–November, 1230] by family friend Li Mizhen, Lower Class Principal Gentleman, Magistrate of Yiling county in Xinxia prefecture [present Xuanchang, Hubei province] and Agriculture Intendant.

The diminished traces of the five tombs described in this chapter are not intended to represent the whole of Middle-Period burial practices. Rather, the selected tombs offer a few concrete, historical constellations of funereal motifs, constituted from regional repertoires by patrons and builders in their construction of coherent, individual, and unpredictable ritual spaces. Shaped by modular building techniques, commodification, sumptuary laws, and shared burial practices, tomb structures and funereal motifs attained a remarkable degree of standardization.[58] Domeshaped brick tombs of similar structure and decoration have been found all across the North, just as parallel-chamber stone-slab tombs have been found across the East, South, and Southwest. From the Tang through the Yuan, filiality scenes increasingly depicted the same deeds of filial devotion, in a standardized iconography that spread from the North to the Southwest.[59] Tomb contracts composed in different centuries and in different parts of the empire, may likewise use identical formulas.[60] Yet the selective modification and idiosyncratic juxtaposition of these standardized structures and commodified artifacts, these conventional iconographies and formulaic inscriptions, allowed a limitless variety of expression. Shi Shengzu (1191–1274), a scholar of the *Book of Changes*, was buried with his second wife, along with his inkstone, his inkstick, cosmological diagrams, a statue of the bodhisattva Guanyin, a lotus-shaped jade cup, and a pair of silver shoes bearing the surname of his first wife.[61] The ashes of Ma Zhiwen and his spouse, Ms. Zhang (d. 1112), were poured into a pair of life-size wooden dolls with movable limbs that sat in meditation on a wooden bed, facing an altar with sacrificial vessels, a circle of wooden zodiac figurines, and a sutra pillar.[62] The express desires of patrons on occasion might even disregard the established repertoires of regional builders, setting thereby an octagonal brick tomb with simulated timber-frame structure in Yangzhou, Jiangsu province, or a parallel-chamber tomb with a connecting corridor in Jia county, Henan province.[63] Tombs, like texts, are coherent traces of conscious human activity. Moreover, the tombs that survive from the Middle Period belong to the same social classes that produced the textual legacy of the period. The "simpler but more ambiguous language of material culture," however, allows a juxtaposition of discursive motifs that the determinate Middle-Period text cannot accommodate, preserving thereby a suggestion of what can never be learned from the writing of Middle-Period weddings.[64]

## THE PRACTICE OF THE TEXT: WRITTEN TRACES OF RITUAL

The practice of wedding ritual survives where writing is a ritual practice and where the text is a ritual object: in the exegetical choreographies of ritual manuals, in the cultural capital of wedding correspondence, and in the cosmological calculations of almanacs and calendars. In those archaist ceremonies, in those displays of wit and erudition, in those prognostications of cosmic danger are lastingly configured living discursive notions of time, space, bodies, and text that forever await their refiguration in ritual performance or in reading. Where writing is not part of the ritual practice of weddings, and where the text is not a ritual object intended for nuptial exchanges, the practice of the text obscures the practice of ritual. Laws and verdicts circulated as ritual objects in the grand ceremony of imperial government. They translate the time, space, bodies, and texts of weddings into the transparent, universal hierarchy of that government, thereby subjecting the local practice of weddings to the universalist practice of the legal text—just as the writing of local customs disperses both the locality and the practicality of local weddings by placing them in the centered literary landscape of a civilizing empire.

The ritual codes and the manuals of letters and ceremonies compiled in the late Tang and early Song merge courtly precedent and contemporary ceremonies with an archaic ritual structure that perpetuates an ancient continuity with the rituals of a remote past. Customs of merit, determined by a hermeneutics of practice, are judiciously embedded in the symmetrical space and time of scriptural rites. The awed study of Shang and Zhou bronzes in the eleventh century invalidated this hermeneutics of practice, inspiring instead visions of an immediate identity of the present with antiquity. Just as the patinated vessels dug from the soil conjured the presence of the men who had made them, the pages of transmitted scripture became a precious membrane through which might be discerned the forms of the ancients, bowing and yielding in permanent conformity with the cosmic order. Sima Guang, Zhang Zai, Cheng Yi, Lü Dajun, and Lü Dalin therefore relied in their manuals on a strict hermeneutics of text, interpreting and rearranging the scriptures in hopes that their times might re-embody the rites of sacred antiquity. These exegetical efforts, endorsed in time by the imperial court, culminated in the acceptance of Zhu Xi's *Family Rituals* as a new scripture. In these codes and manuals, the groom and the bride move through a ritual grammar of gates and stairs, vessels and viands to become husband and wife at the spatial and temporal center of the wedding sequence. Their ascetic imagination of antiquity compelled the stern exegetes of the Song to banish the creation of the sexual bodies of the groom and the bride to the unlit periphery of their nuptial rites.

The exuberant parallel prose of Song wedding correspondence replaced the sober, elegant formality of the engagement letters of earlier eras. Although of lesser currency than official correspondence or funerary inscriptions, wedding letters circulated in the same economy of written exchanges, as watermarked tokens of erudition, originality, and wit. These letters create an anterior space and time, in which caricatures of the groom and the bride contribute to a pretense of social inequality that the form and style of the letters themselves deny. The cultural capital of literary composition and the symbolic capital of matrimonial strategy merge and consolidate in the linear, hierarchical arrangement of writing manuals, where the apt allusions of high officials and the prestigious covenants of examination candidates tower above the apologetic letters of uxorilocal grooms and the cloddish fumbles of invented peasants. In the anterior time and space of the writing manual, too, the approach of the wedding day suspends conventions of literary propriety to allow the inclusion of addresses and song cycles in which the groom slowly penetrates doorways and curtains to unite with his bride amid convulsive volleys of fertile grain. Different from writing manuals, selections of wedding letters in collected works retain some of the horizontality of strategic time, in which bride-givers are also bride-takers, and in which a humbling alliance in one generation enables a prestigious match in the next. However lifelike the grooms and brides in these compositions, and however lively the ceremonies, they are mere creations of the educated hand, figments of the ink and paper that circulated as real ritual objects, in real ritual time.

Almanacs and calendars preserve on their scant pages the traces of a profuse culture of mantic practice that extended from the painted halls of the Bureau of Astronomy to the makeshift stands of village diviners. The taboo days in imperial calendars and the cosmic charts in commercial almanacs trace for the groom and the bride a safe path through the dread hours and threatening doorways of the wedding day, past the numinous well and the wrathful stove. Medical texts explicate the vulnerability and danger of the virginal body, replete with yin blood, and warn of the offensive pollution of sexual intercourse. Miracle tales illustrate the rewards to be gained from the observance of these taboos, and the harm incurred by those who ignore them. Submission to cosmological calculations ensures a prolific marriage and lasting wealth, while disobedience brings spirit possession, destitution, or childless widowhood. Although the lacking prestige of mantic tracts and medical treatises has resulted in their almost complete obliteration, surviving fragments yet suggest the endless variety of calculatory systems generated by a limited number of shared assumptions.

The laws of the Tang, the Song, and the Yuan devise transparent, universal hierarchies of rank, age, kinship, and (in the Yuan) ethnicity that determine the perennial rights and obligations of imperial subjects. Marriage laws protect these hierarchies by containing the temporary instability that engagements and weddings occasion (as betrothal sums are paid and daughters become wives) and by prohibiting alliances that transgress inviolable boundaries of kinship, generation, status, or ethnic difference. Verdicts translate the colloquial practice of local weddings into the classical language of this universal law, thus allowing brief, distorted glimpses of unwritten, unwritable cultures of local practice.

Ritual manuals, wedding letters, almanacs and calendars, and legal texts inscribe wedding ceremonies into discrete discourses. The prefigured notions thus configured in ritual choreographies ensure that these texts will always unfold for the reader their distinct worlds, preserving "the memory of usages and ways of feeling that no longer exist, persistent traces of the past which nothing in the present resembles."[65] *Rites of the Kaiyuan Period* places the reader in the courtyards of the Tang palace or on the steps of aristocratic houses, in a time that perpetuates a dignified memory of antiquity, to perform the ceremonies appropriate to his worldly status. Sima Guang's *Letters and Ceremonies* and Zhu Xi's *Family Rituals* guide the reader through the symmetrical time and centered space of gates and temples (with curtains for walls and feigned stairs of chalk stripes) in a timeless choreography that merges the groom and the bride with the written signs of ritual scripture, and thence with the vanished gestures of the ancients. In their diction and in their references to accompanying gifts, wedding letters preserve a memory of the strategic time of negotiations between men of educated wealth, while nuptial songs lead the reader through a delirious illusion of their vermilion residences, redolent of wine and incense and carnal pleasures. Calendars and almanacs conjure a threatening universe of baleful stars, vindictive spirits, and liminal spaces, through which moves the vulnerable and dangerous body of the virgin bride. In verdicts, the robed official sits ever on his dais, the inked tip of his brush the extremity of imperial government, as he instills the emperor's cosmic order in his besieged courtroom and banishes local disorder to the margins of the written page.

Although certain ceremonies in these scattered, fragmented texts seem at times faintly compatible, their grooms and brides cannot shed the distinct, imperious times and spaces in which their authors have set them. Dark fears of pollution do not afflict the revelers in nuptial songs, and the stately ceremonies of archaic ritual forbid the lewd frivolity of a public consummation. The determinate conventions of the classical text prevent the mergence of discursive spaces, times, and bodies that occurs in tombs. A shared theme of reproduction may have coordinated the confluence of incompatible discursive notions in the ritual practice of weddings, but it is powerless to overcome the immutable generic boundaries within which Middle-Period weddings are forever inscribed and within which grooms and brides forcibly reproduce preordained, generic notions of time and space and bodies and writing. Even in texts that juxtapose fragments of incompatible ceremonies, such as collected works or *A Household Necessity*, or even *Wedding Ritual: A New Edition*, those fragments retain their exclusive discursive contexts, unintegrated and indeed unassimilable into a coordinating ceremonial sequence. The generic boundaries of Middle-Period texts, perpetuated by the practice of writing, have been enhanced by the practice of transmission, since transmission has favored public, generic, printed texts to the exclusion of private, unique manuscripts. Incompatible discourses may have converged in the practice of wedding ritual as they do in tombs, and they may have converged even in the writing of weddings as they do on the stone slabs of funerary inscriptions, but the generic conventions of transmitted text have rendered all such convergence invisible and obsolete.

The tomb is a text, for a tomb, like a text, is a trace of conscious human activity. And yet the tomb is not a text, for its materiality allows a silent juxtaposition of incompatible worlds that the determinate text precludes. The text is a tomb, for a text, like a tomb, preserves in its words, and even in its silences, a forgotten space, a prior time, a faint gesture, ancient ways of seeing and feeling. And yet a text is not a tomb, for generic convention has excluded from the text the multivalence of living practice, the unwritten, unwritable sense of ritual that is forever, irretrievably lost.

## The Practice of History: Toward a Cultural History of the Middle Period

Like the archaeologist, the historian stands in a landscape of diminished traces. Selective transmission has preserved printed, public texts but obliterated unique, private manuscripts. Intellectual fealty and literary preference have protected classicist writings and collected works while ephemera perished and archives were abandoned to fire. The present configuration of Middle-Period texts thus offers but a fragmented record of the original textual landscape. Yet even that original landscape was merely a written surface, shaped by literary traditions and generic conventions. The determinate practice of the classical text excluded the variety and ambiguity of daily life and relegated local practice to the margins of the written page (where it recedes in the damp shrouds of steep cliffs). The Middle-Period historian must therefore recover the past through the historical practice of the text. Only a patient examination of the fissures and outcroppings of the present textual landscape will reveal the accretions and transformations achieved by the practice of transmission, and only a critical hermeneutics will disclose the culture of writing that produced the extant texts. The historian's narrative cannot but follow the accidented terrain of the sources. Not the wide, even flow of a continuous narrative will issue from these labors, but a fragmented description of a unique landscape of cragged discursive formations.

This book demonstrates what Middle-Period history stands to gain from an acknowledgment of the incompleteness of the past and from a narrative accommodation of its fragmented texts. Its descriptions of discursive formations have not only allowed a better understanding of the complex diversity of ritual time, ritual space, and ritual bodies in the writing of Middle-Period weddings, but they have revealed aspects of well-known texts and discourses that the narrow readings of social and intellectual historians have hitherto obscured: the cultural geography of notebooks, the crucial importance of archaeology and archaism in Song and Yuan classicism, the prestige of parallel prose during the twelfth and thirteenth centuries, the semiotics of walls and robes in manuals for local government, and the motifs of filiality and reproduction in funerary inscriptions and burial practices. The improved understanding of discursive practice and generic convention has also contributed to a more effective heuristics, leading to the discovery of passages from wedding books in almanacs and in notebooks.

The dispersal of traditional historical narrative, and its replacement with a fragmented description of segregated discourses, has allowed the preservation of the detailed, contradictory discoveries yielded by this hermeneutics and heuristics: the obfuscation of regional difference in notebooks, the precise exegetical choices in ritual manuals, the mimicry of ritual time in wedding correspondence, the opportunities of betrothals and the dangers of weddings in calendars, the simultaneous intimation and occlusion of local practice in verdicts. The extensive discussion of engagement letters in chapter 2, especially, stands as an impeachment of the methods of the many historians who, aware of the existence of these letters, have been unable to make use of them in their studies of Middle-Period weddings. The abandonment of the universal time of structuralist historiography has also allowed the preservation of the incongruous chronologies and unreconciled simultaneity of discursive formations. Each of the four chapters of this book extends across a different stretch of the Middle Period, and the sequence of chapters (of diminishing length) makes visible the fragmentation of discursive coherence accomplished by the uneven transmission of texts in subsequent centuries. Although the prose of this book cannot match the compact elegance of its erudite sources, its borrowed metaphors and its deliberate approximation of translation and exposition, of analysis and narration, have created a shared textual space, a "fusion of horizons," in which the living discourses of the past may engage the historical discourses of the present.[66] The introduction of texts as historical actors (and as grammatical subjects) and the recognition of the written page as an historical space, moreover, has obviated the fictional characters and artificial settings required by the passive, speculative prose of structuralist history.

The failure of social history, in other words, is not a matter of incidental misinterpretation; it is the structural failure of an unexamined, untenable hermeneutics. Social history (like materialist archaeology) seeks to write an inferior past in the superior, objectivist terms of the modern present. Its universalist notion of the social presumes a linear, commodified time in which scientific bodies inhabit a unified, disenchanted space. This nineteenth-century time, with its steam engines and gunboats, obliterates the intricate discursive multiplicity of the past and ravishes its delicate textual landscape for irreducible facts, whose true meaning and value is understood only by the modern historian. Dislodged from their discursive environment, these meaningless facts fill out the historian's preconceived narrative of a seamless, linear time. The awful power of this nineteenth-century time and its conquering narratives lends the modern historian the authority to proclaim this hermeneutics to be common sense, an infallible standard that condemns premodern discourses as backward and irrelevant. Unlike the natural resources commandeered by colonial industrialists for their tireless factories, however, the texts appropriated by the modern historian do not have universal applicability. The relentless linear time of the modern historian requires a continuous flow of interchangeable data that few Middle-Period texts provide. The dedicated attempt of the social historian to write objective, real history thereby achieves the opposite. The imposition of universalist, modern notions of time, space, bodies, and writing destroys the very historicity of Middle-Period texts and produces only solipsist fictions of a complacent present.

This book has attempted to contribute to a cultural history that accommodates the particularities of Middle-Period practices of writing and transmission. Historians of Europe and the United States are bound to their sources by the organic continuity of a shared literary tradition, with common metaphors and common modes of emplotment. No such continuity exists between the postmodern historian and the Middle Period. The historian of the Middle Period must therefore make an effort to find a language and metaphors and modes of emplotment that accomplish an engagement of the postmodern present with a living past. For in the end, it is not the historian who explains the sources, but the sources that illumine the historian, as they unfold in front of the written page the proposed worlds of the text and the unrealized potentialities of the present.

# Glossary

*A Zhang* 阿張
Ai Changji 哀長吉
*bakai* 八開
Bai 白
*Baiguan liuli ci* 百官六禮辭
*bai men* 拜門
*bai shi* 百事
*bai tang* 拜堂
*baitang zhiyu* 拜堂致語
*bai xianling* 拜先靈
*bangxia* 榜下
Bao Zheng 包拯
*baozi* 抱子
*biji* 筆記
*bishi* 比事
*Bian li* 編禮
*binli* 賓禮
*bu* (plastromancy) 卜
*bujiang* 不將
*bujiang zhi fa* 不將之法
*bu li* 不利
*bu tian* 不腆
*cailiao* 材料
Cai Xiang 蔡襄
Cang Jie 倉頡
*changbai zhiyu* 唱拜致語
Chang'e 嫦娥
Chen Chun 陳淳
Chen Lie 陳烈
Chen Shijun 陳史君
Chen Wei 陳韡
Chen Xiang 陳襄
Chen Zhizhong 陳執中
Chen Zonggui 陳總龜
Cheng Hao 程顥
*cheng hun* 成婚
*chengjie* 承接
*Chengnan lianju yibai wushi yun* 城南聯句一百五十韻
*chengqin* 成親
Cheng Yi 程頤
*ci* 詞
*congchen* 叢辰
Cui Yin 崔駰
*cuizhuang ci* 催妝詞
*Dade lüling* 大德律令
*dafu* 大夫
*dahunshu* 答婚書
*Da Tang xinding jixiong shuyi* 大唐新定吉凶書儀
*Da Tang yili* 大唐儀禮
*Da Yuan tongzhi tiaoli gangmu* 大元通制條例綱目
*dazong* 大宗
Dai Yi 戴翼
*Daodejing* 道德經
*Daotong* 道統
Daoxue 道學
*Daozang* 道藏
Deng Zongwen 鄧宗文
*didi* 滴滴
Di Renjie 狄仁傑
*dinghunshu* 定婚書
*dongwei* 洞微
Du Youjin 杜友晉
Duan Chengshi 段成式
*dunjia* 遁甲, 遁甲
*e'wu* 惡物
*faduan* 發端
*Fali* 法例

*fanren* 凡人
*fanying* 反映
Fan Zhen 范鎮
Fan Zhongyan 范仲淹
Fan Zuyu 范祖禹
*fanzuo* 反坐
Fei Gun 費袞
*fengjian shi zhong* 豐儉適中
Feng Su 馮宿
Feng Zizhen 馮子振
*fu* 賦
*fuchi* 富侈
*fuduo* 富多
*fufu* 夫婦
*fu jian jiugu* 婦見舅姑
*fu jun jiugu* 婦餕舅姑
*furen* 婦人
*fushou* 福壽
*ganhe* 干合
*gong* 工
*gongfa* 公法
Guqi shuo 古器說
*gushi* 故事
*guwen* 古文
*Guwen Shangshu shiwen* 古文尚書釋文
*guai* 怪
*guanfa* 官法
*guanru* 官儒
Guangqi 光啓
*guixi* 軌析
Han Yu 韓愈
*Haoshi jin* 好事近
*he jin* 合巹
*he ti* 合體
Hong Mai 洪邁
*huhun* 戶婚
Hu Qiyu 胡祇遹
Hu Ying 胡穎
*huapan* 花判
Huang Chao 黃巢
*Huangdi shou sanzi Xuannü jing* 黃帝授三子玄女經
Huang Gan 黃榦
Huang Tingjian 黃庭堅
*huiding yizhuang* 回定儀狀
*hui'e* 穢惡
*hunjia* 婚嫁
*hunshu* 婚書
*hunyin* 婚姻
*ji* 記
*Jifu zhidu* 祭服制度
*Jigu lu* 集古錄
*jiji* 及笄
*jili* 吉禮
*jiri* 吉日
*jishu guan* 伎術官
*Jixiong shuyi* 吉凶書儀
Jia Gongyan 賈公彥
*jiali* (joyful rites) 嘉禮
*jiamai* 嫁賣
*jiaqi qixi shi* 佳期綺席詩
*jiaqu* 嫁娶
*jiatong* 嫁痛
*jian* 簡
*jianbian* 簡便
*jianchu* 建除
Jiang Chengwan 江程萬
*jiaojie you jian* 交接有漸
*jiaotong* 交通
*jieba* 結跋
*jiehun* 結婚
*jiejiaofu* 接腳夫
*jing* 經
Jing Fang 京房
*Jingshi dadian xiandian* 經世大典憲典
*jingzhuan* 經傳
*jiugu xiang fu* 舅姑饗婦
*jiuhun* 就婚
*jue* (ditty) 訣
*jue* (tough) 倔
*jueju* 絕句
*junli* 軍禮
*junzi* 君子
*Kaibao tongli* 開寶通禮
*kanyu* 堪輿
Kongzi 孔子
*kouhao* 口號
*lanmen wen* 攔門文
*leishu* 類書
*li* (advantageous) 利
*li* (ritual) 禮
Li (Plum) 李
Li Bing 李丙
Li Fuyan 李復言

*Lige xinbian* 禮閣新編
Li Gonglin 李公麟
*lihun* (divorce) 離婚
*lihun* (ritual wedding) 禮婚
*Liji shuo* 禮記說
*Lijing* 禮經
Li Shangyin 李商隱
*Lizhi ju* 禮制局
Liu Chang 劉敞
Liu Gong 劉珙
Liu Kezhuang 劉克莊
*liu li* 六禮
*liuren* 六壬
Liu Runeng 劉汝能
Liu Xiang 劉向
Liu Yingli 劉應李
Liu Yue 劉岳
Lou Yao 樓鑰
Lu Dian 陸佃
Lu You 陸游
Lü Cai 呂才
Lü Dafang 呂大防
Lü Dajun 呂大均
*lüshi* 律詩
Lü Zuqian 呂祖謙
*maimen qian* 買門錢
*maixiu* 賣休, 買休
*meiren* 媒人
Mi Fu 米芾
*miao jian* 廟見
*mingfu* 命服
*mingqi* 明器
*mingshu* 命書
*nabishu* 納幣書
*na cai* 納采
*nafu* 納婦
*na ji* 納吉
*nayin* 納音
*na zheng* 納徵
*nannü* 男女
*Nan Rong zhi san fu* 南容之三復
*neiluan* 內亂
*nonggong* 農工
*nü xian nan* 女先男
Ouyang Xiu 歐陽修
Ouyang Xuan 歐陽玄
*pudi qian* 鋪地錢
*pu fang* 鋪房
*qi* (curious) 奇
*qi* (energy) 氣
*qilin* 麒麟
*Qian jin fang* 千金方
*qiao* 巧
*qin* 親
Qin Gui 秦檜
*qinjuan* 親眷
*qin ying* 親迎
*qinggai* 青蓋
*qingli* 清理
*Qingming shang he tu* 清明上河圖
*qing qi* 請期
*qiuhun* 求婚
Qiu Jun 丘濬
*renlun* 人倫
*ru* 儒
*ruyi* 如意
*sa gudou* 撒穀豆
*sa zhang* 撒帳
*sanming* 三命
*shanggong* 上宮
*shangliang wen* 上梁文
*shang tou* 上頭
*shaoshu minzu* 少數民族
Shao Yong 邵雍
*shen* 身
*shen li* 甚利
*shi* (achillomancy) 筮
*shi* (poem) 詩
*shi* (*shi* class) 士
*shi'e* 十惡
*shi'er hang qishi* 十二行啓式
*shihua* 詩話
*Shi hunli* 士婚禮
Shi Jiayi 石加議
*shijing* 式經
*shinü* 室女
*shishu* 士庶
Shi Xinwen 始信文
Shi Yingzu 史繩祖
*shupan* 書判
*shuyi* 書儀
*Shuyi jing* 書儀鏡
*sijian* 四撿
*siliu* 四六

*siliu hua* 四六話
Sima Guang 司馬光
Sima Jizhu 司馬季主
*Sitian jian* 司天監
*Sitian tai* 司天臺
*Song huiyao* 宋會要
*song luan* 送鸞
Song Qi 宋祁
Song Shou 宋綬
Song Xiang 宋祥
*su* 俗
Su Guo 蘇過
Su Shi 蘇軾
Su Tianjue 蘇天爵
Sun Simiao 孫思邈
*Suosui lu* 瑣碎錄
*Taichang xinli* 太常新禮
*Taihe lü* 泰和律
*tai jian nan xing* 太簡難行
*taisu* 太素
*taiyi* 太一
*Tang huiyao* 唐會要
*tian* 天
*tianren* 天人
*tonghunshu* 通婚書
*tong lao* 同牢
*tou hu* 投壺
*wanci* 挽辭
*wanshu lianzhu* 婉淑聯珠
*wang* 望
Wang Anshi 王安石
Wang Ang 王昂
Wang Ceng 王曾
Wang Jian 汪鑒
Wang Maochang 汪懋昌
Wang Shen 王詵
Wang Shixian 汪世顯
Wang Weiqin 汪惟勤
Wang Xizhi 王羲之
Wang Xianzhi 王獻之
Wang Yan 王喦
Wang Yuanchang 汪源昌
*wei cheng* 未成
*wei ding* 未定
*Wei gong zhi wu chang* 衛公之五長
Wei Liaoweng 魏了翁
*wen* 文
*wen ming* 問名
*Wenxuan* 文選
Weng 翁
Weng Fu 翁甫
*wudang* 吾黨
*wuhui* 污穢
*Wujun chongxiu Dachengdian ji* 吳郡重修大成殿記
*wuxing* (Five Punishments) 五刑
*wuxing* (Five Stars) 五星
*wuxing* (Five Surnames) 五姓
*wuyin* 五音
*xi* 習
*xizhuo qian* 繫捉錢
*xiagong* 下宮
Xia Song 夏竦
*Xian-Qin guqi ji* 先秦古器記
*Xianqing li* 顯慶禮
*xiang* (to face toward) 向
*xiang* (image) 象
*Xiangding jiaomiao liwen* 詳定郊廟禮文
*Xiangyue* 鄉約
*Xiaoyuan qian jin* 笑苑千金
*xiehouyu* 歇後語
Xie Xuan 謝玄
*xin* 新
*Xinding shuyi jing* 新定書儀鏡
*Xinji jixiong shuyi* 新集吉凶書儀
*xingjia* 行嫁
Xiong Guxi 熊古溪
Xiong He 熊禾
*xiongli* 凶禮
Xiong Penglai 熊朋來
Xiong Puzhai 熊普齋
Xiong Qingzhou 熊慶冑
Xu Hong 徐洪
Xu Kai 徐鍇
*xuli* 序例
*xu niande lian* 敘年德聯
Xu Xuan 徐鉉
*Xu Youguai lu* 續幽怪錄
*yanchang* 延長
*yan ding* 言定
Yan Junping 嚴君平
*yanqin* 衍禽
*yang* (goat) 羊
Yang (Poplar) 楊

Yang Fu 楊復
*yangzhai* 陽宅
Ye Shi 葉適
Ye Wuzi 葉武子
*yi* 異
*yi cheng* 已成
[*yi*] *ding* 已定
*yi jing jiao zi* 一經教子
*Yili* 儀禮
*Yili ju* 議禮局
*Yishi* 逸史
*yinqi shuangbi* 姻契雙璧
*yinyang bujiang* 陰陽不將
*Yinyang shu* 陰陽書
*yinzhai* 陰宅
*yingqu* 迎娶
*Ying xian ke* 迎仙客
Yonghouling 永厚陵
*yu* (fish) 魚
*yu* (metaphor) 寓
*yu* (prosperity) 餘
Yu Fan 虞翻
*Yuanfeng xinli* 元豐新禮
*Yuanhe xinding shuyi* 元和新定書儀
Yuan Jiang 元絳
*Yueling* 月令
*yueyan* 月厭
*yueyu* 樂語
*yunyun* 云云
*zaohua* 造化
Zengzi 曾子
*zha* 劄
Zhai Qinian 翟耆年
Zhang Ao 張敖
Zhang Shaojian 張紹漸
*Zhang shi* 張氏
Zhang Shi 張栻
Zhangsun Wuji 長孫無忌
Zhangtai 章臺
Zhang Yong 張詠
Zhang Yue 張說
Zhang Zai 張載
Zhao Jun 趙頵
*zhaomu* 昭穆
Zhao Renben 趙仁本
Zhen Dexiu 真德秀
*Zhenguan li* 貞觀禮
*zheng* 正
Zheng Juzhong 鄭居中
Zheng Qiao 鄭樵
Zheng Yuqing 鄭餘慶
Zheng Zhong 鄭眾
*zhi* 止
*zhici* 致詞
*zhiyu* 致語
*Zhiyuan xin'ge* 至元新格
*Zhizheng tiaoge* 至正條格
Zhonghe 中和
Zhou Bangyan 周邦彥
Zhou Bida 周必大
Zhou Mi 周密
*zhoutang jiaqu* 周堂嫁娶
Zhou Xu 周諝
Zhu 朱
*zhuhun* 主婚
Zhu Xi 朱熹
Zhu Yizun 朱彝尊
*zhuan* 傳
*zhuo* 拙
*zigui* 子規
*ziliao* 資料
*ziran* 自然
*ziwei* 紫微
*Zong'e* 摠堊
*Zuanyao shuyi* 纂要書儀
*zuodao* 左道

# Notes

## INTRODUCTION

1. Lunyu 20.5a (XX.3).

2. Ricoeur 1981, 113.

3. The term "sense of ritual" is borrowed from Catherine Bell. See Bell 1992, 80–88. Cf. Bourdieu 1977, 113–30 ("sense of practice"); Bourdieu 1990, esp. 10–14 ("practical sense").

4. On text/performance and centering, see Zito 1997.

5. Wedding scenes occur even in the very few fictional works to survive from the Middle Period. The scarcity of Middle-Period fiction, however, encumbers a clear understanding of the relation between the practice of the text and the nuptial ceremonies these texts inscribe. The involuntary bigamy of Liu Zhiyuan in the *In-All-Modes-and-Keys of Liu Zhiyuan* (*Liu Zhiyuan zhugongdiao*), for example, is merely one instance in the parodic sequence of events that leads the oblivious protagonist to his predestined imperial throne. But what does one make of the hairpin, snapped by his first wife into two tallies of engagement on the eve of his departure (and second marriage)? See LZY 1.15. Cf. CZZJ 1.4a. On the *In-All-Modes-and-Keys of Liu Zhiyuan*, see Idema 1995.

6. On the genre of local gazetteers, see Bol 2001; Hargett 1996. On travel essays and travel diaries, see Deborah Rudolph 1996. On notebooks, see Bol 1995.

7. For a similar view of this merging of generic and geographical boundaries in the writing of a threatening, alien landscape, see West 2006.

8. JLB 1.1. The preface to *A Variegated Banquet from the Youyang Mountain Library* (*Youyang zazu*, 9th century) and a 1232 colophon to *Things Heard on Official Travels* (*Youhuan jiwen*, 1232) also compare notebook entries to food. See YHJW 95; YYZZ 1. More commonly, prefaces (and titles) present the gathered notes as records of fading memories jotted down in lonely retirement—matters as marginal as their decrepit author in his rural isolation. See, for example, the prefaces to DXBL, DZJS, GTL, LCLZ, MQBT, MZML, QBZZ, SLYY, SSYTL, YJ, ZhuS.

9. JLB 1.11. Cf. QBZZ 3.100.

10. See Hanshu 54.2447.

11. DSXZ 7.531.

12. Sima Guang and Huang Gan (1152–1221) shared Zhuang Chuo's dismayed mirth about this ceremony. See SY 3.36; ZZYL 89.3b. Cf. also Ebrey 1991b, 82; Ebrey 1993, 94. Some evidence exists to suggest that Song and Yuan literati who performed Tying up the Hair indeed traced it back to authoritative texts such as a poem by Sun Wu in *Selections of Refined Literature* (*Wenxuan*; see WX 29.10b). See, for example, HMQS II.3.11b.

13. The standard text reads, "Someone placed a seat next to the son and the father." Here, I follow a more plausible variant offered in the notes. See JLB 38n9.

14. JLB 1.8.

15. Cf. JLB 1.15, 2.65–66, 3.93, 3.118. In two of these entries (2.65–66 and 3.118), local customs are set not only against canonical ritual, but also against the culture of literary display discussed in the second chapter of this book. For other examples of the writing of weddings in notebooks, see JLJZZ 17b; LXABJ 4.45; MTKH 4.2b–3a; TWSCT 5.93; YJZ XX.7.1273; YYZZ I.1.7–8 (translated in part in chapter 3), II.4.241; ZhuS 3.3ab, 3.4a.

16. GLTJ preface.1–2.

17. GLTJ 22.75. Cf. the similarly curt, comparative statements in LWDD 2.71, 7.251; ZFZ 1.8, 1.12, 1.24, 1.27, 1.28, 2.41, 2.43.

18. LWDD 10.418. Cf. LWDD 4.158, 10.419–23, 10.429–32, 10.447.

19. See Bol 2001; Hargett 1996.

20. WJZ 2.7b. Cf. CAZ 1.6a; WJTJXJ 1.12a.

21. West 2000, 3.

22. DJMHL preface. Cf. West 1985, 70. On the land of Hua Xu, see Liezi 2.13–14.

23. On this painting, see Tsao Hsing-yuan 2003.

24. DJMHL 5.144.

25. At least two of the wedding practices included in the ritual narrative of *A Dream of Hua*, namely the physiognomizing of brides and the use of the nuptial cups as a prognosticatory device, are mentioned elsewhere as unique of Kaifeng. See JLJZZ 17b; ZhuS 3.3ab.

26. West 2000, 14.

27. Cf. Bourdieu 1991, 220–23; de Certeau 1984, 202–203.

28. See GHYHZ 138; LWDD 10.418n1; Netolitzky 1977, xxiii.

29. Many of my insights into the relationships between practice, writing, and discourse cannot be traced to particular pages, but they took shape in the process of reading the following works, to which I therefore owe them: Bell 1992; Bourdieu 1977, 1990, 1991; Chartier 1994, 1997; Connerton 1989; de Certeau 1984, 1988; di Leonardo 1998; Foucault 1972; Hanks 2000; Illich 1993; Ricoeur 1981, 1984–1988; Shanks and Tilley 1992; Spiegel 1997; White 1973; Zito 1997. On the universality of classical genres and the colonization of the vernacular, cf. West n.d., esp. 34–35.

30. Cf. Ricoeur 1984, 52–54. Because Paul Ricoeur (1984–1988) in his *Time and Narrative* pursues a philosophy of time, he applies his central terms "prefiguration," "configuration," and "refiguration" only to the mediation between time and narrative, but space, bodies, and writing are similarly prefigured, configured, and refigured in narrative.

31. On the merging of text and ritual in the configuration of ritual narrative, cf. Kern 1997, 7–22; Zito 1997, 77–94.

32. On the open-ended, undetermined process of refiguration, cf. Hanks 2000, 173–74; Illich 1993; Ricoeur 1988.

33. On the denial of text and the invention of data, cf. LaCapra 2000, 30–72; Ricoeur 1988, 117–18.

34. Cf. Bourdieu 1977, 3–4, 25–29; Bourdieu 1990, 14–17, 25–40; Shanks and Tilley 1992, 59–65.

35. Ricoeur 1981, 295.

36. Only one of the fifty-odd books and five of the twenty-odd articles on the history of weddings and marriage that I have read specifically address Middle-Period wedding ritual. See Cai Weitang 1990; Fang Jianxin 1985; Peng Liyun 1988; Wu Baoqi 1989; Zhou Yiliang 1985; Zhu Ruixi 1988. Zhang Bangwei (1989) has published a book of essays about marriage (not weddings) in the Song dynasty. For a more extensive critique of this literature, see de Pee 2001.

37. See Barlow 1994; Duara 1995; Jensen 1997; Lydia Liu 1995.

38. See Chen Dongyuan 1994 (originally published in 1937); Chen Guyuan 1992 (1936); Dong Jiazun 1995 (a collection of articles originally published between 1934 and 1950); Shang Binghe 1941; Tao Xisheng 1992 (1934); Yang Shuda 1933.

39. See de Pee 2001; Nelson 1997, 120–122; Tong Enzheng 1988.

40. Guo Xingwen 1994, 2. Cf. Bao Zonghao 1990, 1–2; Gou Renmin 1993, 1–2; Li Xiaodong 1986, 2; Su Bing and Wei Lin 1994, 4; Sun Xiao 1988, 1; Wang Jieqing 1988, 1; Wu Baoqi 1989, 92; Wu Cunhao 1986, 1–2; Xu Yangjie 1995, 359.

41. Within the compelling linearity of modern time and space, significant spatial difference can only be misrecognized as temporal difference. Thus, the nomadic peoples of the North and the border tribes of the South lagged behind the Han in their progress toward civilization, perpetuating the practices of primitive times and slave society long after the civilized Han had entered the feudal stage. See, for example, Bao Zonghao 1990, 132–40; Deng Ziqin 1988, 244–49; Gou Renmin 1993, 189; Guo Xingwen 1994, 27–29; Ke Dake 1994, 203–7; Namujila 1994, 128–31; Song Dejin 1988, 80–89; Wang Jieqing 1988, 49–88; Wang Kebin 1988, 30–31. Similarly, practices incongruent with the inexorable linear timeline of scientific anthropology cannot possess a practical meaning, but must be misrecognized as remnants of bygone stages. Thus, uxorilocal marriage must be a remnant of hoary matriarchy, concubinage must be a remnant of the polygamous stage that preceded patrilineal monogamy, and so forth. See, for example, Bao Zonghao 1990, 83–84, 106; Dong Jiazun 1995, 96–103; Guo Xingwen 1994, 53–65; Wang Jieqing 1988,

85; Wu Cunhao 1986, 468–76; Xu Yangjie 1995, 363–67; Yang Zhengwen 1990, 178, 195–96.

42. See, for example, Chen Guyuan 1936, 12–15; Tao Yi 1994, 221–22; Wang Jieqing 1988, 111; Xu Yangjie 1995, 378–79; Zhang Huaicheng 1993, 154–56. The equation of *Family Rituals* with feudal oppression makes it the epitome of a series of attempts at the simplification of the Six Rites of canonical weddings, superseding *Rites of the Kaiyuan Period of the Great Tang* (*Da Tang Kaiyuan li*, 732), Sima Guang's *Letters and Ceremonies* (*Shuyi*, ca. 1081), *New Ceremonies for the Five Rites of the Zhenghe Period* (*Zhenghe wuli xinyi*, 1113), and the sequence preserved in the "Treatise on Ritual" (*Lizhi*) in the *History of the Song* (*Songshi*, 1345). In some Taiwanese studies, *Family Rituals* represents the necessary adaptation of an enduring "Chinese" ritualist essence to the changing times. See, for example, Lin Chunmei 1991, 3–6, 55–59; Ruan Changrui 1982, preface, 101–2. The privileged status accorded to *Family Rituals* also resembles the essentializing designation, common in histories of *hunyin*, of the Song dynasty as the period in which began the promotion of sexual segregation, widow chastity, and footbinding. See, for example, Bao Zonghao 1990, 31–32; Chen Dongyuan 1994, 129–41; Dong Jiazun 1995, 245–74; Lin Chunmei 1991, 151–53; Peng Liyun 1988, 223–30; Shang Binghe 1941, 2; Su Bing and Wei Lin 1994, 260–70; Sun Xiao 1988; Wu Baoqi 1989, 96; Wu Baoqi 1990, 78.

43. See, for example, Ke Dake 1994, 82–87.

44. See, for example, Chen Peng 1990, 186–223, 232–79; Deng Ziqin 1988, 193–225; Guo Xingwen 1994, 259–78; Meng Zhaohua 1992, 171–74; Sun Xiao 1988, 143–45. On the misrecognition of discursive difference as social difference, cf. West n.d., 2. Cf. also Bourdieu 1991, 90–95; Ricoeur 1984, 109.

45. See, for example, Fang Jianxin 1985, 157–74; Guo Xingwen 1994, 236–78; Ma Zhisu 1981, 131–59; Peng Liyun 1988, 187–221; Ruan Changrui 1982, 92–113; Ruan Changrui 1989, 19–32, 45–48, 79–83; Su Bing and Wei Lin 1994, 239–53. Some studies include ceremonies from *A Dream of Hua* and *Family Rituals* in a sequence that spans the entire imperial period. See, for example, Shang Binghe 1941, 233–41; Shi Fengyi 1987, 108–18; Wu Cunhao 1986, 469–79; Yang Zhengwen 1990, 115–85. Other studies do not even attempt to place ceremonies in a sequence at all, but simply list miscellaneous practices gathered from a variety of sources. See, for example, Bao Zonghao 1990, 1–153; Zhu Ruixi 1988, 47–50.

46. See Ebrey 1993, 82–98. In defense of her use of the Ming-dynasty tale "The Shrew," Ebrey refers to H. C. Chang's (1973) translation and his assertion that this story represents a popular, oral tradition. Chang notices similarities between this work and Dunhuang transformation texts in the "naive tone and incoherence, and in its homeliness of language and infelicitous allusions" (23), and he holds that the text has changed only certain details of a much older tradition (30). Patrick Hanan's standard work on Ming vernacular literature, *The Chinese Short Story: Studies in Dating, Authorship, and Composition* (also published in 1973), classifies "The Shrew" under the "middle period" (ca. 1400–1575), adding that it "must genuinely represent Ming dynasty *chantefable* . . . a brilliant match of subject and form" (140–41).

47. See Ebrey 1993, 97.

48. Thus, Richard Davis (1995, 1735) and Linda Walton (1995, 96) commend Patricia Ebrey for reading through the text, and the 1995 Levenson Prize Committee writes in its citation, "Despite daunting problems with sources, she has filled a vast gap in our understanding of Sung civilization by constructing a vivid account of the domestic lives of women."

49. "This is writing that conquers," writes Michel de Certeau (1988, xxv). Cf. Bourdieu 1990, 26; de Certeau 1984, 131–52; de Certeau 1988, 3–12; Shanks and Tilley 1992, 9. The convergence between the cultural geography of "local customs" and the linear time and space of modernity is especially striking in Chinese scholarship on *hunyin* that cites past and present practices of "minority nationalities" (*shaoshu minzu*) as evidence for prehistoric rites. See, for example, Bao Zonghao 1990, 4, 120–31; Guo Xingwen 1994, 27–29, 177; Wang Jieqing 1988, 49–88; Wu Cunhao 1986; Yang Zhengwen 1990, 115–78. Cf. also note 41. In a time of relative academic freedom, anthropologist Tong Enzheng (1988) formulated a sharp critique of this Morganian cultural geography.

50. Paul Ricoeur (1988, 120) writes:

> To say that [history] is a knowledge by traces is to appeal, in the final analysis, to the significance of a passed past that nevertheless remains preserved in its vestiges. . . . On the one hand, to follow a trace is to reason by means of causality about the chain of operations constitutive of the action of passing by. On the other hand, to return from the mark to the thing that made it is to isolate, among all the possible causal chains, the ones that also carry the significance belonging to the relationship of vestige to passage.

51. Ricoeur 1981, 94; Ricoeur 1988, 216.

52. On the description of fragmented discourses, cf. Chartier 1997, 1–22; Foucault 1972, 3–38 *et passim*. This description acknowledges the essential equality of the historical text and the historian's text in their attempt to represent a shared past. It also acknowledges indigenous ritual theory (cf. Chartier 1997, 4–5; Hanks 2000, 3–4; Zito 1997, 56) and the importance of transmission as an integral part of the practice of the text (cf. TZ *jiaochou lüe* 1804; cf. also Foucault 1972, 124).

53. Cf. Ricoeur 1988, 212–213. The preconceived categories of social history provide a limited heuristics and an invalid hermeneutics. Cf. Chartier 1997, 4–5; de Certeau 1988, 137–38.

54. Like the text, the artifact is a "collapsed act" (Richardson 1989, 172), "something that happened in the past" but that survives into the present, where it may be reexperienced (Prown 1993, 2–3). Cf. Hodder 1991, 154; Lubar and Kingery 1993, viii–ix; Shanks and Tilley 1992, 7–9; Tilley 1989, 188.

55. On a critical, reflexive hermeneutics, see Hodder 1991, 125–8, 141–52; Kopytoff 1986, 64–66; Shanks and Tilley 1992, 103–14. On the dialectic between the present and the past, see Hodder 1991; Nelson 1997, 36–48, 169–76; Shanks and Tilley 1992; Tilley 1989, 193. Not surprisingly, the critiques of "processual archaeology" and other objectivist approaches to material remains resemble the critiques of

similar approaches to texts. See, for example, Hodder 1991; Nelson 1997; Shanks and Tilley 1992; von Falkenhausen 1993; von Falkenhausen 1995.

56. Hodder 1991, 191. Cf. Maquet 1993, 35–36; Shanks and Tilley 1992, 133; Tilley 1989, 188–91.

57. In other words, the study of refiguration of the text in reading or in performance must observe the limitations of the configured narrative in order to remain historical.

58. Cf. Chartier 1997, 19–22. The elusive refiguration of inscribed narratives in ritual practice resembles the elusive refiguration of the historical act of reading. On the historical act of reading, see Chartier 1989, 155–71; Chartier 1994, 1–23; de Certeau 1984, 167–76.

59. On emplotment, narrativity, and historicity, see Ricoeur 1981, 274–9, 288–9; Ricoeur 1988, 185–9, 261–73. Since the organic connection between historiography and sources in European and American history is taken for granted, even critical scholars such Roger Chartier, Michel de Certeau, Michel Foucault, Paul Ricoeur, and Hayden White appear never to doubt the suitability of received narrative forms for the writing of history. Phenomena that defy conventional discourse, such as ordinary speech and diabolical possession (de Certeau 1984, 1988), are nondiscursive and unwritable, not alternative discourses.

60. The reflections on emplotment in this book are intended as a contribution to the efforts at a cultural history of imperial times, a history based, not on shifting extraneous questions generated by the political present, as are the paradigms described by Paul Cohen (1984) and Philip Huang (1991), but on indigenous text and discourse. The conceptual changes that Cohen and Huang have identified as shifts in paradigms (from the modernization theory of the 1950s and 1960s, through the anti-imperialism of concerned Asian scholars in the 1960s, to a "China-centered" approach in the 1970s and 1980s) in fact are not paradigmatic shifts at all, but are very similar examples of the homologies that result from the projection of preoccupations and preconceptions of the present onto the sources of the past. In more recent essays, Paul Cohen (2003) has reconfirmed the significance of the "conceptual frameworks" he identified twenty years prior, while failing to detect the more important shift from the structuralist, objectivist history of the 1950s through the 1980s to the post-structuralist, dialectical history of the 1990s. See Paul Cohen 2003, esp. 11, 193. Cf. Farquhar and Hevia 1993; Hevia 1995, 10–28, 225–48; Zito 1997, 5.

61. SCBS 18b.

## One. Ritual Manuals

1. HCLJ 11.12a.

2. YLJShuo preface.3a.

3. JTS 21.3a. Cf. DTXY 7.103; TD 41.1121–2; XTS 11.1b–2a.

4. See SLYY 1.8; SS 98.1a–2a; TCYGL preface.

5. GLXSWJ 19.3b. See also SS 98.2ab.

6. See QBZZ 8.334–6; SLYY 8.116. See also Tsien 1985, 156; Cherniack 1994.

7. See GSJ 36.15a–16b; JGL. Cf. BFDQ 107.12ab; JSLu preface, 12.6b; TWSCT 4.80; XTJGL, preface by Zeng Ji; ZGZDZY, preface by Xiong Penglai; ZhouS 16–18. Cf. also Barnard 1968, 105; Egan 1989, 165–366; Harrist 1995, 240–2.

8. SS 71.11b–12a. Cf. DZJS 2.15–18; SQTY 1b–2a; SS 337.7b.

9. XTS 11.1ab.

10. ZhouS 1.4. Cf. TWSCT 4.80: "Then, at once, the rites and music at the altars and temples of this sacred dynasty had returned to antiquity, leapt in one bound to former times." According to Lu You (1125–1210), Zhai Qinian himself dressed according to the fashions of the Tang dynasty. See LXABJ 8.106. The "Inscription Commemorating the Restoration of the Hall of Great Accomplishment at Wu Prefecture" (*Wujun chongxiu Dachengdian ji*, 1141), at the Temple of Culture in Suzhou, preserves a sample of Zhai Qinian's seal-script calligraphy.

11. See ZhouS 1.4. Zhai Qinian's father, Zhai Ruwen, composed the inscriptions for another set of bronzes, commissioned the following year, in 1115. See ZHJ 10.1a–4b.

12. See Owen 1986, 80–98; West 2006.

13. Liji 61.6b–7a. Cf. Legge 1967, 430.

14. Zhouli 14.13b; ZLDY 23.11a–12a.

15. Guliang 11.4b–5a; Liji 28.20b–21b; Shijing 8C.3a–5b.

16. Waley 1937, 68.

17. On weddings and marriage in the *Spring and Autumn Annals*, see also Granet 1953, 3–62.

18. See Liji 2.13b–14a.

19. See Liji 18.14b–18a.

20. See Liji 26.18b–20a.

21. See Liji 42.18a.

22. See Liji 43.16b–17a.

23. See Liji 49.3a.

24. See Liji 50.5ab.

25. "Duke Ai Asked" also emphasizes the importance of weddings in creating proper differentiation. See Liji 50.7a, 50.9b–10a.

26. See Liji 51.24b–25b.

27. See LJJS 104.2b.

28. WZJ 92.18a–20a. Cf. JTS 21.1a–2a; LCLZ 8.50–52; SCYWL 3.2b; TD 41.1121–2; YLMC 6.103–104. Cf. also Ikeda 1972, 823–9; McMullen 1987, 223.

29. For a more elaborate summary of the contents of *Rites of the Kaiyuan Period*, see McMullen 1987, esp. 190–204.

30. SKQS evaluation, cited in KYL 1. On the Five Rituals, see Shangshu 3.9a; Zhouli 14.6b, 18.1a–30b. Du You recognizes the dual textual basis of *Rites of the Kaiyuan Period* in canon (*jingzhuan*) and precedent (*gushi*). See TD 58.1637. Cf. JTS 21.3a, 21.12a–13b.

31. Cf. McMullen 1987, 196.

32. On the hermeneutics of Fetching the Bride in imperial weddings, cf. TD 58.1633–4.

33. KYL 123.1a.

34. See JTS fascicle 48; TLSY 26.488; XTS fascicle 55.

35. See TD fascicles 106–40. Cf. XTS fascicles 11–20. *Comprehensive Records* collapses the weddings for ranked officials into commentaries on the wedding ritual for imperial princes (fascicle 129). Thereby it disrupts not only the text/performance of *Rites of the Kaiyuan Period*, but also its hierarchical representation of the empire, since ranked officials come to precede imperial princesses.

36. To say that the text/performance of *Rites of the Kaiyuan Period* prohibits abridgment and cross-reference is an overstatement. But the exceptions are significant. The abridgments generally concern either the routine, embodied practice of court ceremonies (which hence existed outside the written practice of exegesis and protocol; cf. MQBT 1.3b) or to choreographies that lie outside ritual proper (such as preparatory arrangements and the host's reception of the guest after the conclusion of the ritual; see, for example, KYL 115.15b–16b, 123.2b, et seq.).

37. The later abridged redactions of *Rites of the Kaiyuan Period* also bear out this emphasis on its exegetical rather than its performative practice. Cf. TD 106.2761. See also TD 4.1121–2.

38. McMullen 1987, 231–2.

39. On these manuals, see Ebrey 1985; Zhao Heping 1993; Zhou Yiliang and Zhao Heping 1995. Apart from the fragments surviving at Dunhuang, a few titles survive in bibliographies. See JTS 46.25a–26b; XTS 58.13a–14b.

40. Liji 1.13a.

41. Note that "auspicious occasions" (*ji*) include ceremonies designated "joyful" (*jia*) in canonical texts and in *Rites of the Kaiyuan Period.*

42. Fragments of several ritual manuals ascribed to Du Youjin have been found at Dunhuang. Zhao Heping (1993, 167–390) has pieced together these fragments into three manuals: *Letters and Ceremonies for Auspicious and Inauspicious Occasions* (*Jixiong shuyi*), *Mirror of Letters and Ceremonies* (*Shuyi jing*), and *New Mirror of Letters and Ceremonies* (*Xinding shuyi jing*). Zhao Heping assumes that Du Youjin during his lifetime compiled a succession of different manuals, ignoring the significant ideological differences that exist not only between the restored manuals, but even between fragments that carry the same title (see especially the radical rhetorical shift in fragment P3849 of *New Mirror*, in Zhao Heping 1993, 360–7). One should better assume a fluid textual environment in which anonymous compilers appropriate the

contents and titles of manuals as well as the names of prestigious authors. The opening sentences of the preface translated here, for example, reappear in the preface to *Newly Compiled Letters and Ceremonies for Auspicious and Inauspicious Occasions* (*Xinji jixiong shuyi*, P2646, in Zhao Heping 1993, 518), ascribed to Zhang Ao—the last sentence of which preface announces that the title of the manual is *Edited Essentials of Letters and Ceremonies* (*Zuanyao shuyi*). Cf. also P3502 (Zhao Heping 1993, 602–3), in which another preface ascribed to Zhang Ao cites a title different from the title of the fragment, and into which a Dunhuang copyist has inserted a Buddhist phrase about the transience of all things.

43. S6537v, in Zhao Heping 1993, 480–1. The officials named in the preface served at court together between 810 and 812. See Zhao Heping 1993, 512. Since the manual elsewhere discusses imperial taboos through the year 827 (Zhao Heping 1993, 492–5), this edition may be a later revision of an earlier manual by Zheng Yuqing (perhaps entitled *Newly Established Letters and Ceremonies of the Yuanhe Period* [*Yuanhe xinding shuyi*]; see P2646, in Zhao Heping 1993, 518–19); in 827, Zheng Yuqing had been dead for seven years. P3849 (in Zhao Heping 1993, 360–7) proposes a similar hermeneutics of canon and current practice.

44. More perhaps than *Rites of the Kaiyuan Period*, this hermeneutics resembles Wang Yan's 726 proposal to use the *Record of Ritual* as a basic text for a contemporary protocol, supplemented with current practice. Cf. also the hermeneutics that underlie the ritual debates summarized by Du You in fascicles 41–105 of his *Comprehensive Records*. Although the Dunhuang fragments obscure the original formats and dates of composition of these manuals, the fluidity of the texts and the shared hermeneutics define the genre very clearly, even if the authors and the exact chronology remain unknown.

45. See S1725, in Zhao Heping 1993, 407–19.

46. S1725, in Zhao Heping 1993, 407–8.

47. See Zhao Heping 1993, 172–3, 250–2, 615–17. The ritual dialogues between the bride and her father (Zhao Heping 1993, 305–6) and between the family of the groom and the family of the bride (Zhao Heping 1993, 674–5) are in many respects comparable to the stylized verbal performance of the letters.

48. P2646, in Zhao Heping 1993, 538–45. On the problematic nature of the title and ascription of this text, see note 42.

49. The ceremonial use of the proposal resembles that of the imperial edicts for the wedding ceremonies of the emperor in *Rites of the Kaiyuan Period*. The style of the proposal (and its reply), too, resembles that of the edicts, with a preference for flowery four-character phrases. Note that *Rites of the Kaiyuan Period* mentions an exchange of letters in the weddings of ranked officials, but that this exchange precedes the wedding ritual proper.

50. P2646, in Zhao Heping 1993, 544.

51. See Ebrey 1985; Zhao Heping 1993; Zhou Yiliang and Zhao Heping 1995.

52. P2646, in Zhao Heping 1993, 545.

53. GTL 2.34–35.

54. See ZGZDZY prefaces.1a–2b, prefaces.3b–4a; ZhouS 1.4–10.

55. See DLJ 6.16a–17a; JSLu preface.1a, 12.6b; SSYTL 7.91; TWSCT 4.80; XTJGL preface.1a–2b. On Song endeavors in archaeology and epigraphy, see Barnard 1968; Harrist 1995; Jin Zhongshu 1995; Mok 1999; Poor 1965; Rawson 1993, 60–66; R. C. Rudolph 1963; Wang Kuo-wei 1927. I am grateful to John Reese for introducing me to the subject of Song archaeology and for providing a helpful introductory bibliography on the subject.

56. JGL preface.1a–2b. Cf. SSYTL 7.91.

57. See, e.g., SSYTL 7.91, where the author recounts how he sought out ancient inscriptions of which he had rubbings made that he intended to send to Ouyang Xiu.

58. Lunyu 7.9a (VII.28), as translated in Ames and Rosemont 1998, 117.

59. GSJ 36.15ab.

60. ZhouS 1.11. Cf. TWSCT 4.80. See also SS 202.29b, 444.15b–16b; Hui-liang Chu 1993, 58–65; Harrist 1993, 44–47. Li Gonglin's *Investigations of Antiquity Illustrated* does not survive as an independent work, but its contents have been incorporated into Lü Dalin's catalogue of the same title (see below).

61. ZhouS 1.11.

62. See Zhuangzi 13.217–18, 14.225–8, translated in Watson 1968, 152–3, 158–61.

63. See Shangshu 2.6a, 3.1b, 4.1b, 4.16b; Lunyu 7.7a (VII.20).

64. KGT preface.1a–4b. Cf. BGT 1.1ab, 18.1ab; MQBT 19.1ab; TWSCT 4.79–80; XTJGL preface.3a.

65. On the collections and publications of the final years of the Northern Song, see JSJW 2.213; JSLu fascicles 11–12; JZGWYH preface.2ab; MZML 7.1b–2a, 7.6ab; XTJGL preface.1a–2b, preface.1b–2a; ZGZDZY prefaces.1a–2b; ZhouS 1.1–4, 1.18–19. Cai Tao's (d. after 1147) "On Ancient Vessels" ("Guqi shuo"; TWSCT 4.79–80), as a partisan defense of his father Cai Jing (1047–1126), is not an objective account of obsessive collecting in the final decades of the Northern Song, but is part of that culture of excess. Notebooks written during or briefly after the Northern Song also contain sections on ancient vessels. See, e.g., MQBT fascicle 19; MZML fascicle 7; ZhuS 3.1b–2b.

66. Quotation from TWSCT 4.80.

67. See DSZ 4.143; QJXZ. Cf. Inaba 1978, 49.

68. JZGWYH preface.1a, referring to the mythical origins of writing according to Zhouyi 8.8a (knotted cords); Han Fei 19.345; LSCQ 17.203; Xunzi 15.267 (Cang Jie). Cf. the prefaces to FGB, EYXY, JZGWYH, PY, and ZGZDZY.

69. LJJS introductions.3a, quoting Liji 1.10b. Similar ideas are expressed in *ibidem*.2b, 3b; LJJS prefaces.2a; ZZYL 84.1a–2a, 84.5ab, 84.7b.

70. See LX; LS.

71. See SLYY 1.8; SS 98.1a–2a; TCYGL preface; ZHWLJY prefaces.1–2.

72. See CMTCL 2.30; SCZCZY 33.321; SS 105.8b–9a. The section on imperial weddings in *Cumulative Rites of the Court of Imperial Sacrifices* (TCYGL fascicle 56) does not survive.

73. See NGZ 12.302.

74. See Bol 1992, chapter 7; de Bary and Bloom 1999, 596–626; Egan 1994, chapter 3; James T. C. Liu 1959, esp. chapter 3.

75. See SS 98.2a–3a; YLMC 12.220–1.

76. See BZJ 10.58–59. Cf. JSJW 1.181–97; LX.

77. See GLXSWJ 19.1a–41b; SS 51.2ab.

78. SSYTL 1.4–5. Cf. SDZLJ 40.214–15; SS 105.9ab, 248.7a–9b.

79. ECJ 15.159. Cited with approval in YLZLBJ 3.26a.

80. GLXSWJ preface.2a. Cf. GLXSWJ appendix.2ab, appendix.16ab; SS 321.3b.

81. SLYY 10.148. Cf. SS 458.4a–5a. Chen Lie cites Shijing 2B.13b (cited in turn in Liji 10.26a and 51.3a), translated after Waley 1960, 101.

82. Lunyu 12.1a (XII.1), translated after Waley 1938, 162. For Yan Yuan's fondness for learning, see Lunyu 6.16 (VI.3).

83. GLXSWJ 8.9ab. In his other letters, too, Chen Xiang consistently upholds the canon and the ancients as practical models. See GLXSWJ fascicles 7–9.

84. For the date of completion, see SMGNP 6.185. Sima Guang, the leading opponent of Wang Anshi's reforms, was recommended to Emperor Shenzong by Chen Xiang. With his friend Fan Zhen he conducted a life-long debate about archaic music that was finally settled (in Sima Guang's favor) with an archaic game of pitch-pot (*tou hu*). See DZJS 2.16–17. Cf. SSYTL 8.102.

85. Sima Guang also shared Chen Xiang's archaist ambitions, as well as Chen Xiang's apprehension about the dangers of this ambition:

> Sima Wengong [i.e., Sima Guang] fashioned a long garment, cap, hat pins, head wrap, and belt, based on the *Record of Ritual*. Whenever he went out on his horse, he wore his court robes, but he would have his long garment carried behind him in a leather case. He would put it on as soon as he entered his Garden of Solitary Enjoyment. He once asked Kangjie [i.e., Shao Yong, 1011–1077], "Would you wear a garment such as this?" But Kangjie answered, "I am a man of the present, and I ought to wear the clothes of the present." With a sigh Wengong admitted the sensibility of these words. (SSWJL 19.210)

86. Cf. Ebrey 1991b, 100. The format of Sima Guang's manual enhances its distinction from earlier manuals of letters and ceremonies. Whereas in earlier manuals letters occupy an important place in the ceremonies, Sima Guang excludes the letters from the ceremonies and confines them to a separate section. The section on letters makes occasional reference to earlier manuals of letters and ceremonies; the section on ceremonies never does.

87. Chunqiu 4.5b–6a, as translated in Legge 1994, 26.

88. Chunqiu 41.3ab, as translated in Legge 1994, 575.

89. SY 3.30.

90. See WGWJ 22.8a–13b, especially 22.8b.

91. SY 2.19. According to Cai Tao, imperial cappings prior to Huizong were called "Unto the Head," after "a ritual in contemporary custom." See TWSCT 2.23.

92. See SY 3.33. Cf. Ebrey 1991a, 54–55. The earliest extant edition of Sima Guang's wedding ritual, in the first fascicle of *Wedding Ritual: A New Edition* (*Hunli xinbian*, ca. 1200), contains a number of superior variants as well as passages not found in more current editions of the text. One such variant is "extravagant wealth" (*fuchi*) for "wealth and opulence" (*fuduo*). See HLXB 1.1a–8a.

93. SY 3.36.

94. SY 3.36.

95. For wedding sequences in which the first meeting of the groom and the bride takes place in the wedding chamber, see chapter 2. Sima Guang's explicit condemnation of contemporary customs such as Tying up the Hair and the playing of music at weddings also involve a translation of practice into text. He condemns the former by reference to the *Old Poems* in *Selections of Refined Literature* (see WX 29.10b) and a biography in the *History of the Han* (see Hanshu 54.2447), and the latter by reference to the *Record of Ritual* (see Liji 18.16b). See SY 3.36, 3.37.

96. On the hermeneutical circle, a concept formulated by Martin Heidegger in *Sein und Zeit* (para. 31), see Ricoeur 1981, pp. 69 et seq.

97. See Yili 5.4b–9a.

98. See Liji 61.5b–6b.

99. See Yili 5.8ab. Zhu Xi quotes Jia Gongyan's commentary in the section on wedding ritual in his *Comprehensive Explanations*, and elsewhere in that work. See YLJZ 2.22ab; YLT 2.14b. Sima Guang must also have been familiar with it, as it was the standard subcommentary on *Ceremonies and Rites* in Song times.

100. For an excellent discussion of the ritual preparation and consumption of food and leftovers, and of ritual symmetry, see Zito 1997, chapters 1, 6, and 7.

101. S1725, in Zhao Heping 1993, 410–11.

102. See SY 3.36. Cf. Zheng Xuan in Yili 5.4b.

103. Cf. the consistent misreading by Zhu Xi of similar themes elsewhere in the canon, suggesting that he associated sexual numerology and yinyang symbolism with illegitimate Daoist readings. See, for example, ZZYL 89.2a. See also Van Gulik 1951, 92–93; Van Gulik 1974, 80, 223.

104. The solemn nature of weddings in the manual of Sima Guang also rests on fundamental conceptions of the body, of marriage, and of the family as a ritual unit. Devotion, self-sacrifice, and chastity characterize proper wifely behavior. In a proper marriage, husband and wife treat each other "like guests." Sima Guang

recounts several anecdotes about such ideal marriages in his *Family Precepts* (*Jiafan*), including one about He Zeng, a high official of the Jin dynasty (265–316), whose "women's quarters were serene and strict." In his old age he and his wife treated each other like guests, impeccably dressed. "He would face south, his wife would face north. They would bow twice, and serve wine. After exchanging toasts, they would part. This took place twice or three times a year. This one may call 'respectful behavior'." See JF 7.20b–21a. Hu Hong (1106–1162) proposed that sex and ritual were not, in fact, mutually exclusive: "Those who are disgusted by the Way of man and wife [i.e., sex] think of it as a matter of unbridled lust. But the sage is at peace with it, because he realizes that the preservation of harmony is a matter of propriety. Thus, he finds ritual in intimacy and perceives the Way in copulation. But only those capable of serious concentration will be able to maintain possession and not lose themselves." See HZZY 1.8b.

105. Cf. the hermeneutical acrobatics performed by Song commentators in their attempts to explain the apparent condonation of elopement in *Rites of Zhou*. See ZLDY 23.13b–14a.

106. SY 3.35.

107. Liji 60.1b. Cf. Chan 1963, 86.

108. Bol 1992, 320.

109. See SS 340.10a–11b; LSYZ 612; SYXA 31.7b. In a mourning poem for Lü Dalin, Cheng Yi praises this same quality with the lines, "The three thousand ritual stipulations/he all practiced in the forty years of his life." Cited in LSYZ 644.

110. See ZZYL 89.1b.

111. See SS 340.1a–11b; LSYZ 587–88. The *Record of Inspecting Public Works* is an ancient text appended to *Rites of Zhou* during the Han dynasty. See KGJJ; Nylan 2001, 183; Zhouli fascicles 39–42.

112. ZZJ 312. Cf. SY 7.82; WGWJ 22.8b. Cf. also a verdict in the collected works of Yu Jing (1000–64) that defends a practitioner of ancient exorcist ritual against accusations of heterodoxy (*zuodao*). See WXJ 13.10ab.

113. Cited in Tillman 1992, 21. Cf. James T. C. Liu 1973, 497; LXABJ 9.118.

114. LSYZ conveniently reprints all of Lü's extant commentaries. Lü Dalin's commentary on "The Meaning of Weddings" emphasizes the solemnity and respect appropriate for a rite that reproduces ritual bodies for the ancestral cult. On *The Edited Rites*, see DSZ 2.81.

115. See LSYZ 598–99.

116. See LXABJ 8.106; QBZZ 1.18–21. Cf. SCZCZY 96.1033.

117. See the fragments in ZZJ 292–302; ECJ 10.620–29. See also Chow 1993.

118. LSYZ 578–79. For the "Community Compact," see LSYZ 563–84.

119. LSYZ 580.

120. See Cheng Yi's manual in ECJ 10.621–22 and his commentary on the prohibitions against music and congratulations in LJJS 26.19b; Lü Dajun's "Community Compact," above; and Lü Dalin's commentaries on "The Meaning of Weddings," in LJJS 154.12a–155.17b.

121. ZHWL imperial preface.3b, citing Lunyu 2.8a (II.23), as translated by Waley 1938, 93. Cf. SHY zhiguan 5.22; ZHWLJY prefaces.

122. See JSJW 2.211–12; SDZLJ 149.552–54; SS 19.11b, 20.2b, 20.5b, 20.6b; TWSCT 1.8.

123. See SLYY 1.8; SS 98.3a.

124. See JZGWYH preface.2ab; SS 98.3ab; TWSCT 4.80; YLMC 7.1b–2a; ZHWL memorials.14b; ZhouS 1.1–4.

125. See SHY zhiguan 5:22; SS 98.3a.

126. See TWSCT 4.80. The extant edition of *Broad Researches* is the recompilation of 1123. See BGT. Cf. DSZ 2.171; ZhouS 1.1. Cf. also Chikusa 1978; Poor 1965. Note that Zheng Qiao places *Broad Researches* under ritual manuals. See TZ *Yiwenlüe* 2.1501. In *Rongzhai's Random Jottings* (*Rongzhai suibi*), Hong Mai (1123–1202) criticizes the scholarship of *Broad Researches of Antiquity Illustrated.* See RZSB I.14.181–82, III.13.565–67. On Song imitations of ancient bronzes, see Cheng Changxin 1989; Erickson 2001; Rawson 2001. The Walters Art Museum in Baltimore owns an archaic bronze bell cast under Huizong.

127. See SS 21.2b–4a, 98.3a. On the *Ritual Canon Illustrated*, see SLT. Cf. SS 98.1ab. On the increasing criticism of the *Ritual Canon Illustrated* during the eleventh century, see MQBT 19.2ab; RZSB II.11.344. Although ancient vessels had been introduced into court debates about ritual vessels and music as early as the 1030s and 1050s (see JSLu 11.3b; MQBT 5.17b–18b; SS 71.1a–12a), the *Ritual Canon Illustrated* remained in use. According to Zhao Yanwei (1140–1210), officials in the provinces in his day still had to make do with vessels copied from the *Ritual Canon Illustrated*, while the imperial court used vessels based on *Broad Researches.* See YLMC 4.57–58.

128. SHY zhiguan 5.23. Cf. SS 98.3ab, 129.1b–2a; TWSCT 1.8, 1.11–12, 4.80, 5.87; YLMC 5.78–79, 12.214; ZHWL memorials.3b–7b *et passim*; ZhouS 1.1–4.

129. The sacredness of the founding emperors of the dynasty and the hallowed first century of stable rule forbade any rigorous criticism of its rites, but the insistence on precedent under Huizong may also have owed something to the political and cultural rivalry between the court and literati, especially between Huizong's court and the men associated with opposition to Wang Anshi's New Policies, such as Sima Guang, the Cheng brothers, and the Lü brothers.

130. ZHWL *shou*.23b–24a. Cf. ZHWL imperial preface, *shou*.8b–9a, *shou*.11b–12a, *shou*.42ab; ZHWLJY preface.1ab, preface.2b.

131. ZHWL preface.1b. Cf. Ye Mengde's (1077–1148) condemnation of *New Ceremonies*: "At the time, there were no old hands with a knowledge of ritual, so that the completed code contained numerous contradictions, and indeed it was later abolished." See SLYY 1.8.

132. See ZHWL *shou*.8b–10a.

133. See ZHWL 178.8ab and 179.4ab; 178.5b–6a and 179.2b–3a.

134. See ZHWL 179.1a–3a. Note that the section on commoner weddings in the current edition of *New Ceremonies* is incomplete. The ritual skips from the groom's entrance into the bride's compound, to the bride's visit to the groom's ancestors. See ZHWL 179.4a. The Ming manuscript in the Fu Ssu-nien Library, Academia Sinica, shows the same lacuna and also hides it in continuous text (179.3a), suggesting an early copying error. The missing passage is preserved (in slightly abridged form) in SS 115.16b–17a.

135. See ZHWL 179.1b–2a. Officials may replace the goose with a goat. See ZHWL 178.2b. The compilers do not explain the hermeneutic rationale for these substitutions. The goat may represent yang, replacing the symbol (the goose and its trek) with the homophone (the word for goat is pronounced *yang*). If the goat represents yang and the turtle dove represents fidelity, the different substitutions of the goose for officials and commoners represent different commentarial interpretations of the goose.

136. See ZHWL 178.7a, 179.3a.

137. See ZHWL 179.3b.

138. See JSJW 2.203; RZSB III.13.571; SS 22.3b, 98.3a.

139. See BZB 10.58–59, 1.67; SS 21.6a–7b, 22.1b, 22.6a–8a, 66.2b–3a, 129.26b; TWSCT 1.8, 4.80. Cf. West 2006.

140. The imperial court of the Southern Song did not issue new comprehensive imperial compilations, despite continued interest and despite endeavors in archaic music. See SS 98.4b; YLMC 3.46, 4.57–58; ZHJ *fulu*.19a–21a. Cf. Lam 1995, 20.

141. See KSFT; TWSCT 4.80; XTJGL; YHJW 5.40–42, 9.79–80; ZhouS.

142. DLJ 6.16a–17a. Cf. the Yuan-dynasty prefaces to KGT and XTJGL.

143. Lunyu 20.5a (XX.3), as translated in Ames and Rosemont 1998, 229.

144. SCBS 18b.

145. See YLSW 4–5.

146. See HAJ 68.13a–26a.

147. See YLSG 1. Cf. Cheng Jiong's (1163 *jinshi*) conviction that the reconstruction of the ancient measures of length, volume, and weight would provide the key to cosmic truth. See SQTY.

148. See, for example, ZZYL 84.9b, 85.2a.

149. According to the "Treatise on Ritual" in the *History of the Song*, Zhu Xi planned the *Comprehensive Explanations* as a "contemporary code," for practice at all levels of society. See SS 98.4b.

150. See YLT. Zhu Xi during his life repeatedly expressed his liking for illustrated editions of ritual texts. See, for example, HAJ 69.18b; YLT preface.3b.

151. For Zhang Shi's manual, see HAJ 83.15a–16a. According to ZZYL 89.1a, Zhang Shi omitted capping ritual from his manual because he considered it too

difficult to practice. For Zhu Xi's compilation, see SS 204.3a; ZZYL 84.6a. Cf. also Lü Zuqian's revision of Sima Guang's wedding ritual. See DLJ *bieji* 2.1a–4a. For other compilations, see the various bibliographical entries in SS 202.14a, 204.3a.

152. See HAJ 69.18ab; SDYT 2–3.

153. ZZYL 84.5b. Cf. ZZYL 90.6a.

154. MZWJ 20.7b–9a. Cf. Cherniack (1994, 24) on "author-based" authority. Patricia Ebrey has written an exhaustive summary of the discussions surrounding the authenticity of *Family Rituals*. See Ebrey 1991b, 102–44, 193–200. See also Ebrey 1995, 107–8.

155. Cf. Zhu Xi's repeated praise for Sima Guang's manual in *Assorted Sayings*, calling it "seventy to eighty percent correct" (ZZYL 84.6a) and the best manual available (ZZYL 89.1a). Zhu Xi deplores Sima's adherence to the detail of *Ceremonies and Rites* only because of its occasional impracticality. See ZZYL 84.8a, 89.1b, 89.2b. But Zhu Xi criticizes Sima Guang severely for some of his departures from *Ceremonies and Rites*. See several entries in ZZYL 89.1b–3a.

156. See Ebrey 1991a, 3; JL 184b.

157. On the magico-cosmological structure of the compound, and the consequent importance of Zhu Xi's manipulation of domestic space, see Bray 1997; Ruitenbeek 1993. For an insightful application of Catherine Bell's concept of "ritualization" to family ritual, see Zito 1993, 327–29, 333–41.

158. The section on family ritual in the *Comprehensive Explanations* follows the same dichotomy: cappings and weddings versus the meaning of cappings and weddings and household regulations. In *Assorted Sayings*, Zhu Xi explains that all good manuals use this dichotomy (see ZZYL 84.10a), and in a memorial advocating the reprint of *New Ceremonies* he stresses the importance of material conditions and clothing in creating ritual unity (see HAJ 69.17a–19a). Yang Fu also observes the similarity between *Family Rituals* and the *Comprehensive Explanations*. See JL 184c.

159. In *Assorted Sayings*, Zhu Xi commends *New Ceremonies for the Five Rites of the Zhenghe Period* for its "simplicity," in contradistinction to Sima Guang's manual. See ZZYL 89.1b.

160. Patricia Ebrey (1991a, 8n19) defines the descent-line system as follows: "A great line (*dazong*) is the line of eldest sons continuing indefinitely from a founding ancestor. A lesser line is the line of eldest sons going back no more than five generations. Great lines and lesser lines continually spin off new lesser lines, founded by younger sons."

161. ZZYL 89.2b. The *loci classici* are Liji 43.16b; Zhouli 14.16a. See also Ebrey 1991a, 53, 53n18. Cf. ZZYL 89.1a, where Zhu Xi remarks that one of the difficulties in persuading prospective affines to follow ritual in a wedding lies in reaching agreement about limiting the betrothal gifts to five pairs of cloth lengths. By contrast, cappings are "easy to practice" because they involve only one family in the seclusion of its own compound.

162. See Ebrey 1991a, 51n10.

163. For other divergences, see Ebrey 1991a, 54–64, especially the footnotes. Zhu Xi's collected works contain an alternative sequence for Fetching the Bride, entitled "Outline for the Ritual of Fetching the Bride for Groom Zhao," which provides guidelines for the steps from Decking the Room to Sharing the Meal. This text largely resembles the equivalent sequence in *Family Rituals*, being also a combination of the protocols by Sima Guang and Cheng Yi. See HAJ 69.31b–32b; Ebrey 1991a, 54n22. One would expect individual protocols of this type to have been more common in circles that attempted the performance of complex, archaic rites. *Assorted Sayings* refers to negotiations about protocol. See ZZYL 89.1a, 89.1b. One passage in *Assorted Sayings* seems to allude to this particular protocol ("The version [of wedding ritual] on which I have decided now . . ."). See ZZYL 89.1b.

164. Fascicle 7 of the *Comprehensive Explanations* discusses the descent-line system, without canonical precedent. According to editor Huang Ruijie, the descent-line system is the crux of *Family Rituals* (JL 185c), and it is difficult to disagree: *Family Rituals* as a whole provides physical form to the patrilineal descent line, and its symmetries and asymmetries inculcate same.

165. See JL 193d. As Ebrey (1991a, 59n43) notes, Zhu Xi seems to have changed his mind on this point. ZZYL 85.4a argues that all ranks in antiquity used a goose as a wedding presentment, but according to ZZYL 85.4a and YLJZ 3.1b, the goose is specific to the *shi* class as it mimics the typical presentment of the *dafu* class. Chen Chun notes some other points on which Zhu Xi revised his stance. See BXDQJ 14.2a–3a, 14.5b–6a.

166. See ZZYL 89.1b. Cf. JL 37a.

167. See ZZYL 89.2b, 89.3a. Note how the third day is at the same time an appropriate condensation of the third month.

168. See ZZYL 84.6a.

169. For Yang Fu's observation about the long garment, see JL 187b. Yang Fu regrets that he has failed to learn the details of Zhu Xi's modifications, because he supposes that the new design bore out a "deep meaning." For the advice against archaic pronunciation, see ZZYL 89.2a. For an injunction to the contrary, see YLJZ 1.16b. Zhu Xi's memorials advising the reprint and enforcement of *New Ceremonies* also discuss the significance of the material culture of the Three Dynasties, and his *Ceremonies for Prefectural and County Sacrifices to the Most Sacred Culture Propagating King* (*Zhouxian shidian Zhisheng Wenxuan wang yi*, 1194) includes illustrations of archaic vessels. See HAJ 69.18b; SDYT 10–39. Zhu Xi's own commentary on the *locus classicus* of "meaning" against "numbers" reads: "If one does not possess the numbers [of ritual objects], one cannot understand the meaning [of ritual]. With what little remains today, probably less than ten percent, we can afford even less the mere approximation [of meaning] that was the task of the Supplicant and the Scribe." See LJJS 67.11b. Cf. ZZYL 84.1b–2a.

170. ZZYL 84.8a. Sima Guang expresses very similar ideas in WGWJ 22.8b–9a. Zhu Xi's commitment to archaism, as perceived by his followers, is also illustrated by an anecdote in which a certain Peng Danxuan, on a walk through the Wuyi Mountains, chances upon two erudite scholars who comment extensively on the ritual choreography of the meal of which they are partaking. Peng gradually realizes that

the two scholars are in fact the spirits of Zhu Xi and Wei Liaoweng, enjoying the sacrifices brought at their shrine. See YWZL 1.13.

171. See ZZYL 84.1b, 84.7b–8b. See especially 84.8a, where one entry combines Zhu Xi's suggestions for a few revisions in Sima Guang's manual with his speculations about the strategies that an imaginary contemporary sage would use to restore ancient ritual.

172. On these matters, see Bol 1997; de Weerdt 1998; Wilson 1995.

173. ZZJL, Qiu Jun's preface.1ab.

174. ZZJL, Wang Jian's colophon.1ab. Cf. all other prefaces gathered in this 1701 edition of *Family Rituals*.

175. See Chen Guyuan 1992, 12–15; Chen Peng 1990, 186–223; Deng Ziqin 1988, 193–99, 223–25; Guo Xingwen 1994, 239; Li Xiaodong 1986; Meng Zhaohua 1992, 171–72; Sun Xiao 1988, 143–45; Tao Yi 1994, 221–22; Wang Jieqing 1988, 111; Xu Yangjie 1995, 378–79; Yang Zhigang 1993; Zhang Huaicheng 1993, 154–56.

176. See Ebrey 1991b, 80–85. Cf. the footnotes in Ebrey 1991a, especially 56n32, 60n53; Ebrey 1993, 82–83.

177. For the association of ritual manuals with the "new elite," see Ebrey 1991b, 45–49, 65–66. The stated aim of *Confucianism and Family Rituals* is to detect "concrete ideas about what to do" or "lower-order ideas" in the ritual manuals. See Ebrey 1991b, 10.

178. Patricia Ebrey (1991a, ix, xxii–xxvi; 1991b, 3–5) emphasizes the ritual life-cycle, and discusses the individual ceremonies that make up these rituals (see the footnotes in Ebrey 1991a; Ebrey 1993, 82–96), but she does not elaborate on the narratives that link individual ceremonies (see especially 1991b, chapter 4). On ceremonies as rules, see Ebrey 1991a, xiv. The dismissal of the exegetical context of ritual manuals appears to be informed by a belief that the meaning of canonical texts was unambiguous (see, for example, Ebrey 1991a, xvi, 44n30, 45n36, 52n15) and by a misconstruction of classicist ideas about ritual and sagehood, due in part to an imposition of inapt binaries from Western religion: "the Confucian tradition recognized that men make rituals. Rituals were not seen as the creation of gods, conveyed to humans through revelation." See Ebrey 1991a, xvii. Cf. Ebrey 1991b, 49, 221–22.

179. See Ebrey 1989, 305–6; Ebrey 1991a, xxix; Ebrey 1991b, 85, 150, 165; Ebrey 1995, 105–6, 129.

180. Ebrey 1991a, xxi. The phrase "modifications and adjustments" quotes Ebrey 1991a, ix. Cf. Ebrey 1991b, 107.

181. Ebrey 1991b, 216. Cf. Ebrey 1989, 304–6; Ebrey 1991b, 80–85; Ebrey 1993, 96–98; Ebrey 1995, 132–36.

182. For the narrative and detail of later revisions, see Ebrey 1991a, xxviii, and footnotes throughout; Ebrey 1991b, 43, 85, 103–4, 149 et seq; Ebrey 1995, 121–27.

183. Ebrey 1991b, 201.

184. Cf. Hevia 1995; Zito 1997. James Hevia (1995, 123 et seq) repeatedly cites an instance of metaphorical, moral centering ("to strike the mean between lavishness and frugality," *fengjian shi zhong*) to stand for the centering of the Macartney embassy in ritual time and space, but his book shows clearly how the Qing empire (the Middle Kingdom) becomes an encompassing ritual space in which a sequence of officials attempt to transform the marginal, uncouth barbarian visitors as they advance toward the imperial center.

## TWO. WEDDING CORRESPONDENCE AND NUPTIAL SONGS

1. GKJ 51.19b–20a; SLCH 500.

2. RZSB III.8.505; RZSL 1.

3. See Ebrey 1978; Johnson 1977. Many of the central concepts in this chapter, such as "cultural capital," "symbolic capital," and "distinction," derive from the work of Pierre Bourdieu, most notably from his *Distinction: A Social Critique of the Judgement of Taste* (1984).

4. See Bol 1992, esp. 6–14; Cherniack 1994, esp. 27–29; Egan 1994, chapter 9; Harrist 1996; McNair 1990; Powers 1995; Powers 1996; Sturman 1996.

5. A select group of Northern Song literati set the terms for a more general divide between literati and the imperial court in Southern Song. See Bol 1992, 58–75, chapter 7; Bol 1993; Bol 1995, 150–51; Bol 2003, 246–56; Hartwell 1982; Powers 1995; Powers 1996; Sturman 1996. On debates and riots, see Chaffee 1995; de Weerdt 1998; Elman 2000; Ho Ping-ti 1962; Kracke 1953.

6. Cf. Powers 1996 for similar discussions on the topic of painting.

7. For marriage, see SSLH 201, 251; YHJW 1.3–4. For release from prison, see SSLH 247; HMQS IX.11.5b–9a. For promotion, see SSLH 247.

8. Cited in SCWJL 1.35–36; SLCH 495.

9. Cf. Jiang Jusong 1977, 7; Langley 1986, 659; Zeng Zaozhuang 1999, 297 et seq.

10. See Hightower 1965, 61–69; Idema and Haft 1985, 102–5; Langley 1986, 657.

11. See CMTCL 3.39–40; HQL 7.4a; RZSL 16; SLCH preface and colophon.

12. See Jiang Jusong 1977, 19–21; Langley, 659.

13. See BMSY 4.25–26; GTL 2.24; HMDQ 1200 preface; HMQS 1307 preface; RZSL 1; SLTZ preface; YLMC 4.63–64. Cf. Zeng Zaozhuang 1999.

14. Fei Gun (1205 *jinshi*) noted in 1192 that these works of criticism were a recent phenomenon. Cited in SLCH 496. See also SLH Qing preface. Extant Song critical works of this kind include CXZN, RZSL, SLH, SLTZ, and YZSL. See also the list of four-six anthologies in Xie Hongxuan 1973, 691–92.

15. QBZZ 5.188; SLCH 491.

16. SLH 3.

17. SLH 1. Hong Mai also espouses the view that some couplets are "natural," since they match phrases that are "found" in the natural world or even in a linguistic environment. See RZSB II.12.362–63; RZSL 8–9. On the ideology of naturalness, see Bourdieu 1984, 68; Powers 1995, 101; Sturman 1996.

18. See, for example, SLCH 500 (citing Lou Yao); SLH preface; SLTZ 1; YZSL 29–30. The secondary literature has replicated the terminology and genealogical claims of traditional criticism, apparently unaware of its polemic nature. This has resulted in an array of contradictory statements about the development of four-six prose (as well as about the development of ancient-style prose). See SLCH preface by Ruan Yuan, 2; SLJZ preface; Jiang Jusong 1977, 17; Jin Juxiang 1965, 110; Xie Hongxuan 1973, 615–16. Compare also William Nienhauser's (1986) essay on ancient-style prose to Langley's (1986) essay on parallel prose, both in the *Indiana Companion to Traditional Chinese Literature.*

19. See, for example, NCJT 1b; LXABJ 3.37; YLMC 8.135. Cf. also the comments by Lou Yao and Ye Shi, above.

20. The exception is Zeng Zaozhuang (1999, 292–335), who recognizes the importance of four-six parallel prose throughout the Song dynasty and presents a reasoned analysis of stylistic shifts during the centuries of its dominance.

21. See YWLJ 40.2a; TD 58.1649–50.

22. See BSJJ 58.38b–39b. See also two engagement letters in the collected works of Yu Fan (164–232 CE), in QSGW 68.3b; also cited in YYZZ II.4.230.

23. See P3442, S329–61, P2646, P3502V, in Zhao Heping 1993. Cf. YYZZ I.11.107.

24. There are even some authors, including Chen Xiang, who eschew parallel prose altogether, preferring instead ancient-style prose. See GLXSWJ 7.29ab; MCWJ 2.4b; SAJ 30.11b–14a. It is possible that wedding letters in parallel prose predate the eleventh century. Although I am not aware of any surviving examples of such earlier letters, there do exist tenth-century divorce contracts whose opening lines are dedicated to a description of marital bliss (and the pain of divorce) in four-six parallel prose. See P3220, P4525, S0343V, P3730V, S6537V, S6417V, S5578, S6537V, in Sha Zhi 1998, 470–88.

25. SZYH 4.4ab. I have not been able to identify Shu Jingzhai and hence have been forced to retain the epithet in the translation. Cf. also CGL 9.111.

26. HLXB 1.11ab; SSWJ 47.1371.

27. BFDQ 86.3ab; HLXB 8.9a; SGWJ 10.37a.

28. Writing manuals list special names for the standard couplets that make up the engagement letter. *A New Book for the Old Man under the Moon* calls its ready-made parallel phrases for the justification of a match between two families "paired gems for marital alliance" (*yinqi shuangbi*), its phrases for praising the bride "linked pearls for female grace" (*wanshu lianzhu*), and couplets juxtaposing the groom and the bride "couplets that state age and virtue" (*xu niande lian*). It also divides engagement letters

into "opening," "continuing," and "closing" couplets (*faduan, chengjie, jieba*). See YLXS I.12.1a–7b, II.2.2a–7b. Cf. HMQS II.7.20b–30a; QZQQ IV.4.522–24.

29. In his analysis of cross-cousin marriage in Kabylia, Pierre Bourdieu (1977, 30–52) detects a tension between "official kinship" and "practical kinship," between collective, public theory and individual, private strategy. The engagement letter combines these two in one text: the naive, conventional surface narrative of the letter denies the symbolic capital displayed in its form and style.

30. See Jinshu 31.963. See also Su Shi's reflections on this episode in DPZL 3.68.

31. Lunyu 11.2ab (XI.6), as translated by Waley 1938, 154.

32. See HCLJ 8.4b.

33. See Jinshu 79.2080.

34. See Bieg 1976. Huang Tingjian's incomplete Yizhou diary, *A Private History of the Year 1105 in Yizhou* (*Yizhou yiyou jiacheng*; YZYYJC), does not make mention of the composition of this letter.

35. For examples of allusions to historical matrimonial ties between two families see, for example, GCG 17.17b; HLXB 3.10a, 6–7.7ab, 8.2b; SLBZ 14.45b–47a.

36. For Cheng Yi's letters see ECJ 9.619. For other letters alluding to the Learning of the Way see, for example, HMQS II.5.3b, II.5.11ab, II.6.6ab, II.6.7b, II.6.12a, II.6.14a, II.7.2a, II.7.21ab; MTJ 17.13a–14b; MZWJ 24.1a–3b; QRJSJ 40.6a–10a; SYWJ 24.3b–6a; YLXS II.4.7b, II.5.6a, II.7.4b, II.10.3b–4a. Cf. also BTJ 81.8b–13b *et passim*; GLXSWJ 7.29ab.

37. HLXB 1.11ab.

38. JLJ 59.16a. Cf., for example, ZYJSJ 11.18ab. For examples of inventory formats, see HLXB 1.11b–13a; YLXS II.1.15b–16b.

39. See Liji 26.18b.

40. See, for example, DongMJ 12.4b–5a; HLXB 9.1b; ZWJ 30.9b.

41. See, for example, YLXS II.5.1a, II.5.2b, II.7.2a ("We set out to seek a peer in the study of the *Songs* and the *Documents*; how could we follow our contemporaries in discussing wealth?"); HMQS II.5.3b ("One concludes a match based on the Way; one does not marry off a daughter by discussing wealth"), II.6.5b, II.6.17a.

42. HLXB 9.3b; YLXS II.5.5ab. "Wrong side of the road," literally "the Ruan family on the south side of the road," refers to a story in *A New Account of Tales of the World* (*Shishuo xinyu*; SSXY 5.179–80) by Liu Yiqing (403–44). For the famous dictum that "only barbarians discuss wealth in concluding a marriage," see WZZ 3.7b. Cited also in SY 3.33; JL 193b. The groom "on the eastern couch" was selected as a son-in-law by a Jin-dynasty official based on nothing more than a description of the young man's composure. The groom was Wang Xizhi, who became the most famous calligrapher of all time. See YLXS I.7.8a.

43. See, for example, SZJ 6.23b–26a; JSSL 20.9ab; MTJ 17.12b–15a. Even the collected works of one author may include different sequences of letters for different

weddings. See, for example, BTJ fascicles 82–86; GCG 17.1a–20a; HCQJ 126.10b–14a.

44. On this phenomenon, cf. Bloch 1992, 75–76.

45. See HLXB 8.10b–11b. Cf. YLXS II.8.5b–6a. Cf. also the instances of uxorilocal marriage in YLXS II.8.10a–11a. Examples of initiative of the bride's family that have not been reinscribed do exist, but they are few and they all date from the early decades of the practice of wedding correspondence. See HQJSJ 28.17ab; SGWJ 10.26ab, 10.27b.

46. See YLXS II.12.1a–2b. A Ming-dynasty manual condemns the practice of Seeing Off the Phoenix as a "Southern custom" for the very reason that it offends the principle of the groom's precedence. See SSJY 3.3a.

47. The earliest wedding *zha* appear to date from the middle of the thirteenth century. See BTJ 83.1a–85.14b; XPJ 26.12a–13a. On the *zha*, see GTL 2.29. On the changing materiality of wedding correspondence, see YLXS II.1.1a, II.1.11b–12a. Cf. HMQS II.5.13a; QZQQ IV.5.525.

The numbers of wedding letters found in the collected works included in the *Complete Books of the Four Treasuries* (*Siku quanshu*) yield an impression of the development of wedding correspondence. Since authors appear to have included only part of their wedding correspondence in their collected works or to have excluded it entirely, and since both the transmission of collected works and their inclusion in the *Complete Books of the Four Treasuries* have been selective, the numbers possess little value except as a general indication of a trend: 101 letters in 23 Northern Song works, 380 in 40 Southern Song works (with a prolific 88 letters in Chen Zhu's *Bentang ji*), 93 in 10 Yuan works (with a disproportionate 51 letters in Xie Yingfang's *Guichao gao*), 39 in 12 Ming works, and 7 in 2 Qing works. The publication of four-six prose anthologies, writing manuals, and anecdote collections during the late twelfth and thirteenth centuries strengthens the impression that the practice of wedding correspondence reached its greatest popularity among literati of the Southern Song. Tantalizing remarks in two engagement letters by Lü Zuqian suggest that the massive dislocation of literati after the Jurchen invasion of 1126, and the resulting reconfiguration of marriage networks, may have created a concrete incentive for the display of cultural capital. See DLJ 4.19b–20b; HLXB 4–5.6a, 8.10b. Cf. also HLXB 8.3b–4a. The style and especially the exorbitant length of the Ming and Qing letters indicate that these were self-conscious efforts in an obsolete practice.

48. Apart from these two specialized writing manuals, anthologies and writing manuals survive that include extensive sections on wedding correspondence among their varied contents. See BFDQ fascicle 86; HMDQ 1307 II.4–18; HMQS I.5.1b–2a, II.3–9; JXWHG I.18.1a–14a; QZQQ II.2.1a–13b, IV.2–5. On *leishu* as a genre, see Bol 1995; Bol 1996, 26–27; Chia 1996; Clunas 1991; de Weerdt 1994; Wilson 1995, esp. introduction and chapter 4. On the exclusiveness of *leishu* and the limits to their use, cf. Jiang Jusong 1977, 30.

49. On the Wuyi Retreat, see Walton 1999, 38, 105–6.

50. See HLXB 1.1a–8a, 11.2a–4b, 11.10b–12a, 15.3b–5b, 18.2b–5a, 19.5b–6a.

51. See HLXB 10.3ab; Wang Deyi 1977, 2644. On the recovery of Zhu Xi's *Family Rituals*, see Ebrey 1991a, 112, 146.

52. This distinction between moral universalism and matrimonial practice owes much to the work of Pierre Bourdieu. See Bourdieu 1977; Bourdieu 1990.

53. See HLXB 1.3a, 1.8ab. *Wedding Ritual* does not provide examples of the letter for Submission of the Choice and Asking the Name stipulated by Sima Guang, and it omits Sima Guang's comment that this letter is intended "to replace the correspondence of current practice." See HLXB 1.1b; SY 3.31.

54. For the wedding correspondence in these works, see BFDQ 86.1a–24b; JXWHG I.18.13a–14a; SLBZ 14.45b–52a.

55. For another description of this imprint, see Chia 2002, 106, 138. The date of this work remains tentative. The identification of Chen Wei (1180–1261) as Bandit-suppression Commissioner draws the *terminus post quem* at 1228, when Chen served in this post. See YLXS II.7.5a in conjunction with HMQS II.6.10b. The repeated identification of Song as the ruling dynasty sets the *terminus ante quem* at 1279. My preference for a date in the final decades of the Southern Song derives from the manual's inclusion of the *zha* format. The earliest *zha* for weddings to be found in collected works were composed by men who passed the examinations in the 1250s. See BTJ 83.1a–85.14b; XPJ 26.12a–13a.

56. Compare, for example, YLXS II.5.1a, II.7.8a, II.7.10a, and II.8.6a with the corresponding entries in the table of contents.

57. YLXS II.1.1a.

58. YLXS II.1.12a. Cf. YLXS II.1.11b–12a.

59. See, for example, YLXS I.11.1a, I.12.1a, II.1.3b, II.2.1a.

60. On the price of writing manuals, cf. Chia 2002, 190–91. On literacy and the book market, see Idema 1974, li–lxiv; Idema 1980, 321–22.

61. The title of the manual, *A New Book for the Old Man under the Moon*, perhaps hints at the practical context in which the work circulated. The eponymous old man was discovered, according to a story in Li Fuyan's *Record of the Mysterious and Strange Continued* (*Xu Youguai lu*), early one morning in 628 by Wei Gu when he set out to discuss a possible betrothal. By the light of the moon the old man was reading a book written in an unintelligible script. When pressed, the old man explained that his book recorded all matches among mankind as predestined in the underworld, and that it was his task to tie red string around the ankles of newborn children to ensure the proper workings of fate. See TPGJ 159.1142–43; Kao 1985, 271–74. See also Ebrey 1993, 56–57. The title *A New Book for the Old Man under the Moon* suggests, in the witty manner of wedding correspondence, that in the thirteenth century letters, not red string, secured marriage alliances, and that the paid scribe had taken the place of the underworld dispatch.

62. See, for example, the engagement letter written by Shen Yuqiu on behalf of Palace Writer Ye, in GXJ 12.19ab.

63. The thesaurus of allusions in the first installment and the ready-made couplets in the second installment are arranged according to a similar social and moral

hierarchy. See YLXS I.7.1a–I.9.9b, II.2.6a–12b. Other writing manuals use similar hierarchical arrangements, but with different choices. *A Complete Book of the Art of Writing* conflates matrimonial strategy with the ideology of the Learning of the Way (see HMQS II.3) and prefaces its section of engagement letters with an explicit rejection of a hierarchy of categories (see HMQS II.6.1a; translated below). In the category of minor marriage, however, appears a letter by compiler Liu Yingli himself, addressed to the family of Xiong He, the author of the manual's preface. The discrepancy between the negative external marking of this letter and the relative absence of negative internal marking strongly suggests the divergence between practical matrimonial strategy and its representation in the manual. In *Amassed Riches for Letters and Writs*, the marriage of stepchildren (*baozi*) precedes uxorilocal marriage, concubinage, and the letters for commoners. See QZQQ IV.3.511–12. See also QZQQ II.2.203–4, IV.3.501–4.522, IV.4.482–88.

64. The risk of marrying one's daughter to a talented student rather than to an examination graduate or an appointed official reduced the price of the match and therefore held a certain appeal for those who trusted their judgment. See especially QBZZ 4.149. Anecdotes about perspicacious fathers-in-law abound in notebooks. See, for example, DXBL 3.28, 14.160; DZJS 1.1; GJLS 6.79, 9.119, 10.122; JWZW 2.36; NGZ 18.447; QJXW 8.1b–2a; SSLY 49.642; SSWJL 9.89; YHJW 4.35; YYZZ 12.118; SLYY 9.139. Some notebooks describe matches in which marriage was contingent upon the betrothed student's success in the examinations. See, for example, CZJW 4.44; YJZ XVII.9.1205. In a pernicious practice known as "underneath the roster" (*bangxia*), wealthy families in the capital attempted to intimidate recent graduates into marrying their daughters. See, for example, DZXL 9a; GJLS 14.176; KCZ 3.27; TZY 3.25; ZGXHS 73. Zhuang Chuo records that investments in a recent examination graduate were called "calculation money" (*pudi qian*), "status-buying money" (*maimen qian*), or "latching money" (*xizhuo qian*). See JLB 2.71. Cf. Bossler 1998, 1–2, 78–94, 155–75; Chen Peng 1990, 140; Ebrey 1993, 72; Wu Xuxia 1990, 90; Zhang Bangwei 1989, chapters 6–7; Zhu Ruixi 1988, 46–47.

65. Emperor Lizong's (r. 1225–64) decree to the Quan family for the marriage of their daughter to his son, the later Emperor Duzong (r. 1265–74), dates from the same period as *A New Book for the Old Man under the Moon* and rather resembles an engagement letter. See XCYS 1.6a–7a.

66. Sima Guang and Yuan Cai (ca. 1140–95) both advice that crippling illnesses and falling fortunes render infant marriage a perilous enterprise. See SY 3.29–30; YSSF 1.24a. Cf. Ebrey 1984, 221–22. Cf. also ZhuS 3.4a. For anthropological studies of the social dynamics of exogamy, endogamy, and minor marriage, see Bourdieu 1977; Bourdieu 1990; Arthur Wolf 1995; Margery Wolf 1972. In *Wedding Ritual* and in collected works, engagement letters for matches that entail a severe loss of symbolic capital exhibit the same increase in narrative tension. See, for example, HLXB 9.6b–7b, 10.7b–9a; BSJ 4.29b; BTJ 82.3ab; DSJ 4.1b–4b; HQJSJ 28.16b; XPJ 24.13b.

67. YLXS II.7.9b. See also HMQS II.6.12b; QZQQ IV.3.507.

68. YLXS II.8.10a.

69. The dearth of surname allusions in letters for commoners contributes to the devaluation of their symbolic capital, leaving the letters generic and depriving their

anonymous users of history and precedent. Perhaps it is significant in this regard that the only puns I have discovered in literati letters have been puns on surnames. See HLXB 4–5.7a (pun on "Weng," the recipient's surname, which also means father-in-law); MXQJ 16.14b (a pun on the surnames of both sender Yang and recipient Li: "Our status has long lapsed, our flowering resembles that of a withered poplar [Yang]; our stature [fragrance] is still compatible, we seek protection underneath your stately plum [Li]").

70. YLXS II.9.1a. Cf. HMQS II.7.4a.

71. YLXS II.9.6a. Cf. QZQQ IV.4.518. The phrase *yi jing jiao zi* ("My son is still mastering his first scripture") appears as a standard self-deprecatory phrase in literati engagement letters, but the context of the present letter suggests the reading of *jing* ("scripture") as "the warp of fabric," hence (inadequately) "not one warped by learning." Black and purple were expensive and therefore dignified colors. Red (actually vermilion: Zhu) and White (Bai) are surnames, apparently of prominent families.

72. YLXS II.9.7a. HLXB 9.10a attributes this letter to Wu Zihou, who is otherwise unknown. The first line of this letter is impossible to translate well. The author uses a device known as *xiehouyu*, a short phrase that implies to the competent reader a second phrase conveying the actual message. Where I have translated "your ability to please your customers," the original says, "your talent for dancing," a reference to the ancient proverb "If you have long sleeves, you'll be good at dancing; if you have lots of money, you'll be good at business" (Han Fei 19.349, as translated in Watson 1964, 114). But in conjunction with the rapidly spreading reputation for services offered on roads and thoroughfares, the abilities of the dancer of course suggest talents other than those of the merchant. The romantic and sexual imagery in the remainder of the letter amplifies this suggestion: clouds and rain (a conventional metaphor for sexual intercourse, here reversed in a *hysteron proteron* to suggest repetition), the moon and the breeze, and crossing a river. The ensuing section on wedding songs discusses these latter images at greater length.

73. Three authors of engagement letters for commoners included in *A Complete Book of the Art of Writing* seem to have belonged to the circle of its compiler, Liu Yingli, and the author of its preface, Xiong He: Xiong Puzhai, Jiang Chengwan, and Xiong Guxi. See HMQS II.7.8a, II.7.9a, II.7.10b. Although only the third name can be identified, namely as a 1214 *jinshi* of Jianyang, the first Xiong is likely another relative of the Jianyang Xiongs, and Jiang Chengwan is credited with several other pieces collected in the manual (see, for example, HMQS II.3.5ab, II.6.15b). Cf. also the sophisticated play on conventional imagery in an acrimonious poem allegedly composed by Huang Tingjian when he learned that the desirable daughter of his humble neighbors had been married to an uncouth bumpkin. See MZML 10.7a.

74. YLXS II.9.5a, II.9.9a. "Extracting one hair for profit" is a frivolous allusion to the philosophy of Yang Zhu (4th century BCE), as caricatured in *Mengzi* and *Liezi*. See Mengzi 13.539 (VIIA.26); Liezi 7.83. Cf. Graham 1989, 60–61.

75. HMQS II.7.19ab. Cf. QZQQ IV.4.523.

76. See, e.g., YLXS II.9.1a, II.9.4b, II.9.5a.

77. Bourdieu 1990, 157.

78. In an amusing anecdote in his *Notebook from the Old Scholar's Studio* (*Laoxue'an biji*; LXABJ 2.17), Lu You (1125–1209) recounts how Qin Gui (1090–1155) ignores polite convention to gloat over his symbolic gains in an engagement letter:

> When Qin Gui married off his granddaughter to Guo Zhiyun, he himself composed the reply to the engagement letter. The letter included the couplets, "The groom: an elegant scion of a noble family; an excellent graduate of the imperial examinations. Yet he deigns to become an uxorilocal groom; how can he renege this binding agreement?" Qin's wife wanted him to delete the words "to become an uxorilocal groom," objecting that the expression was "too repellent." But Lord Qin said, "We have to write it this way, because then he really can't get out of it." Everyone who heard of it derided him.

79. Note also the many inconsistencies and overlaps in the hierarchical arrangement of *A New Book*, such as the inclusion of letters for infant marriage and remarriage under the neutral category of "Matching Surnames." See YLXS II.4.2b–7b.

80. YLXS II.*mulu*.11b. For pastiches of song titles that may replicate the addresses lost from *A New Book*, see HMQS II.9.1b–2b, II.9.5b; SLGJ 1333 I.10.8b; SLGJ 1699 IX.2.16b–17a. The translation of *zhiyu* as "address" combines the public, performative aspect of the genre with the meaning of the characters ("delivery words"). I am not aware of any secondary literature on the genre.

81. See HMQS II.9.1a–5b; GCG 17.3b–4b, 17.24a–25a; JJBY 14th X.27a–28b; MFZYML 37.6a–7a, 38.10ab, 38.11b–12b, 39.3b–4a, 39.18a–19a; QZQQ IV.5.6b–8a; SLGJ 1333 I.10.6a–8b; SLGJ 1699 IX.2.14a–17a; XPJ 45.2a–8a. Cf. DJMHL 5.30–32; MLL 20.304–7. Cf. also Ebrey 1993, 88–98.

82. From early times on, sexual manuals have presented the vagina as a many-layered organ, and architectural metaphors for the vagina and its parts, such as gate, door, palace, gully, and terrace, were common. See Van Gulik 1951, esp. 27–28, 231–32. In a series of lectures at the Metropolitan Museum of Art in New York, in November 1994, art historian James Cahill analyzed the use of visual penetration in erotic painting, a technique used since the tenth century. In such pictures, the painter leads the viewer's gaze through round windows and portals to an eroticized female.

83. This misperception has resulted in part from the condemnations of non-canonical weddings as vulgar by proponents of the Learning of the Way, which modern scholars have misconstrued as a critique of popular practice, instead of recognizing it as a criticism directed at the practices of fellow literati. But it has arisen also from the legacy of Qing prudery, as pointed out by Van Gulik (1951, iv–vi; 1974, xi–xii), which strongly colors the present image of pre-Qing literati.

84. Robert Ashmore (2002, 212) similarly argues that lyrics (*ci*) "only sporadically appear in the 'collected works' of their authors" due to an "enduring distrust of the form."

85. On the theme of the male quest for a female immortal, see Suzanne Cahill 1993; Hawkes 1974; Rouzer 2001.

86. On the *kouhao*, cf. NGZ 2.20–21; SLCH 430; SLJZ 7.

87. According to Hong Mai this form was no longer current in his day. See RZSL 20.

88. See, for example, BFDQ 92.1a–93.27b; HMDQ IV.5, VIII.13, X.7.14a–17b, X.14.8b–12a, X.16.11b–14b, XIV.3.1a–13b. The earliest known examples of such compositions for Hoisting the Ridgepole date from the sixth century, and the Dunhuang manuscripts include several examples of the genre. See Ruitenbeek 1993, 67–71, 164–67. Like Scattering the Grain, the ceremony of Hoisting the Ridgepole consecrates a new social space, with the important difference that the latter assumes a public, less intimate setting. For further parallels between marriage and construction, see chapter 3.

89. Cf. HMQS I.1.10a; RZSL 18, 20; SLCH 429 et seq; SLJZ 4, 7; SSLH 225–40; YZSL 5, 16–17. Both banquet addresses and wedding addresses write their setting into the text.

90. Nongyu and Xiao Shi are a legendary couple from the late Zhou. One day the couple flew away on a pair of phoenixes that Xiao Shi had attracted with his accomplished performance on the flute.

91. SLGJ 1699 IX.2.14b. Cf. HMQS II.9.3a; JJBY 14th X.27b–28a; SLGJ 1333 I.10.6b. Cf. also Ebrey 1993, 91.

92. On public recompense of dowry and sexual privilege, cf. Klapisch-Zuber 1985, 261–82.

93. QZQQ IV.5.536–37. The "romance of the Five Lakes" likely refers to the journey of the legendary beauty Xi Shi and the statesman Fan Li, after their destruction of the state of Wu.

94. See HMQS II.9.1b–2b; JJBY 14th X.27ab; QZQQ IV.5.6ab; SLGJ 1333 I.10.6a; SLGJ 1699 IX.2.14ab. Cf. GCG 17.4ab.

95. SLGJ 1333 I.10.6a. Cf. HMQS II.9.2a; JJBY 14th X.27ab; QZQQ IV.5.6ab; SLGJ 1699 IX.2.14ab. I have lifted this middle section of this address from *A Forest of Facts* in an attempt to reverse the editorializing by the compiler of *The Art of Writing*. In an introductory note (HMQS II.9.1b–2a) he states, "In an older Address at the Prostration of the Bride at the Ancestral Hall the bride first prostrates herself for the King Father of the East, the Queen Mother of the West, and so forth, but this deviates too widely from the canonical rites and is therefore deleted."

96. HMQS II.9.2ab. The collected works of Shi Hao (1106–94) and Yao Mian (1216–62) include addresses for a banquet for the bride, a ceremony for which the writing manuals do not provide. See MFZYML 38.10ab; XPJ 45.5a–6a, 45.7b–8a.

97. See HMQS II.9.2b–4b (twenty-six entries); JJBY 14th IX.27b–28a (ten entries); SLGJ 1333 I.10.6b–8a (twenty-seven entries); SLGJ 1340 II.2.5b–7a (identical to the previous); SLGJ 1699 IX.2.14b–16b (twenty-eight entries). Only the placement of the toast with the nuptial cups differs in these ceremonial sequences. In *The Art of Writing* the groom and the bride drink from the cups after stepping down from the bedstead and bowing to each other, but prior to picking the blossoming branch and opening the fold of each other's clothes. In all editions of *A Forest of*

*Facts*, the toast takes place at the very end of the cycle, before the couple retreats to the bedstead. For Addresses at the Groom's Banquet, see HMQS II.9.1ab; MFZYML 37.6a–7a, 38.11b–12b, 39.3b–4a; XPJ 45.2a–4b, 45.6b–7a. For addresses at other ceremonies, see GCG 17.3b–4b, 17.24a–25a.

98. See Dale Johnson 1980, 310–11. Note that, contrary to convention, the title perfectly fits the contents of the song cycle. The immortal guest is, of course, the groom.

99. "Minor Examination" is an alternative name for a wedding, the "major examination" being the imperial *jinshi* examination. Penghu, also known as Penglai, is a legendary island inhabited by immortals. Heavy clouds allude to the story of King Huan and the Spirit of Wu Mountain. "Young Liu" alludes to the lost fisherman who discovered the Peach Blossom Spring. "Clouds and rain," a common metaphor for sexual intercourse, derives from the tale of King Huan; heavy clouds invoke the ominous preceding stage. "Entwined mandarin ducks" and "dancing phoenix pair," aside from being emblems of marital bliss, also stand for certain positions of sexual intercourse. See Eberhard 1994, 177, 236; Van Gulik 1951, 30. The hibiscus is a common metaphor for the vagina. "The Jade Butterfly" and "The Swaying Flower Heart" are both names of song melodies, apparently invoked here to lend a literary quality to this common metaphor for sexual intercourse. "Golden lotuses" is a flowery expression for bound feet. Curved shoes fit such feet, which ideally take the form of crescent moons.

100. SLGJ 1333 I.10.7a. Cf. HMQS II.9.3a.

101. SLGJ 1699 IX.2.15b.

102. HMQS II.9.4b; SLGJ 1333 I.10.8a. Also translated in Ebrey 1993, 94.

103. SLGJ 1333 I.10.8a; SLGJ 1699 IX.2.16a. The poem given in *The Art of Writing* stares even more intently at the bride's hands, making them appear from her red sleeves. See HMQS II.9.4b.

104. See HMQS II.9.4b–5b; JJBY 14th IX.28ab; MFZYML 39.17b–19a; QZQQ IV.5.6b–7a; SLGJ 1333 I.10.8b; SLGJ 1699 IX.2.16b–17a.

105. HMQS II.9.5b; SLGJ 1333 I.10.8b; SLGJ 1699 IX.2.16b. *A Household Necessity* (JJBY 14th), whose wedding section is in many parts identical to *A Forest of Facts* (SLGJ 1333), contains no prose passages for Scattering the Grain.

106. QZQQ IV.5.6b. See also HMQS II.9.4b–5a. The text brings out the ambiguities present in the original phrasings in the canon.

107. QZQQ IV.5.6b. Although I have not seen "to drip" (*didi*) or "cuckoo" (*zigui*) in these meanings, the context suggests that they refer to ejaculation and the vagina. The cuckoo was believed to cry until it spit blood, so that here, in contrast to other sexual metaphors, the metaphor works by similarity in "function" rather than by similarity in appearance. Perhaps the attraction of the allusion to the cuckoo lies in its automatic evocation in the reader's mind of the word "blood," exempting the author from the obligation to spell out this polluting word. "White jade" refers to the penis (as in common metaphors such as "the jade stalk" or "the jade flute") and "furrows" or "field" stands for the vagina (as in the more common "cinnabar field"). A very similar line appears in a poem for sexual instruction quoted by Charlotte Furth

(1994, 125). "Pearl" and "bee" are, again, common metaphors for the female and male organs. When Chen Ajiao moved into the Yellow-golden Palace, Emperor Wu of the Han dynasty had fulfilled a promise he made as a three-year-old. Although at first sight the rhymes under "Scatter grain to the north" suggest a postcoital stage, the language may actually invoke Daoist sexual techniques. Emperor Wu received, as one of but few mortals, the secret teachings of the Dark Maiden, and according to legend he also accepted an invitation of the Queen Mother of the West to become her lover. See Van Gulik 1951, 39–40; Schipper 1965, 60–64. The perching phoenix pair and the bathing mandarin ducks may stand for sexual positions of the true adepts, invoked by the crowd to wish the newly-weds a healthy sexual life for the duration of their marriage. Cf. the sexual curiosity inscribed onto the bride and the groom in *A Household Necessity* (JJBY 14th IX.28b):

> Scatter grain to the west:
> Soft voices on the pillow
> Inquire about all intimate places,
> Her soft white bosom now stable but still damp.

108. See HMQS II.9.5a; SLGJ 1333 I.10.8b. The rhymes in *The Art of Writing*, perhaps composed by the compilers themselves, largely stress reproduction and proper marital relations. Cf. the lines translated in Ebrey 1993, 93.

109. SLGJ 1699 IX.2.16b–17a.

110. See DSJ 82.5ab; GCG 17.9ab. It must be admitted that both Xie Fangde and Xie Yingfang also use erotic imagery in their engagement letters. See DSJ 84.3ab; GCG 17.1b, 17.7a, 17.9a, 17.27b, 17.28a.

111. See HMQS II.9.6b–7a.

112. HMQS II.8.12a. The author of these lines, identified only by his *hao* may be the 1268 *jinshi* He Hong.

113. HMQS II.8.14a. The groom is still bound to convention, however, and cannot reply in kind, leaving his responses demure and apologetic. See HMQS II.8.11a–27b; QZQQ II.2.2b–7b.

114. See HMQS II.9.7b–11b.

115. See HMQS II.9.8a (by 1220 *jinshi* Ai Changji), II.9.10a.

116. HMQS II.9.10a.

117. HMQS II.9.10b.

118. TZXL 8b. A husband who paints the eyebrows of his wife symbolizes marital bliss. The Terrace of Splendor (Zhangtai) is a generic reference to courtesans and the pleasure quarters, and connotes exceptional female beauty. For other anecdotes about poems composed during weddings, by the groom or by guests, see HQL 7.3ab; HLXB 15.5b–8a, 19.3b; QSLB 8.8ab; YKCS 29.580; YLXS I.8.6ab, I.9.2a, I.9.8a.

119. Howard Levy dedicates an entire section to "The Wedding Occasion" in his *Chinese Sex Jokes in Traditional Times*. See Levy 1974, 73–96.

120. Cf. Levy 1974, 1–2.

121. MXL 4a; ZGXHS 88. Cf. QBZZ 8.346–47. Cf. also SRXH 9; QSTY II.3.8b. In the groom's poem, the bodhisattva (with phallic shaven head) stands for the groom's penis and the bearded face for the bride's vagina. For the beard as vagina, see also SRXH 24–25; Levy 1974, 160, 275–76.

122. YJZ II.2.239–40. While the fecundating blessing of "five sons and two daughters" is conventional (see, e.g., GCG 17.25a; P2646, in Zhao Heping 1993, 542–43; QZ 15.5b), the bride's response is not. I thank Stephen West for his assistance in translating the punch line. West suggests that a fox and a tiger are chosen as protagonists to hint at the disparate sizes of their genitalia (personal communication, December 1995).

123. SRXH 66. Cf. ZGXHS 91; Levy 1974, 82–83.

124. For letters that express affiliation with the Learning of the Way, see YLXS II.4.7b, II.5.6a, II.7.4b, II.10.3b–4a. Several of the sample letters for "Requesting the Date" chide Zhu Xi for the elimination of this ancient ceremony from his *Family Rituals*. See YLXS II.11.5ab, II.11.8a, II.11.8b. One of these remarkable letters (YLXS II.11.5a), an anonymous composition, reads:

> Propriety demands that the time of the Grand Wedding be requested; intention issues from the betrothal that the Six Rites encompass. If the injunctions stress that one should take care to be timely in providing one's son with a wife or one's daughter with a husband; then from the rituals one cannot omit the ceremony of Fetching the Bride when waiting in the hall or waiting at the gate. Dismiss the combination [of the Six Rites] to three: be like Ji [Ran] who opposed abridgment and change! Exhaust the full hundred: follow the Zhou in striving for perfect beginning and completion!

125. Cf. de Weerdt 1998 on the brief popularity that the Learning of the Way achieved in examination essays as a literary style, divorced from its ideological content. On exclusivity as a characteristic of the Learning of the Way, see also de Weerdt 1994.

126. See HMDQ 1307 preface; HMQS 1307 preface; XWXJ 5–7. By 1307, Xiong He and Liu Yingli, the compiler of *The Art of Writing*, had taught together for twelve years at an academy deep in the Wuyi Mountains in Fujian province, committed to spreading Zhu Xi's legacy in the Yuan empire. Xiong He's interest in ritual is evident in his efforts to reprint Zhu Xi's massive rearranged and emended edition of *Ceremonies and Rites*, the *Comprehensive Explanations of the Canon and Commentaries of Ceremonies and Rites*. He also wrote an admiring preface for the collected works of his kinsman Xiong Qingzhou, praising him for his dedication to ancient ritual. See XWXJ 4.56–57; HMDQ IX.3.9b–10b; SYXA 64.9ab, 70.9a.

127. HMQS II.6.1a, quoting Liji 26.18b-19a. Cf. HMQS II.1.1a, II.3.1a, II.4.1a, II.5.13a, II.5.13b, II.8.6b, II.9.1a, II.9.1b–2a, II.9.2b, II.9.5b–6a. Xiong He, in his 1307 preface (HMQS 1307 preface.3b), admits to a similar application of the editorial scissors: "Although it is impossible to remove all vulgar words and deviant

arguments, this doesn't excuse one from the obligation to edit their errors or to investigate their intentions."

128. For the labels "proper," "improper," and "vulgar," see HMQS II.3.1b–12a, II.3.12a–14b, II.9.1a. Editorializing occurs throughout, sometimes marked with an "et cetera" (*yunyun*; see, for example, HMQS II.6.17b, II.7.5a) or announced in an editorial warning (see, for example, HMQS II.9.1b–2a), but many letters and addresses have been curtailed or rewritten without such indication (see, for example, HMQS II.6.12a, II.6.12b, II.7.4a, II.7.7a versus YLXS II.7.8ab, II.7.9b, II.9.1a, II.9.6b; HMQS II.9.5b versus SLGJ 1699 IX.2.16b–17a). For examples of allusions to the surnames of men prominent in the Learning of the Way, see HMQS II.5.3b, II.5.11ab, II.6.6ab, II.6.7b, II.6.12a, II.6.14a, II.7.2a, II.7.21a, II.7.21b. A most remarkable attempt at appropriation presents a congratulatory lyric composed for Zhen Dexiu (1175–1235) which dismisses the conventional imagery of yearning immortals and lush boudoirs to expound philosophical discourse (HMQS II.9.10b):

> Once humaneness and propriety, and the Way of yin and yang have been established,
> And father and mother, and heaven and earth occupy their proper station,
> The six Masters will shine forth. One cannot leave off even for one day;
> This intention asserts itself more strongly as time passes.

129. See the markings in HMQS II.9.6b–8a; HMQS 1307 II.9.1b, II.9.3a–4b, II.9.7a; HMQS GG II.8.14ab. Markings appear in a few other places as well: in selected engagement letters (see HMDQ 1307 II.6.2ab; HMQS 1307 II.6; HMQS GG II.5.15a, II.6.1a–2a, II.6.4a, II.6.7ab), and in the stipulations for Fetching the Bride in government regulations and Zhu Xi's *Family Rituals* (see HMDQ 1307 II.4.5b–7a, II.6.2ab). Although readers' marks are even more difficult to date than the imprints in which they appear, I am confident that in this case they were made by contemporary readers. While Yuan consumers bought these writing manuals on the commercial market as reference guides to the changing conventions of etiquette and style, Ming and Qing collectors prized these (and other) Yuan works for their age and craftsmanship. Ming and Qing booksellers and bibliophiles would appear responsible, rather, for the removal of the smaller marks, in an attempt to increase the value of their holdings (a mended page passing more easily under a critical eye than red marks). A colophon by the proud owner of a fine copy of *The Art of Writing* (now in the Fu Ssu-nien Library, Academia Sinica, Taipei), illustrates the tremendous value that collectors accorded to Yuan imprints as early as 1376:

> Those who in recent times have become known as "antique aficionados" will without exception resort to every means in order to purchase what gives them pleasure. At present, inscriptions, records, calligraphy samples, and rare books will fetch several thousands and hundreds in the blink of an eye. This book I have bought on credit in Wuling [present Changde, Hunan province]. Its characters are straight and neat, and the paper is of remarkable quality. . . . Thus, it is convenient to use as well as a joy for the eye, and I leave it to my sons and grandsons, that they may preserve it for all time and never lose it.

130. See, for example, HMQS I.1.11a; HMQS 1324 preface.

131. Fang Jianxin 1985, 168. Cf. Ebrey 1993, chapter 4; Fang Jianxin 1985, 157–74; Ma Zhisu 1981, 7–14, chapters 1 through 20; Peng Liyun 1988, 193–217; Ruan Changrui 1989, 2–19, 79–83; Shi Fengyi 1987, 115–18; Su Bing and Wei Lin 1994, 239–45, 249–53; Zhu Ruixi 1988, 47–50.

132. See Ebrey 1993, 53–58, 85–86.

133. Ebrey 1993, 86, 97.

134. HQL 7.3a. The poem pretends that its composition proceeds simultaneously with the consummation of Liu Chang's second marriage, which in turn is represented as the composition of a rival poem. The poem also hints at Ouyang Xiu's well-known admiration for Liu Chang's literary skills. See, for example, SS 319.12b.

## Three. Calendars, Almanacs, Miracle Tales, and Medical Texts

1. TZ *Jiaochoulüe* 1809. Zheng Qiao refers to XTS 49.16a, CWZM 8.14ab (the latter entry supplied by Qing editors on the basis of Zheng Qiao's mention), and SKQSM. On these catalogues, including TZ, see Van der Loon 1984, 6–17.

2. JJBY 14th IX.29a.

3. CFYG 160.9ab; cited in Chia 1996, 16.

4. TYL 7.671–72; cited in Deng Wenkuan 1996, 233; also translated in Arrault 2003, 94–95.

5. See JTS 19B.13b, 19B.19a; XTS 9.8a, 9.10a. The reign title Guangqi turned out to possess an unintended inauspicious meaning. See TYL 7.672.

6. YZXZ 5.71. For mnemonic rhymes and tables of dynasties and reign titles see, for example, SLGJ 1340 III.1.1a–25b; SLGJ 1699 I.6.37a–10.59b.

7. See Wechsler 1985; Zito 1997.

8. For the variety of such omens see, for example, JTS fascicles 35–37; SS fascicles 48–67; XTS fascicles 31–36. Auspicious omens were also offered to the throne as tribute and stored in imperial warehouses. See, for example, CMTCL 1.11; DXBL 1.8; DZJS 1.5, 1.8; QXZJ 3.28; YYYML 3.22.

9. See Kalinowski 1983, especially page 311:

> l'absence d'une astronomie géométrique est, en Chine, largement compensée par la présence de traités astro-calendériques qui donnent de l'univers et des mouvements célestes une formulation essentiellement mathématique, sous la forme d'un enchevêtrement complexe de cycles abstraits et de computs extrêmement sophistiqués.

10. The translations "Matching Tone" for *nayin* and "Foundation-Elimination" for *jianchu* must remain tentative, for the names of these divinatory systems and their constituent stages derive from an original device and use that cannot be identified

with certainty. Cf. CGL 20.238–41; MQBT 5.16a–17b; RZSB II.7.297–98, IV.10.732–33; XJBFS 4.3a–6b; XLKY 5.1a–2b.

11. For a fuller description of the elements comprised by imperial calendars, see Arrault 2003.

12. DSHTL 7a.

13. SS 68.1a. Cf. Jinshi 21.1a; XTS 25.1ab. On the use of the calendar in ancient government, cf. Liji fascicles 14–16; Zhouyi 5.18ab. On its cosmic claims in Tang and Song, see the preface to the imperial calendar of 1256 (DSHTL) and the prefaces to the Dunhuang calendars of 834 (P2765), 922 (P3555v), 924 (S2404), 926 (P3247v and san 673), 928 (BD14636), 945 (S681v), 956 (S95), 959 (P2623), 981 (S6886v), 982 (S1473, S11427Bv), and 986 (P3403), in Deng Wenkuan 1996. See also SLYY 9.133–34. Howard Wechsler (1985) describes the Tang calendar as "not primarily a practical but rather a ritual vehicle" (212), and calls its yearly promulgation a "far more ritually and politically potent act" than the adoption of a new reign title (223). Cf. Arrault 2003, 85–86, 95–96.

14. See DSHTL, 1699 colophon; NGZ 2.19.

15. On the recruitment of astronomers for the compilation of calendars, see DTXY 1.10–11, 13.194. On mistakes, see CMTCL 3.48; JTS 32.1b–2a; RZSB III.13.568; SS 74.1a–3a, 80.24a–25a, 82.2a–17a; YJ 6.10ab.

16. On corrections by officials and commoners, see SS 82.11a, 82.15ab. On calendrical reforms, see CMTCL 3.37–38; JTS 32.1a–30a; SS fascicles 67–84; XTS fascicles 25–30. In a particularly embarrassing episode, a calendrical difference between the Song and Liao calendars led to diplomatic irregularities in 1078, until the dispute was resolved in favor of the Liao. See NGZ 12.313–14; SLYY 3.45, 9.133–34; SLYYB 191, 221.

17. See Chia 1996, 15, 41. Counting the numbers of divinatory works recorded in the rubric of the Five Phases in the bibliographical chapters of successive dynastic histories, Klaas Ruitenbeek (1993, 144n36) finds the following trend: "In the *History of the Han*, 31 such works are listed; in the *History of the Sui*, 272; in the *Old History of the Tang*, 113; in the *New History of the Tang*, 160; in the *History of the Song*, 853; in the *History of the Ming*, 104."

18. See S-P10 (Chengdu), S-P12 (Chang'an), and the dozens of Dunhuang calendars in Deng Wenkuan 1996. See also Feng Su's memorial and the anecdote about the dispute between printers of illicit calendars cited at the opening of this chapter.

19. YYBJ 19b. Cf. LZQGY 13a; YLDD volumes 180–81. Cf. also Wu Zeng's (fl. 1157–1170) description of the fate books (*mingshu*) of his day, which used the Five Phases and the twelve Branches to calculate health, life span, and offspring, as well as auspicious days to undertake activities such as washing and official business. See NGZ 5.95–96.

20. See TZ *Yiwenlüe* 6.1678–1703. Cf. JTS 47.7a–8b; SS 206.11a–27a; XTS 59.15a–17b. On competition between *liuren* manuals, see Kalinowski 1983, 402–4.

21. See DLXS prefaces, 15.16a–17b; JTS 47.8b, 79.7a–11b; MQBT 8.2b–3a; SS 294.8b–11a; XTS 59.17a, 107.2b–5a; YLDD 22182.14a. Cf. also other official handbooks named in *A New Book on Geomancy* (DLXS 11.8a, 12.21b, 14.6ab, 14.7b, 14.14a) and the unsuccessful proscription of current almanacs it describes (DLXS 15.17b–18b), and other extant almanacs commissioned by the Song imperial court (LRSDJ, LRDZ). According to Mo Xiufu's *Customs and Scenery of Guilin* (*Guilin fengtu ji*, 899), "Erudite Lü Cai of Our Dynasty had read broadly and deeply. . . . He wrote *Essential Ditties for Yinyang Divination and Geomancy*, in more than fifty fascicles, which is still extant. Today, it is often used for the divination of weddings." See GLFTJ 13. On the appropriation of Lü Cai's work, cf. Huang Zhengjian 2001, 199.

22. See TS 1.2–3. For generic prohibitions against the possession of illicit cosmological and calendrical works, see SXT 9.155–56; YDZ 32.9a–11b.

23. RZSB II.8.307–08; Yan Junping and Sima Jizhu achieved a reputation for efficacious divination during the Han dynasty. Cf. DJMHL 2.66, 3.88–89, 5.131, 6.165; JLB 1.14; LXABJ 2.25; MQBT 22.3ab; QBZZ 3.104–05; RZSB II.15.402, V.6.870–71; SCYWL 5.2ab; TS 3.41–42, 5.53–54; YYZZ I.2.24, I.6.61.

24. Cf. Kalinowski 1994, 39, 66–78.

25. The classic study on pollution is Mary Douglas's *Purity and Danger: An Analysis of Concepts of Pollution and Taboo* (1966). On the house as body and the body as house, see BJQJ 27.11a–12a; QJYF 11.1a–9b, 14.1a–10b; YSLZ 11.1a–9b. Cf. Bray 1997, 91–150. To Klaas Ruitenbeek's (1993) marvelous work on building and carpentry I owe much of my understanding of cosmological discourse. Anthropologists since the 1960s have dedicated much attention to liminality and pollution in weddings, childbirth, and burial in Taiwan, Hong Kong, and (more recently) the Mainland. See, for example, Freedman 1979; Furth 1986; Furth and Ch'en 1992; Martin 1973, 1975; Seaman 1981.

26. For rare explanations of the workings of such systems of prognostication, see Kalinowski 1983; Kalinowski 1994.

27. Cf. Kalinowski 1994, 39–44.

28. QDYY 15.192. Cf. MQBT 18.9ab. One of the calendars compiled by Deng Zongwen survives: see DSHTL preface and postface.

29. JLB 1.6. Cf. MQBT 8.2a–3a, 18.11b–12b; QXZJ 3.30; SCYWL 5.2ab.

30. An anecdote in *Record of Grace and Virtue* (*Houde lu*; HDL 2.18) makes a rare mention of such an archive. The emperor orders the arrest of a diviner whose activities have allegedly infringed upon "palace prohibitions." But after a search, Fan Zhongyan reports,

> I have investigated the writings in the diviner's collection. All pertain to the calculation of fate and the selection of auspicious days, and none of his draft calculations touches upon matters relating to the Court. I have had dealings with this man in the past, and once sent someone to order him to make calculations of the stars and positions. All the documents were still there.

31. Cf. Kalinowski 1994, 37. Cf. also Chia 2002, 143–46.

32. On the uneasy status of texts in medical traditions, cf. JLB 1.25. Cf. also Judith Farquhar 1993, 1–4; Furth 1999, 15, 96–99; Leung 2003, 396–98. Many of Judith Farquhar's observations about Traditional Chinese Medicine in the People's Republic of China seem eminently applicable to medical practice in Song and Yuan, especially the use of the pulse and other non-invasive readings of the patient's body to establish a diagnosis in terms of deregulated processes, and healthy reproduction as the dominant concern in women's medicine. See Farquhar 1991; Farquhar 1993. Cf. Furth 1999.

33. In a chapter dedicated to "Creation and Transformation" (*zaohua*), for example, Liu Xun (1240–1319) concludes a complex exposition on bodily transformations and various cyclical systems with the words, "I have never studied numerology and have not been able to fathom the principles of this phenomenon. I record it for the future reader who may possess the necessary insight." See YJTY 28.298–9. Cf. QDYY 18.263. I call the genre of the miracle tale "marginal" because even its advanced age and apparent popularity did not free its practitioners from the obligation to defend themselves time and again against objections to their pursuits raised by famous canonical passages and by legitimate literati discourse. Cf. Campany 1996, 101–59; Hymes 1997.

34. See, for example, CGL 20.238–41; MQBT 7.1b–4b, 5.16a–17b; NGZ 5.95–96; RZSB II.7.297–98, II.15.410–11, IV.10.732–33, IV.10.733; SCYWL 3.3b; YHJW 7.62–65; YJ 1.9a–10a, 1.11a; YLMC 2.21–23, 9.148, 11.185–90, 11.201, 11.203–06, 13.226–37. Literati maintained, at least in writing, their distance not only from diviners, but also from court astronomers. An edict promulgated in 996 segregated all divinatory officials (*jishu guan*) from the civil and military officials, and relations between these two groups appear to have been acrimonious. See DTXY 3.46–47, 7.105; RZSB III.7.499–500, III.13.568; SS 82.25ab; YYYML 2.14. An occasional notebook entry derides literati for not maintaining their distance from diviners. See, for example, QXZJ 3.104–5; RZSB II.8.307–8.

35. RZSB II.8.307, paraphrasing Shangshu 4.10b–11a and Shiji 3.12ab, and quoting Shangshu 15.1a and Hanshu 30.1770–71. On the divination of weddings in antiquity, cf. RZSB II.6.292, II.8.307–8; YLMC 11.192–98. On the loss of divinatory texts and technologies, cf. RZSB II.15.402, V.6.870–71; TZ *Jiaochoulüe* 1804, 1813. Cf. also the rise and fall of various divinatory systems as reconstructed by Marc Kalinowski (1983, 1994). On the practice of plastromancy in the thirteenth and fourteenth centuries, cf. YLJY, especially 4.65. For literati interest in divinatory systems thought to be ancient, see YJ 1.9a–13a; TS 7.62; XTS 34.1a–2a. On the prestige accorded to the *Book of Changes* by Song literati, see Kidder Smith et al. 1990.

36. RZSB II.4.265, quoting Shiji 127.7b. A Qing imperial almanac (XJBFS preface.1a) adduces the same example for the same argument.

37. See DSHTL. "Great Luminance" was the name of the calendrical system used by the Jin imperial court from 1137 until its fall in 1234. See Jinshi 21.1ab et seq. In his 1669 postface to the *Fully Annotated Huitian Eternal Calendar of the Fourth Year of the Baoyou Reign of the Great Song* (DSHTL, n.p.), Zhu Yizun mentions that the library catalogue of the Ma family lists a copy of such a Jin-dynasty calendar, but

it appears that he did not see the calendar himself, and it does not survive today. Astronomers and mathematicians of the early Qing could learn much about the general principles of earlier calendrical systems, since these were set forth in the astronomical treatises of the dynastic histories and elsewhere, but only individual calendars demonstrate the actual, historical application of these principles.

38. Cf. Arrault 2003, 85–86; Deng Wenkuan 1996; Fujieda 1973. In addition, fragments of Xi Xia calendars of the years 1120, 1144, 1200, and 1211 (the latter printed in movable type) have been unearthed at Heicheng, Inner Mongolia. See Shi Jinbo 2001.

39. See Arrault 2003, 93–95; Deng Wenkuan 1996, 2–4; Deng Wenkuan 2001, 139. The continued use of imperial reign titles and the imperial rhetoric of cosmic order in the prefaces to Dunhuang calendars shows that their compilers (who, moreover, proudly list their official titles) took presumptuous liberties but avoided the treason of an independent reckoning of time. See the calendars of 834 (P2765), 922 (P3555v), 924 (S2404), 926 (P3247v and san 673), 928 (BD14636), 945 (S681v), 956 (S95), 959 (P2623), 981 (S6886v), 982 (S1473 and S11427Bv), and 986 (P3403), in Deng Wenkuan 1996.

40. See, for example, the calendars of 808 or 865 (C106: a month and a half on the reverse of a sutra), 809 (P3900v: three months on the reverse of a ritual manual), 821 (P2583: one month at the end of an annotated sutra), 858 (S1439v: five months on the reverse of a canonical commentary), 864 (P3284v: five abridged months on the reverse of a ritual manual), 888 (P3492: three months interspersed among divinatory texts), 905 (P2506v: a month and a half on the reverse of a chapter from the *Book of Songs*), and an undatable fragment (S1498: two days, preceding a work of Buddhist law), in Deng Wenkuan 1996.

41. See, for example, the calendars of 829 (P2797v: title of the calendar, followed by an abridged copy of the eleventh and twelfth month, on the reverse of a divinatory handbook), 891 (P2832v: one month, discontinued by the copyist), 897 (san 1721: abridged calendar, the majority of entries listing only one auspicious activity per day), 926 (P3247v: *idem*), 928 (BD14636: a calendrical preface copied into the empty space preceding a divinatory text), 981 (S6886v: complete calendar whose full record of activities discontinues after a few days to be replaced by a private record of the dates of ablutions and death rites), and 993 (P3507: the dates and seasonal markings of three months, following upon a divinatory manual), in Deng Wenkuan 1996. A comparison between the entries for the third and fourth months in san 1721 and P3248, two incomplete but overlapping calendars for the year 897, confirms the incompleteness of the former.

42. For marital horoscopes, see the calendars of 877 (S-P6) and 978 (S612), in Deng Wenkuan 1996.

43. See the calendars of 834 (P2765), 858 (S1439v), 864 (P3284v), and 877 (S-P6), in Deng Wenkuan 1996. On changes in the auspiciousness of the stages of the *jianchu* cycle, cf. XLKY 5.1a–2b. Of the importance of the *liuren* system in calendrical calculations, Song Luzhen remarks in the fourteenth century, "the fortunes and disasters as well as the good and evil deities recorded in the calendrical books all have their roots in the *liuren* system." See YYBJ 6a.

44. On the correlation between calendrical spirits and particular activities in the Dunhuang calendars, see Arrault 2003, 114–17.

45. On the Non-infringement System, see JJBY 14th IX.33a; SLCY 20a; XJBFS 4.52a–54b, 9.29b–30a; XLKY 3.35a–36b. Cf. Lu Shixian 1960, 22–23. I thank Jennifer Rudolph for recovering the pertinent passage in *A Household Necessity* whose importance I had failed to recognize in time.

46. I thank Alain Arrault (personal communication, April 2002) for suggesting that Non-infringement at times operates as a calendrical spirit.

47. Patient tabulation has yielded the two groups of auspicious dates for weddings and betrothals, but their identification remains, of necessity, arbitrary. The limited number and the incompleteness of the Dunhuang calendars, and the unexplained divinatory shifts around 900 and in the late tenth century encumber this attempt at a reconstruction of calendrical methods as it hinders other such attempts. The lists of auspicious betrothal and wedding dates in *A Household Necessity* (see below) add to the likelihood that Dunhuang diviners used sets of generic auspicious dates, even if their sets may not have coincided entirely with the two groups identified here. Betrothal dates appear largely to be a subset of wedding dates, but what distinguishes them from wedding dates remains unclear.

48. On the 1256 calendar, see Lu Shixian 1960, 15–59.

49. The specification of particular inauspicious activities on unfavorable days in the calendar of 1256 differs from the blank designations of inauspicious days in the Dunhuang calendars. For most activities, the number of auspicious days balances the number of inauspicious days (13 against 11 for hoisting the ridgepole of a new house, for example). But for activities fraught with liminal danger, such as placing the bed and hanging the bed curtains or cleaning the stove, the calendar lists only unfavorable days. On placing the bed and hanging the bed curtains, see Ruitenbeek 1993, 227.

50. The loss of betrothal dates from the ninth month has reduced the difference between the two numbers. See SLCY 32a.

51. SLCY 8b.

52. SLCY 39b.

53. TZ *Yiwenlüe* 1698–99.

54. See Suishu 34.1036–37.

55. See JTS 47.8a; XTS 59.16a.

56. See CWZM 8.14ab.

57. SS 206.14b, 206.20a.

58. See LRSDJ 2.25, LRDQ 2.40b–42b, 6.30b–33b; XLKY 3.12ab. Cf. Kalinowski 1983, 393.

59. DLXS 1.13ab. The passage flouts ritual by making ceremony dependent on cosmological variables. For other occasional mentions of wedding divination in this work on geomancy, see DLXS 6.1b, 6.10b–11b, 6.13a–14b, 10.1b.

60. KT 16a.

61. See S2729v, P4680, and S4282, in Huang Zhengjian 2001, 148–49. A few Dunhuang calendars also contain marital horoscopes. See S-P6, in Deng Wenkuan 2001, 135–36, 140–41; S0612, in Deng Wenkuan 1996, 521. I thank Alain Arrault for alerting me to the work of Huang Zhengjian, and I thank Michael Nylan for sending me photocopies of the pertinent Dunhuang texts.

62. S2729v, in DHBC vol. 22, 586. See also Huang Zhengjian 2001, 147–48.

63. SF II.109.1a–4a; Daozang no. 285. See also Liu Yongming 1995, vol. 28, 107–13, vol. 29, 801–8.

64. See Kalinowski 1983, 400–2.

65. TYJ 1b.

66. TYJ 2a.

67. The chapter on cappings and weddings, incidentally, follows an elaborate chapter on the rituals associated with the construction and use of domestic space. See JJBY 14th IX.21b–22a. Especially the rites of consecration of a newly built house in this chapter clearly parallel wedding ritual.

68. JJBY 14th IX.30ab.

69. JJBY 14th IX.30b, IX.31b.

70. JJBY 14th IX.32b. Cf. the more detailed explanation of a similar system in XJBFS 36.6b–7b.

71. See JJBY 14th IX.32b–33a. The "Ten Completely and Greatly Auspicious Days" also appear in JJBY 1673 III.45b (without the designation "Greatly"). The same dates appear, as if by mistake, in JJBY 1673 III.44b as "Auspicious Days for Weddings."

72. JJBY 14th IX.33a, citing SLCY 20a. The meaning of the title *Zong'e* (comprehensive mud) is unclear.

73. See JJBY 14th IX.33a. The same graph appears with a differently worded explanation in SLGJ 1478 III.7.32a, which also prints a separate diagram for uxorilocal weddings. Chang Renchun (1993, 20–21) analyzes two similar graphs from later almanacs, but the explanations seem to differ from Yuan understandings. Two imperial almanacs of the Qing dynasty argue that the diagram combines the eight trigrams with the ritual choreography of the ceremonies conducted, in *Rites and Ceremonies*, by the bride and her parents-in-law on the day after the wedding. See XJBFS 35.18ab; XLKY 3.36b–37b.

74. JJBY 14th IX.33b. Cf. XJBFS 36.6b–7b. The wedding section does in fact list another entry here: eleven auspicious cyclical dates for taking a female slave or servant.

75. Improper application of the printing block has blurred the first six of the "Nine Auspicious Matches" in *A Household Necessity*. The captions that appear to read "Matching Stems" (*ganhe*), "Eight Openings" (*bakai*), and "Four Restrictions" (*sijian*) may be identical to the tables in the calendar of 877. See JJBY 14th IX.29ab; Deng Wenkuan 2001, 135, 140–41. Cf. also Chia 2002, 57, 59; LRSDJ 1.6.

76. See JJBY 14th IX.33a; Deng Wenkuan 2001, 138; Huang Zhengjian 2001, 147. Different from *A Household Necessity*, the calendar of 877 instructs the reader to start counting clockwise from the bride in long months and counterclockwise from the groom in short months. The diagram in P2905 is differently constituted, with the door, the road, nobility, and wealth instead of the residence, the hall, the groom, and the bride.

77. Passing mentions of the selection of an "auspicious day" (*jiri*) for a wedding are not uncommon (see, for example, GJLS 16.198–9; YJZ IV.2.548, XV.10.1129), but I know of only one story in which a wedding date achieves a certain prominence in the plot. The day before her marriage, the younger sister of Liu Boshan of Jizhou is punished by the Thunder God for wearing a sandal made of paper on which the character for heaven (*tian*) is inscribed. "The girl subsequently fell ill and missed her wedding date. Not for more than a year were the rituals completed." See YJZ XII.4.827.

78. On the development of the miracle tale from a religious argument in the Six Dynasties to a literary short story with fictional elements in Tang, see Campany 1996; Idema and Haft 1985, 198–204; Kao 1985; Lévi 1986.

79. On the translation of the spoken into the written form, see YJZ XIV. preface.967, XVII.preface.1135, XXVI.preface.1303. On the use of informants, see Hansen 1990, 19–21; ter Haar 1993, 20–21.

80. For an attempt at systematization through a rearrangement of tales from older collections, see GJLS preface.1. For the supernatural as exceeding the comprehension of a single human being, see DZXL 553; YJZ XI.preface.711, XXIX. preface.1467. For a benevolent universe, see HDL. For an eloquent argument on Hong Mai's *Records of Yi Jian* as an exploration of "lower-case truth," see Hymes 1997.

81. For predictions, see GJLS 11.142, 12.146–47. For poems, see GJLS 14.176; YJZ *bu*.18.1720. For dreams, see CZJW 4.44; YJTY 30.312; YJZ I.16.141, I.13.477, I.11.94–95, I.11.98, XI.7.767, XII.2.810, XV.10.1129, *bu*.10.1636, *bu*.22.1750–1, *sanbu*.1806. For physiognomy, see DXBL 2.16–17; SSLY 49.642; YYZZ 12.118. Cf. also DJMHL 5.144 and JLJZZ 17b on the custom of physiognomizing of brides in Northern Song Kaifeng. For omens, see YJZ XII.7.848, *bu*.10.1637. *Classified Anecdotes of Past and Present, Newly Compiled and Arranged by Category* (*Xinbian fenmen gujin leishi*, 1169) dedicates an entire section to predestined marriage, citing anecdotes from the remote and recent past to prove that fate determines one's match. See GJLS 16.193–202. Cf. Ebrey 1993, 58–59.

82. For divorce followed by marriage to the predestined spouse, see GJLS 11.142; KT 16a. For death and fated remarriage, see GJLS 16.194–96, 18.224; YJZ I.13.477, I.11.94–95, XII.7.848, XV.10.1129, *bu*.10.1636, *sanbu*.1806, *sanbu*.1806–7.

83. King Wu possessed seven virtues (see Chunqiu 23.22a; Legge 1994, V.320), and Sage Emperor Yu separated his realm into nine provinces (see Shangshu 1.6b; Legge 1994, III.3). Parallelism requires that *wu* in this passage be King Wu, even though "martial prowess" seems to be the common reading in the locus classicus. Note that Liu Hua replies in the style and idiom of four-six prose, discussed in chapter 2.

84. QXZJ 4.42; also cited in SSLY 49.642.

85. KT 5b–6a. The anecdote, in which Lü Jifu's fortunes finally take a turn for the better, reflects in hilarious fashion on the ambiguous status of Fujian during this period. On this status, cf. Chia 1996, 18.

86. HDL 1.3. For this use of *bu li*, see also HDL 1.2; TYJ 1b.

87. Predictions of the name of the future spouse or the time of marriage are often accompanied by predictions about success in the imperial examinations and in the subsequent career. See, for example, GJLS 11.142; MZML 3.7a; TPGJ 77.489–90; YJZ I.7.767, XII.2.810, *bu*.10.1636, *sanbu*.1806–7; YWZL 4.40; YZXZ 2.34.

88. YJZ XV.2.1064.

89. KYZ 6.71.

90. YYZZ I.1.8. Although Duan Chengshi does not explicate his contempt for contemporary wedding practices in this section (I.1.7–8), he insinuates his condemnation not only by the incoherence of his description, but by the inclusion of practices that appear to the educated reader as ignorant permutations of canonical ritual, such as the three revolutions of the mounted groom around the bride's carriage, replacing the first three revolutions of the wheels of the carriage by the groom as driver. Elsewhere Duan Chengshi explicitly criticizes a number of contemporary wedding ceremonies for their deviation from the canon. See YYZZ II.4.241.

91. The difficulties in assessing views on the pollution of defloration during that distant era need not cause surprise. During fieldwork in Taiwan, Emily Martin was unable to ascertain her informants' ideas about the pollution associated with sexual intercourse. See Martin 1975, 209. On the yin bride as the center of wedding ritual, cf. Granet 1953 (1912), 65–66, 84–85. Maurice Freedman (1979, 288–89) notes that in generic practice, marriage rites are based on virilocal virgin marriage, regardless of the actual circumstances of individual weddings.

92. Furth 1999, 16.

93. See, for example, BJQJ preface.1ab, colophon.6a; QJBY preface.1a–3b; QJYF. FRLF and WTMY claim to be compilations of the best methods from an array of earlier texts. On the legendary Sun Simiao, see DTXY 10.155–56; YYZZ I.2.19. Cf. Furth 1999, 70–92; Angela Leung 2003, 374 *et passim*.

94. Furth (1999, 70–93) similarly draws attention to the asymmetry in Song learned medical discourse, in which (male) *qi* remained at the apex (92) of the yinyang system, encompassing (female) Blood. On yang as encompassing yin, cf. also Zito 1987; Zito 1997.

95. The locus classicus of this opinion seems to be QJYF 5.1a. Many Song and Yuan manuals accord to this dictum a prominent place in their sections on women's medicine. BJQJ (colophon.6a) even cites it as the reason for placing women's medicine in the opening section of the book. See also BJQJ 1.12a, 2.1a–2a; FRLF 9.3ab; NKBW 1.2; XDCYF 9.1a. Cf. Furth 1999, chapter 2.

96. See BJQJ 2.1a–2a; FRLF 2.1b–2a, 9.3ab; NKBW 1.2; XDCY 9.1a. Cf. Furth 1999, chapter 2.

97. See FRLF 1.2a–3a, 6.6ab; NKBW 1.1, 1.47–48; NKWJF "Menstruation"; WSBJ 18.5b–6a.

98. For medical concern with loss of semen, see BJQJ 19.1a–36b; WTMY 16.36a–41a; YSLZ 7.6a–7b. Cf. NGZ 8.211. For techniques for the containment of semen during intercourse, emission control, and emission quotas, see BJQJ 27.26b–29b; QJYF 12.1b–3b; YSLZ 7.6a–8b. See also Van Gulik 1951, chapters 2–3. BJQJ 1.12a argues that male weakness resulting from loss of semen is still ten times easier to cure than the diseases of adult women. On the female conditions resulting from lack of intercourse, see FRLF 6.12a and NKBW 1.47–48, both of which quote ZBYH 40.2a. See also ZBYH 42.6b–7a. The only women who have to fear for overexposure to yang are prostitutes. See NKWJF "Menstruation."

99. NKBW 1.2.

100. For sexual possession and rape of adult women by deities and demons, see GD 4.6b–7a; YJZ IV.19.699–700, IV.20.703, IV.20.705–6, XII.1.796–97, XII.1.797, XIII.2.890–91, XIII.6.926, XIV.3.986, XIV.6.1011, XVII.7.1191, XVII.8.1195, XXVIII.5.1425.

101. See BGL 3.21.

102. For impregnated virgins, see KCZ 3.29; KYZ 9.103; YJZ III.6.417, IV.19.694, IV.20.703, XIV.8.1033–34; YYZZ II.2.213. For possession of virgins "without harm," see BGL 3.23 (at entering a new house); YJZ III.7.421, III.10.446–47, IV.5.574, IV.18.684–85, XIV.2.982, XIV.6.1011, XXVIII.2.1396–97. For impregnated married women, see YJZ I.14.121–22, IV.19.695–97, IV.20.702–03, XII.4.824, XII.6.836, XIII.8.940, XX.3.1238, XX.3.1240, XXVI.2.1316–17, *bu*.9.1627; YWZL 3.28. Even statues and paintings of women may be impregnated. See YJZ I.17.146, I.19.166.

103. YJZ III.10.452–53. Cf. KCZ 5.41–42; YJZ III.1.370–71, IV.20.708, XVII.3.1158–59, XVII.7.1191–92, *bu*.10.1642, *bu*.22.1750–51. For examples of weddings as haunted liminal occasions, see DPZL 2.45–46; GD 3.9b–10b, 4.10a; MJ 2.21; NGZ 18.442; SLYY 7.98; SLYYB 211; YJZ III.2.373–74, III.10.448; YYZZ I.13.120.

104. YSLZ 7.7b. On the pollution of sexual intercourse, cf. BJQJ 2.2ab, 27.29b–31a; FRLF 9.2a, 9.4a–6b, 9.14b–15a; NKBW 1.1; NKWJF "Delivery"; QJYF 12.1b–3a; WTMY 33.3b; YSLZ 7.5a–8b, 11.5a; ZBYHF 38.7b. Cf. also Furth 1994, 139; Van Gulik 1951, 55–57, 59–61. As in the divination of weddings, the shared assumptions underlying prohibitions on sexual intercourse yield disparate results (BJQJ 27.29b–31a; the italics render the underlinings and emphatic dots left by an early owner of this book, as shown in the facsimile reproduction of the Song original):

> The method of mounting women requires that one avoid having intercourse on certain occasions. If a man mounts a woman on *even* days, or during the *crescent, full, last, or new moons*; *during heavy wind, heavy rain, or heavy fog*; *during great cold or great heat*; *during thunder or lightning*; *when heaven and earth are covered in unnatural darkness*; *during a solar or a lunar eclipse*; *under a rainbow or during an earthquake*; then he will harm his Internal Deity.

> This is not auspicious. It harms the male a hundred times, and it causes illness to the female. If a child result of this union, it will be idiotic or stupid; dumb, deaf, or dim-sighted; hunchbacked or blind; of ill health and short-lived; unfilial and inhumane. One should also avoid copulating under *the sun, the moon, or the stars, or by the light of a fire*; *in a temple or monastery*; *by the side of a well, a stove, or a latrine*; *next to a grave or an encoffined body*. None of this is allowed.

105. See BJQJ 3.38ab; FRLF 7.45a–46a; WTMY 34.47b–48b. Cf. Van Gulik 1951, 64.

106. BJQJ 2.29ab. Cf. WTMY 33.32b–34b, 34.2b–3a. The "day of the counter-branch" (*fanzhi ri*) is the day whose number conflicts with the branch of the first day of the moon (see XJBFS 6.72a–73a), but the meaning of the "month of the counter-branch" is uncertain. *Methods from the Essential Secrets of the Palace Library* (*Waitai miyao fang*; WTMY 33.34b–48a) prints delivery charts of the kind mentioned in the translated passage (one for every month of the year, each indicating the positions of baleful stars and auspicious directions), as well as tables of auspicious and inauspicious times and directions for every year of a woman's reproductive years (ages thirteen through forty-nine) and a chart for the calculation of the "travel of Taiyi" (*riyou*). Cf. also the explanation of the cycle of the Internal Deity and of the travel of Taiyi in calendars (DSHTL 27a):

> Whenever in the above entries the whereabouts of the Internal Deity reaches [the evil stars] Blood's Taboo or Blood's Branch, one cannot practice acupuncture or moxibustion, or draw blood. When the sun travels in the bedroom, a woman in labor should avoid the specified direction. Placing the bed and hanging the bed curtains, and sweeping the room are also inauspicious.

Cf. the calendars of 986 (P3403) and 989 (S3985 and P2705), and the undated fragment P3054, in Deng Wenkuan 1996. On the internal deity and the travel of Taiyi, see Arrault 2006.

107. Furth and Ch'en (1992, 41) mention that Taiwanese women who washed rags stained with menstrual blood in ditches and streams risked "polluting stream water and offending the gods or their neighbors or both." For a powerful miracle tale about birth pollution, see YWZL 2.21–22. KCZ 3.22 mentions the Bloody Pond, the generic punishment in the hells for female pollution by menstruation and childbirth. On this belief, see Seaman 1981.

108. YJZ *bu*.17.1712–13.

109. See, for example, Granet 1953, 65–69; Granet 1975, 56; Granet 1994, 24–40.

110. See Granet 1919; Granet 1953, 67, 84; Granet 1975, 44. Bernard Karlgren (1950) and Arthur Waley (1960) refined Granet's approach to the *Book of Songs*, always acknowledging their debt to their predecessor's work.

111. See Karlgren 1930. Karlgren (1930, 2) surmises that certain insights into ancient ritual had been lost so early, that even in Zhou times men handled ritual objects without realizing their origins in phallic cults.

112. See Van Gulik 1951, 92–93; Van Gulik 1974, 80, 223.

113. See Liji 15.5a–6a. On ancient beliefs about thunder and reproduction, see also Karlgren 1930, 35.

114. See Liji 4.22b–23b, 5.11b–13a, 28.10a–11a, 61.10a–11a. Cf. Shijing 2C.12a–14b. Cf. also YKCS 29.329–30.

115. See Liji 61.10a–12a. Van Gulik (1974, 17) writes about this passage, "In the human sphere the union of king and queen, the man and woman *par excellence*, epitomizes the balance of the positive and negative elements in the realm and the world. If their union lacks harmony, the effects will be felt throughout the land in droughts, floods and other natural disasters." Cf. Granet 1953, 26–27, 67; Granet 1994, 2–3; Waley 1960, 81.

116. See YJTY 28.288. Since *zi* (creation) is associated with the east, and *si* (conception) with the west, *yin* (three places removed from *zi* by inclusive count) is "three yang," while *shen* (three places removed from *si*) is "three yin." Cf. FRLF 9.1b–2a, 10.6ab, 10.9b; NKBW 1.1–2; NKWJF "Delivery"; RZSB II.15.400–401; SCYWL 3.3b; YJTY 28.288–89. Lü Dalin, much admired by Zhu Xi, also reads thirty and twenty as absolute ages (see LJJS 2.19b), and he accords much importance to the dynamic of yin and yang in wedding ritual: "The 'wedding' [also: 'dusk'] is the time when yang goes and yin comes, when yang crouches and yin expands. This means that the male is inferior to the female." See LJJS 154.13a.

117. Early in my research I read an anecdote in which a Song expert on the *Book of Changes* was much in demand for the calculation of auspicious wedding dates, but I lost the reference. For general examples of active use of the *Changes* by Song and Yuan experts see, for example, LZQGY 10ab; NGZ 10.260, 18.447; TZ *Jiaochoulüe* 1804, 1813; YYBJ 1ab. Liu Xun relates theories of contemporary diviners to the *Record of Ritual* and the *Rites of Zhou*. See YJTY 28.291. On ambivalence among Song literati about divination as practice, see Smith et al. 1990. On Daoist readings of the *Book of Changes*, see Kalinowski 1989–1990.

## Four. Legal Codes, Verdicts, and Contracts

1. YDFLYC 88.

2. QMJ 12.479.

3. JTS 50.2a.

4. JTS 50.4a.

5. See JTS 50.1a–6a. This narrative of the establishment of the dynasty's laws is by no means unique (see, for example, the comparable narratives collected in TZ *Xingfalüe* 1332–54) and contains evident literary tropes. But though one may doubt the historicity of the tropical narrative, one should recognize the tropes themselves as an intrinsic part of the historical practice of legal discourse.

6. See TLSY 1.3–6. Several of these punishments were nominal. Penal servitude was automatically converted into strokes with the heavy rod, and strokes with the light and the heavy rod were automatically converted into lower numbers.

7. See TLSY 1.16–39.

8. See TLSY 1.6–16.

9. DTYL 4.56, citing Lunyu 13.2a (XIII.3). Cf. DTYL 4.55; JTS 50.6ab.

10. JTS 50.7a.

11. On the dependence of the Song Code on the Tang Code, see SS 199.2a; SXT 5–6. See also Langlois 1981, 169; McKnight 1992a, 334.

12. McKnight 1989, 113.

13. McKnight 1989, 114.

14. Cf. de Pee 1997; Langlois 1981, 165; Miyazaki 1992, 144–57. Brian McKnight imputes the increasing number of laws in Song times to the proliferation of criminal opportunities in an expanding urban economy. See McKnight 1985, 124; McKnight 1992a, 68, 94, 284–89, 515–18.

15. TLSY 663–64, paraphrasing Lunyu 11.56 (XI.16). On the laws as scripture, cf. YLMC 4.57. On the laws as cosmic truth, cf. SXT 5, 502–4; TLSY 577–79, 616.

16. Lunyu 6.10a (VI.29), second sentence as translated by Waley 1938, 121–22.

17. I doubt that many of these ideas would have occurred to me had I not made the gratifying acquaintance of Angela Zito and her work (1987, 1993, 1997).

18. XSZX 2. Cf. GZ 1; LXZN 151–52; ZLXL 22–23; ZXTG 1.1–3; ZYZZ 1.1b–2b. Monika Übelhör's (1990) transparent reading of these manuals as "recht offenherzige Einblicke" (84) into Song local government ignores their potent metaphors and ontological assumptions to suggest an unwarranted rationalist interpretation of their contents.

19. See GZ 1–2; LXZN 145–46; XSZX 2–5; ZLXL 1–2, 22–23; ZWGZX 4; ZXTG 1–3; ZYZZ 1.1b–2b. Cf. the admiring anecdotes about model officials such as the legendary Zhang Yong (946–1015) and Bao Zheng (999–1062) in notebooks. See, for example, DXBL 10.110–11, 11.126; DZJS *buyi*.45; HDL 1.10; MQBT 22.3b–4a; NGZ 12.316; RZSB III.5.470; SLYY 7.100–101.

20. ZXTG 1.3. Cf. ZLXL 22–23.

21. GZ 5.

22. See GZ 3; LXZN 146; ZLXL 2; ZXTG 1.4–5; ZYZZ 1.3a–4a.

23. See ZXTG 1.7–8.

24. See GZ 2–5; TYBS; XSZX 2–3, 7–8; XYJL; YYJ; ZZ 256–57; ZXTG 2.11–21, 3.28–32; ZYGJ. Cf. also the anecdotes about perspicacious judges in notebooks: DXBL 11.128; DZJS 4.34, *buyi*.46–47, *buyi*.52–53; HDL 1.1–2; MQBT 12.1b–2a; NCJT 3a; NGZ 12.316, 12.321; QBZZ 2.47–48. On casebooks, see de Pee 1997, 44–49, 55; McKnight 1981; Van Gulik 1956; Waltner 1990.

25. ZYGJ 5.17b.

26. For admonitions against anger and inebriation, see ZLXL 9, 19; ZXTG 1.2, 1.8–9. For advice against torture see, for example, ZGFJ 42.796; ZXTG 3.6, 3.29.

27. GLXSWJ 7.12a–13a. On the distortion by clerks of truth and the official's perception, cf. GZ 2; QMJ 11.435; XSZX 10; ZLXL 9b–11a; ZXTG 3.29.

28. YYYML 4.33. Cf. QMJ 12.452–80; MZWJ 38.1a–9b, 39.8b, 39.15a–16a, 39.17ab, 40.1a–6b, 40.8a–9a; ZGFJ 42.790–91; ZLXL 21.

29. ZLXL 21–22. On the conflict between private passions and the public Way, cf. XSZX 5. Cf. also anecdotes in notebooks that attribute disgrace in office to personal weakness. See, for example, DXBL 7.77–78; MJ 3.39–40.

30. The official residences of County Magistrates and Prefects represented the imperial center not only in function, but also in form, being modeled on the imperial palace. See DLXS 7.2a; QBZZ 1.10. Cf. Bray 1997, 52–53; Zito 1997, 4–6.

31. On the genre of the verdict, see de Pee 1997. According to Fan Zhen (1007–1088), Song Shou (991–1040) refused to speak in colloquial language even during interrogations, which severely limited their efficacy. See DZJS 3.27–28.

32. GLXSWJ 7.10ab; ZLXL 7. Zhu Xi recommended that his disciples hold court sessions every day. See ZWGZX 15. On the archives and paperwork of legal administration, cf. JWZW 3.41; QBZZ 2.47–48; SLYY 3.37; YYYML 4.40–41.

33. Cf. Birge 2002, 66–76, 208–17.

34. See TLSY 13.253–14.274; SXT 13.212–14.229. Apart from a number of misprints and taboo characters, the differences between Tang and Song stipulations on weddings are limited to one four-character phrase omitted from the Song Code (see TLSY 13.256 *versus* SXT 13.215) and the inclusion in the Song Code of a law that limits litigation, including wedding disputes, to the period from the first day of the tenth lunar month through the thirtieth day of the third lunar month (see SXT 13.207).

35. See, for example, SSYY 358; SXT 13.207; ZZ 258; ZYZZ 2.8b, 4.17a, 6.29b, 9.47b.

36. SXT 13.212–13; TLSY 13.253–54. Cf. SXT 14.227–29; TLSY 14.271–74.

37. Undue postponement of the wedding voids the betrothal. See SXT 14.227; TLSY 14.271.

38. SXT 1.9; TLSY 1.9.

39. See SXT 13.215. Cf. Ebrey 1993, 47.

40. See SXT 13.214–16, 14.223; TLSY 13.256–57, 14.267.

41. See SXT 12.199–200.

42. See SXT 1.8–9, 1.12–13, 17.273–75, 22.345–46; TLSY 1.8–9, 1.14–16, 18.327–29, 22.409–11. The laws against fornication also illustrate this ritual hierarchy: fornication with a married woman (who has attained her proper station in her husband's ancestral cult) carries a heavier penalty than fornication with an unmarried girl, and the punishment increases with the status of the female as well as the status of her husband or master. See SXT 26.421; TLSY 26.493.

43. Ann Waltner (1996) has examined similar issues in a perceptive study of the family as a social construct in the Ming Code.

44. On expulsion by the husband and divorce by mutual consent, see SXT 14.223–24; TLSY 14.268–69. On compulsory divorce mandated by the authorities, see SXT 14.227–28; TLSY 14.272. On a wife's mourning obligations for her husband, see SXT 1.13, 13.216; TLSY 1.15–16, 13.257.

45. See SXT 17.275; TLSY 17.328–29.

46. See SXT 14.227–28; TLSY 14.272.

47. See SXT 13.214–14.227; TLSY 13.255–14.271. Cf. DXBL 1.2; DZJS *buyi*.61. Since the status of concubine or servant is not hereditary, one man's former concubine (or servant) may become another man's wife, and vice versa.

48. On the androcentrism of the law, cf. Ebrey 1993, 47–50.

49. See SXT 14.218–20; TLSY 14.262–64. Cf. RZSB II.8.318.

50. Relatives of a widow other than parents and grandparents who force her into remarriage are punished according to their degree of kinship to the widow. See SXT 14.220–21; TSLY 14.265. The responsibility for an illegal marriage contracted by family members other than parents or grandparents is shared by these family members with the bride and the groom, and in some cases with the go-between. See SXT 14.228–229; TLSY 14.272–74. The guarantor (*zhuhun*) always carries greater legal responsibility than the go-between (*meiren*), who in some cases bears no responsibility at all for infractions upon the law (*ibidem*).

51. See SXT 14.227; TLSY 14.272. For this reason the prohibitions that void marriages apply to concubinage as well.

52. SXT 5. In this 963 preface to the *Song Penal Code*, Dou Yi (914–966) paraphrases Chunqiu 42.30b on leniency and greed. Cf. Zhangsun Wuji's 653 preface to the *Annotated Tang Code*, especially TLSY 579.

53. See HCQJ fascicles 192–93; MZWJ fascicles 38–40; QMJ.

54. See BJYJ fascicles 66–67; HCWJ 129.10a–15b; LJFSP; WYYH fascicles 503–52; WXJ fascicles 12–13. Cf. DTXY 10.152–54; GJSWLJ IV.11.7a–14a; RZSB I.10.127, II.12.358–59.

55. See, for example, DXBL 8.88; LXABJ 2.17; MQBT 15.8a, 23.1a; SLGJ 1699 X.13.67b–71b; SRXH 53, 65; ZWTL VII.2. Cf. RZSB I.10.127.

56. ZWTL VII.2.78–79. The river Xiang flows through Hunan province. Yue refers to Ms. Dai's hometown, present Shaoxing, in Zhejiang province.

57. See TYBS; YYJ; ZYGJ. On these works and on their influence on later fiction, cf. de Pee 1997, 44–49; Van Gulik 1956; Waltner 1990. These casebooks cite marital laws in a total of four cases, in all instances subsidiary to other accusations: voidance of a marriage by the murder of affinal kin (TYBS 2.17ab; cf. MQBT 17.4a; ZYGJ 4.14b; translated in Van Gulik 1956, 163); a forged marriage contract (TYBS 2.27a–28a; cf. ZYGJ 6.6b–7a; translated in Van Gulik 1956, 181–82); bigamy (ZYGJ 2.16b–17b; cf. YJTY 14.148–49; YFLG 17.2b–4a); and voidance of a marriage due to an illegal guarantor (ZYGJ 6.26ab; cf. DXBL 11.128).

58. For the continuous reprinting and study of casebooks and verdict collections, see, for example, the Ming and Qing prefaces to LJFSP; TYBS; YYJ. Cf. RZSB

II.12.358–359. Cf. also the inclusion of parallel cases (*bishi*) among the specialized encyclopedias printed in Fujian, listed in a 1250 preface to *Variegated Banquet from the Youyang Mountain Library*. See YYZZ 292.

59. On the nature of *A Collection of Pure and Lucid Verdicts*, see Birge 2002, 67–76; Chen Zhichao 1986, 659–63; de Pee 1997, esp. 52–57; Linck 1986; McKnight 1995; McKnight and Liu 1999; Niida Noboru 1981; Sadachi Haruto 1993; Suto Yoshiyuki 1969; Umehara Kaoru 1986.

60. By "marital cases" I mean all verdicts that refer to the laws pertaining to marriage in the *Song Penal Code*. In *A Collection of Pure and Lucid Verdicts* such verdicts appear in the main toward the end of the ninth fascicle, in the sections "Weddings" (*hunjia*), "Divorce" (*lihun*), and "Immediate Remarriage" (*jiejiaofu*: "husbands who follow upon the heels of the deceased"), and in the tenth fascicle ("Husbands and Wives" [*fufu*]). Betrothal sums, wedding contracts, and void marriages, however, also add to the complications of verdicts classified under other categories, such as property disputes or false accusations.

61. See QMJ 9.345–46, 9.356, 10.379, 12.442. Cf. QMJ 8.273–74, 9.344–45, 9.353–56, 14.527–28. The designation *A Zhang* or *Zhang shi* (Ms. Zhang) lacks a proper equivalent in English usage. It identifies a married woman by her maiden name. Contrary to what recent scholars have assumed, the prefix *A* as it appears in the verdicts of *A Collection of Pure and Lucid Verdicts* does not mimic colloquial speech, but is an archaic usage peculiar to Song legal writing. See YLMC 10.168.

62. QMJ 12.443, quoted slightly out of context.

63. QMJ 13.499. False accusations are punishable by "reversal of the penalty" (*fanzuo*), that is, the punishment for the crime of which the plaintiff has falsely accused the defendant befalls the plaintiff (see SXT 23.361–363)—in this case three years of penal servitude for the abduction of commoners and their sale as wives (see SXT 20.312–14). For the discretion of officials in determining the severity of the penalty, see SS 200.1a. Note that Zhu Yuanyi and Zhu Qiansan are not related to Zhu Qian'er and Zhu Wanwu; their surnames are written with a different character.

64. QMJ 9.351. Cf. QMJ 9.343.

65. See SXT 14.223.

66. QMJ 9.352. Two years of penal servitude was automatically converted into seventeen blows with the heavy rod on the spine. Here, Weng Fu converts two years of penal servitude into a hundred blows with the heavy rod, automatically converted into twenty blows on the buttocks. For these conversions, see SXT 1.4–5.

67. Cf. QMJ 7.230–32, 7.234–35, 9.343, 9.344, 9.348. Cf. also QMJ 10.384–85. Magistrate Zhao's condonation, elsewhere in *A Collection of Clear and Lucid Verdicts*, of Fu Shijiu's remarriage prior to having obtained a divorce from his adulterous wife (see QMJ 12.443–44), but especially the occasional mention in other sources of "divorce by sale" and the rental of wives as the established customs of certain regions of the empire (see below), confirm that Ye Si and Lü Yuanwu did not act in ill faith (at least not on this account) but were ignorant that their agreement violated imperial law. See JLB 2.58. See also Ruan Changrui 1989, 19; Wu Baoqi 1990, 78.

68. For marriage across social boundaries, see QMJ 7.230–32, 9.344. For widows remarrying during the mourning period for their late husband, see QMJ 6.177–80, 7.234, 8.273, 8.294–95, 9.348, 10.377, 10.389.

69. See QMJ 9.348.

70. See QMJ 5.141–42, 13.501–3. Cf. also the inclusion of parallel-cousin marriage in the hierarchies of matrimonial strategies constructed by writing manuals, discussed in chapter 2 of this book.

71. See SXT 26.422. Cf. SXT 1.13. Fornication with the wife of one's brother is, in fact, punishable by exile at a thousand kilometers (*ibidem*).

72. QMJ 10.389–90. Cf. QMJ 11.415; ZWGZX 13.

73. QMJ 9.344. For other examples, see QMJ 8.273–74, 10.365–66, 10.377–78, 10.378–80, 10.389. Many of these verdicts inscribe the plaintiff or defendant into a literary discourse that isolates her from contemporary society and thereby obliterates the legitimacy of her actions. Cf. Barthes 1993; de Pee 1997; Gravdal 1991, chapter 5.

74. QMJ 5.141. Cf. MZWJ 40.10b–12a, 40.14b–16b. Other verdicts (QMJ 5.140, 9.316), including one by Weng Fu, do cite the law that separates the possession of the wife from her husband's patrimony (see SXT 12.197), while many other verdicts, including one by Huang Gan, silently acknowledge them (see QMJ 10.365–66; MZWJ 40.9a–10b). Bettine Birge (2002) has published a book-length study on the "Confucian reaction" against widow remarriage, based in large part on *A Collection of Pure and Lucid Verdicts.*

75. See QMJ 10.387–89. For a translation and detailed analysis of these verdicts, see de Pee 1997. Cf. Ebrey 1993, 252–253; Jennifer Jay 1991, 50–54.

76. See QMJ 9.346–51.

77. See QMJ 10.379–81.

78. See QMJ 9.348–49.

79. See MZWJ 40.9b–10b.

80. QMJ 5.144. Although Ye Wuzi's ignorance of Hu Wujie's marital status may be due to the early stage of his investigation, it stands in stark contrast with his detailed knowledge of the sales of Weng Tai's lands, as well as with the certainty other judges display in distinguishing concubines from wives (see especially QMJ 7.232–33, 8.252–53).

81. In 1272, Khubilai founded an imperial dynasty that allowed him some independence from the Mongol empire. On the legal activity prior to the abolition of the Jin code, see Paul Ch'en 1979, 13–15; Huang Shijian 1988, 254. The narrative of this paragraph draws on the work of these two scholars, as well as on the materials collected in YDFLZL and on the surviving fragments and compendia themselves, especially YDZ table of contents.1a and YDZXJ table of contents.1a. Cf. also Birge 2002, 208–17.

82. For the continued study of the Tang, Song, and Jin codes see LXZN 4, 52–54, 92; TLSY 616; YDFLZL 83, 164; and numerous instances in the TZTG and YDZ. Cf. also Paul Ch'en 1979, chapter 1, esp. 39–40; Langlois 1981, 174–76.

83. YDFLZL 85, citing a proposal by Su Tianjue (1294–1352) for a supplement to the *Comprehensive Institutions*. Cf. prefaces to other compilations, cited in YDFLZL 82–83, 87.

84. See SLGJ 1333 IV.3.1a–9a (laws); SLGJ 1340 V.1.20a–26b (laws); TZTG (precedents). The *Comprehensive Institutions* originally comprised four parts: laws, precedents, decrees and amnesties, and miscellaneous ordinances. See TZTG preface; YDFLZL 87. See also Paul Ch'en 1979, 25–30; Huang Shijian 1986, 1; Huang Shijian 1988, 260–64.

85. For fragments of *New Regulations of the Zhiyuan Reign*, see SLGJ 1699 IX.1.5a–11b; YDFLZL 9–34. For a fragment of *Laws and Ordinances of the Dade Reign*, see YDFLZL 53–58. For fragments of the *Great, Comprehensive Legal Compendium for Ordering the World*, see YS fascicles 102–5; YDFLZL 89–90. Of *Regulations of the Zhizheng Reign* only a preface remains. See YDFLZL 87–88.

86. These features suggest that the surviving Yuan edition of the *Imperial Canon* may in fact be a commercial re-edition by Jianyang printers. Lucille Chia, personal communication, April 1997. Cf. Chia 1996, 28–29, 33.

87. See Paul Ch'en 1979, 30–32. Perhaps the Ming copyist who prepared the manuscript of *Comprehensive Institutions of the Great Yuan* diluted its format and contents; perhaps the lost sections of the work explained the structure and intention of the precedents. The laborious compilation by Zhang Shaojian of an *Outline and Commentary to the Precedents in the Comprehensive Institutions of the Great Yuan* (*Da Yuan tongzhi tiaoli gangmu*) suggests, however, that during the Yuan, too, these fascicles required the use of an index. See YDFLZL 82–83.

88. Cf. Dardess 2003, 123–28; Endicott-West 1989; David Farquhar 1981; McKnight 1989, 125; Paul J. Smith 1990–1992; Paul J. Smith 2003, 91–96.

89. See YDFLZL 9–10, 82–83, 85–90, 94, 127; LXZN 3, 143–46.

90. See TZTG 4.2a. Cf. TZTG 4.2b, 4.3a. In the latter case, a Prefect actually receives a humiliating rebuke for memorializing about an obvious case. For Su Tianjue's metaphor, see YDFLZL 85.

91. On multiethnicity in Yuan law, see Birge 1995; Birge 2002; Paul Ch'en 1979; Hansen 1995, 117–20. For the concern with litigation, see LXZN 52, 90, 147–48; SSYY 357–58; TZTG 4.16a, 16.3a; YDFLZL 18, 34, 39, 89; YDZXJ *hunyin*.1a; ZZ 256, 258. Some previous dynasties had issued sumptuary laws, and the Tang imperial court in 712 had shown concern with the ritual practice of weddings, but no earlier dynastic house had attempted such detailed regulations. See TD 58.1651, 58.1653. Cf. also chapter 1.

92. For binding betrothals, see SLGJ 1333 IV.3.5ab; SLGJ 1340 V.1.23b; YDZ 18.1b, 18.11a–12a, 45.13a; YDZXJ *hunyin*.1ab; YS 103.22b. For the expiration of betrothals, see HMQS II.4.3b; JJBY 14th IX.28b; SLGJ 1333 IV.3.5b; SLGJ 1340 V.1.23b–24a; TZTG 4.1a; YDZ 18.2b, 18.11a–12a; YS 103.22b.

93. For the rights and obligations of marriage, see the mourning tables and tables of penal measures in YDFLZL 53–58; YDZ 30.4a–7b, 42.1a–2b, 42.20b, 45.1ab. For legal divorce, see SLGJ 1333 IV.3.5b–6a; SLGJ 1340 V.1.24a; TZTG

4.7ab, 4.12ab; YDZ 18.1b, 18.6a–7a; YS 103.24a. For mandatory divorce, see YDZ 18.1b and, especially, 41.21b. For fulfillment of mourning obligations, see JJBY 14th IX.28a; SLGJ 1340 V.1.24b–25a; TZTG 3.17ab; YDZ 18.13b–14b.

94. For marriage during mourning periods, see HMQS II.4.3b; SLGJ 1699 IX.1.5b; YDFLZL 36–37, 66; YDZ 18.1ab, 18.9a, 18.33ab, 41.17ab; YDZXJ *hunyin*.1a–3b; YS 103.22b. For marriage to close kin or wives of close kin, see TZTG 3.20b; YDZ 18.17a; YS 103.23ab. For marriage between people of the same surname, see HMQS II.4.3b; JJBY 14th IX.28a; SLGJ 1333 V.1.23b; YDZ 18.2ab. For laws prohibiting officials from marrying within their jurisdiction, see TZTG 3.23b–24a, 4.6b–7a; YDZ 18.15a, 18.16ab. For bigamy, see HMQS II.4.3b; JJBY 14th IX.28a; SLGJ 1333 IV.3.5b; SLGJ 1340 V.1.23b; TZTG 4.1a, 4.1b; YDZ 18.1b–2b, 18.29ab; YS 103.22b–23a. For marriage across class boundaries, see TZTG 3.21a, 3.22ab, 3.23a–25b, 4.20ab; YDZ 17.7b, 18.1b, 18.30a–32b; YS 103.22b, 103.23b. For unauthorized guarantors, see TZTG 3.17a, 3.21b–22a; YDZ 18.4a, 18.14ab.

95. For the laws on levirate marriage and other ethnic distinctions in marital law, see TZTG 3.14b–15a, 3.18a–20b, 4.1b, 4.8a; YDZ 18.1a, 18.21ab, 18.23a–28a, 18.26b, 18.33a; YDZXJ *hunyin*.4ab.

96. For canonical rhetoric on marriage see, for example, TZTG 3.2a–3a, 4.18b; YDZ 18.7b–8a, 18.11ab, 18.16b, 18.33a. The limitation of litigation to the agricultural off-season, adopted in April 1269 from the *Song Penal Code* (see SXT 13.207) and affirmed in 1299 (see SLGJ 1699 IX.1.6b; TZTG 4.16a–17a; YDZXJ *songsong*.1a) was amended in November 1317. Whereas the original law excepted public matters and difficult cases from this stipulation, the 1317 amendment allows wedding cases to be brought to court as they occur and forbids officials from barring them with reference to the time limits, as they would all other suits. If after two appeals, however, the case fails to be resolved due to intentional prolongation by one of the parties, the Surveillance Commissioner will take measures. This amended law is found in the subsection "How to Stop Litigation" of *Precedents of the Zhizhi Reign*. See YDZXJ *songsong*.1a. Cf. YS 103.21ab.

97. On uxorilocal marriage, see TZTG 2.16b–18a, 2.26a, 3.16a, 4.3ab, 4.8b–10b; YDZ 17.7ab, 18.1a, 18.2b–3a, 18.5b–8a, 18.18a. On rights to the betrothal sum in case of the death of one of the betrothed, see TZTG 4.4ab; YDZ 18.1a, 18.21ab, 34.4b. On the marriage of officials, see TZTG 4.6b–7a; YDZ 18.15a–16b. On the remarriage of military wives, see YDZ 18.18ab. Cf. also the explicit laws against the marriage of monks (YS 103.23a) and against the rental and sale of wives (see below).

98. See TZTG 3.17a; YDZ 8.14ab, 18.22a. Cf. also the laws on the fornication of betrothed women (YS 103.22a) and on criminal transgressions by betrothed and married men (TZTG 4.2a–3a; YS 103.22a).

99. See YDZ 18.11a–12a; YDZXJ *hunyin*.1ab.

100. YDZ 57.8b–9a. Cf. TZTG 4.17b–19a; YDZ 57.8a–10a; YS 103.21b. Cf. also the "rampant urban phenomenon" of husbands prostituting their wives. See SLGJ 1333 IV.3.3a; SLGJ 1340 V.1.22a; YDZ 45.7a–8a.

101. See TZTG 4.7b–8a, 4.19a; YDZ 18.12b–13b, 18.19ab; YS 103.21b, 103.23a, 103.24a.

102. YDZ 18.14a. Cf. TZTG 4.5b; YDZ 18.9ab, 18.15b–16a, 18.33ab, 41.17ab; YDZXJ *hunyin*.3ab.

103. See YDZ 18.33ab; YDZXJ *hunyin*.3b. A law from the Zhiyuan period (1264–1295) permits families to proceed with weddings immediately after the death of a relative if the ailing relative has expressed a wish to this effect, but the law still prohibits banquets in such cases. See YDFLZL 36–37. Sources throughout imperial times record instances of weddings in the presence of a corpse, occurring under different names in all parts of the empire. Such rites either rely on the auspicious powers of weddings to drive out the inauspicious airs of disease and death, or attempt to draw on the powers of the inauspicious event of death for the benefit of the wedding. See Ma Zhisu 1981, 23–27. Cf. also SY 6.65; YLXS I.9.9b. An early Ming author, ironically, condemns the practice as a "barbaric Yuan custom"; cited in Ma Zhisu 1981, 23.

Several precedents also void marriages to close kin—two cases of an aunt marrying a nephew (see TZTG 3.20b; YDZ 18.17a), and four cases of men marrying their late brother's wife (see 18.26ab; YDZXJ *hunyin*.4ab)—that would be acceptable among Mongols and aliens but that among Han "throw into disorder the great relations" and "greatly harm proper customs."

104. See YDZ 18.9b–10a; 45.9ab.

105. See YDZ 18.9ab, 18.12b–13a. For other irregular condonations of irregular betrothals and marriages, see YDZ 18.4ab, 18.10a–11a, 42.20b–21a. In 1279, the Censorate refuses to persecute a widow for fornication during the mourning period for her late husband with the statement, "If considered as adultery by consent, the male and the female are liable to severe punishment. This woman, however, committed her crime while in the home of her late husband. Since she has already married someone else, *her body now belongs to her second husband* and it has become impossible to prosecute her." See YDZ 45.13a (emphasis added).

106. See YDZ 30.2ab. See also TZTG 27.16b.

107. YDZ 18.2ab.

108. See YDZ 18.2b–3a. Since betrothal sums are a form of brideprice, their amount diminishes as the period for which the bride (and the groom) is committed to living in her own household increases. Cf. YDZ 30.2a, where the legislative authorities surmise that poor families engage in uxorilocal marriage because they cannot afford a full bride. For the sumptuary laws of 1270–71, see also HMQS II.4.3a–4a; JJBY 14th IX.28b–29a; TZTG 4.1a, 27.16b. Cf. also YS 103.22a, 105.16b–17a.

109. See YDZ 30.9ab. For sumptuary laws pertaining to funerals see, for example, YDFLZL 74–75.

110. See ZZ 222-23. The phrase "Those who wish to set their own [sum] are free to do so" presumably meant to emphasize that the prescribed sums were upper limits, not obligatory amounts. The clause has been deleted from subsequent compilations, but a similar phrase, without the ambiguity, appears in the 1304 sumptuary laws.

111. See HMQS II.4.3a–4a; JJBY 14th IX.28b–29a; SLGJ 1333 I.10.9ab; SLGJ 1340 II.2.7b–8a; TZTG 3.15ab; YDZ 18.1a.

112. See TZTG 27.19b; YDZ 30.2b–3a. The Tang court prohibited similar practices as early as the eighth century. See TD 58.1654. Cf. YYZZ 1.8; CYQZ 3.77. The appellation "Blocking the Bride's Carriage" in the Yuan laws may actually derive from Tang sources rather than from contemporary practice. Cf. HMQS II.9.2b. The description of gangs of young, disruptive, single men who demand their share of the economy of marriage bears a strong resemblance to the charivari discussed by Natalie Zemon Davis (1975: 104–8) and Christiane Klapisch-Zuber (1985: 261–82). The poems for Blocking the Gate found in writing manuals (see chapter 2) suggest a controlled and ritualized version of this practice. Cf. also TZY 10.115.

113. YDZ 30.1a. See also HMQS II.4.1ab; TZTG 3.12ab. On the ceremony of Bowing at the Gate, see DJGZ 39.553; SMJW 28–29.

114. See YDZ 30.1a–2a. Cf. HMQS II.4.1a–3a; SLGJ 1333 IV.3.5b; SLGJ 1340 V.1.23b; TZTG 3.12a–14b.

115. See TZTG 3.14b–15a; YDZ 18.2b.

116. TZTG 4.4b–5b. The Shaanxi custom resembles Bowing to the Gate because, like the latter practice, it requires a substantial expenditure prior to the conclusion of any formal agreement.

117. YDZ 18.2a, 18.6b. Cf. TZTG 3.15b–16a. Cf. also SSYY 357–58.

118. See JJBY 14th IX.28b; SLGJ 1333 IV.3.5b; SLGJ 140 V.1.23b; TZTG 3.15b–16a; YDZ 18.1a, 18.2a.

119. See TZTG 4.3b; YDZ 30.2a; YS 103.22a.

120. See TZTG 4.1b.

121. See TZTG 4.7ab; YDZ 18.1b; YS 103.24a.

122. SLGJ 1333 IV.3.5b; SLGJ 1340 V.1.23b. For other laws and regulations, see JJBY 14th IX.26b; SLGJ 1333 I.10.9b; SLGJ 1340 II.2.8ab; YLXS II.1.1a ("Use varicolored paper and standard script for all letters and documents related to wedding ritual. It is not allowed to write two rows of characters on one line").

123. See YDZ 45.5a. For the reputation of go-betweens in Yuan sources see, for example, CGL 10.10b–11a; LXZN 146. Cf. the jokes about go-betweens in SRXH 22; translated in Levy 1974, 75–76, 80–81. Cf. Leung 1999, 101–5.

124. YDZ 18.3a. See also TZTG 4.9a.

125. TZTG 4.6ab.

126. YDFLZL 34. On *New Statutes*, see Paul Ch'en 1979.

127. YDZ 30.1a. TZTG 3.12ab gives a slightly abridged version but adds that poor families "may do as they please." See also HMQS II.4.1ab.

128. See, for example, YDZ 18.4b, 18.5a, 18.24a. One might counter that the very absence of a contract brought such cases to court, but many cases in *A Collection of Pure and Lucid Verdicts* demonstrate the untruth of that assumption.

129. TZTG 4.6b–7a. Cf. TZTG 3.23a–24a.

130. See SDRJ 8.86–87; cited by Fang Jianxin 1985, 159–60. See also Birge 2002, 33–35; Ebrey 1993, 99.

131. SDRJ 8.87. If Zheng Qingyi was born at the age of one *sui* on the 11th day of the 12th month and turned two a few weeks later, the year of her birth according to the Western calendar was 1248, and her age at marriage was 14, by a Western count. According to Patricia Ebrey (1993, 99), 500 *mu* equals "nearly a hundred acres." The note about the "three ritual letters" must have occurred on a separate sheet. Cf. the discussion of the formats of wedding correspondence in chapter 2.

132. Li Yiyou 1992, 30. I thank Morris Rossabi for supplying the proper transliterations of the Mongol names.

133. For the three Dunhuang divorce contracts, dated 957 (tentative date), 977, and 985, see Dx3002, P3220, and P4525, in Sha Zhi 1998, 468–74. On divorce contracts, see also Hansen 1995, 63–64, 101–3; Niida 1937, 483–510; Niida 1959, 27–37; Zhou Yiliang and Zhao Heping 1995, 2.

134. Li Yiyou (1992, 31) succumbs to this temptation when he writes that the 1365 contract shows how the fate of the poverty-stricken Mongol families in this negotiation "follows the gradual collapse of the Yuan dynasty"—as though the wealth of Han families were increasing with the devastating conquests of Zhu Yuanzhang. For similar misreadings, see Birge 2002; Paul J. Smith 1998.

135. For model wedding contracts, see HMDQ I.5.2a–5b; HMQS I.5.2b–5a, II.9.6ab; HMQS GG I.5.2b–5a; JJBY 14th IX.26ab; QZQQ IV.2.489–92; SLGJ 1333 I.10.5ab; SLGJ 1340 II.2.4ab; YLXS II.1.1a–3a, II.1.16a. For model trousseau lists, see HMQS II.9.6ab; YLXS II.1.16ab. Even the great majority of the divorce contracts found at Dunhuang are model contracts, describing in four-six parallel prose the painful estrangement of generic spouses. See S0343v, P3730v, S6537v, S6417v, S5578, S6537v, P3212v, P4001, in Sha Zhi 1998, 475–91.

136. Ebrey 1993, 47.

137. Birge 2002, 64, 1. Cf. Birge 2003.

138. See Birge 2002, 64–229. See also Birge 1995; Birge 2003.

139. Birge 2002, 237–38.

140. Birge 2002, 280.

141. In 1068, Ms. Yun of Dengzhou, Shandong province, attempted to stab to death her fiancé Wei Ada, asleep in the fields, because she did not wish to marry a man whose appearance disgusted her. The sources on this case include LCLZ 4.19–20; SS 201.1b–3a; WGWJ 38.11b–13b; WXTK 170.1475a–1476b; XCB 411.13a; XCBSB 3I.15b–17b; YYJ 4.5ab. Shen Jiaben presents a convenient collection of most of the relevant materials. See JYWC 4.2161–2169. The best discussion of this case provides Langlois 1981, 200–217. See also McKnight 1992a, 502; Miyazaki 1992, 167–68.

142. On the practice of levirate marriage during the Five Dynasties, Liao, and Jin, see Dong Jiazun 1995, 63–71; Franke 1981, 227–29. Franke (1981, 228) notes that the Jin dynasty explicitly prohibited the practice of levirate marriage among the

Han (and Bohai) in 1169—a hundred years before the promulgation of a similar law by the Mongol court.

143. See QMJ 11.414–16. Cf. JSJW 1.197; ZWGZX 12–13.

144. Despite the efforts of Bettine Birge (1995, 2002) and Patricia Ebrey (1991c, 1993), marriage finance in the Tang, Song, and Yuan remains poorly understood. The *Song Penal Code* clearly defines the betrothal sum as a public marriage payment, and hints that the dowry is a form of premortem inheritance for daughters. See SXT 12.197, 13.212–214. In Southern Song verdicts, proponents of the Learning of the Way maintain that the dowry belongs to the public marriage payments and condemn the private property of women as divisive and disruptive. It is my impression that dowries were never universal but existed besides betrothal sums, as one means for wealthy families to attract desirable grooms. In a tale in the *Records of Yi Jian* (YJZ *sanbu*.1806), for example, Deng Yi of Nancheng, Jiangxi, dismisses a dream that promises him a rich dowry, because "he reasoned that since he was poor, without a square inch of land, and did not lead the scholar's life, he possessed none of the attributes that could fetch a generous dowry." On the coexistence of betrothal gifts and dowries, see Harrell and Dickey 1985, esp. 116.

145. For laws on chastity and remarriage, see HMQS II.4.3b; TZTG 3.17ab, 17.17b–20a; YDZ 11.25a, 18.2b, 18.16b, 18.33a. For the format of an official request for widow remarriage, see SLGJ 1333 IV.4.6b; SLGJ 1340 V.1.31ab.

146. See TZTG 4.4b, 4.6a; YDZ 18.21b–22a; YS 105.12a. Cf. Birge 2002, 276–77.

147. For betrothal gifts in Southern Song verdicts, see QMJ 9.344–45, 9.379. For general mentions of dowries, see MZWJ 40.10a–11b; QMJ 5.141–42, 5.147, 6.184–85, 7.215, 8.248, 8.257–60, 9.315–16, 9.356, 10.381–83, 13.502. For the rhetoric of the Learning of the Way on dowries, see HCQJ 193.10ab; MZWJ 39.1a–3a, 39.13b–14b, 40.14b–16b; QMJ 7.229–32, 7.234–35, 7.242–43, 8.272, 8.275, 9.296, 9.353–56, 10.360, 10.365–66.

148. By lack of a critical assessment of the relationship between the transmission of legal texts and the writing of legal texts, and of the relationship between the writing of legal texts and their enforcement, the haphazard collection of extant verdicts and precedents comes to represent universal social practice: "In conclusion, the military structure of Yuan society resulted in the marginalization of women in matters of family inheritance" (Birge 2002, 229), and: "In 1321 the Ministry of Punishments cited [two rulings, of 1277 and 1308] as precedents in a case from Yinzhou, in the Yangzi delta. . . . The location shows that Chinese in the south by this time also practiced levirate marriage" (Birge 2002, 256).

149. Birge 2002, 278. Cf. Birge 2003, 239.

150. HCQJ 192.6ab.

## Conclusion

1. Tilley 1991, 20.

2. Proust 1972, 65.

3. See Gansusheng bowuguan and Zhangxian wenhuaguan 1982; Zhangxian wenhuaguan 1982. See also Wu Jingshan 1999. I thank Thomas Hahn and Wu Xian of the East Asian Library at Cornell University for procuring the latter article at very short notice.

4. See Jinshi 124.15ab; YS 155.1a–10a; YWL 35.12b–13b. See also the epigraphic materials gathered in LYJSL 5.7a–16a; Wu Jingshan 1999.

5. The description of Wang Maochang's tomb in these pages assembles in a coherent narrative the various details scattered throughout the two often unsatisfactory site reports.

6. The capstone mirror (*qinggai*) appears to be a material pun, since the installation of this "bronze mirror cover" assists the descendants in attaining to the "dark canopy" (also *qinggai*) that is the ceremonial prerogative of the Chancellor (hence: "noble canopy").

7. Cf. Kern 1997, 11–13; Zito 1997, 202–3.

8. Angela Zito, personal communication.

9. Cf. Wu Hung 1995, 122.

10. Since ethnic identity in the Middle Period was a matter of cultural expression rather than phenotype, it was eminently malleable. The early tombs in the Wang graveyard accomplished the ethnic transformation of the family by omitting any mention of tribal affiliation and by avoiding all narrowly Mongol or Jurchen burial practices. The ethnic transformation culminates in an extensive false genealogy in the fifteenth-century funerary inscription of Wang Zhao (1417–1499). See Gansusheng bowuguan and Zhangxian wenhuaguan 1982, 1–2; Wu Jingshan 1999, 248–49. Although in certain parts of her essay in *Differences Preserved: Reconstructed Tombs from the Liao and Song Dynasties*, Hsingyuan Tsao appears to imply that enduring, prior Han and Qidan ethnicities determined cultural expression, the more convincing passages of the essay argue the reverse: that tombs afforded an occasion for a conscious, nuanced expression of a malleable cultural ethnicity. See Tsao 2000, 13. For a balanced, intelligent analysis of ethnic identity in tombs and archaeology see also Stevenson 1999.

11. Cf. DLXS 14.11b; ECJ 10.623 (also quoted in JL 201a); ZD. Cf. also Ebner von Eschenbach 1995, 174–75. In miracle tales, grave trees sometimes lend form to the mood or longings of the dead. See, for example, BZB 2.83; CZZJ 1.1b, 1.3a; TPGJ 389.3099–3100, 389.3103–104, 390.3113–114. The importance of grave trees is borne out also by their explicit inclusion in the legal protection of tombs. See, for example, DXBL 8.88; QMJ 9.330–34; SXT 19.298; YDZ 50.8b.

12. Cf. Ruitenbeek 1993, 38, 58–62. For examples of competing theories about the geomancy of burial see, for example, CGL 20.239–41; CYQZ *buji*.164–165; DLXS; DTXY 13.195; ZJ. Cf. also the many titles of geomantic treatises on burial in SS 206.13a–25b; TZ *Yiwenlüe* 1699–1703.

13. For other examples of the burial of archaist vessels in Song and Yuan tombs, see Liu Bao'ai and Zhang Dewen 1992; Luoyangshi tielu beizhan bianzuzhan lianhe kaogu fajuedui 1996; Shaanxisheng wenwu guanli weiyuanhui 1958; Ye Hong 1983.

On burial according to generational order, see DLXS 13.1b; ECJ 10.623; ZL 605. Classicists such as Cheng Yi and Wang Anshi buried their ancestors according to this arrangement. See ECJ 22a.290; QBZZ 12.514. Cf. Ebrey 1991b, 72, 93.

14. Hsingyuan Tsao (2000, 12) notes a similar discordance between the coffins inscribed with sutra passages (and containing cremated remains) and the ample sacrifices provided for an afterlife in the 1093 Liao tomb of Zhang Wenzao and his wife at Xuanhua, Hebei province. On this tomb, see also Hebeisheng wenwu yanjiusuo 2001.

15. Cf. SSWJL 19.215:

> My late father Kangjie [i.e., Shao Yong, 1011–1077] . . . performed the vernal and autumnal sacrifices as a combination of ancient and contemporary rituals, and this included the burning of spirit money. When Cheng Yichuan [i.e., Cheng Yi] expressed surprise about this, my father replied, "This is the purpose of funereal goods (*mingqi*). The untoward omission of one item would compromise my filiality as a son and my gratitude as a grandson."

16. On the significance of the truncated-pyramidal shape of funerary inscription, see Zhao Chao 1999. For the format of funerary inscriptions according to *Family Rituals*, see JL 201c. Cf. SY 7.80; ZZYL 89.11b–12a. Although Yuan law does not appear to have upheld the funeral rites in *Family Rituals* as it did (in distorted form) its wedding ceremonies, the pertinent laws accrued in the *Imperial Canon of Sacred Governance* are written in much the same strident classicist rhetoric, prohibiting cremation in 1278, condemning music at funerals in 1310, enforcing universal Han observance of a sober three-year mourning period for parents in 1314 and 1315, and fulminating against geomantic practices in 1318. See YDZ 30.9a–10b, 33.12b–13a. Not only the shape of the cover of Wang Maochang's funerary inscription, but also many of the grave goods, and especially the structure of the tomb ignore the injunctions of *Family Rituals*, which demands a straight, unadorned cement pit without a ramp, and a small compartment with wooden figurines and miniature furniture. See JL 200d–203d.

17. See Gansusheng bowuguan and Zhangxian wenhuaguan 1982.

18. See, for example, Beijingshi wenwu gongzuodui 1980; Handanshi wenguansuo 1984; Luoyangshi wenhua gongzuodui 1996. Cf. Zhao Chao 1999, 78. Occasionally, too, archaeologists find a coin stuck between the cover and the inscription. See, for example, Li Yufeng 1984.

19. Song literati were aware that funerary inscriptions originated in the Han dynasty and that the ancients had not placed such objects in their tombs. See, for example, SWJY 9.343–44; SY 7.80–81; YFL 12.5a; ZZYL 89.14a. For an example of the use of epigraphic models for the composition of funerary inscriptions, see JSLi. On Song literary fashions in funerary inscriptions, see BTL 4.39; LXABJ 1.5, 1.9; JWGBJ 1.2; YLMC 8.134–35. See also Schottenhammer 1994; Schottenhammer 1995.

20. According to Zhou Hui, the famous calligrapher Mi Fu wrote out three funerary inscriptions composed by Wang Anshi, and one of these was copied onto

stone. See QBZZ 5.231. Zhuang Chuo recounts that Zhou Bangyan (1058–1123) was once offered "several dozen pounds of gold to moisten his brush" for the composition of a funerary inscription. See JLB 2.70. Cf. TS 6.70. On the economics of funerary inscriptions, cf. also Clunas 1991, 14.

21. Peng Jinhua 1995, 84–85.

22. Cf. also the final couplet of the eulogy of this funerary inscription: "As he finds rest in this dark tomb, /This carved inscription secures his place."

23. On the mimicry of funerary inscriptions in tomb contracts, cf. Asim 1994, 362–63. On tomb contracts, see also Chen Boquan 1987; Hansen 1995, 149–229. For examples of illicit funerary inscriptions, see Cheng Jihong 1993; Wang Jinxian and Shi Weiguo 1994 (discussed below); Wangjiangxian bowuguan 1997.

24. The contrast between printed and carved funerary inscriptions may be perceived most clearly when both happen to survive. See, for example, Dai Zunde 1990 (Wei Xian); Anhuisheng bowuguan 1980 (Bao Zheng). Cf. TS 6.70. Cf. also Ebner von Eschenbach 1995, 22; Schottenhammer 1994; Schottenhammer 1995.

25. Hanks 2000, 11.

26. By the "denial of text" I mean the unspoken, unargued (and indeed indefensible) assumption that the cunning historian may catch a glimpse of an unmediated past through transparent texts. Cf. LaCapra 2000, 30–72.

27. WLXSJ 32.2a. Mei Yaochen (1002–1060) composed this dirge (*wanci*) for the joint burial of the late Ms. Xie with her predeceased husband, Chen Zhizhong (991–1059).

28. On paper houses and other paper grave goods, see YDZ 30.8b, 33.11b–12a; YLMC 5.83. See also Tao Fuhai 1988, 1121. The occasional Middle-Period tomb that has preserved its paper and textiles indicates how their common decay affects the legibility of other tombs. See, for example, Chongqingshi bowuguan 1986; Feng Puren 1986; Jiangxisheng wenwu kaogu yanjiusuo and De'anxian bowuguan 1990; Shandongsheng Jining diqu wenwuju 1983.

29. Cf. Appadurai 1986, 16 (paraphrasing Jacques Macquet; emphasis in the original): "a special, sharp case of commodities by metamorphosis are commodities by *diversion*, objects placed into a commodity state though originally specifically protected from it."

30. The inauguration of a market economy in the 1980s, combined with an exceedingly successful tourist industry, has encouraged grave robbery in the People's Republic of China on an unprecedented scale. Cf. Ji Guang 1983. Cf. also von Falkenhausen 1993, 844. Where grave robbery was previously confined to small, inconspicuous items, it now extends to funerary inscriptions and entire murals. See, for example Nei Menggu wenwu kaogu yanjiusuo and Aluke'erqinqi wenwu guanlisuo 1998; Hangzhoushi wenwu kaogusuo and Lin'anshi wenwuguan 2000. Incidentally, the epigraphic interest of Northern Song literati also led to a widespread desecration of tombs by turning steles, funerary inscriptions, and ancient bronzes into valuable commodities. See JLB 1.35; SCWJL V.206–207. On Middle-Period robbery of contemporary graves (which included grave lands and grave trees), see QMJ

9.322–34; TPGJ 389.3100–3103, 390.3112–122; YDZ 50.7a–8b; YYZZ 13.122–26. Cf. Ebner von Eschenbach 1995, 108–12.

31. See TPGJ 390.3122, and many site reports. Wei Tai and Zhuang Chuo warned their contemporaries that frugal burial not only failed to prevent grave robbery, as some believed, but that it endangered the peace of the dead, since vindictive intruders would scatter their bones. See DXBL 7.78; JLB 1.24.

32. TPGJ 390.3117. The story, taken from *Unofficial Histories* (*Yishi*), is set in the late eighth century, when Fan Ze served as Military Commissioner of Xiangyang (present Xiangfan, Hubei province).

33. The political uses of archaeology under the Communist government differ from those under the Nationalist government of the Republic of China in detail, but not in kind. See Clunas 1997, 18–19; Rawson 1993, 68–69; von Falkenhausen 1993, 841–42. On the politics of Chinese archaeology, see Evasdottir 2004; von Falkenhausen 1993; von Falkenhausen 1995.

34. See, for example, Sichuansheng bowuguan 1959 (a six-page report on two Song sites and eighteen tombs). For a notable exception, see Su Bai 1957.

35. See, for example, Chaoyang diqu bowuguan 1973; Zhejiangsheng wenwu guanli weiyuanhui 1975. The emphasis on class during the 1970s did at times contribute to insightful site reports. See, for example, Wang Renbo 1973.

36. See, for example, Liaoningsheng bowuguan and Liaoning Tieling diqu wenwuzu fajue xiaozu 1975.

37. See, for example, Anonymous 1991; Bai Yunxiang and Gu Zhijie 1989; Su Bingqi 1995; Yu Weichao 1999; Zhou Weizhou 1980. Cf. also the blatantly political theme issues dedicated to Tibet (*Kaogu* 1994.7, *Wenwu* 1997.9), Hong Kong (*Huaxia kaogu* 1997.2, *Kaogu* 1997.6, *Wenwu* 1997.6), "multi-nationality" Guangxi (*Kaogu* 1998.11), and Macau (*Wenwu* 1999.11).

38. Monographs on royal and imperial tombs include Feng Hanji 2002; Henansheng wenwu kaogu yanjiusuo 1997. Monographs on Middle-Period tombs with interesting architecture and artifacts include Fujiansheng bowuguan 1982 (textiles); Hebeisheng wenwu yanjiusuo 2001 (murals); Su Bai 1957 (architecture and murals). Nei Menggu zizhiqu wenwu kaogu yanjiusuo and Zhelimumeng bowuguan 1993 fits both categories. An admirable exception is the extensive monograph on a Northern Song charitable graveyard in Shaanzhou, Henan province. See Sanmenxiashi wenwu gongzuodui 1999. On the nationalist, Marxist, and antiquarian interests in Chinese archaeology, see von Falkenhausen 1993.

39. The unawareness of these correlations is especially apparent in summary articles about filiality scenes and about the mimicry of timber-frame structures. Articles on filiality scenes chart their iconographic development and ponder their ideological and religious affiliations, but none comments on their more general associations with joint burial, reproduction, and immortality. See Duan Pengqi 1995; Zhao Chao 1998. Discussions of the mimicry of timber-frame structures in Middle-Period tombs emphasize the importance of this phenomenon for the study of vernacular architecture, of which so few examples survive above ground. Liao Ben

(2000) proposes to link the mimicry of wood architecture to commoner status, the representation of drama scenes, and government by "minority nationalities."

40. For filiality scenes represented by figurines, see Jiangxisheng wenwu gongzuodui and Nanfengxian bowuguan 1988.

41. The Elder Princess Xincheng of the Tang dynasty received especial imperial honor and was buried in the vicinity of Emperor Taizong, in a tomb mimicking a timber structure, even though her first spouse died in exile and her second spouse was executed. See Shaanxisheng kaogu yanjiusuo, Shaanxi lishi bowuguan, and Zhaoling bowuguan 1997. Empress Li of the Song dynasty was buried in a separate tomb, but within the precinct of Emperor Taizong, in accordance with the particular form of joint burial implemented in the Northern Song imperial cemetery at Gongyi. See Henansheng wenwu kaogu yanjiusuo 1997, 7, 308–37. For the tombs of Buddhist monks, see Han Guoxiang 2000; *Lishi nianjian* (*Historical Yearbook*) 1994, 393; Nei Menggu wenwu kaogu yanjiusuo, Wulanchabu bowuguan, and Qingshuihexian wenwu guanlisuo 1997; and possibly Shanxisheng kaogu yanjiusuo and Taiyuanshi wenwu guanli weiyuanhui 1990. For the tomb of a Daoist priest, see Datongshi bowuguan 1978.

42. See Ji'nanshi wenhuaju wenwuchu and Changqingxian bowuguan 1991; Linyixian bowuguan 1997. Cf. Fu Xinian 2002, 122.

43. For single burial amid simulated wood architecture in unusual Qidan aristocratic tombs of the early Liao dynasty, see Nei Menggu Chifengshi Aohanqi bowuguan 1998; Nei Menggu wenwu kaogu yanjiusuo and Aluke'erqinqi wenwu guanlisuo 1998. The possibility of archaeological oversight is suggested not merely by the general tenor of the superficial reports of salvage excavations, but also by an article that describes the discovery of a single skeleton along with a funerary inscription that specifies joint burial. See Changzhishi bowuguan 1989.

44. See Fujiansheng bowuguan and Sanmingshi wenguanhui 1995; Fujiansheng bowuguan, Youxixian wenguanhui, and Youxixian bowuguan 1988.

45. See Wang Jinxian and Shi Weiguo 1994.

46. The use of the verb *wang* (to look out on), rather than *xiang* (to face toward) or *zhi* (to extend to), suggests an interpretation of geomancy that emphasizes the scenic view from the tomb as its prime concern. Cf. ECJ 10.623. Cf. also Martin 1973, 182.

47. See Zhou Dao 1964; Henansheng wenwu kaogu yanjiusuo 1997, 198–203.

48. See Henansheng wenwu kaogu yanjiusuo 1997, 15–17, 173–208.

49. See Henansheng wenwu kaogu yanjiusuo 1997.

50. See Feng Jiren 1994; Henansheng wenwu kaogu yanjiusuo 1997, 4.

51. For an attempted reconstruction of the temples at the upper palaces, see Feng Jiren 1992.

52. Wang Shen, "Inscription for the Pagoda for the late Reverend Bianzheng, Abbot of the Monastery of Luminous Filiality, of the Great Song" ("Da Song gu Zhaoxiao chanyuanzhu Bianzheng dashi ta ming," 1093), transcribed in Henansheng wenwu kaogu yanjiusuo 1997, 512.

53. See Chongqingshi bowuguan lishizu 1961. See also Kuhn 1996, 343; Stahl 1994, 177.

54. See Dexingxian bowuguan 1990.

55. See, for example, Chen Dingrong and Xu Jianchang 1988; Jiangxisheng wenwu gongzuodui and Nanfengxian bowuguan 1988; Zhejiangsheng wenwu guanli weiyuanhui 1975.

56. On the meaning of the prone and supine figurines, see Chen Dingrong and Xu Jianchang 1988. On the rooster and the dog, see DLXS 11.5ab, 13.4a.

57. Scenes of musicians, dancers, and actors are common in Middle-Period tombs. Although Chinese archaeologists tend to associate such scenes with a popular culture of urban entertainment, it seems more likely that they instantiate and perpetuate the musical and theatrical performances at funerals and temple festivals.

58. Cf. Fu Xinian 2002, 122, 127–130; Guo Daineng 2002, 187–88; Ledderose 2000, chapter 5.

59. See Duan Pengqi 1995; Zhao Chao 1998.

60. See Hansen 1995, 159–73.

61. See Quzhoushi wenguanhui 1983.

62. See Beijingshi wenwu gongzuo dui 1980. Cf. Hebeisheng wenwu yanjiusuo 2001, 69–125; Hebeisheng wenwu yanjiusuo, Zhangjiakoushi wenwu guanlichu, and Xuanhuaqu wenwu guanlichu 1996. Cf. also Tsao 2000, 9–15.

63. See Li Shaolian 1973; Wu Wei 1995.

64. Hodder 1991, 191. Cf. Shanks and Tilley 1992, 133.

65. Proust 1972, 63.

66. The phrase "fusion of horizons" is Hans-Georg Gadamer's. See Gadamer 1989, 306–7 et seq.

# Bibliography

## Abbreviations


BJXSDG — *Biji xiaoshuo daguan* 筆記小說大觀. Taipei: Xinxing shuju, 1978–1985.

CSJCCB — *Congshu jicheng chubian* 叢書集成初編. Beijing: Zhonghua shuju, 1985.

DHBC — *Dunhuang baocang* 敦煌寶藏, ed. Huang Yongwu 黃永武. Taipei: Xin wenfeng, 1981–1986.

GJZBCK — *Beijing tushuguan guji zhenben congkan* 北京圖書館古籍珍本叢刊. Beijing: Shumu wenxian, 1988–1991.

HKBLS — *Hekeben leishu jicheng* 和刻本類書集成. Shanghai: Shanghai guji, 1990.

SBCK — *Sibu congkan* 四部叢刊. Shanghai: Shanghai shudian, 1984–1985.

SKQS — *Wenyuange Siku quanshu* 文淵閣四庫全書. Taipei: Taiwan Commercial Press, 1983.

SSJZS — *Shisanjing zhushu* 十三經注疏. Taipei: Xin Wenfeng, 1988.

SYFZ — *Song-Yuan fangzhi congkan* 宋元方志叢刊. Beijing: Zhonghua shuju, 1990.

WWBC — *Xuanyin wanwei biecang* 選印宛委別藏. Shanghai: Commercial Press, 1935.

ZGFSGG — *Zhongguo fangshu gaiguan* 中國方術概觀. Beijing: Renmin Zhongguo chubanshe, 1993.

ZZJC — *Xinbian zhuzi jicheng* 新編諸子集成. Taipei: Shijie shuju, 1991.


## Primary sources


BFDQ — *Sheng Song mingxian wubaijia bofang daquan* 聖宋名賢五百家播芳大全, comp. Wei Qixian 魏齊賢 and Ye Fen 葉棻. 1190. SKQS edition.

BGL — *Baoguang lu* 葆光錄, by Chen Longmingzi 陳龍明子 (*hao*). 10th century. CSJCCB edition.

| | |
|---|---|
| BGT | *Bo gu tu* 博古圖, comp. Wang Fu 王黼. Yuan edition (ca. 1123). National Central Library, Taipei. |
| BJQJ | *Beiji qianjin yaofang* 備急千金要方, by Lin Yi 林億. Song edition (11th century). Reprint, Osaka: Orient Press, 1989. |
| BJYJ | *Bai Juyi ji* 白居易集, by Bai Juyi 白居易. Ca. 846. Beijing: Zhonghua shuju, 1979. |
| BMSY | *Beimeng suoyan* 北夢瑣言, by Sun Guangxian 孫光憲. 10th century. Shanghai: Shanghai guji, 1981. |
| BSJ | *Beishan ji* 北山集, by Zheng Gangzhong 鄭剛中. Ca. 1154. SKQS edition. |
| BSJJ | *Han Wei Liuchao baisan jia ji* 漢魏六朝百三家集, comp. Zhang Pu 張溥. Ca. 1641. SKQS edition. |
| BTJ | *Bentang ji* 本堂集, by Chen Zhu 陳著. Ca. 1297. SKQS edition. |
| BTL | *Bin tui lu* 賓退錄, by Zhao Yushi 趙與時. 1224. CSJCCB edition. |
| BXDQJ | *Beixi daquanji* 北溪大全集, by Chen Chun 陳淳. Ca. 1217. SKQS edition. |
| BZB | *Bozhai bian* 泊宅編, by Fang Shao 方勺. 12th century. Beijing: Zhonghua shuju, 1983. |
| CAZ | *Chang'an zhi* 長安志, by Song Minqiu 宋敏求. 1076. Reprint, SYFZ. |
| CFYG | *Cefu yuangui* 冊府元龜, comp. Wang Qinro 王欽若 et al. 1013. Beijing: Zhonghua shuju, 1960. |
| CGL | *Nancun chuogeng lu* 南村輟耕錄, by Tao Zongyi 陶宗儀. 1366. SBCK edition. |
| Chunqiu | *Chunqiu* 春秋. SSJZS edition. |
| CLJ | *Culai ji* 徂徠集, by Shi Jie 石介. Ca. 1045. SKQS edition. |
| CMTCL | *Chunming tuichao lu* 春明退朝錄, by Song Minqiu 宋敏求. 1070s. Beijing: Zhonghua shuju, 1980. |
| CWZM | *Chongwen zongmu* 崇文總目, by Wang Yaochen 王堯臣 et al. 1042. SKQS edition. |
| CXZN | *Cixue zhinan* 辭學指南, by Wang Yinglin 王應麟. *Yuhai* edition (13th century). Beijing: Wenwu, 1987. |
| CYQZ | *Chaoye qianzai* 朝野僉載, by Zhang Zhuo 張鷟. 8th century. Beijing: Zhonghua shuju, 1979. |
| CZJW | *Chunzhu jiwen* 春渚紀聞, by He Wei 何薳. Ca. 1140s. CSJCCB edition. |
| CZZJ | *Chengzhai zaji* 誠齋雜記, by Lin Kun 林坤. Yuan dynasty. BJXSDG edition. |
| DJGZ | *Da Jin guozhi jiaozheng* 大金國志校證, by Yu Wenmao 宇文懋. 1234. Beijing: Zhonghua shuju, 1986. |

DJMHL *Dongjing meng Hua lu* 東京夢華錄, attr. to Meng Yuanlao 孟元老. 1147. Beijing: Zhonghua shuju, 1982.

DLJ *Donglai ji* 東萊集, by Lü Zuqian 呂祖謙. 1204. SKQS edition.

DLXS *Dili xinshu* 地理新書, comp. Wang Zhu 王洙 et al. 1192 edition (1184; 1050s). Reprint, Taipei: Jiwen shuju, 1985.

DongMJ *Dongmou ji* 東牟集, by Wang Yang 王洋. Ca. 1154. SKQS edition.

DPZL *Dongpo zhilin* 東坡志林, by Su Shi 蘇軾. Ca. 1100. Beijing: Zhonghua shuju, 1981.

DSHTL *Da Song Baoyou sinian bingchen sui Huitian wannian juzhu li* 大宋寶祐四年丙辰歲會天萬年具注曆, comp. Jing Zhili 荊執禮 et al. 1155. WWBC edition.

DSJ *Dieshan ji* 疊山集, by Xie Fangde 謝枋得. Ca. 1289. SKQS edition.

DSXZ *Dushi xiangzhu* 杜詩詳注, by Du Fu 杜甫. 1703 (8th century). Beijing: Zhonghua shuju, 1979.

DSZ *Junzhai dushu zhi* 郡齋讀書志, by Chao Gongwu 晁公武. 1187. Shanghai: Shanghai guji, 1990.

DTXY *Da Tang xinyu* 大唐新語, by Liu Su 劉肅. 807. Beijing: Zhonghua shuju, 1984.

DuanMJ *Duanming ji* 端明集, by Cai Xiang 蔡襄. Ca. 1090. SKQS edition.

DXBL *Dongxuan bilu* 東軒筆錄, by Wei Tai 魏泰. 1094. Beijing: Zhonghua shuju, 1983.

DZJS *Dongzhai jishi* 東齋記事, by Fan Zhen 范鎮. 11th century. Beijing: Zhonghua shuju, 1980.

DZXL *Dunzhai xianlan* 遯齋閒覽, by Fan Zhengmin 范正敏. 11th century. SF edition.

ECJ *Er Cheng ji* 二程集, by Cheng Yi 程頤 and Cheng Hao 程顥. 1112. Beijing: Zhonghua shuju, 1981.

EYXY *Erya xinyi* 爾雅新義, by Lu Dian 陸佃. 1808 edition (1099). Reprint, GJZBCK.

FGB *Fugubian* 復古編, by Zhang You 張有. 1114. SKQS edition.

FRLF *Furen daquan liangfang* 婦人大全良方, by Chen Ziming 陳自明. 1237. SKQS edition.

GCG *Guichao gao* 龜巢稿, by Xie Yingfang 謝應芳. 1379. SBCK edition.

GD *Guidong* 鬼董. Anonymous. Late 9th century. BJXSDG edition.

GHYHZ *Guihai yuheng zhi* 桂海虞衡志, by Fan Chengda 范成大. 1175. Beijing: Zhonghua shuju, 2002.

| | |
|---|---|
| GJLS | *Xinbian fenmen gujin leishi* 新編分門古今類事, by Weixinzi 委心子 (pseud.). 1169. CSJCCB edition. |
| GJSWLJ | *Xinbian gujin shiwen leiju* 新編古今事文類聚, by Zhu Mu 祝穆. Yuan edition. Reprint, Beijing: Shumu wenxian, 1991. |
| GKJ | *Gongkui ji* 攻媿集, by Lou Yao 樓鑰. Ca. 1213. SBCK edition. |
| GLFTJ | *Guilin fengtu ji* 桂林風土記, by Mo Xiufu 莫休符. 899. CSJCCB edition. |
| GLTJ | *Xuanhe fengshi Gaoli tujing* 宣和奉使高麗圖經, by Xu Jing 徐兢. 1124. CSJCCB edition. |
| GLXSWJ | *Guling xiansheng wenji* 古靈先生文集, by Chen Xiang 陳襄. Song edition (ca. 1135). Reprint, GJZBCK. |
| GSJ | *Gongshi ji* 公是集, by Liu Chang 劉敞. Ca. 1068. SKQS edition. |
| GTL | *Guitian lu* 歸田錄, by Ouyang Xiu 歐陽修. 1067. Beijing: Zhonghua shuju, 1981. |
| Guliang | *Guliang zhuan* 穀梁傳. SSJZS edition. |
| GXJ | *Guixi ji* 龜溪集, by Shen Yuqiu 沈與求. 1191. SKQS edition. |
| GZ | *Guanzhen* 官箴, by Lü Juren 呂居仁. 1227 (1130). CSJCCB edition. |
| HAJ | *Hui'an ji* 晦庵集, by Zhu Xi 朱熹. 1532 (ca. 1200). SBCK edition. |
| Han Fei | *Han Feizi* 韓非子. ZZJC edition. |
| Hanshu | *Hanshu* 漢書, by Ban Gu 班固. 92 CE. Beijing: Zhonghua shuju, 1962. |
| HCLJ | *Han Changli xiansheng ji* 韓昌黎先生集, by Han Yu 韓愈. 1227 (ca. 824). SBCK edition. |
| HCQJ | *Houcun xiansheng da quanji* 後村先生大全集, by Liu Kezhuang 劉克莊. 1272. SBCK edition. |
| HCWJ | *Huangchao wenjian* 皇朝文鑑, comp. Lü Zuqian 呂祖謙. 12th century. SBCK edition. |
| HDL | *Houde lu* 厚德錄, by Li Yuangang 李元綱. 12th century. CSJCCB edition. |
| HLXB | *Hunli xinbian* 婚禮新編, by Ding Shengzhi 丁昇之. Southern Song edition (ca. 1200). Reprint, GJZBCK. |
| HMDQ_1200 | *Sheng Song qianjia mingxian biaoqi hanmo daquan* 聖宋千家名賢表啓翰墨大全, by Wu Huanran 吳奐然. 1200. Nara: Tenri daigaku shuppanbu, 1981. |
| HMDQ_1307 | *Xinbian shiwen leiju hanmo daquan* 新編事文類聚翰墨大全, attr. to Liu Yingli 劉應李. 14th century. National Central Library, Taipei. |

HMQS — *Xinbian shiwen leiju hanmo quanshu* 新編事文類聚翰墨全書, attr. to Liu Yingli 劉應李. 14th century. Fu Ssu-nien Library, Academia Sinica, Taipei.

HMQS 1307 — *Xinbian shiwen leiju hanmo daquan* 新編事文類聚翰墨大全, attr. to Liu Yingli 劉應李. 14th century. National Palace Museum Library, Taipei.

HMQS GG — *Xinbian shiwen leiju hanmo daquan* 新編事文類聚翰墨大全, attr. to Liu Yingli 劉應李. 14th century. National Palace Museum Library, Taipei.

HQJSJ — *Hongqing jushi ji* 鴻慶居士集, by Sun Di 孫覿. Ca. 1169. SKQS edition.

HQL — *Houqing lu* 侯鯖錄, by Zhao Delin 趙德麟. Early 12th century. BJXSDG edition.

HZL — *Huizhu lu* 揮麈錄, by Wang Mingqing 王明清. 1166. Beijing: Zhonghua shuju, 1961.

HZZY — *Huzi zhiyan* 胡子知言, by Hu Hong 胡宏. 12th century. BJXSDG edition.

JF — *Jiafan* 家範, by Sima Guang 司馬光. 11th century. SKQS edition.

JGL — *Jigu lu ba wei* 集古錄八尾, by Ouyang Xiu 歐陽修. 1070. SKQS edition.

Jinshi — *Jinshi* 金史, comp. Toghto 脫脫 et al. 1344. Baina edition.

Jinshu — *Jinshu* 晉書, comp. Fang Xuanling 房玄齡 et al. 646. Beijing: Zhonghua shuju, 1974.

JJBY 14th — *Jujia biyong* 居家必用. Anonymous. 14th century. National Palace Museum Library, Taipei.

JJBY 1673 — *Jujia biyong shilei* 居家必用事類. Anonymous. 1673. Reprint, Kyoto: Zhongwen, 1984.

JL — *Jiali* 家禮, by Zhu Xi 朱熹. 1341 (1216). Reprint, Ebrey 1991a.

JLB — *Jilei bian* 雞肋編, by Zhuang Chuo 莊綽. 1133. Beijing: Zhonghua shuju, 1983.

JLJ — *Jilei ji* 雞肋集, by Chao Buzhi 晁補之. Ca. 1110. SKQS edition.

JLJZZ — *Jiang Linji zazhi* 江鄰幾雜志, by Jiang Xiufu 江休復. 11th century. BJXSDG edition.

JSHL — *Jinsi houlu* 近思後錄. Anonymous. Southern Song edition (13th century). National Central Library, Taipei.

JSJW — *Jiashi jiuwen* 家世舊聞, by Lu You 陸游. Ca. 1060s. Beijing: Zhonghua shuju, 1993.

JSLi — *Jinshi li* 金石例, by Pan Angxiao 潘昂霄. 1345. SKQS edition.

JSLu — *Jinshilu* 金石錄, by Zhao Mingcheng 趙明誠. Southern Song edition (1119–1125). Reprint, Beijing: Zhonghua shuju, 1983.

| | |
|---|---|
| JSSL | *Jushan siliu* 橘山四六, by Li Tingzhong 李廷忠. 12th century. SKQS edition. |
| JTS | *Jiu Tang shu* 舊唐書, comp. Liu Xu 劉煦 et al. 941–945. Baina edition. |
| JWGBJ | *Song Jingwengong biji* 宋景文公筆記, by Song Qi 宋祁. 11th century. CSJCCB edition. |
| JWJ | *Jingwen ji* 景文集, by Song Qi 宋祁. Ca. 1061. CSJCCB edition. |
| JWZW | *Jiuwen zhengwu* 舊聞證誤, by Li Xinchuan 李心傳. 13th century. Beijing: Zhonghua shuju, 1981. |
| JXWHG | *Jinxiu wanhua gu* 錦繡萬花谷. Anonymous. Southern Song edition (1188). Reprint, GJZBCK. |
| JYWC | *Jiyi wencun* 寄簃文存, by Shen Jiaben 沈家本. *Lidai xingfa kao* edition. Beijing: Zhonghua shuju, 1985. |
| JZGWYH | *Jizhuan guwen yunhai* 集篆古文韻海, by Du Conggu 杜從古. 1796 manuscript (1119). Reprint, GJZBCK. |
| KCZ | *Kuiche zhi* 睽車志, by Guo Tuan 郭彖. Ca. 1181. CSJCCB edition. |
| KGJJ | *Kao gong ji jie* 考工記解, by Lin Xiyi 林希逸. 13th century. Tongzhi tang edition. |
| KGT | *Kao gu tu* 考古圖, by Lü Dalin 呂大臨. 1299 edition. National Central Library, Taipei. |
| KSFT | *Lidai zhongding yiqi kuanshi fatie* 曆代鐘鼎彝器款識法帖, by Xue Shanggong 薛尚功. 1144. SKQS edition. |
| KT | *Ke tan* 可談, by Zhu Yu 朱彧. 11th century. BJXSDG edition. |
| KYL | *Da Tang Kaiyuan li* 大唐開元禮, comp. Xiao Song 蕭嵩 et al. 732. Tokyo: Koten kenkyūkai, 1972. |
| KYZ | *Kuoyi zhi* 括異志, by Zhang Shizheng 張師正. 11th century. BJXSDG edition. |
| LCLZ | *Longchuan lüezhi* 龍川略志, by Su Che 蘇轍. 11th century. Beijing: Zhonghua shuju, 1982. |
| Liezi | *Liezi* 列子. ZZJC edition. |
| Liji | *Liji* 禮記. SSJZS edition. |
| LJAZ | *Lijing aozhi* 禮經奧旨, by Zheng Qiao 鄭樵. 12th century. CSJCCB edition. |
| LJFSP | *Longjin fengsui pan* 龍筋鳳髓判, by Zhang Zhuo 張鷟. 7th century. CSJCCB edition. |
| LJJS | *Liji jishuo* 禮記集說, by Wei Shi 衛湜. 1240. Tongzhi tang edition. |
| LJJYT | *Liji juyao tu* 禮記舉要圖. Anonymous. Song edition. National Central Library, Taipei. |

LJYY *Liji yaoyi* 禮記要義, by Wei Liaoweng 魏了翁. 13th century. SBCK edition.

LNZ *Huitu gu lienü zhuan* 繪圖古列女傳, by Liu Xiang 劉向. Ming edition (1st century BCE). Reprint, Taipei: Guangwen shuju, 1978.

LRDQ *Liuren daquan* 六壬大全. Anonymous. Ming dynasty. SKQS edition.

LRDZ *Liuren dazhan* 六壬大占, by Zhu Mi 祝泌. 1239. WWBC edition.

LRSDJ *Jingyou liuren shendingjing* 景祐六壬神定經, comp. Yang Weide 楊維德 et al. 1030s. CSJCCB edition.

LS *Lishu* 禮書, by Chen Xiangdao 陳祥道. 1092. SKQS edition.

LSCC *Lüshi chunqiu* 呂氏春秋. ZZJC edition.

LSYZ *Lantian Lüshi yizhu jijiao* 藍田呂氏遺著集校, comp. Chen Junmin 陳俊民. Beijing: Zhonghua shuju, 1993.

Lunyu *Lunyu* 論語. SSJZS edition.

LWDD *Lingwai daida* 嶺外代答, by Zhou Qufei 周去非. 1178. Beijing: Zhonghua shuju, 1999.

LX *Lixiang* 禮象, by Lu Dian 陸佃. 12th century. YLDD edition.

LXABJ *Laoxue'an biji* 老學庵筆記, by Lu You 陸游. 1190s. Beijing: Zhonghua shuju, 1979.

LXZN *Lixue zhinan* 吏學指南, by Xu Yuanrui 徐元瑞. 1673 (1301). Reprint, Hangzhou: Zhejiang guji, 1988.

LYJSL *Longyou jinshi lu* 隴右金石錄, by Zhang Wei 張維. 1943. Reprint, *Lidai shike shiliao huibian* 曆代石刻史料彙編, vol. 13. Beijing: Beijing tushuguan, 2000.

LZQGY *Lizuan qian guiyu* 曆纂千圭玉, comp. Yu Yuanxiang 余元祥. Yuan dynasty? YLDD edition.

LZY *Liu Zhiyuan zhugongdiao jiaozhu* 劉知遠諸宮調校注. Anonymous. 12th century. Jianyang: Ba Shu shushe, 1989.

MCWJ *Mocheng wenji* 默成文集, by Pan Lianggui 潘良貴. Ca. 1150. SKQS edition.

Mengzi *Mengzi* 孟子. ZZJC edition.

MFZYML *Maofeng zhenyin manlu* 鄮峰真隱漫錄, by Shi Hao 史浩. Ca. 1194. SKQS edition.

MJ *Moji* 默記, by Wang Zhi 王銍. 12th century. Beijing: Zhonghua shuju, 1981.

MLL *Meng Liang lu* 夢粱錄, by Wu Zimu 吳自牧. 14th century. In *Dongjing meng Hua lu wai sizhong*. Taipei: Dali, 1980.

MQBT *Mengqi bitan* 夢溪筆談, by Shen Gua 沈括. 1305 edition (1086–1093). Reprint, Beijing: Wenwu chubanshe, 1975.

MTJ *Mantang ji* 漫塘集, by Liu Zai 劉宰. Ca. 1239. SKQS edition.

MTKH *Maoting kehua* 茅亭客話, by Huang Xiufu 黃修復. 11th century. BJXSDG edition.

MXL *Man xiao lu* 漫笑錄, by Xu Zao 徐慥. 12th century. SF edition.

MXQJ *Meixi qianji* 梅溪前集, by Wang Shiming 王十明. Ca. 1171. SKQS edition.

MZML *Mozhuang manlu* 墨莊漫錄, by Zhang Bangji 張邦基. 12th century. BJXSDG edition.

MZWJ *Mianzhai xiansheng Huang Wensugong wenji* 勉齋先生黃文肅公文集, by Huang Gan 黃榦. 1315 edition (ca. 1221). Reprint, GJZBCK.

NCJT *Nanchuang jitan* 南窗紀談. Anonymous. 12th century. BJXSDG edition.

NGZ *Nenggai zhai manlu* 能改齋漫錄, by Wu Zeng 吳曾. 1157. CSJCCB edition.

NKBW *Nüke baiwen* 女科百問, by Qi Zhongfu 齊仲甫. Ca. 1200. Zhenben yishu jicheng edition. Taipei: Shijie shuju, 1962.

NKWJF *Nüke wanjin fang* 女科萬金方, by Xue Guyu 薛古愚. Ming edition (Song). Microfilm, Fu Ssu-nien Library, Academia Sinica.

PY *Piya* 埤雅, by Lu Dian 陸佃. 1479 (1125). Reprint, GJZBCK.

QBZZ *Qingbo zazhi* 清波雜志, by Zhou Hui 周煇. 1192. Beijing: Zhonghua shuju, 1983.

QDYY *Qidong yeyu* 齊東野語, by Zhou Mi 周密. 1291. CSJCCB edition.

QJBY *Qianjin baoyao* 千金寶要, by Guo Si 郭思. 1849 manuscript based on a 1444 edition (1124). National Central Library, Taipei.

QJXW *Qijiu xuwen* 耆舊續聞, by Chen Hu 陳鵠. 13th century. BJXSDG edition.

QJXZ *Qijing xiaozhuan* 七經小傳, by Liu Chang 劉敞. 11th century. SBCK edition.

QJYF *Qianjin yifang* 千金翼方, by Sun Simiao 孫思邈. 1310s (ca. 682). Reprint, Osaka: Orient Press, 1989.

QMJ *Minggong shupan qingmingji* 名公書判清明集. Anonymous. 1261, 1569. Beijing: Zhonghua shuju, 1987.

QRJSJ *Qingrong jushi ji* 清容居士集, by Yuan Jue 袁桷. Ca. 1327. SKQS edition.

QSGW *Quan shanggu sandai Qin Han Sanguo Liuchao wen* 全上古三代秦漢三國六朝文, comp. Yan Kejun 嚴可均. 1836. Beijing: Zhonghua shuju, 1958.

QSLB *Qunshu leibian gushi* 群書類編故事. Anonymous. Date unknown. WWBC edition.

QSTY *Qunshu tongyao* 群書通要. Anonymous. 1341–1368 (1299). WWBC edition.

QSYL *Qunshu yilan* 群書一覽. Anonymous. Yuan edition. National Palace Museum Library, Taipei.

QXZJ *Qingxiang zaji* 青箱雜記, by Wu Chuhou 吳處厚. 1087. Beijing: Zhonghua shuju, 1985.

QYTF *Qingyuan tiaofa shilei* 慶元條法事類, comp. Xie Shenfu 謝沈甫. 1202. Taipei: Xin wenfeng, 1976.

QZ *Quanzhi* 泉志, by Hong Zun 洪遵. 12th century. Wanli edition (12th century). National Central Library, Taipei.

QZQQ *Xinbian shiwen leiyao qizha qingqian* 新編事文類要啓劄青錢. Anonymous. 1324. Reprint, Tokyo: Koten kenkyūkai, 1963.

RZSB *Rongzhai suibi* 容齋隨筆, by Hong Mai 洪邁. 12th century. Shanghai: Shanghai guji, 1996.

RZSL *Rongzhai siliu congtan* 容齋四六叢談, by Hong Mai 洪邁. 1192–1202. CSJCCB edition.

SAJ *Si'an ji* 俟菴集, by Li Cun 李存. Ca. 1354. SKQS edition.

SCBS *Songchuang baishuo* 松窗百說, by Li Jike 李季可. Ca. 1158. BJXSDG edition.

SCTSM *Suichu tang shumu* 遂初堂書目, by You Mao 尤袤. 12th century. CSJCCB edition.

SCWJL *Sichao wenjian lu* 四朝聞見錄, by Ye Shaoweng 葉紹翁. Ca. 1225. Beijing: Zhonghua shuju, 1989.

SCYWL *Soucai yiwen lu* 搜采異聞錄, by Yong Heng 永亨. 13th century. BJXSDG edition.

SCZCZY *Songchao zhuchen zouyi* 宋朝諸臣奏議, comp. Zhao Ruyu 趙汝愚. 1186. Shanghai: Shanghai guji, 1999.

SDRJ *Shuidong riji* 水東日記, by Ye Sheng 葉盛. 15th century. Beijing: Zhonghua shuju, 1980.

SDYT *Shaoxi zhouxian shidian yitu* 紹熙州縣釋奠儀圖, by Zhu Xi 朱熹. 1194. CSJCCB edition.

SDZLJ *Song da zhaoling ji* 宋大詔令集. Anonymous. 1131–1162. Beijing: Zhonghua shuju, 1962.

SF *Shuofu sanzhong* 說郛三種, by Tao Zongyi 陶宗儀. Ca. 1360 and ca. 1500. Shanghai: Shanghai guji, 1988.

SGWJ *Shangu waiji* 山谷外集, by Huang Tingjian 黃庭堅. Ca. 1105. SKQS edition.

Shangshu *Shangshu* 尙書. SSJZS edition.

Shiji *Shiji* 史記, by Sima Qian 司馬遷. 1st century BCE. Baina edition.

Shijing *Shijing* 詩經. SSJZS edition.

SHY — *Song huiyao jigao* 宋會要輯稿, comp. Xu Song 徐松 et al. Ca. 1820 (Song). Reprint, Taipei: Xin wenfeng, 1976.

SJZL — *Dade Shengji zonglu* 大德聖濟總錄, comp. Emperor Huizong 宋徽宗. 1300 (1118). Reprint, Osaka: Orient Press, 1994.

SKQSM — *Bishusheng xubiandao siku queshu mu* 秘書省續編到四庫闕書目. Anonymous. 1903 (1145). *Shumu leibian* edition.

SLBZ — *Siliu biaozhun* 四六標準, by Li Liu 李劉. 13th century. SKQS edition.

SLCH — *Siliu conghua* 四六叢話, comp. Sun Mei 孫梅. 1789. Wanyou wenku huiyao edition.

SLCY — *Sanli cuoyao* 三曆撮要. Anonymous. Southern Song. Reprint, *Sui'an Xushi congshu xubian* 隨庵徐氏叢書續編. Nanling: privately published, 1916.

SLGJ 1333 — *Xinbian zuantu zenglei qunshu leiyao shilin guangji* 新編纂圖增類群書類要事林廣記, attr. to Chen Yuanjing 陳元靚. 1330–1333. Reprint, Kyoto: Zhongwen, 1988.

SLGJ 1340 — *Zuantu zengxin qunshu leiyao shilin guangji* 纂圖增新群書類要事林廣記, attr. to Chen Yuanjing 陳元靚. 1340. Reprint, Beijing: Zhonghua shuju, 1999.

SLGJ 1478 — *Zuantu zengxin qunshu leiyao shilin guangji* 纂圖增新群書類要事林廣記, attr. to Chen Yuanjing 陳元靚. 1478. National Central Library, Taipei.

SLGJ 1699 — *Xinbian qunshu leiyao shilin guangji* 新編群書類要事林廣記, attr. to Chen Yuanjing 陳元靚. 1699 (1325). Reprint, Beijing: Zhonghua shuju, 1999.

SLH — *Siliu hua* 四六話, by Wang Zhi 王銍. 12th century. CSJCCB edition.

SLJZ — *Siliu jinzhen* 四六金針, by Chen Weisong 陳維崧. Qing dynasty. CSJCCB edition.

SLT — *Sanli tu* 三禮圖, by Nie Chongyi 聶崇義. Ca. 960. Shanghai: Shanghai tongwen shuju, n.d.

SLTZ — *Siliu tanzhu* 四六談塵, by Xie Ji 謝伋. 12th century. CSJCCB edition.

SLYY — *Shilin yanyu* 石林燕語, by Ye Mengde 葉夢得. 1128. Beijing: Zhonghua shuju, 1984.

SLYYB — *Shilin yanyu bian* 石林燕語辨, by Wang Yingchen 汪應辰. 12th century. Beijing: Zhonghua shuju, 1984.

SMGNP — *Sima Guang nianpu* 司馬光年譜, by Gu Donggao 顧棟高. 1733. Beijing: Zhonghua shuju, 1990.

SMJW — *Songmo jiwen* 松漠紀聞, by Hong Hao 洪皓. 1156. Changchunshi: Jilin wenshi, 1986.

SQTY — *Sanqi tuyi* 三器圖義, by Cheng Jiong 程迥. 1183. SF edition.

SRXH — *Songren xiaohua* 宋人笑話, comp. Lou Zikuang 婁子匡. Folklore and Folkliterature Series, vol. 6. Taipei: Chinese Association for Folklore, 1970.

SS — *Songshi* 宋史, comp. Toghto 脫脫 et al. 1345. Baina edition.

SSJY — *Songshi jiayi* 宋氏家儀, by Song Xu 宋詡. 1504. GJZBCK edition.

SSLH — *Song siliu hua* 宋四六話, by Peng Yuanrui 彭元瑞. 1803. CSJCCB edition.

SSLY — *Songchao shishi leiyuan* 宋朝事實類苑, by Jiang Shaoyu 江少虞. 12th century. Shanghai: Shanghai guji, 1981.

SSWJ — *Su Shi wenji* 蘇軾文集, by Su Shi 蘇軾. 12th century. Beijing: Zhonghua shuju, 1986.

SSWJL — *Shaoshi wenjian lu* 邵氏聞見錄, by Shao Bowen 邵伯溫. 1151. Beijing: Zhonghua shuju, 1983.

SSXY — *Shishuo xinyu* 世說新語, by Liu Yiqing 劉義慶. 5th century. Hong Kong: Zhonghua shuju, 1973.

SSYTL — *Shengshui yantan lu* 澠水燕談錄, by Wang Pizhi 王闢之. Ca. 1095. Beijing: Zhonghua shuju, 1981.

SSYY — *Shansu yaoyi* 善俗要義, by Wang Jie 王結. Ca. 1336. LXZN edition.

Suishu — *Suishu* 隋書, comp. Wei Zheng 魏徵 et al. 7th century. Beijing: Zhonghua shuju, 1973.

SWJY — *Shiwu jiyuan* 事物紀原, by Gao Cheng 高承 and Li Guo 李果. 1472 (1447; ca. 1078–1085). CSJCCB edition.

SXT — *Song xingtong* 宋刑統, comp. Dou Yi 竇儀. 963. Beijing: Zhonghua shuju, 1984.

SXZN — *Shuxu zhinan* 書敘指南, by Ren Guang 任廣. 1649 (1126). HKBLS edition.

SY — *Shuyi* 書儀, by Sima Guang 司馬光. Ca. 1081. CSJCCB edition.

SYWJ — *Shanyuan wenji* 剡源文集, by Dai Biaoyuan 戴表元. Ca. 1310. SKQS edition.

SYXA — *Song-Yuan xue'an* 宋元學案, by Huang Zongxi 黃宗羲. 17th century. SBBY edition.

SZJ — *Shengzhai ji* 省齋集, by Liao Xingzhi 廖行之. Ca. 1189. SKQS edition.

SZYH — *Shuzhai yehua* 書齋夜話, by Yu Yan 俞琰. Yuan dynasty. WWBC edition.

TCYGL — *Taichang yinge li* 太常因革禮, comp. Ouyang Xiu 歐陽修 et al. Ca. 1064. CSJCCB edition.

| | |
|---|---|
| TD | *Tongdian* 通典, by Du You 杜佑. 801. Beijing: Zhonghua shuju, 1988. |
| TLSY | *Tanglü shuyi* 唐律疏議, comp. Zhangsun Wuji 長孫無忌. 653. Beijing: Zhonghua shuju, 1983. |
| TPGJ | *Taiping guangji* 太平廣記, comp. Li Fang 李昉. 978. Taipei: Wenshizhe, 1987. |
| TS | *Tingshi* 桯史, by Yue Ke 岳珂. 1214. Beijing: Zhonghua shuju, 1981. |
| TWSCT | *Tieweishan congtan* 鐵圍山叢談, by Cai Tao 蔡絛. Ca. 1130. Beijing: Zhonghua shuju, 1983. |
| TYBS | *Tangyin bishi* 棠陰比事, by Gui Wanrong 桂萬榮. 1211. SBCK edition. |
| TYJ | *Taiyi jing* 太乙經. Anonymous. Six Dynasties? SF edition. |
| TYL | *Tang yulin jiaozheng* 唐語林校證, by Wang Dang 王讜. Ca. 1106. Beijing: Zhonghua shuju, 1987. |
| TZ | *Tongzhi* 通志, by Zheng Qiao 鄭樵. 1161. Beijing: Zhonghua shuju, 1995. |
| TZTG | *Tongzhi tiaoge* 通制條格. Anonymous. Late 14th-century manuscript (1323). Reprint, Beijing: Huawen shuju, 1930. |
| TZTG 1986 | *Tongzhi tiaoge* 通制條格. Hangzhou: Zhejiang guji, 1986. |
| TZXL | *Taozhu xinlu* 陶朱新錄, by Ma Chun 馬純. 12th century. SF edition. |
| TZY | *Tang zhiyan* 唐摭言, by Wang Dingbao 王定保. Ca. 954. Shanghai: Shanghai guji, 1978. |
| WGWJ | *Wenguo Wenzhenggong wenji* 溫國文正公文集, by Sima Guang 司馬光. 1190s (ca. 1086). SBCK edition. |
| WJTJXJ | *Wujun tujing xuji* 吳郡圖經續記, comp. Zhu Changwen 朱長文. Song edition (1084). Reprint, SYFZ. |
| WJZ | *Wujun zhi* 吳郡志, by Fan Chengda 范成大. Ming edition (1192). Reprint, SYFZ. |
| WLXSJ | *Wanling xiansheng ji* 宛陵先生集, by Mei Yaochen 梅堯臣. Ca. 1060. SBCK edition. |
| WSBJ | *Weisheng baojian* 衛生寶監, by Luo Tianyi 羅天益. 1418 (Yuan). Palace Museum Library, Taipei. |
| WTMY | *Waitai miyao fang* 外台秘要方. Anonymous. Song edition (752). Reprint, Osaka: Orient Press, 1981. |
| WX | *Wenxuan* 文選, comp. Xiao Tong 蕭統. 1809 facsimile reprint of a 12th-century edition (6th century). Reprint, Taipei: Yiwen yinshuguan, 1990. |
| WXJ | *Wuxi ji* 武溪集, by Yu Jing 余靖. Ca. 1064. SKQS edition. |

WXTK *Wenxian tongkao* 文獻通考, by Ma Duanlin 馬端臨. Ca. 1308. Taipei: Taiwan shangwu yinshuguan, 1988 (1959).

WYYH *Wenyuan yinghua* 文苑英華, comp. Li Fang 李昉 et al. 986. SKQS edition.

WZJ *Wenzhong ji* 文忠集, by Zhou Bida 周必大. 1205. SKQS edition.

WZZ *Wenzhongzi* 文中子, by Wang Tong 王通. 7th century. Taipei: Shijie shuju, 1970.

XCB *Xu Zizhi tongjian changbian* 續資治通鑑長編, by Li Dao 李燾. 1183. Shanghai: Shanghai guji, 1986.

XCBSB *Xu Zizhi tongjian changbian shibu* 續資治通鑑長編拾補, by Huang Yizhou 黃以周. 1883. Shanghai: Shanghai guji, 1986.

XCYS *Xianchun yishi* 咸淳遺事. Anonymous. 13th century. BJXSDG edition.

XDCYF *Xin dacheng yifang* 新大成醫方, by Wang Yuanfu 王元福. Song edition. Microfilm, National Central Library, Taipei.

XJBFS *Xieji bian fang shu* 協紀辨方書. Anonymous. 1741. C. V. Starr East Asian Library Rare Book Collection, Columbia University.

XLKY *Yuding xingli kaoyuan* 御定星曆考原, comp. Li Guangdi 李光地 et al. 1713. SKQS edition.

XPJ *Xuepo ji* 雪坡集, by Yao Mian 姚勉. 1264. SKQS edition.

XSZX *Xishan zhengxun* 西山政訓, by Zhen Dexiu 真德秀. 13th century. CSJCCB edition.

XTJGL *Xiaotang Jigu lu* 嘯堂集古錄, by Wang Qiu 王俅. Ming facsimile reprint of a Song edition (early Southern Song). National Central Library, Taipei.

XTS *Xin Tang shu* 新唐書, comp. Ouyang Xiu 歐陽修 et al. 1060. Baina edition.

Xunzi *Xunzi* 荀子. ZZJC edition.

XWXJ *Xiong Wuxuan xiansheng wenji* 熊勿軒先生文集, by Xiong He 熊禾. 1351. CSJCCB edition.

XYCS *Xiangyan congshu* 香艷叢書, comp. Chongtianzi 蟲天子 (pseud.). Shanghai: Zhongguo tushu, 1909.

XYJL *Xiyuan jilu* 洗冤集錄, by Song Ci 宋慈. 1247. CSJCCB edition.

YDFLZL *Yuandai falü ziliao jicun* 元代法律資料輯存, ed. Huang Shijian 黃時鑒. Hangzhou: Zhejiang guji, 1988.

YDZ *Da Yuan shengzheng guochao dianzhang* 大元聖政國朝典章. Anonymous. Yuan edition (1317). Reprint, Taipei: National Palace Museum, 1976.

YDZXJ *Da Yuan shengzheng dianzhang xinji* 大元聖政典章新集. Anonymous. Yuan edition (1322). Reprint, in YDZ.

| | |
|---|---|
| YFL | *Yan fanlu* 演繁露, by Cheng Dachang 程大昌. 1201 (1180). Ruxue jingwu edition. |
| YFLG | *Yuanfeng leigao* 元豐類稿, by Zeng Gong 曾鞏. Ca. 1083. SBCK edition. |
| YHJW | *Youhuan jiwen* 遊宦紀聞, by Zhang Shinan 張世南. 1232. Beijing: Zhonghua shuju, 1981. |
| Yili | *Yili* 儀禮. SSJZS edition. |
| YJ | *Yujian* 寓簡, by Shen Zuozhe 沈作哲. 1174. BJXSDG edition. |
| YJTY | *Yinju tongyi* 隱居通議, by Liu Xun 劉壎. Yuan dynasty. CSJCCB edition. |
| YJZ | *Yi Jian zhi* 夷堅志, by Hong Mai 洪邁. 12th century. Taipei: Mingwen shuju, 1994. |
| YKCS | *Yeke congshu* 野客叢書, by Wang Mao 王楙. 1202 (1195). Beijing: Zhonghua shuju, 1987. |
| YL | *Yili* 儀禮. SSJZS edition. |
| YLDD | *Yongle dadian* 永樂大典. 15th century. Reprint, Beijing: Zhonghua shuju, 1960. |
| YLJShi | *Yili jishi* 儀禮集釋, by Li Rugui 李如圭. Ca. 1200. CSJCCB edition. |
| YLJShuo | *Yili jishuo* 儀禮集說, by Ao Jigong 敖繼公. 1677 (1301). Tongzhi tang edition. |
| YLJY | *Yuling juyi* 玉靈聚義, by Lu Sen 陸森. 1315. ZGFSGG edition. |
| YLJZ | *Yili jingzhuan tongjie* 儀禮經傳通解, comp. Zhu Xi 朱熹 et al. 1217. SKQS edition. |
| YLMC | *Yunlu manchao* 雲麓漫鈔, by Zhao Yanwei 趙彥衛. 1206. Beijing: Zhonghua shuju, 1996. |
| YLSG | *Yili shigong* 儀禮釋宮, by Li Rugui 李如圭. Ca. 1190. CSJCCB edition. |
| YLSW | *Yili shiwu* 儀禮識誤, by Zhang Chun 張淳. Ca. 1172. CSJCCB edition. |
| YLT | *Yili tu* 儀禮圖, by Yang Fu 楊復. 1228. Tongzhi tang edition. |
| YLXS | *Xinbian hunli beiyong yuelao xinshu* 新編婚禮備用月老新書. Anonymous. Southern Song edition (ca. 1260). National Central Library, Taipei. |
| YLZLBJ | *Gujin yuanliu zhilun bieji* 古今源流至論別集, by Huang Lüweng 黃履翁. 13th century. SKQS edition. |
| YS | *Yuanshi* 元史, comp. Song Lian 宋濂 et al. 1370. Baina edition. |
| YSLZ | *Yangsheng leizuan* 養生類纂, by Zhou Shouzhong 周守忠. 1474 (Song). Microfilm, National Central Library, Taipei. |

YSSF *Yuanshi shifan* 袁氏世範, by Yuan Cai 袁采. 1178. SKQS edition.

YWL *Yuan wenlei* 元文類, by Su Tianjue 蘇天爵. 1334. SKQS edition.

YWLJ *Yiwen leiju* 藝文類聚, by Ouyang Xun 歐陽詢. Southern Song edition (7th century). Reprint, Shanghai: Zhonghua shuju, 1959.

YWZL *Yiwen zonglu* 異聞總錄. Anonymous. Yuan dynasty. CSJCCB edition.

YYBJ *Xinkan Yinyang baojian keze tongshu* 新刊陰陽寶鑑剋擇通書, by Song Luzhen 宋魯珍. 14th century. YLDD edition.

YYJ *Yiyu ji* 疑獄集, by He Ning 和凝 and He Meng 和巘. 10th century. SKQS edition.

YYYML *Yanyi yimou lu* 燕翼詒謀錄, by Wang Yong 王栐. 1227. Beijing: Zhonghua shuju, 1981.

YYZZ *Youyang zazu* 酉陽雜俎, by Duan Chengshi 段成式. 9th century. Beijing: Zhonghua shuju, 1981.

YZSL *Yunzhuang siliu yuhua* 雲莊四六餘話, by Yang Yuandao 楊囦. 13th century. CSJCCB edition.

YZXZ *Yuzhao xinzhi* 玉照新志, by Wang Mingqing 王明清. 1198. CSJCCB edition.

YZYYJC *Yizhou yiyou jiacheng* 宜州乙酉家乘, by Huang Tingjian 黃庭堅. 1105. CSJCCB edition.

ZBYH *Chaoshi Zhubing yuanhou lun* 巢氏諸病源候論, by Chao Yuanfang 巢元方 et al. 11th-century edition (early 7th century). Reprint, Osaka: Orient Press, 1981.

ZD *Zangdu* 葬度, by Wang Wenlu 王文祿. 16th century. SF edition.

ZFZ *Zhufan zhi* 諸蕃志, by Zhao Rugua 趙汝括. 1225. CSJCCB edition.

ZGFY *Zhiguan fenji* 職官分紀, by Sun Fengji 孫逢吉. 1092. Beijing: Zhonghua shuju, 1988.

ZGXHS *Zhongguo xiaohuashu* 中國笑話書, comp. Yang Jialuo 楊家駱. Taipei: Shijie shuju, 1996.

ZGZDZY *Zengguang Zhongding zhuanyun* 增廣鐘鼎篆韻, by Yang Jun 楊鈞. Qing manuscript (14th century). Reprint, GJZBCK.

ZHJ *Zhonghui ji* 忠惠集, by Zhai Ruwen 翟汝文. Ca. 1141. SKQS edition.

Zhouli *Zhouli* 周禮. SSJZS edition.

ZhouS *Zhoushi* 籀史, by Zhai Qinian 翟耆年. 1140s. CSJCCB edition.

Zhouyi *Zhouyi* 周易. SSJZS edition.

Zhuangzi *Zhuangzi* 莊子. ZZJC edition.

ZhuS *Zhushi* 麈史, by Wang Dechen 王得臣. 1115. BJXSDG edition.

| | |
|---|---|
| ZHWL | *Zhenghe wuli xinyi* 政和五禮新儀, comp. Zheng Juzhong 鄭居中 et al. 1113. SKQS edition, and Ming manuscript in Fu Ssu-nien Library, Academia Sinica. |
| ZHWLJY | *Huangchao Zhenghe wuli jingyi zhu* 皇朝政和五禮精義註, by Wei Tong 韋彤. 1113. Qing manuscript based on a 1335 imprint. National Central Library, Taipei. |
| ZJ | *Zhaijing* 宅經. Anonymous. Date unknown. SF edition. |
| ZL | *Zanglu* 葬錄. Anonymous. Date unknown. DHBC edition. |
| ZLDY | *Zhouli dingyi* 周禮訂義, by Wang Yuzhi 王與之. 1243. SKQS edition. |
| ZLXL | *Zhoulian xulun* 晝簾緒論, by Hu Taichu 胡太初. 1235. CSJCCB edition. |
| ZWGZX | *Zhu Wengong zhengxun* 朱文公政訓, by Zhu Xi 朱熹. 1476 (12th century). CSJCCB edition. |
| ZWJ | *Ziwei ji* 紫微集, by Zhang Nie 張嵲. Ca. 1148. SKQS edition. |
| ZWTL | *Zuiweng tanlu* 醉翁談錄, by Luo Hua 羅燁. Yuan dynasty? Shanghai: Gudian wenxue, 1957. |
| ZXTG | *Zhouxian tigang* 州縣提綱. Anonymous. 1158. CSJCCB edition. |
| ZYGJ | *Zheyu guijian* 折獄龜鑒, by Zheng Ke 鄭克. 12th century. SKQS edition. |
| ZYJSJ | *Zhuyin jishi ji* 竹隱畸士集, by Zhao Dingchen 趙鼎臣. 11th century. SKQS edition. |
| ZYZZ | *Zuoyi zizhen* 作邑自箴, by Li Yuanbi 李元弼. 1179 (1117). SBCK edition. |
| ZZ | *Zazhu* 雜著, by Hu Qiyu 胡祇遹. Late 13th century. LXZN edition. |
| ZZJ | *Zhang Zai ji* 張載集, by Zhang Zai 張載. 11th century. Beijing: Zhonghua shuju, 1978. |
| ZZJL | *Zhuzi jiali* 朱子家禮, by Zhu Xi 朱熹. 1701 edition (1216). N.p. |
| ZZYL | *Zhuzi yulei* 朱子語類, comp. Li Jingde 黎靖德. 1270. Kyoto: Zhongwen chubanshe, 1979. |

## SECONDARY SOURCES

Ames, Roger T., and Henry Rosemont, trans. *The Analects of Confucius: A Philosophical Translation*. New York: Ballantine Books, 1998.

Anhuisheng bowuguan 安徽省博物館. "Hefei dongjiao Daxing ji Bei Song Bao Zheng jiazu muqun fajue baogao" 合肥東郊大興集北宋包拯家族墓群發掘報告. *Wenwu ziliao congkan* 3 (1980): 154–78.

Anonymous. "Zhongguo kaoguxuehui di ba ci nianhui zai Huhehaote zhaokai" 中國考古學會第八次年會在呼合浩特召開. *Kaogu* 12 (1991): 1146.

Appadurai, Arjun. "Introduction: Commodities and the Politics of Value." In *The Social Life of Things*, edited by A. Appadurai, 3–63. Cambridge: Cambridge University Press, 1986.

Appadurai, Arjun, ed. *The Social Life of Things: Commodities in Cultural Perspective*. Cambridge: Cambridge University Press, 1986.

Arrault, Alain. "Les calendriers de Dunhuang." In *Divination et société dans la Chine médiévale: Étude des manuscrits de Dunhuang de la Bibliothèque nationale de France et de la British Library*, edited by Marc Kalinowski, 85–123. Paris: Bibliothèque nationale de France, 2003.

———. "Jiu zhi shi shiji Dunhuang liri zhong de xuanzeshu yu yixue huodong" 九至十世紀敦煌曆日中的選擇術與醫學活動. *Dunhuang Tulufan yanjiu* 9 (2006): 423–443.

Ashmore, Robert. "The Banquet's Aftermath: Yan Jidao's *ci* Poetics and the High Tradition." *T'oung Pao* 88 (2002): 211–50.

Asim, Ina. "Status Symbol and Insurance Policy: Song Land Deeds for the Afterlife." In *Burial in Song China*, edited by Dieter Kuhn, 307–70. Heidelberg, Germany: Edition Forum, 1994.

Bai, Yunxiang 白雲翔, and Gu Zhijie 顧智界. "Zhongguo wenming qiyuan zuotan jiyao" 中國文明起源座談紀要. *Kaogu* 12 (1989): 1110–20, 1097.

Bakhtin, M. M. *Speech Genres and Other Late Essays*. Translated by Vern McGee. Edited by Caryl Emerson and Michael Holquist. Austin: University of Texas Press, 1986.

Balazs, Étienne, and Yves Hervouet, eds. *A Sung Bibliography*. Hong Kong: Chinese University Press, 1978.

Bao, Zonghao 鮑宗豪. *Hunsu wenhua: Zhongguo hunsu de guiji* 婚俗文化：中國婚俗的軌跡. Shanghai: Shanghai renmin chubanshe, 1990.

Barlow, Tani E. "Theorizing Woman: *Funü*, *Guojia*, *Jiating* (Chinese Woman, Chinese State, Chinese Family)." In *Body, Subject, and Power in China*, edited by Angela R. Zito and Tani E. Barlow, 253–89. Chicago: University of Chicago Press, 1994.

Barnard, Noel. "The Incidence of Forgery amongst Archaic Chinese Bronzes: Some Preliminary Notes." *Monumenta Serica* 27 (1968): 91–168.

Barnhart, Richard M., ed. *Li Kung-lin's Classic of Filial Piety*. New York: Metropolitan Museum of Art, 1993.

Barthes, Roland. 1957. "Dominici, or the Triumph of Literature." In *The Cultural Studies Reader*, edited by Simon During, 44–48. London: Routledge, 1993.

Beijingshi wenwu gongzuodui 北京市文物工作隊. "Beijingshi faxian de jizuo Tang mu" 北京市發現的幾座唐墓. *Kaogu* 6 (1980): 498–505, plate 9.

———. "Beijingshi Daxingxian Liaodai Ma Zhiwen fuqi hezang mu" 北京市大興縣遼代馬直溫夫妻合葬墓. *Wenwu* 12 (1980): 30–37.

Bell, Catherine. *Ritual Theory, Ritual Practice.* New York: Oxford University Press, 1992.

———. *Ritual: Perspectives and Dimensions.* New York: Oxford University Press, 1997.

Bieg, Lutz. "Huang T'ing-chien." In *Sung Biographies,* edited by Herbert Franke, 454–61. Wiesbaden, Germany: Franz Steiner Verlag, 1976.

Birge, Bettine. "Levirate Marriage and the Rise of Widow Chastity in Yüan China." *Asia Major* 8, no. 2 (1995): 107–46.

———. *Women, Property, and Confucian Reaction in Sung and Yüan China (960–1368).* Cambridge: Cambridge University Press, 2002.

———. "Women and Confucianism from Song to Ming: The Institutionalization of Patrilineality." In *The Song-Yuan-Ming Transition in Chinese History,* edited by Paul Smith and Richard von Glahn, 212–40. Cambridge, MA: Harvard University Asia Center, 2003.

Blum, Susan D. "Ethnic Diversity in Southwest China: Perceptions of Self and Other." *Ethnic Groups* 9, no. 4 (1992): 267–79.

Bol, Peter K. *"This Culture of Ours": Intellectual Transitions in T'ang and Sung China.* Stanford: Stanford University Press, 1992.

———. "A Literary Miscellany and Sung Intellectual History: The Case of Chang Lei's *Ming-tao tsa-chih.*" *Journal of Sung-Yuan Studies* 25 (1995): 121–51.

———. "Intellectual Culture in Wuzhou ca. 1200: Finding a Place for Pan Zimu and the *Complete Source for Composition.*" In *Proceedings of the Second Symposium on Sung History,* edited by Sung Shee, 1–51. Taipei: National Culture University, 1996.

———. "Examinations and Orthodoxies: 1070 and 1313 Compared." In *Culture and State in Chinese History: Conventions, Accommodations, and Critiques,* edited by Theodore Huters, R. Bin Wong, and Pauline Yu, 29–57. Stanford: Stanford University Press, 1997.

———. "The Rise of Local History: History, Geography, and Culture in Southern Song and Yuan Wuzhou." *Harvard Journal of Asiatic Studies* 61, no. 1 (June 2001): 37–76.

———. "Neo-Confucianism and Local Society, Twelfth to Sixteenth Century: A Case Study." In *The Song-Yuan-Ming Transition in Chinese History,* edited by Paul J. Smith and Richard von Glahn 241–83. Cambridge, MA: Harvard University Asia Center, 2003.

Bossler, Beverly J. *Powerful Relations: Kinship, Status, and the State in Sung China (960–1279).* Cambridge, MA: Council on East Asian Studies, Harvard University, 1998.

Bourdieu, Pierre. 1972. *Outline of a Theory of Practice.* Translated by Richard Nice. Cambridge: Cambridge University Press, 1977.

———. 1979. *Distinction: A Social Critique of the Judgement of Taste.* Translated by Richard Nice. Cambridge, MA: Harvard University Press, 1984.

———. 1980. *The Logic of Practice.* Translated by Richard Nice. Stanford: Stanford University Press, 1990.

———. *Language and Symbolic Power.* Edited by John B. Thompson. Translated by Gino Raymond and Matthew Adamson. Cambridge, MA: Harvard University Press, 1991.

Bray, Francesca. *Technology and Gender: Fabrics of Power in Late Imperial China.* Berkeley: University of California Press, 1997.

Cai, Weitang 蔡偉堂. "Guanyu Dunhuang bihua 'hunlitu' de jige wenti" 關於敦煌壁畫〈婚禮圖〉的幾個問題. *Dunhuang yanjiu* 1 (1990): 54–59.

Campany, Robert F. *Strange Writing: Anomaly Accounts in Early Medieval China.* Albany: State University of New York Press, 1996.

Chaffee, John W. 1985. *The Thorny Gates of Learning in Sung China: A Social History of Examinations.* New ed. Albany: State University of New York Press, 1995.

Chan, Wing-tsit. *A Sourcebook in Chinese Philosophy.* Princeton, NJ: Princeton University Press, 1963.

Chang, H. C. *Chinese Literature: Popular Fiction and Drama.* Edinburgh: Edinburgh University Press, 1973.

Changzhishi bowuguan 長治市博物館. "Shanxi Changzhishi Tangdai Feng Kuo mu" 山西長治市唐代馮廓墓. *Wenwu* 6 (1989): 51–57.

Chaoyang diqu bowuguan 朝陽地區博物館. "Liaoning Chaoyang Tang Han Zhen mu" 遼寧朝陽唐韓貞墓. *Kaogu* 6 (1973): 356–61, plates 11–12.

Chartier, Roger. "Texts, Printing, Readings." In *The New Cultural History*, edited by Lynn Hunt, 154–75. Berkeley: University of California Press, 1989.

———. 1992. *The Order of Books: Readers, Authors, and Libraries in Europe between the Fourteenth and Eighteenth Centuries.* Translated by Lydia G. Cochrane. Stanford: Stanford University Press, 1994.

———. *On the Edge of the Cliff: History, Language, and Practices.* Translated by Lydia G. Cochrane. Baltimore: Johns Hopkins University Press, 1997.

Chen, Boquan 陳柏泉. "Jiangxi chutu diquan zongshu" 江西出土地券綜述. *Kaogu* 3 (1987): 223–31, 219.

Chen, Dingrong 陳定榮, and Xu Jianchang 徐建昌. "Jiangxi Linchuanxian Song mu" 江西臨川縣宋墓. *Kaogu* 4 (1988): 329–34, plates 3–4.

Chen, Dongyuan 陳東原. 1937. *Zhongguo funü shenghuo shi* 中國婦女生活史. Taipei: Taiwan Commercial Press, 1994.

Chen, Guyuan 陳顧遠. 1936. *Zhongguo hunyin shi* 中國婚姻史. Taipei: Taiwan Commercial Press, 1992.

Chen, Peng 陳鵬. *Zhongguo hunyin shi gao* 中國婚姻史稿. Beijing: Zhonghua shuju, 1990.

Chen, Zhichao 陳智超. "Songshi yanjiu de zhengui shiliao: Ming keben *Minggong shupan qingmingji* jieshao" 宋史研究的珍貴史料：明刻本《名公書判清明集》介紹. In QMJ (1987): 645–86.

Ch'en, Paul. *Chinese Legal Tradition under the Mongols: The Code of 1291 as Reconstructed.* Princeton, NJ: Princeton University Press, 1979.

Cheng, Changxin 程長新, Wang Wenchang 王文昶, and Cheng Ruixiu 程瑞秀. "Tongqi bianwei qianshuo" 銅器辨僞淺說. *Wenwu* 8 (1989): 36–43, plates 6–8; 11 (1989): 28–38, plates 7–8; 12 (1989): 40–47, plate 6.

Cheng, Jihong 程霽紅. "Anhui Wangjiang faxian yizuo Bei Song mu" 安徽望江發現一座北宋墓. *Kaogu* 2 (1993): 141–43, plates 5–8.

Cherniack, Susan. "Book Culture and Textual Transmission in Sung China." *Harvard Journal of Asiatic Studies* 54, no. 1 (June 1994): 5–125.

Chia, Lucille. "The Development of the Jianyang Book Trade, Song-Yuan." *Late Imperial China* 17, no. 1 (June 1996): 10–48.

———. *Printing for Profit: The Commercial Publishers of Jianyang, Fujian (11th–17th Centuries).* Cambridge, MA: Harvard University Asia Center for the Harvard-Yenching Institute, 2002.

Chikusa, Masaaki. "Ch'ung-hsiu Hsüan-ho Po ku t'u lu ('Drawings and Lists of all the antiquities known at the Hsüan-ho period. Rev. ed.)." In *A Sung Bibliography*, edited by Étienne Balazs and Yves Hervouet, 200–01. Hong Kong: Chinese University Press, 1978.

Chongqingshi bowuguan 重慶市博物館. "Sichuan Chongqing Ming Yuzhen mu" 四川重慶明玉珍墓. *Kaogu* 9 (1986): 827–33, plate 8.

Chongqingshi bowuguan lishizu 重慶市博物館歷史組. "Chongqing Jingkou Song mu qingli jianbao" 重慶井口宋墓清理簡報. *Wenwu* 11 (1961): 53–60, plates 7–8.

Chow, Kai-wing. "Ritual, Cosmology, and Ontology: Chang Tsai's Moral Philosophy and Neo-Confucian Ethics." *Philosophy East and West* 43, no. 2 (1993): 201–28.

Chu, Hui-liang J. "The Calligraphy of Li Kung-lin in the *Classic of Filial Piety*." In *Li Kung-lin's Classic of Filial Piety*, edited by Richard M. Barnhart, 53–71. New York: Metropolitan Museum of Art, 1993.

Clunas, Craig. *Superfluous Things: Material Culture and Social Status in Early Modern China.* Urbana and Chicago: University of Illinois Press, 1991.

———. *Art in China.* Oxford: Oxford University Press, 1997.

Cohen, Paul A. *Discovering History in China: American Historical Writing on the Recent Chinese Past.* New York: Columbia University Press, 1984.

———. *China Unbound: Evolving Perspectives on the Chinese Past.* London: RoutledgeCurzon, 2003.

Comaroff, John, and Jean Comaroff. *Ethnography and the Historical Imagination.* Boulder: Westview Press, 1992.

Connerton, Paul. *How Societies Remember.* Cambridge: Cambridge University Press, 1989.

Dai, Zunde 戴尊德. "Sima Guang zhuan Wei Xian muzhi zhi yanjiu" 司馬光撰魏閑墓志之研究. *Wenwu* 12 (1990): 83–85.

Dardess, John W. "Did the Mongols Matter? Territory, Power, and the Intelligentsia in China, from the Northern Song to the Early Ming." In *The Song-Yuan-Ming Transition in Chinese History*, edited by Paul J. Smith and Richard von Glahn, 111–34. Cambridge, MA: Harvard University Asia Center, 2003.

Datongshi bowuguan 大同市博物館. "Datong Jindai Yan Deyuan mu fajue jianbao" 大同金代閻德原墓發掘簡報. *Wenwu* 4 (1978): 1–13, plates 1–2.

Davis, Natalie Zemon. *Society and Culture in Early Modern France*. Stanford: Stanford University Press, 1975.

Davis, Richard. Review of *The Inner Quarters*, by Patricia Ebrey. *American Historical Review* 99, no. 5 (December 1994): 1735–6.

de Bary, Wm. Theodore, and Irene Bloom, eds. *Sources of Chinese Tradition*, 2nd ed., Vol. 1. New York: Columbia University Press, 1999.

de Certeau, Michel. *The Practice of Everyday Life*. Translated by Steven Randall. Berkeley: University of California Press, 1984.

———. *The Writing of History*. Translated by Tom Conley. New York: Columbia University Press, 1988.

Deng, Wenkuan 鄧文寬. *Dunhuang tianwen lifa wenxian jijiao* 敦煌天文曆法文獻輯校. Nanjing: Jiangsu guji chubanshe, 1996.

———. "Dunhuang ben *Tang Qianfu sinian dingyou sui (877 nian) juzhu liri* 'zazhan' bulu" 敦煌本《唐乾符四年丁酉歲877年具注曆日》〈雜占〉補錄. In *Dunhuangxue yu Zhongguo shi yanjiu lunji: jinian Sun Xiushen xiansheng shishi yi zhounian* 敦煌學與中國史研究論集：紀念孫修身先生逝世一周年, edited by Duan Wenjie 段文傑 and Mao Muya 茂木雅, 135–45. Lanzhou: Gansu renmin chubanshe, 2001.

Deng, Ziqin 鄧子琴. *Zhongguo fengsu shi* 中國風俗史. Chengdu: Ba Shu shushe, 1988.

de Pee, Christian. "Cases of the New Terrace: Canon and Law in Three Southern Song Verdicts." *Journal of Sung-Yuan Studies* 27 (1997): 27–57.

———. "Premodern Chinese Weddings and the Divorce of Past and Present." *positions: east asia cultures critique* 9, no. 3 (Winter 2001): 559–84.

———. "Material Ambiguity and the Hermetic Text: Cities, Tombs, and Middle-Period History." *Journal of Song-Yuan Studies* 34 (2004): 81–94.

de Weerdt, Hilde. "Aspects of Song Intellectual Life: A Preliminary Inquiry into Some Southern Song Encyclopedias." *Papers on Chinese History* 3 (Spring 1994): 1–27.

———. "The Composition of Examination Standards: *Daoxue* and Southern Song Dynasty Examination Culture." PhD diss., Harvard University, 1998.

Dexingxian bowuguan 德興縣博物館. "Jiangxi Dexingxian Xiangtun Song mu" 江西德興縣香屯宋墓. *Kaogu* 8 (1990): 737–40, plates 5–6.

di Leonardo, Micaela. *Exotics at Home: Anthropologies, Others, American Modernity*. Chicago: University of Chicago Press, 1998.

Dong, Jiazun 董家遵. *Zhongguo gudai hunyin shi yanjiu* 中國古代婚姻史研究. Fanyu: Guangdong renmin chubanshe, 1995.

Douglas, Mary. *Purity and Danger: An Analysis of Concepts of Pollution and Taboo.* New York: Frederick A. Praeger, 1966.

Duan, Pengqi 段鵬琦. 1993. "Woguo gu muzang zhong faxian de xiaoti tuxiang" 我國古墓葬中發現的孝悌圖象. In *Zhongguo kaoguxue luncong* 中國考古學論叢, edited by Zhongguo shehui kexueyuan kaogu yanjiusuo 中國社會科學院考古研究所, 463–73. Beijing: Kexue chubanshe, 1995.

Duara, Prasenjit. *Rescuing History from the Nation: Questioning Narratives of Modern China.* Chicago: University of Chicago Press, 1995.

Eberhard, Wolfram. "Auspicious Marriages: A Statistical Study of a Chinese Custom." *Sociologus* 13, no. 1: 49–55.

———. 1983. *A Dictionary of Chinese Symbols.* Taipei: SMC Publishing, 1994.

Ebner von Eschenbach, Silvia Freiin. *Die Sorge der Lebenden um die Toten: Thanatopraxis und Thanatologie in der Song-Zeit (960–1279).* Heidelberg, Germany: Edition Forum, 1995.

Ebrey, Patricia B. *The Aristocratic Families of Early Imperial China: A Case Study of the Po-ling Ts'ui Family.* Cambridge: Cambridge University Press, 1978.

———. *Family and Property: Yüan Ts'ai's Precepts for Social Life.* Princeton, NJ: Princeton University Press, 1984.

———. "T'ang Guides to Verbal Etiquette." *Harvard Journal of Asiatic Studies* 45, no. 2 (December 1985): 581–613.

———. "Education through Ritual: Efforts to Formulate Family Rituals during the Sung Period." In *Neo-Confucian Education*, edited by Wm. Theodore de Bary and John W. Chaffee, 277–306. Berkeley: University of California Press, 1989.

———, trans. *Chu Hsi's* Family Rituals: *A Twelfth-Century Chinese Manual for the Performance of Cappings, Weddings, Funerals, and Ancestral Rites.* Princeton, NJ: Princeton University Press, 1991a.

———. *Confucianism and Family Rituals in Imperial China: A Social History of Writing About Rites.* Princeton, NJ: Princeton University Press, 1991b.

———. "Shifts in Marriage Finance from the Sixth to the Thirteenth Centuries." In *Marriage and Inequality in Chinese Society*, edited by Rubie S. Watson and Patricia B. Ebrey, 97–132. Berkeley: University of California Press, 1991.

———. *The Inner Quarters: Marriage and the Lives of Chinese Women in the Sung Period.* Berkeley: University of California Press, 1993.

———. "The Liturgies for Sacrifices to Ancestors in Successive Versions of the *Family Rituals.*" In *Ritual and Scripture in Chinese Popular Religion: Five Studies*, edited by David Johnson, 104–36. Berkeley: Publications of the Chinese Popular Culture Project, 1995.

Ebrey, Patricia B., and James L. Watson, eds. *Kinship Organization in Late Imperial China, 1000–1940.* Berkeley: University of California Press, 1986.

Egan, Ronald C. "Ou-yang Hsiu and Su Shih on Calligraphy." *Harvard Journal of Asiatic Studies* 49, no. 2 (December 1989): 365–419.

———. *Word, Image, and Deed in the Life of Su Shi.* Cambridge, MA: Council on East Asian Studies, Harvard University, 1994.

Elman, Benjamin A. *A Cultural History of Civil Examinations in Late Imperial China.* Berkeley: University of California Press, 2000.

Endicott-West, Elizabeth. *Mongolian Rule in China: Local Administration in the Yuan Dynasty.* Cambridge, MA: Harvard University Press, 1989.

Erickson, Susan N. "Investing in the Antique: Bronze Vessels of the Song Dynasty (960–1279)." In *Die Gegenwart des Altertums*, edited by Dieter Kuhn and Helga Stahl, 423–35. Heidelberg, Germany: Edition Forum, 2001.

Evasdottir, Erika E. S. *Obedient Autonomy: Chinese Intellectuals and the Achievement of Orderly Life.* Vancouver, BC: University of British Columbia Press, 2004.

Fang, Jianxin 方建新. "Songdai hunyin lisu kaoshu" 宋代婚姻禮俗考述. *Wenshi* 24 (April 1985): 157–78.

Farquhar, David M. "Structure and Function in the Yüan Imperial Government." In *China Under Mongol Rule*, edited by John D. Langlois, Jr., 25–55. Princeton, NJ: Princeton University Press, 1981.

Farquhar, Judith. "Objects, Processes, and Female Infertility in Chinese Medicine." *Medical Anthropology Quarterly*, n.s., 5, no. 4 (December 1991): 370–99.

———. *Knowing Practice: The Clinical Encounter of Chinese Medicine.* Boulder, CO: Westview Press, 1994.

Farquhar, Judith, and James Hevia. "Culture and Postwar American Historiography of China." *positions: east asia cultures critique* 1, no. 2 (Fall 1993): 487–525.

Feng, Hanji 馮漢驥. *Qian Shu Wang Jian mu fajue baogao* 前蜀王建墓發掘報告. Beijing: Wenwu chubanshe, 2002.

Feng, Jiren 馮繼仁. "Gongxian Song ling xiandian de fuyuan gouxiang" 鞏縣宋陵獻殿的復原構想. *Wenwu* 6 (1992): 63–71.

———. "Lun yinyang kanyu dui Bei Song huangling de quanmian yingxiang" 論陰陽勘輿對北宋皇陵的全面影響. *Wenwu* 8 (1994): 55–68.

Feng, Puren 馮普仁. "Wuxishi Xihuiqiao Bei Song mu" 無錫市錫惠橋北宋墓. *Kaogu* 12 (1986): 1140–1.

Foucault, Michel. 1969, 1971. *The Archaeology of Knowledge, and the Discourse on Language.* Translated by A. M. Sheridan Smith. New York: Pantheon Books, 1972.

Franke, Herbert. "Jurchen Customary Law and the Chinese Law of the Chin Dynasty." In *State and Law in East Asia: Festschrift für Karl Bünger*, edited by D. Eikemeier and H. Franke, 215–33. Wiesbaden, Germany: Otto Harrassowitz, 1981.

Freedman, Maurice. 1967. *The Study of Chinese Society: Essays by Maurice Freedman.* Edited by G. William Skinner. Stanford: Stanford University Press, 1979.

Fu, Xinian. "The Sui, Tang, and Five Dynasties." In *Chinese Architecture*, edited by Nancy S. Steinhardt, 90–133. New Haven, CT: Yale University Press, 2002.

Fujiansheng bowuguan 福建省博物館. *Fuzhou Nan Song Huang Sheng mu* 福州南宋黃昇墓. Beijing: Wenwu chubanshe, 1982.

Fujiansheng bowuguan 福建省博物館 and Sanmingshi wenguanhui 三明市文管會. "Fujian Sanmingshi Yanqiancun Songdai bihua mu" 福建三明市巖前村宋代壁畫墓. *Kaogu* 10 (1995): 909–14.

Fujiansheng bowuguan 福建省博物館, Youxixian wenguanhui 尤溪縣文管會, and Youxixian bowuguan 尤溪縣博物館. "Fujian Youxi chengguan Songdai bihua mu" 福建尤溪城關宋代壁畫墓. *Wenwu* 4 (1988): 71–5.

Fujieda, Akira 藤枝晃. "Tonkō rekijitsu fu" 敦煌曆日譜. *Tōhō gakuhō* 45 (September 1973): 377–441.

Furth, Charlotte. "Blood, Body, and Gender: Medical Images of the Female Condition in China, 1600–1850." *Chinese Science* 7 (1986): 43–66.

———. "Rethinking Van Gulik: Sexuality and Reproduction in Traditional Chinese Medicine." In *Engendering China: Women, Culture, and the State*, edited by Christina K. Gilmartin, Gail Hershatter, Lisa Rofel, and Tyrene White, 125–46. Cambridge, MA: Harvard University Press, 1994.

———. *A Flourishing Yin: Gender in China's Medical History, 960–1665.* Berkeley: University of California Press, 1999.

Furth, Charlotte, and Ch'en Shu-yueh. "Chinese Medicine and the Anthropology of Menstruation in Contemporary Taiwan." *Medical Anthropology Quarterly*, n.s., 6, no. 1 (March 1992): 27–48.

Gadamer, Hans-Georg. 1986, 1960. *Truth and Method*, 2nd ed. Translated by Joel Weinsheimer and Donald G. Marshall. New York: Continuum, 1989.

Gan, Huaizhen 甘懷真. *Tangdai jiamiao lizhi yanjiu* 唐代家廟禮制研究. Taipei: Taiwan Commercial Press, 1991.

Gansusheng bowuguan 甘肅省博物館 and Zhangxian wenhuaguan 漳縣文化館. "Gansu Zhangxian Yuandai Wang Shixian jiazu muzang: jianbao zhi yi" 甘肅漳縣元代汪世顯家族墓葬：簡報之一. *Wenwu* 2 (1982): 1–12, plates 1–2.

Gao, Guofan 高國藩. *Dunhuang minsu xue* 敦煌民俗學. Shanghai: Shanghai wenyi chubanshe, 1989.

Gou, Renmin 苟人民. *Jin Yuan suqu* 金元俗趣. Beijing: Beijing shifan daxue chubanshe, 1993.

Graham, Angus C. *Disputers of the Tao: Philosophical Argument in Ancient China.* La Salle, IL: Open Court, 1989.

———. 1958. *Two Chinese Philosophers: The Metaphysics of the Brothers Ch'eng.* La Salle, IL: Open Court, 1992.

Granet, Marcel. *Fêtes et chansons anciennes de la Chine.* Paris: Ernest Leroux, 1919.

———. *Catégories matrimoniales et relations de proximité dans la Chine ancienne.* Paris: Librairie Félix Alcan, 1939.

———. *Études sociologiques sur la Chine.* Edited by Louis Gernet and R.-A. Stein. Paris: Presses Universitaires de France, 1953.

———. 1922. *The Religion of the Chinese People.* Edited and translated by Maurice Freedman. New York: Harper and Row, 1975.

———. 1926. *Danses et légendes de la Chine ancienne.* Edited by Rémi Mathieu. Paris: Presses Universitaires de France, 1994.

Gravdal, Kathryn L. *Ravishing Maidens: Writing Rape in Medieval French Literature.* Philadelphia: University of Pennsylvania Press, 1991.

Guo, Daineng. "The Liao, Song, Xi Xia, and Jin Dynasties." In *Chinese Architecture*, edited by Nancy S. Steinhardt, 134–97. New Haven, CT: Yale University Press, 2002.

Guo, Xingwen 郭興文. *Zhongguo chuantong hunyin fengsu* 中國傳統婚姻風俗. Xi'an: Shaanxi renmin chubanshe, 1994.

Han, Guoxiang 韓國祥. "Chaoyang Xishangtai Liao mu" 朝陽西上台遼墓. *Wenwu* 7 (2000): 50–64.

Hanan, Patrick. *The Chinese Short Story: Studies in Dating, Authorship, and Composition.* Cambridge, MA: Harvard University Press, 1973.

Handanshi wenguansuo 邯鄲市文管所. "Hebei Damingxian faxian He Hongjing muzhi" 河北大名縣發現何弘敬墓志. *Kaogu* 8 (1984): 721–25, 729.

Hangzhoushi wenwu kaogusuo 杭州市文物考古所 and Lin'anshi wenwuguan 臨安市文物館. "Zhejiang Lin'an Wudai Wuyueguo Kangling fajue jianbao" 浙江臨安五代吳越國康陵發掘簡報. *Wenwu* 2 (2000): 4–34, 4 plates.

Hanks, William F. *Intertexts: Writings on Language, Utterance, and Context.* Lanham: Rowman and Littlefield, 2000.

Hansen, Valerie. *Changing Gods in Medieval China, 1127–1276.* Princeton, NJ: Princeton University Press, 1990.

———. *Negotiating Daily Life in Traditional China: How Ordinary People Used Contracts, 600–1400.* New Haven, CT: Yale University Press, 1995.

Hargett, James M. "Song Dynasty Local Gazetteers and Their Place in the History of *Difangzhi* Writing." *Harvard Journal of Asiatic Studies* 56, no. 2 (December 1996): 405–42.

Harrell, Stevan, and Sara A. Dickey. "Dowry Systems in Complex Societies." *Ethnology* 24, no. 2 (April 1985): 105–20.

Harrist, Robert E. "The Hermit of Lung-mien: A Biography of Li Kung-lin." In *Li Kung-lin's Classic of Filial Piety*, edited by Richard M. Barnhart, 31–51. New York: Metropolitan Museum of Art, 1993.

———. "The Artist as Antiquarian: Li Gonglin and His Study of Early Chinese Art." *Artibus Asiae* 55, 3–4 (1995): 237–80.

———. "Art and Identity in the Northern Sung Dynasty: Evidence from Gardens." In *Arts of the Sung and Yüan*, edited by Maxwell K. Hearn and Judith G. Smith, 147–63. New York: Metropolitan Museum of Art, 1996.

Hartwell, Robert M. "Demographic, Political, and Social Transformations of China, 750–1550." *Harvard Journal of Asiatic Studies* 42, no. 2 (December 1982): 365–442.

Hawkes, David. "The Quest of the Goddess." In *Studies in Chinese Literary Genres*, edited by Cyril Birch 42–68. Berkeley: University of California Press, 1974.

Hearn, Maxwell K., and Judith G. Smith, eds. *Arts of the Sung and Yüan*. New York: Metropolitan Museum of Art, 1996.

Hebeisheng wenwu yanjiusuo 河北省文物研究所. *Xuanhua Liao mu: 1974–1993 nian kaogu fajue baogao* 宣化遼墓：1974–1993 年考古發掘報告, 2 vols. Beijing: Wenwu chubanshe, 2001.

Henansheng wenwu kaogu yanjiusuo 河南省文物考古研究所. *Bei Song huangling* 北宋皇陵. Zhengzhou: Zhongzhou guji chubanshe, 1997.

Hevia, James. *Cherishing Men from Afar: Qing Guest Ritual and the Macartney Embassy of 1793*. Durham, NC: Duke University Press, 1995.

Hightower, James. "Some Characteristics of Parallel Prose." In *Studies in Chinese Literature*, 108–39. Cambridge, MA: Harvard University Press, 1965.

Ho, Ping-ti. *The Ladder of Success in Imperial China: Aspects of Social Mobility, 1368–1911*. New York: Columbia University Press, 1962.

Hodder, Ian. 1986. *Reading the Past: Current Approaches to Interpretation in Archaeology*, 2nd ed. Cambridge: Cambridge University Press, 1991.

Hodder, Ian, ed. *The Meanings of Things: Material Culture and Symbolic Expression*. London: Unwin Hyman, 1989.

Huang, Philip C. C. "The Paradigmatic Crisis in Chinese Studies: Paradoxes in Social and Economic History." *Modern China* 17, no. 3 (July 1991): 299–341.

Huang, Shijian 黃時鑑. "Dianjiao shuoming" 點校說明. In TZTG, 1986, 1–5.

———. "*Da Yuan tongzhi* kaobian" 大元通制考辨. In YDFLZL, 1988, 253–78.

Huang, Zhengjian 黃正建. *Dunhuang zhanbu wenshu yu Tang-Wudai zhanbu yanjiu* 敦煌占卜文書與唐五代占卜研究. Beijing: Xueyuan chubanshe, 2001.

Hymes, Robert P. *Statesmen and Gentlemen: The Elite of Fu-chou, Chiang-hsi, in Northern and Southern Sung*. Cambridge: Cambridge University Press, 1986.

———. "Truth, Falsity, and Pretense in Sung China: An Approach through the Stories of Hung Mai." Unpublished paper, 1997.

Idema, Wilt L. *Chinese Vernacular Fiction: The Formative Period*. Leiden, Netherlands: E. J. Brill, 1974.

———. Review of *Education and Popular Literacy in Ch'ing China*, by Evelyn S. Rawski. *T'oung Pao* 66, 4–5 (1980): 314–24.

———. "Satire and Allegory in All Keys and Modes." In *China Under Jürchen Rule*, edited by Hoyt C. Tillman and Stephen H. West, 238–280. Albany: State University of New York Press, 1995.

Idema, Wilt L., and Lloyd Haft. *Chinese letterkunde: Inleiding, historisch overzicht en bibliografieën*. Utrecht and Antwerpen: Uitgeverij Het Spectrum, 1985.

Ikeda, On 池田溫. "*Dai Tō Kaigen rei* kaisetsu" 大唐開元禮解說. In *KYL*, 1972, 822–32.

Illich, Ivan. *In the Vineyard of the Text: A Commentary to Hugh's Didascalicon*. Chicago: University of Chicago Press, 1993.

Inaba, Ichiro. "Kung-shih hsien-sheng ch'i-ching hsiao-chuan ('Short Commentaries on the Seven Classics, by Master Kung-shih'), by Liu Ch'ang." In *A Sung Bibliography*, edited by Étienne Balazs and Yves Hervouet, 49. Hong Kong: Chinese University Press, 1978.

Jay, Jennifer. "Prefaces, Jottings, and Legal Proceedings on Women in Thirteenth-Century South China." *Chinese Culture* 32, no. 4 (December 1991): 41–56.

Jensen, Lionel M. *Manufacturing Confucianism: Chinese Traditions and Universal Civilization*. Durham, NC: Duke University Press, 1997.

Ji, Guang 紀光. "Renzhen xuexi, qieshi zhixing: Zhongguo shehui kexue yuan kaogu yanjiusuo zuotan wenwu baohu fa" 認真學習, 切實執行：中國社會科學院考古研究所座談文物保護法. *Kaogu* 4 (1983): 384.

Jiang, Jusong 江菊松. *Song siliuwen yanjiu* 宋四六文研究. Taipei: Huazheng shuju, 1977.

Jiangxisheng wenwu gongzuodui 江西省文物工作隊 and Nanfengxian bowuguan 南豐縣博物館. "Jiangxi Nanfengxian Sangtian Song mu" 江西南豐縣桑田宋墓. *Kaogu* 4 (1988): 318–28, plates 1–2.

Jiangxisheng wenwu kaogu yanjiusuo 江西省文物考古研究所 and De'anxian bowuguan 德安縣博物館. "Jiangxi De'an Nan Song Zhoushi mu qingli jianbao" 江西德安南宋周氏墓清理簡報. *Wenwu* 9 (1990): 1–13, 3 plates.

Jin, Juxiang 金秬香. *Pianwen gailun* 駢文概論. Taipei: Taiwan Commercial Press, 1965.

Jin, Zhongshu 金中樞. 1983. "Songdai de jingxue dangdaihua chutan: Nie Chongyi de *Sanli tu* xue" 宋代的經學當代化初探：聶崇義的《三禮圖》學. *Songshi yanjiu ji* 24 (1995): 1–37.

Ji'nanshi wenhuaju wenwuchu 濟南市文化局文物處 and Changqingxian bowuguan 長清縣博物館. "Shandong Changqingxian Songdai Zhenxiangyuan Shijiashelita digong" 山東長清縣宋代真相院釋迦舍利塔地宮. *Kaogu* 3 (1991): 217–23, plates 2–3.

Johnson, Dale. *Yuarn Music Dramas: Studies in Prosody and Structure and a Complete Catalogue of Northern Arias in the Dramatic Style*. Ann Arbor: Center for Chinese Studies, University of Michigan, 1980.

Johnson, David. *The Medieval Chinese Oligarchy*. Boulder, CO: Westview, 1977.

Kalinowski, Marc. "Les instruments astro-calendériques des Han et la méthode *liu ren*." *Bulletin de l'École Française d'Extrême Orient* 72 (1983): 309–419.

———. "La littérature divinatoire dans le *Daozang*." *Cahiers d'Extrême Asie* 5 (1989–1990): 85–114.

———. "La divination par les nombres dans les manuscrits de Dunhuang." In *Nombres, astres, plantes et viscères: sept essais sur l'histoire des sciences et des techniques en Asie orientale*, edited by Isabelle Ang and Pierre-Étienne Will, 37–88. Paris: Collège de France, Institut des Hautes Études Chinoises, 1994.

Kao, Karl S. Y., ed. *Classical Chinese Tales of the Supernatural and the Fantastic: Selections from the Third to the Tenth Century.* Bloomington: Indiana University Press, 1985.

Karlgren, Bernard. "Some Fecundity Symbols in Ancient China." *Bulletin of the Museum of Far Eastern Antiquities* 2 (1930): 1–65.

———. *The Book of Odes.* Stockholm, Sweden: Museum of Far Eastern Antiquities, 1950.

Ke, Dake 柯大課. *Zhongguo Song, Liao, Jin, Xia xisu shi* 中國宋遼金夏習俗史. Beijing: Renmin chubanshe, 1994.

Kern, Martin. *Die Hymnen der chinesischen Staatsopfer: Literatur und Ritual in der politischen Repräsentation von der Han-Zeit bis zu den Sechs Dynastien.* Stuttgart, Germany: Franz Steiner Verlag, 1997.

Klapisch-Zuber, Christiane. *Women, Family, and Ritual in Renaissance Italy.* Translated by Lydia Cochrane. Chicago: University of Chicago Press, 1985.

Kopytoff, Igor. "The Cultural Biography of Things: Commoditization as Process." In *The Social Life of Things,* edited by Arjun Appadurai, 64–91. Cambridge: Cambridge University Press, 1986.

Kracke, E. A. *Civil Service in Early Sung China.* Cambridge: Cambridge University Press, 1953.

Kuhn, Dieter. *A Place for the Dead: An Archaeological Documentary on Graves and Tombs of the Song Dynasty (960–1279).* Heidelberg, Germany: Edition Forum, 1996.

Kuhn, Dieter, ed. *Burial in Song China.* Heidelberg, Germany: Edition Forum, 1994.

Kuhn, Dieter, and Helga Stahl, eds. *Die Gegenwart des Altertums: Formen und Funktionen des Altertumsbezug in den Hochkulturen der Alten Welt.* Heidelberg, Germany: Edition Forum, 2001.

LaCapra, Dominick. *History and Reading: Tocqueville, Foucault, French Studies.* Toronto: University of Toronto Press, 2000.

Lam, Joseph S. C. "Musical Relics and Cultural Expressions: State Sacrificial Songs from the Southern Song Court." *Journal of Sung-Yuan Studies* 25 (1995): 1–27.

Langley, Bradford. "*P'ien-wen.*" In *The Indiana Companion,* edited by William H. Nienhauser, Charles Hartman, Y. W. Ma, and Stephen H. West, 656–60. Bloomington: Indiana University Press, 1986.

Langlois, John D. Jr. "'Living Law' in Sung and Yüan Jurisprudence." *Harvard Journal of Asiatic Studies* 41, no. 1 (June 1981): 165–217.

Ledderose, Lothar. *Ten Thousand Things: Module and Mass Production in Chinese Art.* Princeton, NJ: Princeton University Press, 2000.

Legge, James, trans. 1885. *Li Chi: Book of Rites.* 2 vols. New Hyde Park, NY: University Books, 1967.

———. 1893. *The Four Books.* Taipei: Wenhua tushu, 1985.

———. 1872. *The Chinese Classics.* Taipei: SMC Publishing, 1994.

Leung, Angela Ki-che. "Women Practicing Medicine in Premodern China." In *Chinese Women in the Imperial Past: New Perspectives*, edited by Harriet T. Zurndorfer, 101–34. Leiden, Netherlands: E. J. Brill, 1999.

———. "Medical Learning from the Song to the Ming." In *The Song-Yuan-Ming Transition in Chinese History*, edited by Paul J. Smith and Richard von Glahn, 374–98. Cambridge, MA: Harvard University Asia Center, 2003.

Lévi, Jean. "Les fonctionnaires et le divin: Luttes de pouvoirs entre divinités et administrateurs dans les contes des Six Dynasties et des Tang." *Cahiers d'Extrême Asie* 2 (1986): 81–110.

Levy, Howard S. 1974. *Chinese Sex Jokes in Traditional Times*. Folklore and Folkliterature Series, vol. 58. Taipei: Chinese Association for Folklore, 1974.

Li, Shaolian 李紹連. "Song Su Kuo muzhi ji qita" 宋蘇适墓志及其他. *Wenwu* 7 (1973): 63–69.

Li, Xiaodong 李曉東. *Zhongguo fengjian jiali* 中國封建家禮. Xi'an: Shaanxi renmin chubanshe, 1986.

Li, Yiyou 李逸友. "Heicheng chutu de Yuandai hetong hunshu" 黑城出土的元代合同婚書. *Wenwu tiandi* 2 (1992): 30–31.

Li, Yufeng 李宇峰. "Liaoning Chaoyangxian faxian Liaodai Zhang Rang muzhi" 遼寧朝陽縣發現遼代張讓墓志. *Kaogu* 5 (1984): 480.

Liao, Ben 廖奔. "Song, Liao, Jin fangmu jiegou zhuandiao mu ji qi yuewu zhuangshi" 宋遼金仿木結構磚雕墓及其樂舞裝飾. *Wenwu* 5 (2000): 81–7.

Liaoningsheng bowuguan 遼寧省博物館 and Liaoning Tieling diqu wenwuzu fajue xiaozu 遼寧鐵嶺地區文物組發掘小組. "Faku Yemaotai Liao mu jilüe" 法庫葉茂台遼墓記略. *Wenwu* 12 (1975): 26–36, plates 1–4.

Lin, Chunmei 林春梅. *Songdai jiali, jiaxun de yanjiu* 宋代家禮, 家訓的研究. Master's thesis, Furen University, 1991.

Linck, Gudula. *Zur Sozialgeschichte der chinesischen Familie im 13. Jahrhundert: Untersuchungen am Ming-gong shu-pan qing-ming ji*. Stuttgart, Germany: Franz Steiner Verlag, 1986.

Linyixian bowuguan 臨猗縣博物館. "Shanxi Linyi Shuangtasi Bei Song taji digong qingli jianbao" 山西臨猗雙塔寺北宋塔基地宮清理簡報. *Wenwu* 3 (1997): 35–53, plate 2.

Liu, Bao'ai 劉寶愛, and Zhang Dewen 張德文. "Shaanxi Baoji Yuan mu" 陝西寶雞元墓. *Wenwu* 2 (1992): 28–33, 43, plate 4.

Liu, James T. C. *Reform in Sung China: Wang An-shih (1021–1086) and His New Policies*. Cambridge, MA: Harvard University Press, 1959.

———. "How Did a Neo-Confucian School Become the State Orthodoxy?" *Philosophy East and West* 23 (1973): 483–505.

Liu, Lydia H. *Translingual Practice: Literature, National Culture, and Translated Modernity—China, 1900–1937*. Stanford: Stanford University Press, 1995.

Liu, Yongming 劉永明, ed. *Siku weishou shushulei guji daquan* 四庫未收數術類古籍大全. Hefeishi: Huangshan shushe, 1995.

Lu, Shixian 魯實先. *Lishu zhiyan* 曆術卮言, vol. 1. Taizhong: Donghai daxue, 1960.

Lubar, Steven, and W. David Kingery, eds. *History from Things: Essays on Material Culture.* Washington, DC: Smithsonian Institution Press, 1993.

Luoyangshi tielu beizhan bianzuzhan lianhe kaogu fajue dui 洛陽市鐵路北站編組站聯合考古發掘隊. "Yuan Saiyinchidahu mu de fajue" 元賽因赤答忽墓的發掘. *Wenwu* 2 (1996): 22–33.

Luoyangshi wenwu gongzuodui 洛陽市文物工作隊. "Luoyangshi beijiao Tangdai muzang de fajue" 洛陽市北郊唐代墓葬的發掘. *Huaxia kaogu* 1 (1996): 8–12, 16.

Ma, Zhisu 馬之驌. *Zhongguo de hunsu* 中國的婚俗. Taipei: Jingshi shuju, 1981.

McKnight, Brian E. *The Washing Away of Wrongs.* Ann Arbor: Center for Chinese Studies, University of Michigan, 1981.

———. "Song Legal Privileges." *Journal of the American Oriental Society* 105, no. 1 (1985): 95–103.

———. "From Statute to Precedent: An Introduction to Sung Law and Its Transformation." In *Law and the State in Traditional East Asia: Six Studies on the Sources of East Asian Law*, edited by Brian E. McKnight, 111–31. Honolulu: University of Hawai'i Press, 1989.

———. *Law and Order in Sung China.* Cambridge: Cambridge University Press, 1992.

———. "Riot at a Song Dynasty Boat Race: A Settlement of Legal Cases from the *Minggong shupan qingming ji.*" *Journal of Sung-Yuan Studies* 25 (1995): 229–40.

McKnight, Brian E., and James T. C. Liu, trans. *The Enlightened Judgments (Ch'ing-ming Chi): The Sung Dynasty Collection.* Albany: State University of New York Press, 1999.

McMullen, David. "Bureaucrats and Cosmology: The Ritual Code of T'ang China." In *Rituals of Royalty: Power and Ceremonial in Traditional Societies*, edited by David Cannadine and Simon Price, 181–236. Cambridge: Cambridge University Press, 1987.

McNair, Amy. "Su Shih's Copy of the *Letter on the Controversy over Seating Protocol.*" *Archives of Asian Art* 43 (1990): 38–48.

Macquet, Jacques. "Objects as Instruments, Objects as Signs." In *History from Things*, edited by Steven Lubar and W. David Kingery, 30–40. Washington, DC: Smithsonian Institution Press, 1993.

Martin, Emily (Emily M. Ahern). *The Cult of the Dead in a Chinese Village.* Stanford: Stanford University Press, 1973.

———. "The Power and Pollution of Chinese Women." In *Women in Chinese Society*, edited by Margery Wolf and Roxane Witke, 193–214. Stanford: Stanford University Press, 1975.

Meng, Zhaohua 孟昭華, Wang Minghuan王明寰, and Wu Jianying 吳建英. *Zhongguo hunyin yu hunyin guanli shi* 中國婚姻與婚姻管理史. Beijing: Zhongguo shehui chubanshe, 1992.

Miyazaki, Ichisada 宮崎市定. "The Administration of Justice During the Sung Dynasty." In *Essays on China's Legal Tradition*, edited by J. A. Cohen, R. Randle Edwards, and Fu-mei Chang Chen, 56–75. Princeton, NJ: Princeton University Press, 1980.

———. 1954. "Sō-Gen jidai no hōsei to saiban kikō: *Gen tenshō* seiritsu no jidaiteki, shakaiteki haikei" 宋元時代の法制と裁判機構:《元典章》成立の時代的·社會的背景. In *Miyazaki Ichisada zenshu*. Tokyo: Iwanami Shokyoku, 1992.

Mok, Harold. "Seal and Clerical Scripts of the Song Dynasty." In *Character and Context in Chinese Calligraphy*, edited by Cary Y. Liu, Dora C. Y. Ching, and Judith G. Smith, 174–98. Princeton, NJ: Art Museum, Princeton University, 1999.

Morita, Kenji 森田憲司. "Guanyu zai Riben de *Shilin guangji* zhuben" 關於在日本的《事林廣記》諸本. In *Guoji Song shi yantaohui lunwen xuanji* 國際宋史研討會論文選集, edited by Deng Guangming 鄧廣銘 and Qi Xia 漆俠, 266–80. Xianghe: Hebei daxue, 1992.

Namujila 那木吉拉. *Zhongguo Yuandai xisu kao* 中國元代習俗考. Beijing: Renmin chubanshe, 1994.

Nei Menggu Chifengshi Aohanqi bowuguan 內蒙古赤峰市敖漢旗博物館. "Nei Menggu Aohanqi Pijianggou 1, 2 hao Liao mu" 內蒙古敖漢旗皮匠溝1, 2 號遼墓. *Wenwu* 9 (1998): 46–52, 63.

Nei Menggu wenwu kaogu yanjiusuo 內蒙古文物考古研究所 and Aluke'erqinqi wenwu guanlisuo 阿魯科爾沁旗文物管理所. "Nei Menggu Chifeng Baoshan Liao bihua mu fajue jianbao" 內蒙古赤峰寶山遼壁畫墓發掘簡報. *Wenwu* 1 (1998): 73–95, plates 1–6.

Nei Menggu wenwu kaogu yanjiusuo 內蒙古文物考古研究所, Wulanchabu bowuguan 烏蘭察布博物館, and Qingshuihexian wenwu guanlisuo 清水河縣文物管理所. "Nei Menggu Qingshuihexian Shantiaomao mudi" 內蒙古清水河縣山跳峁墓地. *Wenwu* 1 (1997): 20–35.

Nei Menggu zizhiqu wenwu kaogu yanjiusuo 內蒙古自治區文物考古研究所 and Zhelimumeng bowuguan 哲里木盟博物館. *Liao Chenguo gongzhu mu* 遼陳國公主墓. Beijing: Wenwu chubanshe, 1993.

Nelson, Sarah Milledge. *Gender in Archaeology: Analyzing Power and Prestige*. Walnut Creek, CA: Alta Mira Press, 1997.

Netolitzky, Almut. *Das* Ling-wai tai-ta *von Chou Ch'ü-fei: Eine Landeskünde Südchinas aus dem 12. Jahrhundert*. Wiesbaden, Germany: Franz Steiner Verlag, 1977.

Nienhauser, William H., Charles Hartman, Y. H. Ma, and Stephen H. West, eds. *The Indiana Companion to Traditional Chinese Literature*. Bloomington: Indiana University Press, 1986.

Niida, Noboru 仁井田陞. *Tō-Sō hōritsu bunsho no kenkyū* 唐宋法律文書の研究. Tokyo: Tōhō bunka gakuin, 1937.

———. "Sutain Tonkō hatten no Tō-Sō kazokuhō kankei bunsho" スタイン敦煌發見の唐宋家族法關係文書. *Tōyō bunka kenkyūjo kiyō* 17 (March 1959): 1–41.

———. 1964. "*Seimeishū* kokonmon no kenkyū" 《清明集》戶婚門の研究. In: Niida Noboru, *Chūgoku hōseishi kenkyū* 中國法制史研究. Tokyo: Tokyo University Press, 1981.

Nylan, Michael. *The Five "Confucian" Classics.* New Haven, CT: Yale University Press, 2001.

Owen, Stephen. *Remembrances: The Experience of the Past in Classical Chinese Literature.* Cambridge, MA: Harvard University Press, 1986.

Peng, Jinhua 彭錦華. "Song gongfengguan Liu fujun muzhiming" 宋供奉官劉府君墓志銘. *Wenwu* 7 (1995): 84–5.

Peng, Liyun 彭利芸. *Songdai hunsu yanjiu* 宋代婚俗研究. Taipei: Xin wenfeng, 1988.

Poor, Robert. "Notes on the Sung Dynasty Archaeological Catalogues." *Archives of the Chinese Art Society of America* 19 (1965): 33–43.

Powers, Martin. "Discourses of Representation in Tenth- and Eleventh-Century China." In *The Art of Interpreting*, edited by Susan C. Scott, 88–125. University Park: Department of Art History, Pennsylvania State University, 1995.

———. "Humanity and 'Universals' in Sung Dynasty Painting." In *Arts of the Sung and Yüan*, edited by Maxwell K. Hearn and Judith G. Smith, 135–45. New York: Metropolitan Museum of Art, 1996.

Proust, Marcel. 1906. *On Reading.* Edited and translated by Jean Auret and William Burford. London: Souvenir Press, 1972.

Prown, Jules David. "The Truth of Material Culture: History or Fiction?" In *History from Things*, edited by Steven Lubar and W. David Kingery, 1–19. Washington, DC: Smithsonian Institution Press, 1993.

Quzhoushi wenguanhui 衢州市文管會. "Zhejiang Quzhoushi Nan Song mu chutu qiwu" 浙江衢州市南宋墓出土器物. *Kaogu* 11 (1983): 1004–11, 1018, plates 6–7.

Ratchnevsky, Paul. *Un Code des Yuan.* Paris: Presses Universitaires de France, 1972.

Rawson, Jessica. "The Ancestry of Chinese Bronze Vessels." In *History from Things*, edited by Steven Lubar and W. David Kingery, 51–73. Washington, DC: Smithsonian Institution Press, 1993.

———. "The Many Meanings of the Past in China." In *Die Gegenwart des Altertums*, edited by Dieter Kuhn and Helga Stahl, 397–421. Heidelberg, Germany: Edition Forum, 2001.

Richardson, Miles. "The Artefact as Abbreviated Act: A Social Interpretation of Material Culture." In *The Meanings of Things*, edited by Ian Hodder, 172–77. London: Unwin Hyman, 1989.

Ricoeur, Paul. *Hermeneutics and the Human Sciences: Essays on Language, Action, and Interpretation.* Edited and translated by John B. Thompson. Cambridge and Paris:

Cambridge University Press and Éditions de la Maison des Sciences de l'Homme, 1981.

———. 1983–1985. *Time and Narrative*, 3 vols. Translated by Kathleen McLaughlin Blamey and David Pellauer. Chicago: University of Chicago Press, 1984–1988.

Rouzer, Paul. *Articulated Ladies: Gender and the Male Community in Early Chinese Texts*. Cambridge, MA: Harvard University East Asia Center, 2001.

Ruan, Changrui 阮昌瑞. *Zhong-wai hunyin lisu zhi bijiao yanjiu* 中外婚姻禮俗之比較研究. Taipei: Zhongyang wenwu gongying she, 1982.

———. *Zhongguo hunyin xisu zhi yanjiu* 中國婚姻習俗之研究. Taipei: Taiwan shengli bowuguan, 1989.

Rudolph, Deborah Marie. "Literary Innovation and Aesthetic Tradition in Travel Writing of the Southern Sung: A Study of Fan Ch'eng-ta's *Wu ch'uan lu*." PhD diss., University of California at Berkeley, 1996.

Rudolph, R. C. "Preliminary Notes on Sung Archaeology." *Journal of Asian Studies* 22, no. 1 (1963): 169–77.

Ruitenbeek, Klaas. *Carpentry and Building in Late Imperial China: A Study of the Fifteenth-Century Carpenter's Manual* Lu Ban jing. Leiden, Netherlands: E. J. Brill, 1993.

Sadachi, Haruto 佐立治人. "*Seimeishū* no 'hōi' to 'ninjō': Soshō tōjisha ni yoru hōritsu kaishaku no konseki" 《清明集》の〈法意〉と〈人情〉：訴訟當事者による法律解釋の痕跡. In Umehara Kaoru 梅原郁, ed. *Chūgoku kinsei no hōsei to shakai* 中國近世の法制と社會. Kyoto: Kyōto daigaku jinbun kagaku kenkyūjo, 1993.

Sanmenxiashi wenwu gongzuodui 三門峽市文物工作隊. *Bei Song Shanzhou louzeyuan* 北宋陝州漏澤園. Beijing: Wenwu chubanshe, 1999.

Schipper, Kristofer M. *L'empereur Wou des Han dans la légende taoïste, Han Wou-ti nei tchouan*. Paris: École Française d'Extrême Orient, 1965.

Schirokauer, Conrad. "Neo-Confucians Under Attack: The Condemnation of *Wei-hsüeh*." In *Crisis and Prosperity in Sung China*, edited by John Winthrop Haeger, 163–98. Tucson: University of Arizona Press, 1975.

Schottenhammer, Angela. "Characteristics of Song Epitaphs." In *Burial in Song China*, edited by Dieter Kuhn, 253–306. Heidelberg, Germany: Edition Forum, 1994.

———. *Grabinschriften in der Song-Dynastie*. Heidelberg, Germany: Edition Forum, 1995.

Seaman, Gary. "The Sexual Politics of Karmic Retribution." In *The Anthropology of Taiwanese Society*, edited by Emily Martin Ahern and Hill Gates, 381–96. Stanford: Stanford University Press, 1981.

Sha, Zhi 沙知. *Dunhuang qiyue wenshu jijiao* 敦煌契約文書輯校. Nanjing: Jiangsu guji chubanshe, 1998.

Shaanxisheng kaogu yanjiusuo 陝西省考古研究所, Shaanxi lishi bowuguan 陝西歷史博物館, and Zhaoling bowuguan 昭陵博物館. "Tang Zhaoling Xincheng zhanggongzhu mu fajue jianbao" 唐昭陵新城長公主墓發掘簡報. *Kaogu yu wenwu* 3 (1997): 3–38, 4 plates.

Shaanxisheng wenwu guanli weiyuanhui 陝西省文物管理委員會. "Xi'an Qujiang Chixicun Yuan mu qingli jianbao" 西安曲江池西村元墓清理簡報. *Wenwu cankao ziliao* 6 (1958): 57–61, 1 plate.

Shandongsheng Jining diqu wenwuju 山東省濟寧地區文物局. "Shandong Jiaxiangxian Yuandai Cao Yuanyong mu qingli jianbao" 山東嘉祥縣元代曹元用墓清理簡報. *Kaogu* 9 (1983): 803–9, plates 5–6.

Shang, Binghe 尙秉和. *Lidai shehui fengsu shiwu kao* 曆代社會風俗事物考. Shanghai: Commercial Press, 1941.

Shanks, Michael, and Christopher Tilley. 1987. *Re-Constructing Archaeology: Theory and Practice*, 2nd ed. London: Routledge, 1992.

Shanxisheng kaogu yanjiusuo 山西省考古研究所 and Taiyuanshi wenwu guanli weiyuanhui 太原市文物管理委員會. "Taiyuan Jinshengcun 337 hao Tangdai bihua mu" 太原金勝村337 號唐代壁畫墓. *Wenwu* 12 (1990): 11–15, color plate 1, plate 5.

Shi, Fengyi 史鳳儀. *Zhongguo gudai hunyin yu jiating* 中國古代婚姻與家庭. Hubei: Hubei renmin chubanshe, 1987.

Shi, Jinbo 史金波. "Heishuicheng chutu huoziban Hanwen lishu kao" 黑水城出土活字版漢文曆書考. *Wenwu* 10 (2001): 87–96.

Sichuansheng bowuguan 四川省博物館. "Sichuan Dongshan guangaiqu Songdai yizhi ji gumu qingli jianbao" 四川東山灌溉渠宋代遺址及古墓清理簡報. *Kaogu* 8 (1959): 430–5, plate 7.

Smith, Kidder, Peter K. Bol, Joseph A. Adler, and Don J. Wyatt. *Sung Dynasty Uses of the I-Ching*. Princeton, NJ: Princeton University Press, 1990.

Smith, Paul J. Review of *Mongolian Rule in China: Local Administration in the Yuan Dynasty*, by Elizabeth Endicott-West. *Journal of Sung-Yuan Studies* 22 (1990–1992): 215–23.

———. "Fear of Gynarchy in an Age of Chaos: Kong Qi's Reflections on Life in South China under Mongol Rule." *Journal of the Economic and Social History of the Orient* 41, no. 1 (February 1998): 1–95.

———. "Impressions of the Song-Yuan-Ming Transition: The Evidence from *Biji* Memoirs." In *The Song-Yuan-Ming Transition in Chinese History*, edited by Paul J. Smith and Richard von Glahn, 71–110. Cambridge, MA: Harvard University Asia Center, 2003.

Smith, Paul J., and Richard von Glahn, eds. *The Song-Yuan-Ming Transition in Chinese History*. Cambridge, MA: Harvard University Asia Center, 2003.

Song, Dejin 宋德金. *Jindai de shehui shenghuo* 金代的社會生活. Xi'an: Shaanxi renmin chubanshe, 1988.

Spiegel, Gabrielle M. *The Past as Text: The Theory and Practice of Medieval Historiography*. Baltimore: Johns Hopkins University Press, 1997.

Stahl, Helga. "Su Shi's Orthodox Burials: Interconnected Double Chamber Tombs in Sichuan." In *Burial in Song China*, edited by Dieter Kuhn, 161–214. Heidelberg, Germany: Edition Forum, 1994.

Steele, John, trans. *The I-li, Or Book of Etiquette and Ceremonial.* London: Probsthain, 1917.

Steinhardt, Nancy S., ed. *Chinese Architecture.* New Haven, CT: Yale University Press, 2002.

Stevenson, Miwha Lee. "Webs of Signification: Representation as Social Transformation in the Muraled Tombs of Koguryo." PhD diss., Columbia University, 1999.

Sturman, Peter. "In the Realm of Naturalness: Problems of Self-Imaging by the Northern Sung Literati." In *Arts of the Sung and Yüan*, edited by Maxwell K. Hearn and Judith G. Smith, 165–85. New York: Metropolitan Museum of Art, 1996.

Su, Bai 宿白. *Baisha Song mu* 白沙宋墓. Beijing: Wenwu chubanshe, 1957.

Su, Bing 蘇冰, and Wei Lin 魏林. *Zhongguo hunyin shi* 中國婚姻史. Taipei: Wenjin, 1994.

Su, Bingqi 蘇秉琦. "Jianli you Zhongguo tese de kaogu xuepai" 建立有中國特色的考古學派. *Kaogu* 6 (1995): 561–3.

Sun, Xiao 孫曉. *Zhongguo hunyin xiaoshi* 中國婚姻小史. Beijing: Guangming ribao chubanshe, 1988.

Sutō, Yoshiyuki 周藤吉之. 1964. "Koten Kenkyūkai kan Seikadō bunkozō *Meikō shohan seimeishū* ni tsuite" 古典研究會刊靜嘉堂文庫藏《名公書判清明集》について. In Sutō Yoshiyuki, *Sōdaishi kenkyū* 宋代史研究, 647–54. Tokyo: Tōyō bunko, 1969.

Tao, Fuhai 陶富海. "Shanxi Xiangfenxian de sizuo Jin, Yuan shiqi muzang" 山西襄汾縣的四座金元時期墓葬. *Kaogu* 12 (1988): 1116–21.

Tao, Xisheng 陶希聖. 1934. *Hunyin yu jiazu* 婚姻與家族. Shanghai: Shanghai shudian, 1992.

Tao, Yi 陶毅, and Ming Xin 明欣. *Zhongguo hunyin jiating zhidu shi* 中國婚姻家庭制度史. Beijing: Dongfang chubanshe, 1994.

ter Haar, Barend J. "Newly Recovered Anecdotes from Hong Mai's (1123–1202) *Yijian zhi*." *Journal of Sung-Yuan Studies* 23 (1993): 19–41.

Tilley, Christopher. "Interpreting Material Culture." In *The Meanings of Things*, edited by Ian Hodder, 185–94. London: Unwin Hyman, 1989.

———. *Material Culture and Text: The Art of Ambiguity.* London: Routledge, 1991.

Tillman, Hoyt C. *Confucian Discourse and Chu Hsi's Ascendancy.* Honolulu: University of Hawai'i Press, 1992.

Tong, Enzheng 童恩正. "Mo'ergen moshi yu Zhongguo de yuanshi shehui shi yanjiu" 摩爾根模式與中國的原始社會史研究. *Zhongguo shehui kexue* 3 (1988): 177–96.

Tsao, Hsingyuan. *Differences Preserved: Reconstructed Tombs from the Liao and Song Dynasties.* Portland: Douglas F. Cooley Memorial Art Gallery, Reed College, 2000.

———. "Unraveling the Mystery of the Handscroll 'Qingming shanghe tu.'" *Journal of Sung-Yuan Studies* 33 (2003): 155–79.

Tsien, Tsuen-hsuin. *Science and Civilization in China V.1: Paper and Printing.* Cambridge: Cambridge University Press, 1985.

Übelhör, Monika. "Problematische Situationen im Alltag eines Kreisbeamten: nach sungzeitlichen Handbüchern für korrekte Amtsführung." In *Lebenswelt und Weltanschauung im frühzeitlichen China*, edited by Helwig Schmidt-Glintzer, 83–96. Stuttgart, Germany: Franz Steiner Verlag, 1990.

Umehara, Kaoru 梅原郁, trans. *Meikō shohan seimeishū* 名公書判清明集. Tokyo: Shushiki kaisha dōbōsha, 1986.

van der Loon, Piet. *Taoist Books in the Libraries of the Sung Period: A Critical Study and Index.* London: Ithaca Press, 1984.

van Gulik, Robert H. *Erotic Colour Prints of the Ming Period.* Tokyo (privately published), 1951.

———. *T'ang-yin-pi-shih: Parallel Cases From Under the Pear Tree: A 13th Century Manual of Jurisprudence and Detection.* Leiden, Netherlands: E. J. Brill, 1956.

———. 1961. *Sexual Life in Ancient China: A Preliminary Survey of Chinese Sex and Society from ca. 1500 B.C. till 1644 A. D.* Leiden, Netherlands: E. J. Brill, 1974.

von Falkenhausen, Lothar. "On the Historiographical Orientation of Chinese Archaeology." *Antiquity* 67, no. 257 (December 1993): 839–49.

———. "The Regionalist Paradigm in Chinese Archaeology." In *Nationalism, Politics, and the Practice of Archaeology*, edited by Philip L. Kohl and Clare Fawcett, 198–217. Cambridge: Cambridge University Press, 1995.

Waley, Arthur. *The Analects of Confucius.* New York: Macmillan, 1938.

———. 1937. *The Book of Songs.* New York: Grove Press, 1960.

Waltner, Ann. "From Casebook to Fiction: *Kung-an* in Late Imperial China." *Journal of the American Oriental Society* 110, no. 2 (April–June 1990): 281–89.

———. "Breaking the Law: Family Violence, Kinship, and Gender in the Legal Code of Ming Dynasty China." *Ming Studies* 36 (1996): 29–43.

Walton, Linda A. "Kinship, Marriage, and Status in Song China: A Study of the Lou Lineage of Ningbo, c. 1050–1250." *Journal of Asian History* 18 (1984): 35–77.

———. Review of *The Inner Quarters*, by Patricia Ebrey. *Journal of Asian History* 29, no. 1 (1995): 95–6.

———. *Academies and Society in Southern Sung China.* Honolulu: University of Hawai'i Press, 1999.

Wang, Deyi 王德毅, Chang Bide 昌彼得, Cheng Yuanmin 程元敏, and Hou Junde 候俊德, comp. *Songren zhuanji ziliao suoyin* 宋人傳記資料索引. 6 vols. Taipei: Dingwen shuju, 1977.

Wang, Jieqing 王潔卿. *Zhongguo hunyin: Hunsu, hunli, yu hunlü* 中國婚姻：婚俗, 婚禮, 與婚律. Taipei: Kunji, 1988.

Wang, Jinxian 王進先, and Shi Weiguo 石衛國. "Shanxi Changzhishi Wumacun Song mu" 山西長治市五馬村宋墓. *Kaogu* 9 (1994): 815–17, 778, plates 5–7.

Wang, Kebin 王可賓. *Nüzhen guosu* 女真國俗. Changchunshi: Jilin daxue chubanshe, 1988.

Wang, Kuo-wei. "Archaeology in the Sung Dynasty." *The China Journal* 6, no. 5, (1927): 222–31.

Wang, Renbo 王仁波. "Tang Yide taizi mu bihua ticai de fenxi" 唐懿德太子墓壁畫題材的分析. *Kaogu* 6 (1973): 381–93, 371, plates 6–9.

Wangjiangxian bowuguan 望江縣博物館. "Anhui Wangjiangxian faxian liangjian Bei Song muzhi" 安徽望江縣發現兩件北宋墓志. *Kaogu* 12 (1997): 88–9.

Watson, Burton, trans. *Han Fei Tzu: Basic Writings.* New York: Columbia University Press, 1964.

———. *The Complete Works of Chuang Tzu.* New York: Columbia University Press, 1968.

Wechsler, Howard J. *Offerings of Jade and Silk: Ritual and Symbol in the Legitimation of the T'ang Dynasty.* New Haven, CT: Yale University Press, 1985.

West, Stephen H. "Textual Typography and Cultural Palimpsests: A Mediaeval Encyclopaedia in China." Unpublished paper, n.d.

———. "The Interpretation of a Dream: The Sources, Evaluation, and Influence of the *Dongjing meng Hua lu.*" *T'oung Pao* 71 (1985): 63–108.

———. "Empresses and Funerals, Pigs and Pancakes: *The Dream of Hua* and the Rise of Urban Literature." Unpublished paper, 2000.

———. "Deconstructing History: Huizong in the Afterglow, Or the Deaths of a Troubling Emperor." In *Emperor Huizong and Late Northern Song China: The Politics of Culture and the Culture of Politics*, edited by Patricia B. Ebrey and Maggie Bickford, Cambridge, MA: Harvard University Asia Center, 2006.

West, Stephen H., and Wilt L. Idema. *The Story of the Western Wing.* Berkeley: University of California Press, 1995.

White, Hayden. *Metahistory: The Historical Imagination in Nineteenth-Century Europe.* Baltimore: Johns Hopkins University Press, 1973.

Wilson, Thomas A. *Genealogy of the Way: The Construction and Uses of the Confucian Tradition in Late Imperial China.* Stanford: Stanford University Press, 1995.

Wolf, Arthur P. *Sexual Attraction and Childhood Association: A Chinese Brief for Edward Westermarck.* Stanford: Stanford University Press, 1995.

Wolf, Margery. *Women and the Family in Rural Taiwan.* Stanford: Stanford University Press, 1972.

Wu, Baoqi 吳寶琪. "Shixi Songdai yu, hun, sang su de chengyin" 試析宋代育, 婚, 喪俗的成因. *Beijing shifan daxue xuebao* 5 (1989): 92–8, 91.

———. "Songdai de lihun yu funü zaijia" 宋代的離婚與婦女再嫁. *Shixue jikan* 1 (1990): 77–8.

Wu, Cunhao 吳存浩. *Zhongguo hunsu* 中國婚俗. Ji'nan: Shandong renmin chubanshe, 1986.

Wu, Hung. *Monumentality in Early Chinese Art and Architecture.* Stanford: Stanford University Press, 1995.

Wu, Jingshan 吳景山. "Yuandai Wang Shixian jiazu beizhi ziliao jilu" 元代汪世顯家族碑志資料輯錄. *Xibei minzu yanjiu* 1 (1999): 233–52.

Wu, K. T. "The Development of Printing in China." *T'ien-hsia Monthly* 3 (1936): 137–60.

Wu, Wei 吳煒. "Jieshao Yangzhou faxian de lianghe Song muzhi" 介紹揚州發現的兩合宋墓志. *Wenwu* 4, 78–2, 15.

Xie, Hongxuan 謝鴻軒. *Pianwen henglun* 駢文衡論. Taipei: Guangwen shuju, 1973.

Xu, Yangjie 徐揚傑. *Song-Ming jiating zhidu shilun* 宋明家庭制度史論. Beijing: Zhonghua shuju, 1995.

Yang, Shuda 楊樹達. *Handai hun sang lisu kao* 漢代婚喪禮俗考. Shanghai: Commercial Press, 1933.

Yang, Zhengwen 楊正文, and Ma Chengjun 馬成俊. *Zhongguo hunsu wenhua* 中國婚俗文化. Shenyang: Liaoning daxue chubanshe, 1990.

Yang, Zhigang 楊志剛. "*Simashi shuyi* he *Zhuzi jiali* yanjiu" 《司馬氏書儀》和《朱子家禮》研究. *Zhejiang xuekan* 1 (1993): 108–13.

Ye, Hong 葉紅. "Zhejiang Pingyangxian Song mu" 浙江平陽縣宋墓. *Kaogu* 1 (1983): 80–1.

Zeng, Zaozhuang 曾棗莊. *Tang Song wenxue yanjiu: Zeng Zaozhuang wencun zhi er* 唐宋文學研究：曾棗莊文存之二. Chengdu: Ba Shu shushe, 1999.

Zhang, Bangwei 張邦煒. *Hunyin yu shehui (Songdai)* 婚姻與社會（宋代）. Chengdu: Sichuan renmin chubanshe, 1989.

Zhang, Huaicheng 張懷承. *Zhongguo de jiating yu lunli* 中國的家庭與倫理. Beijing: Zhongguo Renmin daxue chubanshe, 1993.

Zhangxian wenhuaguan 漳縣文化館. "Gansu Zhangxian Yuandai Wang Shixian jiazu muzang: jianbao zhi er" 甘肅漳縣元代汪世顯家族墓葬：簡報之二. *Wenwu* 2 (1982): 13–21, plates 1–2.

Zhao, Chao 趙超. "Shi, qionglongding mushi yu doufuxing muzhi: jiantan gudai muzang zhong 'xiang tiandi' de sixiang" 式，穹窿頂墓室與斗覆形墓志：兼談古代墓葬中〈象天地〉的思想. *Wenwu* 5 (1999): 72–82.

———. "Shanxi Huguan Nancun Songdai zhuandiao mu zhuandiao ticai shixi" 山西壺關南村宋代磚雕墓磚雕題材試析. *Wenwu* 5 (1998): 41–50.

Zhao, Heping 趙和平. *Dunhuang xieben shuyi yanjiu* 敦煌寫本書儀研究. Taipei: Xin wenfeng, 1993.

Zhejiangsheng wenwu guanli weiyuanhui 浙江省文物管理委員會. "Hangzhou Lin'an Wudai mu zhong de tianwentu he miseci" 杭州臨安五代墓中的天文圖和秘色瓷. *Kaogu* 3 (1975): 186–94, plates 9–10.

Zhou, Dao 周到. "Song Wei wang Zhao Jun fuqi hezang mu" 宋魏王趙頵夫妻合葬墓. *Kaogu* 7 (1964): 349–54, plate 8.

Zhou, Yiliang 周一良. "Dunhuang xieben shuyi zhong suo jian de Tangdai hunsang lisu" 敦煌寫本書儀中所見的唐代婚喪禮俗. *Wenwu* 7 (1985): 17–25.

Zhou, Yiliang 周一良, and Zhao Heping 趙和平. *Tang, Wudai shuyi yanjiu* 唐, 五代書儀研究. Beijing: Zhongguo shehui kexue chubanshe, 1995.

Zhu, Ruixi 朱瑞熙. "Songdai de hunyin liyi" 宋代的婚姻禮儀. *Wenshi zhishi* 12 (1988): 46–50.

Zito, Angela R. "City Gods, Filiality, and Hegemony in Late Imperial China." *Modern China* 13, no. 3 (July 1987): 333–71.

———. "Ritualizing *Li*: Implications for Studying Power and Gender." *positions: east asia cultures critique* 1, no. 2 (1993): 321–48.

———. *Of Body and Brush: Grand Sacrifice as Text/Performance in Eighteenth-Century China*. Chicago: University of Chicago Press, 1997.

# Index